Anthropology & Mass Communication

Anthropology &

General Editors: William O. Beeman and David Kertzer, Department of Anthropology, Brown University

Anthropology & Law
James M. Donovan and H. Edwin Anderson, III

Anthropology & Mass Communication: Media and Myth in the
   New Millennium
Mark Allen Peterson

ANTHROPOLOGY & MASS COMMUNICATION
Media and Myth in the New Millennium

Mark Allen Peterson

Berghahn Books
New York • Oxford

First published in 2003 by
Berghahn Books
www.BerghahnBooks.com

First paperback edition published in 2005

The author and publisher greatly acknowledge the right to reproduce
the extract on pages 122-123 from *Nice Work* © David Lodge.
Used by permission of The Random House Group Limited
and Viking Penguin, a division of Penguin Group (USA) Inc.

Library of Congress Cataloging-in-Publication Data

Peterson, Mark Allen.
    Anthropology & mass communication : media and myth in the new millenium / Mark
Allen Peterson.
        p. cm. -- (Anthropology &)
    Includes bibliographical references and index.
    ISBN 1-57181-277-6 (alk. paper) -- ISBN 1-57181-278-4 (pbk.: alk. paper)
    1. Mass media and anthropology. I. Title. II. Series.

P96.A56P48 2003
302.23'4--dc21   2003052307

British Library Cataloguing in Publication Data
A catalogue record for this book is available from the British Library

Printed in Canada on acid-free paper

CONTENTS

To Dawna, of course

ACKNOWLEDGMENTS

This manuscript owes a debt to many people.

Much of my thinking about media was shaped by two three-year stints as a political journalist in Washington, DC. I would like to thank everyone there who helped me learn, and learn about, American journalism, especially Howard Haugerud, John Carroll, Fred Geiger, and Dick Maggrett. I have also drawn heavily on my fieldwork in India, where I owe a debt of gratitude to many reporters and editors at *Times of India*, *Nav Bharat Times*, *Sandhya Times*, *Indian Express*, *Janasatta*, *Milap*, *Pratap*, and others.

Many of my ideas were refined during the Media Anthropology Summer School at the University of Hamburg in 1999. I would like to thank Dorle Dracklé, who organized the summer school, the Volkswagen Foundation, who sponsored it, my fellow faculty members, especially David Hakken, Debra Spitulnik, Merry Bruns, Penelope Harvey, and Mark Pedelty, and the students, especially John Postill and Barbara Zang. Special thanks go to Mark and John for their reading and careful comments on early drafts of some of the chapters.

My thanks go out to Marion Berghahn, for her enthusiasm about this project, to Shearin Abdel-Moneim and Christy Ferguson, who spent a hefty part of their graduate education locating citations and entering my copyediting corrections, and to my secretary, Safaa Sedky, for her contributions.

I would like to thank my colleagues at the American University in Cairo, especially Donald Cole, who commented on an early draft of chapter 2. Many of the ideas expressed here were first tried out in my course on media, culture, and society in the Islamic world. I thank all my students, but especially Dalia al-Amroussey, Ahmed Bassiouni, Frederic Copper-Royer, Elizabeth Cooper, Jack Dolph, Yasmine el-Dorghamy, Yvette Fayez, Mamdouh Hakim, Samar Ibrahim, Natalia Kasprzak-Suit, Sandra Khalifa, James Lejukole, Ivan Panović, Sridevi Raman, Louly Seif, and Wesam Younis for asking tough questions and bringing to class their own insights and examples.

My anthropological perspective on media—and on everything else—has been primarily shaped by three superb mentors: William O. Beeman, Jon Anderson, and Phyllis Chock. All of my best work in anthropology is in some way derived from their teaching and example; the errors and lapses, alas, are mine alone.

I thank my daughters, Madison, Thea, and Sophie, for their open and insightful discussions of their own and their peers' encounters with media, for introducing me to the world of Pokémon, and for their constant encouragement, even when the manuscript for this book consumed time that would have been better spent with them.

Finally, my greatest debt is owed to my wife, Dawna, who has supported me in this, and in all my projects, for over eighteen years.

INTRODUCTION

I have dabbled in media at least since junior high school, when my father bought me a used 8mm movie camera. My productions were fundamentally intertextual, pastiches and parodies of the television and films I enjoyed viewing. They were also fundamentally social activities, ways for a loud, socially inept adolescent to bring together a group of male and female comrades, some of whom might not otherwise have wanted anything to do with me. I went to Mayo High School in Rochester, Minnesota, one of the first secondary schools in America to have a fully fledged television production studio, and at sixteen I was producing (with a crew of six) a daily, two-minute humorous segment for the school's daily ten-to-fifteen minute broadcast, *The Spartan Scene.*

While an undergraduate majoring in the study of religion at UCLA, I freelanced for magazines and newspapers, and discovered a lucrative niche producing institutional newsletters. I was hired to write a screenplay treatment for a movie about King David, which was never made (the funding collapsed when *Variety* announced Dino DeLaurentis was planning a movie on the same subject starring Richard Gere). Accompanying my wife to the east coast to pursue her M.Ed., I learned computer typesetting as a text editor for law books at the Michie Company in Virginia. When my wife found a job in Washington, DC, I began taking classes in anthropology at the Catholic University of America, and I became assistant editor of *Anthropological Quarterly*. Needing a job, I lucked into an assistant editorial position at the National Tribune Co., where for three years I learned the mysteries of the Washington Press Corps. The "Trib," as we affectionately called it, published watchdog publications on the U.S. Department of Veterans Affairs (and its predecessors), several congressional committees and some departments of the Pentagon. It was a great place to work. Hours were flexible, pay was low, and turnover high; an assistant editor might find himself off to cover a congressional hearing or interviewing a senator because no reporters were available.

I kept my anthropology and my journalism as separate as possible during this period, in part because I recognized that their epistemologies were incompatible. Journalism is founded on common sense, while anthropology scrutinizes common sense and analyzes it. My concerns about mixing the two were realized when I began taking a course from Jon Anderson on performance and practice theories in anthropology, and realized that the mythmaking of the peoples I was studying and the mythmaking by which I made my livelihood were too similar to ignore. Things came to a head after President Reagan announced that the United States was fighting a "war on drugs" and I was confronted with the ways my own institutionalized practices as a journalist were objectifying a metaphor I absolutely did not believe in.

Even as I sought to critically examine my own journalistic praxis from an anthropological perspective, my friendship with Randy Fillmore drew me into his "Center for Anthropology and Journalism." Each month I met anthropologists critical of media representations of the peoples they studied. Ironically, their criticisms led them to reify the sprawling and complicated constellation of institutions and practices we call "the media" in the same ways they were accusing media of doing to "their" people. My M.A. thesis project extended my thinking on these issues. I received a telephone call from a theater in Denver, Colorado, saying that they wanted to produce a play I had written as an undergraduate as part of their summer theater festival. They wondered if I could fly out to attend the rehearsal process. I did, and the resulting thesis examined the process of mediation as a social practice through which scripts were turned into shows.

I went to Brown University intending to abandon the media and return to my interests in religion and religious performance. My hopes to study *taziyeh* performances in Iraq under the guidance of Bill Beeman ended shortly after I arrived when the United States declared war on its former ally. At the recommendation of Lina Fruzetti, I switched from studying Persian to Hindi, and began planning to go to India. But where I had spent *years* reading about Islam and its performative traditions, I felt completely unprepared to plunge into the depths of Indian ritual performance. Nor, I felt, would a year's intensive study of Hindi and Urdu—leaving me with a reading knowledge and a smattering of conversation—prepare me to conduct fieldwork. There was, however, the Indian press.

Almost everything I read about the Indian press—including some things by Indian journalists—turned out to be wrong. Like me, many of these writers assumed the press had certain essential, rather than cultural and historical, characteristics. This was in part because journalism education in India, which often uses British and American textbooks, has little to do with actual practice. Then there was the sheer number of newspapers to be explained—more than forty *daily* newspapers in New Delhi alone (a city with a literacy rate of 69 percent). And there were the stories people tell *about* newspapers to think about. And the vast number of oral and social reading practices to be described and related to one another. What I found was a complex ecology of media forms, and a set of domains into which newspapers entered and around which meaningful action was (in part) organized. The language I had to describe this was insufficient.

Between 1993 and 1997 I returned to political journalism in Washington, DC, a place that now looked fundamentally different to me. In 1996 I filed a workable but ultimately unsatisfying dissertation, and knew that at least part of my professional work would involve finding a language and set of conceptual models that could describe the kinds of things I found in India and which, with my sensitivity heightened by that experience of difference, I now saw all around me.

I was not alone. A number of scholars had been increasingly engaged since 1985 with the kinds of problems that beset me in India. I met some of them in 1999, when I was invited by Dorle Dracklé to be on the faculty of the Media Anthropology Summer School in Hamburg, sponsored by the Volkswagen Foundation. My discussions with them, and with the students, were fruitful and exciting. Meanwhile, in 1997 I had accepted a position as assistant professor of anthropology at the American University in Cairo. This gave me another site within which to reflect; my reflections were guided by the questions, comments, and insights of students in my course, "Media, Culture, and Society in the Islamic World."

I offer this personal and intellectual biography because my experiences dabbling in media, both professionally and academically, shape much of what follows. The model I will unpack in this text is a model that allows me to answer the kinds of questions I have been asking about the media, and about my own engagements with it, for many years. This is a synthetic model, derived from the work of many anthropologists in many sites around the world. There is an overabundance of examples from the United States, not because the United States is typical but because I, like so many anthropologists writing about media, am an American, and because the United States is the site of my own amateur and professional work in media production. South Asia and the Middle East also loom large, not only because these are the places where I have lived, worked and taught, but because these regions have each inspired a large and prolific body of anthropological work on media.

A couple of years ago, as I was beginning to work on this book, I received an e-mail from a woman who had worked with me years ago on the high-school television program. Now a radio producer, she was surprised to find I'd become a university professor, and wondered if I still had my sense of humor. I responded that giving up one's sense of humor was one of the requirements for the Ph.D.—which I hoped she'd find funny.

The real answer is more difficult. I am certainly less innocent about media than I was at sixteen. There are many aspects of the media industries in the United States, Egypt and India about which I am deeply disturbed. Much of what I see makes me laugh; other things make me too angry even for irony. Yet I remain an avid consumer and sometime producer of media, someone who continues to derive pleasure from mediated communication, even those media messages I do not think are particularly good for me or for my children. That pleasure and power coexist, that critical understanding and gratification struggle with one another, that guilty laughter and embarrassed tears may be simultaneously evoked by the same messages, these are fundamental to the human condition. Anthropology offers me a perspective for looking at media without losing sight of this. It offers me a critical perspective on the world, but also insights into my own practice. If this book captures some sense of this, I will be more than satisfied.

— Mark Allen Peterson
Cairo, Egypt, 2002

Chapter 1

MASS MEDIATIONS

In the rainforests of Brazil, members of the Kayapo tribe are preparing for a ritual performance. The performers have shed their T-shirts and shorts and donned ceremonial garb while the musicians gathered their instruments and took their places. There is a brief delay while they wait for another necessary participant. Finally, he arrives, the son of one of the community's political leaders, carrying a videocamera. He takes a position, looks through the viewfinder, and gives a wave. The ritual can now start. The tape of this ritual will join the others in the community's video library of ceremonies.[1]

In Cairo, a young man and woman alight from a taxi and push their way through the crowd milling about outside the theater, waiting to see the newest comedy by 'Adil Imam, one of Egypt's most famous actors. The young man slides a handful of pound notes to the ticketseller and takes his two tickets. He looks about. Already some of the young men in the crowd are making eyes and not-too-quiet remarks about his date. Like many Egyptian women, she pretends they do not exist—that she cannot hear what they are saying—while she keeps her eyes firmly fixed on her boyfriend. Forcing a smile, he takes her inside to get a table in the lobby, which is reserved for those who buy refreshments. The prices are three times what they would cost anywhere else but at least they can be alone for a few minutes before the show starts. This night will cost him a week's pay. In a society where middle class young people are bombarded with mixed messages about premarital behavior and modern romance, the movies—at least, certain theaters showing certain kinds of films—offer one of the few places where unmarried couples can go to "try out" dating and being together.[2]

Notes for this section begin on page 25.

In a suburban neighborhood in the eastern United States, three nine-year-old boys are hammering out the framework of their play. As they argue about which child will be which Mighty Morphin Power Ranger, they are approached by two neighbor girls who demand to be included in the play. For a moment the boys are nonplussed; there *are* girl power rangers, after all. They quiz the two sisters: who will be the pink ranger and who the yellow? Do they know the characters' names? Which *zords* do the respective girls drive? Do the girls have action figures of "their" rangers? The last question is not answered at once; now it is the girls' turn to be at a loss. Their tastes run more to Barbie dolls than superhero action figures. They run to their house and emerge triumphantly a few moments later: they have action figures, recent acquisitions courtesy of McDonald's Happy Meals. Theirs are half the size and possess fewer joints than those of the boys, but they are unmistakably the right characters. Play commences, to be interrupted fifteen minutes later when the mother of one of the boys calls out that the television series *Goosebumps* is starting. All five children race to the boy's house and clamber inside, speculating loudly as to which of the popular paperback books will be dramatized in this afternoon's episode.[3]

Throughout the world, media have become a part of the rhythms of human life. As means of communication, as symbols for modernity and transformation, and as resources for cultural action, they have become part of human culture. Media consumption throughout the world involves not only passive viewing but ritual activity, ways of speaking, play, and forms of social organization. In recent decades, anthropologists, as students of human culture, have begun to pay increasing attention to the ways media operates in the lives of human beings throughout the world. If the mass media have not yet created a "global village" (McLuhan 1989), they have nonetheless touched the lives of everyone on the globe—albeit in very different ways and at different levels.

In spite of the ubiquity of mass media, anthropologists have until recently done an astoundingly good job of ignoring it. There is a well-known Gary Larson cartoon that shows a group of grass-skirted hut-dwelling "natives" scrambling to hide their technological appliances—including a television set—before the anthropologists arrive. But in real life, the "natives," whoever they may be, have not needed to hide their televisions. Anthropologists have done it for them by selectively choosing what they will or will not pay attention to in their ethnographies. Even as anthropologists spent decades insisting that their discipline was *not* the study of "primitive" cultures, and criticizing notions of unchanging tradition and stable authenticity, they have collectively as a discipline "selected out" or marginalized many aspects of the social lives of the people they studied, particularly where these involved the media.

Since the mid 1980s, however, anthropologists have begun to pay increasing attention to the mass media. A number of statements have appeared describing what an anthropology of mass communication might look like or how it should proceed (Lyons 1990; Drummond 1992; Spitulnik 1993; Abu-Lughod 1997; Dickey 1997; Herzfeld 2001; Askew 2002; Ginsburg 2002a). At the turn of the millennium, more than one hundred academically employed anthropologists declared mass media or popular culture as among their research and teaching interests in the American Anthropological Association's *Guide to Departments.* Several major anthropology journals routinely publish articles on mass media and the number of interdisciplinary journals to which anthropologists contribute media studies continues to grow.

Yet as anthropology rediscovers the mass media, there are already in place a series of disciplines for which the mass media have long been objects of study. Mass communication, sociology, gender studies, political science, performance theory, cultural studies, and critical theory have all developed methods for defining the mass media as objects of study and have formulated theories for understanding media's roles in social life. In the face of the longstanding theoretical positions and commitments established by these disciplines, what does anthropology have to offer?

This book will attempt to answer this question by offering a systematic overview of the themes, topics, and methodologies emerging in this dialogue between anthropologists studying mass communication and media analysts turning to ethnography and cultural analysis. In this chapter I will focus on three primary elements that anthropology brings to the study of mass media: ethnography, cross-cultural comparison, and alternative theoretical paradigms. First, however, it is necessary to clarify what we will mean here by *media* and by *mass communication.*

Mediations and Meanings

Media is the plural of *medium* which, according to the *New American Heritage Dictionary,* is an "agency … by means of which something is accomplished, conveyed, or transferred." Communications media are vehicles for the transmission of symbols. The natural medium for human communication, given to us by our own evolutionary biology, is the *vocal-auditory apparatus,* that complex of lungs, larynx, ears, cranial cavities, teeth, lips, palate, and so forth which enable speech to take place. Other media are technological enhancements or modifications of this primary medium.

The vocal-auditory medium of speech has certain implications for how people typically communicate in face-to-face interaction. Several of these implications have been described by Charles Hockett (1977) as "design features of human language." One such implication is that linguistic signals are broadcast in all directions, although they are heard as coming from one particular place. This feature, which Hockett calls *broadcast transmission and directional reception*, means that a message intended for a particular person can nonetheless be overheard by anyone within the range of the speaker's voice, including people of whom the speaker may be unaware. The sender of a linguistic signal also receives the message he or she sends—a feature Hockett calls *complete feedback*. Speakers can therefore adjust their messages—control volume, pitch, and so forth—in response to their assessments of their own voices. A third feature of the vocal-auditory apparatus is *rapid fading*. The sounds of spoken signals cannot be heard for long—they vanish as discrete units almost as soon as they leave our mouths. And because almost all human beings are born with the same biological equipment, speaker and listener positions are *interchangeable*; adult members of any speech community can be both senders and receivers of linguistic signals. Finally, human language is *specialized* for communication. Linguistic signals meet no human needs except communication; they have little direct physical effect on the environment. As Hockett observed, the "sound of a heated conversation does not raise the temperature of a room enough to benefit those in it" (1977: 134).[4]

The normal setting for human speech is the dyadic or small group speech act, in which a speaker addresses a small number of other listeners (all of whom are also at least potential speakers). In this setting, physical cues come into play alongside verbal signals. People negotiate their meanings not only through talk but through facial expression, gesture, stance, and physical proximity. Speakers not only receive feedback by hearing their own voices but through the myriad signals being sent to them through nonverbal means. These physical cues serve as metamessages, telling senders how others are interpreting their messages, and, because they take place in a different channel, are capable of being generated at the same time as, and parallel to, the spoken message. Face-to-face interaction involves multiple levels of communication—visual, aural and kinesic—which provide multiple levels of feedback loops. Conversation analysts and ethnographers of communication have emphasized the fundamentally interactive nature of face-to-face human communication, drawing our attention to the overlaps, repairs, and clarifications that emerge in even the smoothest of casual conversations. The sheer volume of information expressed in even the shortest conversations is staggering. Thus Moerman (1988) can build a lengthy article out of the analysis of a three-minute conversation between a handful of Thai villagers, a district official and himself, while

Tannen (1984) can construct an entire book around a two-hour Thanksgiving dinner conversation.

Mass media involve technological transformations of this system of communication in various ways and to different ends. The media thus include not only books, films, television, videos, magazines, newspapers, and radio, but billboards, comic books, e-mail, the World Wide Web, telephones, and many other technologies. The key questions for the anthropologist are how these technologies operate to mediate human communication, and how such mediation is embedded in broader social and historical processes.

In this sense, something as simple as a soapbox can be understood as media. By raising the speaker above his or her audience, the soapbox extends the feature of broadcast transmission, allowing the voice to penetrate further. But even while extending the speaker's auditory reach, the soapbox at the same time constrains the speaker. The subtle cues that are available in small-group interactions are muted here; the speaker may be able to see only those nearest to the soapbox and must rely less on immediate feedback cues and more on general assumptions about how to best communicate with an audience. Successful speakers must develop special knowledge—special competence in "oration"— which is quite different than the skills required to hold a conversation. In turn, societies enable and constrain mediated communication technologies as places are made to accommodate new media. In Edwardian England, orating from a soapbox in the middle of Hyde Park was not only permissible, but served as a form of entertainment and as a sign of Britain's commitment to free speech. Orating from a soapbox in the heart of the financial district was illegal, a deliberate challenge to orthodoxy that was likely to get one arrested as a "public nuisance."

The breach between the sender and the receiver is central to most forms of technological mediation. One of the fundamental reasons for mediating communication through technology is to increase the number of persons to whom a sender can transmit messages. The term "mass" in mass communication was intended in this way to refer to the large, undifferentiated aggregate of people whom technologically mediated communication was supposed to reach. The idea of the mass audience assumes an aggregate of individuals who are largely unconnected to one another except through their common reception of mediated messages. So defined, it was assumed that mass communication was a means of joining disparate people, whether to sell products or increase social control.

But there are serious problems with this assumption. If media texts carry with them their own contexts of interpretation, then it means something to speak of a mass audience because all receivers will interpret, or be affected by, the same messages in very similar ways. If, on the other hand, people interpret the same messages differently, the idea becomes much more problematic. The total number of receivers of a set of messages, already differentiated by gender, class, ethnicity, language, caste, status, age, education, and other distinctions, cannot be said to constitute an audience in any meaningful sense of the term if these distinctions affect the ways they interpret the messages. If the social experience of growing up as a woman gives an individual a different set of interpretive frames for making sense of messages than one who has grown up as a man, in what sense are they "joined" by mass communication?[5] In what sense is their experience common? Multiply this example by considering the possible intersections of social identities—contrasting, for example, the interpretation of a particular television program by a poor, black woman with that of a rich, white man or that of a female bilingual Hispanic college professor with that of a white, rural male high school dropout—and we begin to see what Raymond Williams meant when he said "there are no masses, only ways of seeing people as masses" (1958: 289).

What is important about the mass concept is not its notion about the aggregation of the audience but its recognition that the break between sender and receiver is crucial to understanding mass media as different from face-to-face communication. A better name for this design feature might be *anonymity,* since the breach allows the possibility of persons to send messages to unknown receivers and vice versa. Anonymity engages the imagination in a very different way than face-to-face communication. It is a feature possessed equally by broadcast media (such as television and radio), circulated media (such as magazines, newspapers, and books), displayed media (such as billboards, posters, hoardings, and wall newspapers) and interactive media (such as internet chat rooms).

This typology—broadcast, circulated, displayed, and interactive—is dependent on the presence or absence of another design feature of many forms of mass media, that of *fixedness.* Many media produce physical texts that are not subject to the rapid fading of human speech. Such messages are not lost after having been produced; they hang about in various forms. Not all media possess this feature—live television broadcasts and telephone conversations may have the same rapid fading as speech. Other media, like Web pages, offer texts which are extraordinarily malleable, and which can be changed without leaving traces, each text having the appearance of completeness. Unfixed media can often be readily transformed into fixed media through various technologies: a Web page can be saved or printed, and later compared with the version that replaces it on the Web. Chat room dialogues can be (and frequently are) archived. Telephone conversations can be recorded by one party or the other, or by an outside party unknown to either conversant. Television and radio broadcasts are recorded on tape, and so forth. Such "fixing" however, involves transforming texts of one kind into another.

Finally, it is worth noting that Hockett described other design features less directly related to the organs of speech that may be nonetheless affected by different technologies. One of these is *arbitrariness*, the fact that there is no necessary connection between a spoken sound and the concept to which it refers. In spoken language, the words *horse, hassan, equus* and *cheval* can thus all refer to the same category of animal. However, many media depend not on verbal arbitrariness but on resemblance. The photographic image of a horse does not bear the same relation to the subject that the words *horse, hassan, equus,* and *cheval* do. Many of the visual images of television and movies, or the sound effects on the radio, resemble the things to which they refer. It may not be unreasonable to consider *iconicity* a central feature of mediated communication.

Thus far I have focused on the immediate affects of technology on the act of communicating. In speaking of mass communication as mediated by the technologies that enable it, however, it is useful to speak of at least two levels of technological mediation. I refer to the extensions and disruptions of the design features of language as *primary mediation*. The enhancement of broadcast reach and the disabling of complete feedback for the soapbox orator are examples of this primary mediation. But there is a secondary form of mediation as well. Communication is also mediated by the relations of production that are associated in a given time and place with particular media technologies. Mass communication technologies are embedded in particular modes of production that tie the specific means of production—the technologies and knowledge of how to use them—to social relations of production: jobs, values, networks. The example of the organization of space to create appropriate and inappropriate social contexts for soapbox oration is an example of this *secondary mediation*.

Secondary mediation involves the ways these social relations of production shape the meanings of the messages they create. Telling a fairy tale as a bedtime story is one kind of communicative act; reading the fairy tale aloud from a book is yet another. A radio broadcast of the same fairy tale is yet another kind of act, as is a theatrical performance. A Hollywood movie representation of that fairy tale is different from all of these, and is also different from an Indian film version of the same tale, despite the fact that both involve the same technologies. Understanding the ways such things as fairy tales are transformed from one site of production to another requires an empirical study of the social systems within which production

technologies are embedded. Understanding the ways that different audiences are constructed in their acts of consumption, and the multiple ways
that media texts may be interpreted, requires a study of consumption and
interpretation as social actions. Understanding communication—actual
connections between senders and receivers created by the exchange of
media—requires attention not only to these sites, but to wider discourses
about media that circulate in society. For anthropologists, as for an
increasing number of scholars in other disciplines, the most effective way
of coming to these understandings is through ethnography.

Ethnography and Media

By *ethnography* I mean description based on intimate, long-term reflexive encounters between scholars and the peoples they are studying.
Anthropological knowledge is largely *situated* knowledge, deriving from
an intimate understanding of the structures of everyday life. The classic
model of ethnography is participant-observation, which involves relatively long-term relationships between the ethnographer and his or her
host community,[6] in which researchers attempt to situate themselves
within quotidian situations and events. Through such fieldwork, ethnographers seek to capture a sense of life as it actually happens, not just
as people recount it in interviews, surveys, focus groups, or other quasi-
experimental situations. Anthropologists may gather census data, conduct
interviews, and do surveys, but these methods are usually subsumed
within a broader fieldwork encounter. It is their knowledge of the lives
and lifestyles of their informants that allows anthropologists to contextualize and interpret these other forms of information in a comprehensive and holistic fashion.

Ethnography involves a thickly contextual mode of detailed description arising out of the encounter of different cultural codes. The majority of audience studies in mass communication research are marked by
"thin description," accounts of media consumption extracted from the
contexts of everyday life, rather than built up of layers of detail. Even
some of those studies that set out to examine media consumers in such
places as "the dust and dirt of rural India" (Hartmann, Patil and Dighe
1989: 35) tend to extract data *from* this dust and dirt, instead of attempting to bring the dust and dirt into the understanding of everyday media
consumption. Ethnographic fieldwork seeks to record everyday life in as
much of its complexity as the ethnographer can capture, because
anthropology seeks not to reduce complexity to something understand-
able, but rather to accept that human life is complex and to understand
life in its complexity.

Ideally, ethnography involves continuing reflexive encounters with people in the situations of their everyday life, situations that increasingly include mass media. Ethnography is empirical in that it requires anthropologists to physically situate themselves in sites where they can observe and record human action as it happens. At the same time, ethnographic fieldwork seeks to avoid the reductionistic stance associated with positivistic methodologies that seek to "control" social variables or seek a "fly on the wall" position. Because we are studying people like ourselves, scientific accuracy as well as respect for human dignity requires us to treat our "subjects" as the human beings they are.

Ethnography is intimate in its efforts to enter into the situations of everyday life, to engage with people in their homes, their workplaces, their markets, and their places of leisure, rather than limiting research to the quasi-experimental methods of interview, survey, or focus group. This intimacy has several consequences in addition to the opportunities it affords for observation of contextual details. One of the most important of these is that ethnography allows the researchers to learn *from* their hosts, rather than only learning about them. Indeed, ethnography provides opportunities for researchers to learn what the host community believes it is important to know, rather than merely seeking answers to questions the researcher assumes are important. Ethnographers seek to learn from the host community by allowing their hosts to partially shape not only the answers but the questions being asked.[7]

Ethnography is also intimate in that it recognizes that research takes place in a web of social relationships. In any social research, the physical appearance, ethnicity, mode of speaking, style of dress, and other intimate details of a researcher's person intersect with situational constraints and local knowledges to determine who will answer their questions and how. There is no neutral way to dress, no mode of speech that does not signify social meaning, and these elements therefore frame the research encounter and help construct the kinds of answers surveyors and interviewers receive. Instead of seeking to minimize or "control" the sociality of their research, ethnography seeks to make this sociality central. Scientific accuracy is handled in anthropology through reflexivity, the ethnographers' thinking about the ways they think about their engagement with their hosts. Ethnography seeks to make explicit the nature of the data-gathering situation. Since this involves an "I" in interaction with various others, it is sometimes misunderstood as "subjective." Yet pretending that research is *not* interactive, adopting the language of laboratory experiments, does not produce accuracy or "objectivity", it merely disguises and mystifies the nature of the research, deceiving both the researcher and his or her publics. Anthropological reflexivity involves not a slide into self-indulgent solipsism but a pragmatic effort to refine our analytic sensitivity by foregrounding the encounter of different systems of knowledge and selfhood between researcher and hosts. Ideally, fieldwork seeks to produce data by describing information produced in the situation of interaction. Ethnography does not pretend to produce abstract knowledge on the level of natural laws of humanity but situated knowledge at various levels of generalization. This knowledge is produced through an ongoing dialectical encounter between anthropologists and their hosts.

Decentering the West

Anthropology continues to be associated in popular representation with the study of tribal societies, isolated villages or island communities. While this is not an accurate perception, it does arise from the fact that peoples in such communities are often seen as "different," and understanding how people imagine difference is central to anthropology. Anthropology, that is, studies "otherness." Although anthropologists are as likely to study the culture of biological reproduction in urban America (Martin 1992) or the political culture of Italy (Kertzer 1980), or the social practice of biotechnology (Rabinow 1997), all anthropological work remains shaped by disciplinary attention to the ways people are constituted as "same" and "other," and sees *all* forms of knowledge (including "scientific" knowledge) as situated and local.

This approach diverges sharply from many mass communication approaches, which have often tended to assume that the ways media technologies have emerged and become normalized in North America and Western Europe are somehow "natural" or inevitable and thus capable of being extended universally. Mass communication literature has always included cross-cultural work, of course, as in the case of the famous study by Leibes and Katz (1994) of the ways families in different countries watch the American TV series *Dallas* or the work by James Lull (1988, 1990) on television viewing in different parts of the world. But such studies tend to replicate methods developed in Europe and North America (such as interviewing) and apply them in countries where different understandings of social relations and the purposes of talk may distort their comparability or even render them invalid (Briggs 1986).

What anthropology brings from its cross-cultural perspective is a healthy skepticism toward universalism and essentialism. Anthropology, that is, tends to be suspicious of claims about how "the media" operate when the models are derived from data gathered entirely from within Western, post-Enlightenment societies. Anthropology offers mass communication data on societies where the positions of media in the social field differ from those we know, data that challenge mass communication to test and rethink many of the things it has tended to take for granted. At the same time, anthropology offers these accounts as alternative models that can be examined in the contexts of Western societies: *what else is this like?*

The skepticism engendered by such cross-cultural comparison leads to the questioning of fundamental paradigms in mass communication. Under the anthropological gaze, the sender-message-receiver model that has organized most of the work in mass communication and its related disciplines for decades shrinks to become one model among many, applicable with some forms of media in some settings and not in others. Instead of a top-down theoretical apparatus, anthropology invites scholars to consider a bottom-up apparatus that uses models and metaphors grounded in empirical observations of media in everyday life.

This last point is particularly important in the face of the changing world in which we live. In a world marked by vast diasporas of peoples, by global flows of symbols and ideologies, by a worldwide network of unbelievably complex financial transactions and by an explosion of technologies, new models and metaphors are needed as never before. These transformations are equally challenging to anthropology and mass communications. Even as mass communication is seriously rethinking its "dominant paradigm" (McQuail 1992), so anthropology is being forced to abandon the comfort of its traditional assumptions about the congruence of people, culture, and place.

The Problem of Pokémon

> Well it's not just a game! It's a whole *world*. There's TV shows, comic books, little figures and card games. ...
>
> —10-year-old Scott Levine (Joyce 1999)

One example of the kinds of social, technological, and economic transformations anthropology and mass communications must deal with is the phenomenon of Pokémon. Pokémon began as a Nintendo electronic game in Japan in 1996 and quickly became wildly successful. It was exported to the United States in 1998, by which time it had already become marketed in multiple Japanese consumer niches. In the Pokémon game, a player becomes a trainer who has to capture one of each species of wild Pokémon to advance to higher levels of mastery. The trainer whips his or her Pokémon into fighting shape, then sends them into one-on-one matches against another trainer's Pokémon. Pokémon who lose a fight don't die, they faint. Each Pokémon has a special power of attack, and as they use these successfully, they "evolve" into more powerful forms. The Gameboy technology for which Pokémon was designed invites certain forms of sociability, since separate Gameboy machines can be connected by a cable to allow dual play. What's more, in the original version of the game, two machines *must* be connected in order for players to capture the rare 151st Pokémon species.

Pokémon itself also evolved into multiple forms. Roughly categorized by media form, we can group these into four primary domains: electronic games, cards, animation and figurines. "Electronic games" include not only the original Nintendo game and its supplemental editions but also various computer CD-ROM games and web site-mounted games. The category "cards" includes game cards, which can be used to play a competitive strategy game in which players seek to capture one another's cards, and also collecting/trading cards in multiple sets and series (with each new release of a game or movie resulting in the release of a new series of cards). "Animation" refers to the Japanese television series available in various dubbed and re-edited versions throughout Europe and North America and, via satellite, the rest of the world. But it also includes a highly lucrative movie series. Both the television shows and the movies moved quickly from broadcast and theater release to video. Some children collected the videos as avidly as the cards or other goods. "Figurines" include various plastic figures as well as stuffed animals and other material forms of the Pokémon.

In addition to these four primary media, a vast secondary domain of production emerged that fed off of and commented on the primary domains. This secondary domain includes books on collecting various Pokémon products; illustrated books recounting stories from the animated series; posters enumerating the total number of monsters; "studio" computer programs that allow owners to produce Pokémon stationery, tattoos, greeting cards, stickers, and t-shirts; Halloween costumes; school supplies; apparel; and so on, ad infinitum.

Pokémon is a transnational phenomenon of astonishing complexity that defies simple labels or explanations. It is, as ten-year-old fan Levine says, "a whole world." But what kind of world is it?

It is an economic world in which billions of dollars flow within and across national boundaries, a world in which images and texts are commodities that can be owned by corporations which in turn lease them to other corporations, which in turn transform them into other kinds of commodities. Acquisition of such a license can completely alter a company's status in the economic hierarchy expressed by stock exchanges. Topp's, the trading card company with the Pokémon license for the United States and Canada, had its stock rise from $1.69 to $10.81 on

Nasdaq after it announced its first-quarter Pokémon sales (between $80 and $100 million) (Reuter's 1999). In the first three years after the release of the initial games, Nintendo grossed over $5 billion worldwide (Wapshott 1999)

It is a political world in which schools ban student Pokémon card trading and related activities because their carnivalesque nature threatens the institutional order, and in which students run for school office on campaign promises to revoke such bans (Wood 1999). It is a world in which passions run high and beatings and stabbing incidents occur as students struggle over issues of honor, fair play, and injustice expressed through Pokémon card play (Associated Press 1999).

It is a legal world in which ownership of texts and images, and the uses to which they are put, can be the subject of lawsuits and contestations. In the United States, several families have filed a class action suit against Nintendo and its trading card licensees alleging that because more of some cards are printed than others, card transactions become a form of illegal gambling (Halbfinger 1999). And in Saudi Arabia the Mufti issued a *fatwa* against Pokémon card play as a form of gambling, leading to the ban of all Pokémon products in several Gulf states (Al Korey 2001)

It is a public world in which adults and children debate the pleasures and moral dangers of Pokémon-centered play across the mediascape. Parents and psychologists debate whether Pokémon teaches positive values or mere materialism and whether it is a damaging obsession or fulfills fundamental needs for this age group (Strom 1999; Wood 1999).

It is a social world in which Pokémon-centered discourse and play can mediate social and cultural boundaries. To quote Scott Levine again: "there was this one time and I was at a place and I was nervous and shy and I found out everyone liked Pokémon and I became everyone's friend and they became my friends, because I like Pokémon, too. So it's a good way to collect friends. A *lot* of people like Pokémon" (Joyce 1999). Pokémon is about collecting friends by collecting commodities. But it is also a social world in which economic or geographic inaccessibility to Pokémon goods can mark and socially isolate children.

Above all, it is a visual world, one in which Pokémon icons—particularly the ubiquitous electric yellow mouse Pikachu—serve as indexical signs that connect diverse activities and goods across social, political and economic boundaries.

At the dawn of the new millennium, Pokémon was arguably *the* media phenomenon of the period. Yet it poses a particular problem for scholars of mass communication and media. A discipline whose origins lie in the study of powerful senders transmitting coherent messages to mass audiences connected perhaps only by their viewing habits is here faced with the situation of multiple producers simultaneously (and at least somewhat independently) creating myriad texts in dozens of different media for consumers speaking different languages and occupying different social positions in at least a dozen countries. The Pokémon players are not only consumers, however; they in turn use the media they acquire to create their own texts, to engage in play, to generate social relations, and to resist institutional authority. Children consume Pokémon, but in turn, Pokémon becomes a resource through which they become producers of social worlds.

Pokémon constitutes what Arjun Appadurai has called an "imagined world" (1996). Children encounter Pokémon not as a game or a television show, or a card game or a motion picture, but as a lived totality; it serves as an intertextual resource for their play, for their art, for their discourse. It serves as a reference point for myriad social activities as well as a resource for private fantasies. Efforts to make sense of Pokémon by approaching it chronologically (as *Time* magazine did), or by analyzing the cartoons, films, and games individually as media texts, are not useful in understanding the place of Pokémon in people's lives. Such approaches ignore the way people actually encounter Pokémon, ways that include not only individual "readings" of various kinds of media texts—both Pokémon texts and texts *about* Pokémon—but face-to-face discourses that try to articulate coherence between media texts, related commodities, and the play organized around them.

I use the example of Pokémon here not because of its intrinsic cultural importance or its transformative capacity or its permanence. (Indeed, the phenomenon peaked in 2000 and has been declining worldwide as this book goes to press). Rather, I invoke Pokémon as an example of the kind of transnational multimedia phenomena that students of media, culture, and society will be increasingly faced with in the twenty-first century. Mass communications models may be ill-equipped to explain these kinds of phenomena. From the first, mass communication theories have been shaped by a transmission model that has served as a central paradigm for the entire project. While other models based on other metaphors have also emerged—ritual, spectacle, reception, and so forth—these have tended to be defined and explicated in relation to the transmission model. So deeply rooted is this metaphor, that in one comprehensive and widely read textbook all the "alternate" models are compared using a rubric based on components of the transmission model, thus unintentionally privileging this model and reducing the others to variations on it (McQuail 1992: 54-55).

The rich body of media theory can discuss Pokémon in bits and pieces—studies of television reception, studies of uses and gratifications, studies of advertisements. Yet if it is not to be reductionistic, what is mass communication theory to make of young children pretending to be Pikachu, of trading-card play, of the social uses of drawing pictures of the Pokémon monsters, and the way all these actions overlap and intertwine? How can it relate this level of consumption to that of parents who must reflect on Pokémon in its many forms, on their children's Pokémon-based play, and on media commentaries by psychologists, sociologists and religious leaders warning against or giving license for parents' continued economic investment in their children's Pokémon worlds? What kinds of theories can encompass the multiplicity and mutability not only of consumption but of messages and senders?

Like many other social sciences, anthropology is struggling to come to terms with the changing nature of the social world in the age of globalization (Kearney 1995; Appadurai 1996; Gupta and Ferguson 1997). Yet anthropology's models—derived originally from studying societies without market metaphors and centralized systems of cultural production—may prove quite adaptable for understanding phenomena like Pokémon. Anthropologists have always recognized the tension between cultural representations (myth, ritual, media) and social formations (families, communities, polities). But they have also significantly focused on systems of exchange as the third leg of a theoretical triad.[8]

An exchange model differs from a transmission or producer/consumer model. Exchanges may be of many types—exchanges of spouses, linguistic exchanges, sharing of food. Exchanges may take place in markets, involve redistribution, or be organized by forms of reciprocity. Anthropological models have traditionally examined cultural representation, exchange, and social formation in tension. The elements of this triad are not separate or separable: exchanges occur only according to a set of cultural representations that renders them meaningful, and it is through exchanges that social formations are created, reproduced, and contested. Exchange produces and reproduces social formations. Cultural representations provide scripts and schemas for understanding the values of things exchanged as well as models for exchange. Yet cultural representations exist only insofar as they are themselves exchanged—if not shared, they are not social and collective. Although anthropology has developed many methods and theoretical approaches privileging one element in the system or another, all three are always present in some fashion; each element presupposes the others.

It is certainly as meaningful to speak of media in terms of the ways messages are exchanged as to speak of texts (cultural representations) or of media imperialism (social formation). After all, media technologies are always, in part, technologies of distribution. Texts can be broadcast, circulated, and displayed, or they can be produced through interaction. Each of these modes of distribution engages different modes of production and is employed to different ends. Many interesting aspects of media involve shifts between modes of distribution and the ways these engage representation and social formation. In the United States, e-mails are generally experienced by users as ephemeral exchanges but may not be; not only may senders or receivers archive messages but the Internet service providers routinely archive messages. These can be subpoenaed by a court as evidence to confound oral accounts of events that happened in the past. For this purpose, the messages will be transformed into printed text. It is the printed versions of what were assumed by the original senders to be ephemeral which are subsequently quoted, or even reproduced, in newspapers and circulated widely as part of stories about the trial. As we study these transformations, we see not merely exchanges of messages, but transformations, shifts in modes of production, the involvement of different social institutions with different powers, rights, and obligations, the transformation of complexes of interactions into narrative "stories" and more. What become central to this mode of analysis are the acts people perform with and through media, acts which simultaneously involve representation, exchange and social formation.

This a model can handle complex systems like that of the Pokémon phenomenon better than the sender—message—receiver model can. Yet to make it fit, anthropology will need to delve deep within the theoretical lexicon of mass communication for much of its conceptual vocabulary. Otherwise, it may find itself in the position of reinventing the wheel. With a few exceptions, anthropology has consistently refused, at least since the late 1950s, to look at the media and its roles in the lives of the peoples anthropologists have studied.

Interdisciplinary Dilemmas

In describing the interdisciplinary relations between anthropology and studies of mass communication, what I propose here is to see the relationship between the fields as one of cross-fertilization. In doing so, I wish to distance myself from some other notions of cross-disciplinary work. The term "interdisciplinary" has been much prized in academic circles for some time. The concept seems sound viewed from the outside: an historian will tackle the historical component, an anthropologist the cultural component, a political scientist the political component and so on. But such interdisciplinary work is fraught with danger and must be handled cautiously. Academic disciplines are cultural systems with different sets of values and different practices. They have different methods and theoretical assumptions that lead them to pay attention to different things, or to understand (and value) the same things in different ways. The assumption that if you combine the analyses of the six blind men you'll get a complete picture of the elephant has not been shown to be true.

Rather, what I am advocating in this book is retheorizing through interdisciplinary reading, discussion and collaboration. Mass communication scholars who must, by their own disciplinary definitions, put the mass media at the center of their analysis may find the work of anthropologists—for whom ordinary people are not just receivers and consumers of media but producers of culture—refreshing and invigorating.

Consider, for example, Stuart Hall's early book with Paddy Whannell, *The Popular Arts* (Hall and Whannell 1965). This textbook used anthropology (including arguments from Margaret Mead's *And Keep Your Powder Dry*) to complicate and resist the transmission model. Whannel and Hall described cultural values within which media consumption was located, and discussed how these would affect the reception of mass media. Later, Hall, recognizing the lack of attention to power in this approach, politicized this notion of reception and constructed his famous "dominated, negotiated, resistant" model (Hall 1977). In turn, this model has been appropriated and transformed by many other scholars, including some anthropologists.

But the flow of theoretical engagement scarcely flows only in one direction. Anthropologists studying people engaged in the practices of everyday life have likewise found in the vast conceptual lexicon of mass communication research tools to help them articulate cultural processes and social practices in the field. In Gail Landsman's 1988 study of the Ganienkah uprisings in New York and Canada, for example, she drew heavily on studies of news production by mass communications scholars. Her study is not a study of mass communication per se; rather, it focuses on the ways the Ganienkah attempted to construct themselves socially, legally, and politically as a people with national sovereignty in a particular time and place. This ethnographic study inevitably includes—as one element among many—dealings between the Ganienkah and various news media during their insurrection. Landsman uses the work of mass communication theorists like Tuchman, Gans, Fishman, and Schudson to help her theorize her ethnographic data on the relations between the Indians and the press, their mutual uses and representations of one another, and their role in the larger process of schismogenesis, the differentiation of society through the working out of cultural distinctions.

Mass communication scholars who want to be able to connect media texts to the social and cultural worlds of the people who produce and consume media must find contextual models that allow them to examine the interplay between technologies, social formations and texts. Anthropologists have perhaps an even more difficult task as they seek to integrate mass communication studies into the discipline. An anthropology of mass media, in the fullest sense of the term, must be more than just ethnography; it requires theorizing media to understand it as a part of everyday human life in the modern world. Both anthropology and mass communication can benefit from cross-reading and appropriating concepts and language. This kind of interdisciplinary work is what will allow for broader, deeper, and more comprehensive understandings of the place(s) of mass communication in contemporary lives. It is to this sense of interdisciplinary cross-fertilization I hope this book can contribute.

Media and Expressive Culture

This book takes as its starting point a consideration of media as a form of expressive culture, which we take to mean the public display of symbols or enactment of symbolic action for performative effect. We will follow William O. Beeman in using the term "expressive culture" to refer to those institutions and practices through which people enact, display, and manipulate symbolic materials "with the implicit [or explicit] expectation that other individuals will be directly affected by such presentations" (1982: xiii). That media have as one of their primary and manifest functions the expression of social and cultural information, clearly makes them part of the field of expressive culture. All media, moreover, explicitly seek to affect human beings, and consumers of media intentionally constitute themselves as audiences in order to be affected. Media messages can persuade (seduce, compel) us. They can inform (educate, provoke, brainwash) us. And they can give us pleasure in the form of escape, laughter, or insight.

Treating media as expressive culture is not a way to isolate it from other forms of cultural practice. Every social practice has an expressive aspect; when we marry, we not only undergo a ritual transformation of our own and our families' social realities, but the marriage itself always stands as a public sign, a representation of (some of) the norms and values that constitute social life in the community. The marriage expresses, at the least, the continuing validity of the ritual in the society, the reproduction of the social form of the family through the ritual, and as such, expresses the success of the society itself to those people who participate in the wedding, talk about it, hear about it, read about it or look at photographs of it. The same can be said of any other social practice: going to work, brushing our teeth, cooking a meal, dining with friends.

In other words, we not only act according (or in reaction) to cultural values and norms, but in doing so, we serve as signs to ourselves and those around us of the validity of those cultural practices, values, and norms. We are most aware of this when we are surrounded by children, who learn far more about how to live and act from such expressions than they ever do from any formal schooling. But this process, usually labeled "socialization," should not be seen as limited to childhood. "Socialization should be understood as an element of *the continuity of social reproduction*—of the inherent temporality of the social process— rather than just referring to the personality formation of the child" (Giddens 1979: 128, my italics). Socialization is an ongoing practice and the expressive dimension of culture is a primary system through which this process takes place. Expressive culture not only provides people with privileged spaces within which to contemplate and even "try out" alternative ways of viewing the world, but also provides resources in the form of alternative metaphors, schemas, and frames for analysis. In every society, some institutions seem to foreground the expressive aspect of culture. Anthropologists drawn to the study of symbolism and expressive culture have accordingly devoted a great deal of attention to such domains of human action as drama, art, play, myth, and ritual— and, increasingly, mass communication.

Not all scholars would agree with this positioning of mass media as part of expressive culture. Clifford Geertz's felicitous phrase describing public and expressive aspects of culture as where we "show ourselves to ourselves" (1973) has obvious problems in the contemporary world in which performances—packaged, commoditized, and advertised—travel from their places of origin to new sites where they can be consumed, recontextualized and interpreted. A viewing of the television show *Dallas* in America is not the same as a viewing of *Dallas* in Israel, while a Moroccan viewing differs from both of these (Liebes and Katz 1994).

These examples express two aspects of mass media that have made many scholars insist on its distinctness from such forms of expressive media as play, spectacle, art, drama, and ritual. First, whereas most anthropological studies of expressive culture have involved the physical co-presence of producers and audiences, mass media generally involves the consumption of messages by audiences separate from the sources and sites of production. Second, whereas most forms of expressive culture studies by anthropologists are specific to a time and place, mass media often exist in commodified and textualized forms that can circulate among various sets of audiences completely unrelated to one another.

The separateness of mass media from the interactive elements that mark face-to-face interactions is, as we have seen, a defining characteristic of many of the forms of communication we call mass media. Mass mediation disrupts the rich multichannel feedback that occurs in face-to-face discourse. Recipients have no immediate, apparent effect on the media they consume through subtle feedback cues. This returns us to the concept of the mass audience. Insofar as the function of mass media is seen as transmission, it would seem they can only be recipients, never participants. This apparently allows a small group of producers to join together and affect a vast number of people who may have no social connection in common, save for their mutual consumption of the media.

The objectification of mass media also distinguishes it from face-to-face interaction. Nearly all media forms involve discrete texts that exist not only as messages but as objects. When the media text leaves the producer to be received by audiences, it takes on a social life of its own as a thing, and at some point in its social biography, the text is usually a commodity (Appadurai 1988). One can pay for access to a specified reception site such as a movie theater, rent or purchase a media text (such as a book, magazine, or videotape) or choose a channel (and hence, the commercial surround of the text). The objectification and commodification of mass media forms is a crucial distinction since it allows for radical recontextualization of cultural symbols. This distinction is significant enough that Marie Gillespie has attempted to distinguish between "expressive culture"—mass media produced by certain groups as a means of establishing, challenging or maintaining a cultural identity—and "cultures of consumption," efforts by groups to construct identities from cultural expressions they consume but to whose production they do not contribute (1995: 4).

I do not want to minimize these problems. Nonetheless, too great an attention on the former—now apparently being followed by a reactionary overattention to the latter—threatens to blind us from a more reasoned position: to see mass media not as radically new technologies of expression but to recognize the kinship, as well as the differences, between the mass media and the other common forms of expressive media.

The distinctiveness between the ways audiences view a text are, after all, applicable to drama and spectacle as well as to mass media. A Manipuri production of Shakespeare's *Macbeth* in Brentford, England, during the Golden Jubilee celebrations of India's independence from Britain not only means something very different than a production of the same play by a British company but means something quite different to the Manipuri performers than to the British audiences attending the Jubilee celebrations—and likely means something different to Brentford audiences of South Asian origin than those who see themselves as Anglo-Saxons (Bhatia 1998).

Following this line of thought, we can follow ethnographic film-maker Jay Ruby in regarding a media text as "a culturally coded communicative event *designed* to function in a particular context." Media producers employ various codes they deem culturally appropriate for the context in which they wish the film seen. Like performers, producers assume that viewers share their cultural codes and interpretive competencies, and that therefore the film will have its intended impact. "Lacking a convenient or common means of feedback, producers must hypothesize their viewers' ability to understand with little hope of ever really knowing whether their assumptions are correct. In other words, producers make cultural assumptions about their viewers' cultural assumptions about codes and their contexts" (Ruby 1995: 194-195).

This in no way assumes that producers are correct in their assumptions or that viewers are passive recipients shaped by the design of these culturally coded media events. On the contrary, usually viewers have an active and powerful role in interpreting media in part because they come to media in a context, a situation that frames the interpretations and uses they will make of symbols. Depending on their cultural background—that is, their own codes for interpreting not only symbols in a media text but for understanding how to interpret a media text, media recipients will interpret and understand media differently. Both media production and media consumption are performances, that is, interpretive *events*. They occur in situations, defined by different sets of norms, with participants who have different identities, roles, and statuses. What is more, people do more with these media than read or view and interpret them. Buying a nonfunctional antique radio for decoration, displaying videos, books or records one doesn't actually enjoy in the belief that they exemplify a particular taste, wearing clothing decorated with media figures, and giving technologies or media texts as gifts are also all part of media(ted) culture. The goal of looking at media as a form of expressive culture is to understand mass media in the everyday practices of both producers and its consumers (and producers are always also consumers); that is, as a part of human social life interconnected to the many other dimensions of human life.

Understanding media in this multidimensional way is all the more necessary in that the boundaries between the domains of expressive culture are not sharp but blurred. Scholarly commentary and analysis is (like myth) usually marked by categorization and clarity but the everyday lives of producers, consumers and texts themselves are marked by messiness and hybridity. The Kayapo capture their rituals on video as a means of passing them on to their children (T. Turner 1992a). Indian children in Los Angeles learn South Asian dance from watching movies made in Bombay (Ghei 1988). Myths are retold as comic books (Pritchett 1995). The compression of time and space made possible by the mass media result in an ever-increasing number of such hybrids. Far from exceeding the criteria for the study of expressive culture, media analysis constitutes a fascinating new twist on it: through mass media, representations become commodities in a world in which social formation and identity are increasingly expressed through commodities. Consuming—purchasing, displaying, using (and using up)—is itself a form of expressive culture insofar as it is public and functions to construct, reproduce, or contest individual or collective identities.

Seeing media as a form of expressive culture fits well with an emerging model in media studies, a dynamic model in which public symbolic configurations are selectively appropriated by various culture industries, that is, social organizations and institutions that control the technology, skills, and knowledge needed for media production. These culture industries, large and small, transform these symbolic configurations and return them to public circulation in new, textualized and commodified (or otherwise objectified) forms. This production process is mirrored by the consumption process. Audiences selectively appropriate symbols from the sets of media texts available to them and employ these in their practices of social formation. The circuit is completed as the culture industries become aware of and evaluate consumer choices through various means of surveillance (not the least of which are the observations and intuitions of producers who, after all, are also media consumers). Through this circuit, not only content but processes of selection and transformation may themselves be selectively transformed.[9]

From Word to World

The purpose of this book is to describe the emergence of an anthropology of media, and the ways in which this field connects with, and challenges, other approaches to media and mass communications. This project will take us from the word to the world, from the analysis of media texts, to the study of audiences and the parallel study of producers, to a model of exchange that seeks to examine local and global mediascapes.

At the heart of media analysis is the media text: the news story, the film, the show, the ad, the snapshot. The text is at once an object of exchange, a vehicle for cultural representation, and a resource for social formation. Chapter 3 explores text and textual analysis; it introduces the concept of the text and describes the six sets of relations through which texts are usually analyzed. Textual analysis, to be effective, however, inevitably ties the text to the social relations of its production and consumption. In most theories of media, these links center around relations of power. Chapter 4 continues this focus by examining theories about the power of media texts and their effects on consumers, from theories of linear reception to audience gratification theories. In Chapter 5, I argue that shifts in media theory toward the text as a site of struggle over meaning have created a theoretical space for connecting with anthropological metaphors of media as myth, a conceptualization that sees peoples' reception, interpretation, and use of media as at once embedded in broader cosmological orientations, and continuous with other domains of social life. I suggest the outlines of an emerging theory of spectatorship.

In the hands of its main proponents, however, this is a theory of spectatorship without spectators. Chapter 6 examines how assumptions made about the effects of texts and the nature of the interpretive encounter can be challenged and extended by examining emerging work in the ethnography of audience. The rise of ethnography draws our attention to the *situation* of interpretation. Audiences are here seen neither as free agents in a free market nor as mesmerized units mindlessly consuming the messages they are force-fed, but rather as agents who selectively appropriate and interpret media according to their positions within social fields. Media interpretation is conceived here as an active process through which social actors become (as they have always been) producers of culture. Audience ethnography seeks to enter intimately into people's lives, to see how media representations become part of the cultural construction of identities, both social and individual.

Yet it is not only media consumers who are productive of identity and sociality. If audiences are now seen as performers of text-acts, rather than as receivers of messages, a retheorizing of producers is also necessary. Chapter 7 looks at how ethnographies of media producers dislodge some of the more extreme theories of media domination by illustrating the ways that media production inevitably forms a (sub)culture, a symbolic system with its own practices, identities, and social formations, which have consequences for the kinds of texts it produces.

This approach is particularly relevant in the light of the changes in theory required by the rise of the so-called emancipatory media (Enzenberger 1970), in which means of reception and means of production are contained in the same technologies. The rise of small-scale media industries and "indigenous media" are the subject of chapter 8, which raises the question of how we can theorize media in a world where, with video recorders, cassettes, faxes, the Internet, and the World Wide Web, the means of reception and the means of production are becoming the same technologies.

Yet if we are to conceive of producers and consumers as both being engaged in "text-acts," we must recognize the degree to which conti-

nuities and discontinuities exist through shared (but unequally distributed) interpretive codes, the ways in which producers and consumers
mutually imagine one another, the ways in which they use technologies
of consumption and production, and the web of intertextuality that
links media texts across time and space. Chapter 9 explores these issues
by examining the organization of cultural practices, associated with
specific media literacies, around particular technologies. These clusters
form niches within interconnected communications ecologies, which
are, in turn, embedded in mediascapes.

I conclude with some reflections on the role of the mass media in
social transformation, and particularly the increasing collapse of perceptions of time and space that are labeled "postmodernity" and "globalization." The circulation of media and its incorporation into multiple
spheres of everyday life has become simultaneously a principle vehicle
for the flow of ideas and symbols across time and space, but also one of
the dominant signs of the modernities it produces. The rise of so-called
new media and of phenomena that transcend a single medium to sprawl
across the mediascape in myriad commoditized forms, also pose significant challenges for media ethnography and anthropological theory.

Before we can examine the emerging anthropology of media, however, we must first examine what contemporary anthropology is emerging from. The notion that anthropologists must examine the mass media
as a part of the lives of their subjects is not a new idea. It is easy to overestimate the novelty of anthropology's interest in mass communication.
Chapter 2 offers a critical historical overview of anthropological
approaches to mass communication research stretching back over
eighty years. My approach here is not to criticize the inadequacies of
these early approaches; rather, I aim to reformulate the questions that
underlie such works so that they shed light on current theories and
problematics. Such an engagement seems to me to be the best way to
understand what is new in the anthropology of media, and what are
reformulations of anthropology's perennial concerns.

Notes

1. This vignette is derived from the writings of Terrence Turner (1991, 1992a, 1992b)
2. This vignette is based on Armbrust 1998b and personal observations by the author.
3. This vignette is based on an observation by the author, recorded in College Park, MD, summer 1996.
4. Hockett does not compare these design features of human communication to technological transformations but rather to the design features of the communication systems of other animal species. Ants, which leave scent trails, do not have rapid fading. Stickleback fish, which communicate by changing the colors of the scales on their bellies, lack immediate feedback since they cannot see their own abdomens. As males and females cannot send the same messages, stickleback communication also lacks interchangeability.
5. I use *frame* throughout this book to refer to a general interpretive context established by participants in an interpretive activity through which events, objects and actions are made meaningful. On frames and framing, see Goffman 1981.
6. Although I will occasionally speak of research "subjects" or "informants," I prefer the term *hosts* because it better captures the nature of the fieldwork experience. Ethnography is essentially parasitic; although members of the host community may gain something from it, their gains are rarely balanced by the gains of the ethnographer in terms of pleasures, pay, and promotions. "Host" emphasizes this essential inequality of giver and receiver. "Host" also reverses the assumption of authority implied in terms such as "subject," and emphasizes the ethical obligations of the ethnographer to those who make his or her research possible.
7. For a fascinating account of a psychologist's realization of the importance of this kind of dialogue in human research, see Gilligan and Brown 1992. A renowned psychologist, Gilligan discovers that the resistance of her subjects to the forms of interviewing are not obstacles to be overcome but indicate real efforts toward dialogue: indeed, the resistance reveals the subjects' desires to be recognized as persons by the researcher and to have some say in the shaping of the research into their lives and feelings. Sadly, Gilligan and her colleagues never use the term "ethnography," and seem unaware they are reinventing the wheel.
8. For this observation, I am indebted to Jon Anderson and Debra Spitulnik, who suggested it in different words on very different occasions.
9. This circuit model is different from, but consonant with, the "cultural circuit" model of Johnson (1986-1987) and scholars at Britain's "Open University" (du Gay 1996; du Gay et al. 1997).

◦‿◦

WHATEVER HAPPENED TO THE ANTHROPOLOGY OF MEDIA?

In 1989 I took a short break from participation in Brown University's Pembroke Seminar on "cultural literacies" to attend the American Anthropological Association meetings in New Orleans, where I was on one of three panels dealing with topics of mass media, then a record for the organization. On my return to Brown, one of the Pembroke fellows, a recent Ph.D. in communications from the University of Illinois, told me, "I hear the anthropologists have finally discovered the mass media."

The jest was both unkind and, unfortunately, true. The literature on mass media in mass communications, communication, sociology, political science, cultural studies, American studies and similar disciplines is vast and has a long and intricate history. Anthropological interest in mass media seems scant by comparison. Nonetheless, anthropological interest in media goes back at least to Franz Boas's brief reflections on the value of Native American newspapers in 1911. Anthropological writing on media grew steadily during the depression and World War II, continuing in various forms through the 1960s.

Yet just as mass communication research was taking off in other disciplines, and mass communication was emerging as a field of study in its own right, anthropology seemed to lose interest in it. Disciplinary attention to mass communication, never strong, faltered for a quarter century, between about 1960 and 1985, with only a few scattered publications outside of the development communications arena. Since 1985, however, anthropological interest in mass media has been growing exponentially.

Notes for this section begin on page 56.

Communities and Communication

The earliest work by anthropologists to touch on mass communication involved the application of the functionalist methods associated with the anthropology of Malinowski and Radcliffe-Brown to American and European cities and villages. This anthropological approach included taking a residential community as the unit of analysis, using participant-observation methods, and focusing on "institutions" as the primary analytical unit within the community. These studies paid attention both to how these institutions functioned to meet social and psychological needs of the members of the community, and to how these institutions functioned to maintain overall social cohesion. Among the earliest and best known studies were Robert and Helen Merrell Lynd's *Middletown* studies and William Lloyd Warner's five-volume *Yankee City*.

Media in Middletown

Neither of the Lynds was a professional anthropologist. Robert Lynd was a graduate of a divinity school, while Helen Merrell Lynd had a B.A. from Wellesley College. In 1924 they received a grant from New York's Institute of Social and Religious Research (ISRR) to study religion in America through the medium of a single community. Both the ISRR and Presbyterian Board of Home Missions were sponsoring quantitative studies of the changing place of religion in American society, some of which offered sophisticated methodologies for the time.[1] The Lynds, however, were not satisfied with these quantitative methods. Claiming to borrow the methods of social anthropology,[2] the Lynds set out to examine religion in "the total social context of the community" of Muncie, Indiana. Although their final report was rejected by their funders as unpublishable, *Middletown* (1929) was picked up by the mainstream publisher Harcourt Brace, reviewed on the front page of the *New York Times* and has remained in print for more than seventy years. This work both established the principle of, and set the benchmark for, studies of cities as communities. On the strength of the book, Columbia University granted Robert Lynd a Ph.D. and a position in its sociology department, while Helen Merrell Lynd became a professor at Sarah Lawrence College.

Within its broad depiction of the institutions of an American city, *Middletown* examines mass media under two functions: "using leisure" and "getting information." According to the Lynds, leisure poses a cultural problem for Middletowners. Although one of the purposes of making a living is to afford leisure, Middletowners worry that "too much leisure" might lead to shiftlessness and a decline in community cohesion and prosperity. Middletowners thus spend[3] most of their time engaged in "marshaled pursuits" such as "getting a living, home-making, receiving training in school or carrying on religious or communal practices." The remaining leisure time is used to "break the routines" of these other activities (Lynd and Lynd 1929: 225).

The fundamental form of leisure activity is reading. Comparing the Middletown of their study with the Middletown of 1890 through examination of old newspapers and diaries, they note that in 1924, people read as much as in 1890, and subscribed to more magazines and newspapers than previously, but social discourse *about* books and news had declined considerably. In interviews, Middletowners described their interest in magazines as stemming from their inability to find time for more extended reading. Public lectures were in decline in 1924, as were literary clubs. Whereas the 1890 data suggested that literary and scientific subjects formed a considerable part of social discourse, in both public discussion and private conversation,[4] the Lynds found in 1925 that people pointed to time spent in social activities as reasons they *couldn't* spend more time reading (Lynd and Lynd 1929: 234)—implying that a distinct breach had developed between reading as an individual activity and conversation as a social one. Moreover, there was less social agreement about what people *should* read, and many interviewees complained that they didn't know how to organize "courses" of reading. Reading was thus constructed as a kind of intellectual work rather than a pleasurable activity or a social obligation.

The Lynds also examined the transformation of leisure through technological innovation. While they regarded the most significant transformation of leisure in Middletown to be the automobile, which liberated members of the community from the community, new forms of media—movies and radio—were also seen as having a growing impact on family life. The automobile and the radio combined to increase nuclear-family activity at the expense of extended social relations. The radio kept families from scattering in the evenings after dinner, while the family car provided them with the opportunity to get away from the community *as* a family. Both automobiles and radio were the subject of public moral discourse, as the community sought to sort out whether they were "good" or "bad" in terms of the effects their introduction was having on the community.

Motion pictures, on the other hand, represented a decentralizing tendency, since young people of all classes tended to go to the movies without their families. While family filmgoers preferred comedies, the primary interest of young people was in modern-society films "with burning 'heart interest'" (Lynd and Lynd 1929: 266).[5] Public discourse about the effects of movies on society was less uniform than it was about automobiles or radio. Members of social agencies dealing with

young people—high-school teachers, the judge of the juvenile court—
made claims for the pernicious effects of these films on the city's youth,
but most Middletowners took them at "face value" as entertainment
(267). In sum, "[i]n 1925 leisure was becoming more passive, more formal, more organized, more mechanized, and more commercialized"
(Lynd 1937: 245).

The second function of media, "getting information," was conceived by the Lynds as a central part of engaging in community activities. In 1924, the local newspaper was ubiquitous; scarcely a single
home did not receive either the morning or the evening newspaper. The
function of the newspaper assumed by the Lynds is that ascribed to it
by the Middletowners themselves: to provide information about the
community on the basis of which citizens can intelligently construct the
community politically (as informed voters), socially (as knowledgeable
citizens), and economically (as thoughtful consumers). However, the
Lynds argue that because newspapers are dependent on advertising
from the business class, the interests of this class shape editorial policy.
Juvenile crimes (particularly violations of liquor laws) are not reported
when the culprits are children of local businessmen, for example, but
culprits are identified by name when they are members of the working
class (Lynd and Lynd 1929: 476). Newspapers served to unify the diver-
sified city, but they do so through frameworks that reinforce the class
structure of Middletown (conceived by the Lynds' as a simple duality).

Ten years later, in 1935, Robert Lynd revisited Muncie for a follow-
up study, to examine the effects of the depression on the community. In
general, Lynd found few fundamental changes in Middletown, although
two of his observations on media are interesting. The first is the increasing function of leisure activities in differentiating between generations.
Using the federal funding made available during the depression, play-
grounds and parks were renovated and improved, and a public swim-
ming pool was constructed. Social activities—dances, concerts, plays,
talent shows—were organized, primarily aimed at children and young
adults. In this atmosphere, Lynd notes that movies were being used differently by different generations. For adults, the films were escapist
entertainment, an "anodyne" for the trials of everyday life. For children,
the Saturday matinee is an "exciting weekly event" offering hours of
entertainment including a cartoon, serial, newsreel, and one, or even
two, features. For adolescents, Lynd claims the movies offer an education in how to be an adult, particularly for girls learning how to present
"the confidence of a Joan Crawford." Lynd notes that this education is
not simply absorbed from the movies; it is transferred from the movies
and tried out in the everyday social worlds of movie viewers. He offers
the following as a typical sample of adolescent discourse in which high-

school girls "stroll with brittle confidence in and out of 'Barney's'soft drink parlor 'clicking' with the 'drugstore cowboys' at the tables; while the tongue-tied young male learns the art of the swift, confident come-back in the face of female confidence" (Lynd 1937: 262):

> *Scene in Barney's: A boy drinking a coke is joined by a girl.*
> *Boy*: You see the Strand? [Joan Crawford in *No More Ladies.*]
> *Girl*: Yes, it's swell. [They both light cigarettes.]
> *Boy*: They were the best wisecracks I've heard in this town.
> *Girl*: Remember when he said—[then a repetition of the wisecrack]
> [The girl goes out, and soon the same boy is joined by another girl]
> *Boy*: You been to the Strand?
> *Girl*: Sure!
> *Boy*: Ever heard such wonderful wisecracks?
> *Girl*: They were *mar*-velous.
> *Boy*: You remember when—[and out comes the wisecrack again, gaining more confidence of tone in the retelling] (Lynd 1937: 262-263).

Media thus differentiates between the generations not only as a marker of demographic differences in taste but because it serves different kinds of functions for audiences of different age groups who live in different social worlds. Through their use of media, people construct generational differences.

Lynd's second observation concerned the dual function of media in at once producing local social cohesion, and at the same time, serving as a channel through which Middletowners feel linked to a wider world. The local radio station, established in Muncie during the decade between the two studies, served the former function with its coverage of local high-school sports and the broadcast of a local amateur program, while it serves the latter function through such syndicated programs as Walter Winchell's *On Broadway* with its heavily localized New York lingo and subject matter (Lynd 1937: 263-265). Newspapers as well mixed local news (20 percent of their total column inches) with national (10 percent) and international (10 percent) news and blended local advertising with advertisements from outside Muncie, offering Middletowners a sense of connectedness to the world outside.

The Middletown studies are at their weakest when they attempt to elaborate on the ways in which media come to support the local power structure. *Middletown* offers no real theory of class,[6] loosely dividing the population into a "working class" and a "business class." Lynd recognizes in *Middletown Revisited* that class tensions are reflected in the media but he is unable to offer any real theorization of this. He recognizes the conundrum that "the operation of a profitable newspaper depends on securing at one and the same time maximum circulation from the working class and maximum advertising and credit from the business class" is resolved in Middletown by framing news and editorials within regular appeals to such slogans as "civil unity" and "radicalism is un-American" (Lynd 1937: 382-383). But while his data demonstrates that working-class men are perfectly able to engage in alternative discourses of class, Lynd doesn't know what to do with such resistance, or how to locate it with regard to their consumption of texts.

The Lynds' arguments about media technologies prefigure by forty years Raymond Williams's argument about "mobile privatization" (1974: 171). Like the Lynds, Williams argued that mass media and the automobile function together to privatize the family while transporting it, both literally and figuratively, beyond the home. Yet the nature of the technologies are such that the consumers carried their domestic "shell" of family privacy with them. What Williams insists on, but is missing from the Lynds' studies, is comprehensive exploration of the real and imagined worlds outside Middletown to which the Middletowners travel and the pleasures they derive thereof. Joan Crawford films and Walter Winchell reports are symbolic reservoirs from which Middletowners appropriate symbols, and they are also powerful performances that transport their listeners out of Middletown to other, imagined communities. The failure to explore this is, to a large extent, an artifact of the method of treating the community as a self-contained whole.

Yankee City and Beyond

Not long after Lynd revisited Muncie, William Lloyd Warner, who had already published an ethnography on Australian Aboriginal communities, set out to study an American city—Newburyport, Massachussetts—in a manner similar to that adopted by the Lynds. Although *Yankee City* resembles the earlier *Middletown* in some ways, it is a larger (five volumes), more complex, and more theoretically sophisticated study. In particular, Warner greatly expands the focus on class. Whereas Middletown is rather simply divided into the working class and the business class, Warner's study divides society into six classes based on distinctions not only of wealth and property but on the basis of complex social distinctions, including those of taste in consumption and use of leisure.

Warner's interest in media began in a minor vein but grew over the years. In the first volume of the Yankee City series, Warner claimed that the newspaper served the field research because it provided (1) descriptions of events which took place in the community, (2) indications of the sentiments and attitudes of certain groups, (3) research leads for interviewing, and (4) materials for the study of the paper as a mechanism of communication (Warner and Lunt 1941: 68)

By 1959 Warner's position had shifted so that he now regarded newspapers primarily as symbolic artifacts:

> Despite the intrusion of modern canons of accuracy and the infusion of the spirit of rationality into newspapers and other mass media, a casual listing of the prevailing selection of stories and the simplest analysis of the criteria of a "good story" that will hold readers and perhaps build circulation demonstrate that the "objective" coverage of what happens every day to the people of the world is dominated by the basic wishes, the hopes and fears, the non-logical symbolic themes and folk-beliefs of the people who buy and read the papers. ... the reporter must put the mark of empirical truth on the story—over the whole of his plot, its dramatis personae, and its solutions—as if it all really happened.... [but] Although the events of the news story may have all occurred in the form in which they are set forth, the relations of the major and minor characters, the arrangements of the incidents, and the symbols used to refer to them must be part of the storyteller's art. (1959: 55)

Beginning with the first volume of the Yankee City study, Warner offered a detailed analysis of media consumption as "symbolic behavior," mapping tastes in consumption to class (Warner and Lunt 1941: 378-421). Warner examined taste in book genres, magazine subscriptions, newspaper reading, and movie going, finding all of these to be "highly influenced by class values" (379), and he examined ethnicity as well as class in consumption of magazines and movies.

Although foreshadowing later work by Bourdieu (1984) and others in examining how taste constructs social distinctions, Warner's study is considerably less theorized. In his analysis of reading, for example, the genres into which he categorizes literature are his own categories; they are not derived from interviews or observations and do not reflect a "natives' point of view." Warner notes, for example, that of the six classes of Yankee City it is the two extreme opposites—upper upper and lower lower—who read the bulk of "detective stories," in which fact he sees "an obvious likeness." What he misses is the fact that *for consumers* there is a world of difference between the works of, say, Dorothy L. Sayers and S.S. van Dine, on the one hand, and E. Phillips Oppenheimer and Sax Rohmer on the other. Warner lumps them all together. The supposed likenesses are thus partly an artifact of the sociological method of analysis. Ultimately, Warner uses his surveys to illustrate how consumption marks preexisting class distinctions rather than seeing media consumption as one form of action (among many) through which people engage in an ongoing (re)construction of class distinctions.

By 1959, and the final volume of the Yankee City study, Warner had shifted his attention from the study of texts to analyzing the role of media, particularly the press, in social action. *The Living and the Dead* traces the role of symbolism in political action, social organization, public ceremony, death ritual, and religion. In three lengthy chapters, Warner examines the way a local political actor, "Biggy" Muldoon, employed symbols that played with the cultural contradictions of American society to transform himself "in the minds of many in Yankee City from the mundane referential image they had of him as another tough kid from the wrong side of the tracks into a type of symbolic hero much beloved of Americans ... the strong man who attacks the proud and powerful and protects the poor and lowly" (1959: 15).

In particular, Warner offers a contrast between the ways Muldoon's public performances were cast by local and national presses. While locally Muldoon could not be but an ambiguous figure, at the national level he was consistently framed as a kind of trickster hero, the bright young man fighting the stultifying bureaucrats of City Hall. Since many residents of Newburyport were also consumers of national media (50 percent of newspapers read in Newburyport came from outside), these external representations of Muldoon began to transform local understandings of him as a public figure. In his rise to power and through his first terms as mayor, Warner argues, representations of Muldoon held the symbols of the hero and the clown in successful tension. During Muldoon's second term, however, the national press began to tire of Muldoon's antics. Performances appropriate for a man fighting the powers that be were not read in the same ways once that man *became* one of the powers that be. The frame of clown increasingly began to replace that of hero. As the frame in the national press came to echo (and be echoed in) the local press, Muldoon's popularity waned and he lost his third election bid. In this story, Warner offers an account of a social drama (V. Turner 1974a, 1980) in which semiotic agency shifts as the social and political stakes shift. It prefigures similar, more sophisticated descriptions of media social dramas in which the press is both a channel and an agent (Wagner-Pacifici 1986; Landsman 1987; Scherer 1988). It also pays careful attention to the *bifocality* of media (Peters 1997), the ways in which media provide local communities with frames for imagining themselves in relation to larger national or even global worlds.

Although the Lynds cited anthropologists as their inspiration, their work was most influential with sociologists, as was that of Warner. The works by Warner and the Lynds served as models for an entire genre of community studies that followed, mostly conducted by sociologists.[7] As these accumulated, they led to a series of synthetic sociological accounts of the United States as a national community, texts that combined statistical analysis with information drawn from community studies, as well as original research. Many of these included critiques of mass media as a central institution in contemporary American society.

One of these, by anthropologist Jules Henry, argued that Americans were constructing a national "culture of death" (1963: 475). Henry combined analysis of media texts with ethnographic studies of a series of American institutions to offer a "passionate ethnography" of American society. Henry argues that the United States possessed a "pecuniary culture" of drive (in the sense of unending desire and the need to work ceaselessly toward fulfillment of these desires), acquisition (the need to meet unquenchable desires with acquisition and possession of an unending stream of goods and services), and fear (of loss). The "philosophies" of fear and desire he elicits from advertising and political discourses are explored in accounts of American childrearing and care for the elderly, based on detailed ethnographic accounts of schools, family homes, and nursing-care facilities (1963).

Henry's work, which sought to connect community study with larger, national cultural patterns, was something of a last hurrah by American anthropologists doing community studies in the United States. While studies based on participant observation within communities abroad continued to play a significant role in anthropology, community studies in the United States became increasingly focused on demographics and subsumed into sociology.

Community studies like those of Warner and the Lynds were marred by their devotion to functionalist assumptions and fell out of fashion as the notion of the clearly bounded social community fell out of fashion in anthropology, and as many of the fundamental principles of functionalism became questioned in social thought.[8] Primary among these was the question of whether an American city truly constituted a homogenous community in the functionalist sense, that is, a collection of social institutions whose interconnections created a complete and bounded whole. The American cities studied in this period were geographically distinct from one another but they were not distinguished by cultural boundaries of language, kinship rules, or religious practice. Their economic, social, and communicative interconnections with other cities and with other polities—the state, the region, the nation—were significantly underplayed in many cases.

Closely related to this is the issue of the conservative bias of functionalist studies. While *Middletown* clearly puts the community into a historical perspective, the nature of the critique seems to be based on an assumption that the community is declining as the city moves more clearly away from the homogenous ideal-type postulated by structural-functionalism and projected into the past. The Lynds certainly seem to see the automobile and the radio as threatening social order by diminishing community networks, rather than as strengthening the nuclear family by increasing time spent together. The only basis for the evaluative nature of their comments seems to be the general functionalist preference for closed rather than open systems.[9]

Finally, many functionalist arguments concerning media also suffer from a teleological fallacy, which confuses origins and functions. When Warner speaks of the "needs" of contemporary societies for communication and describes the mass media as answering these needs, he seems to be treating society as a goal-oriented entity which acts to meet these goals. Yet most of the mass media in Yankee City, as in Middletown, comes from beyond the community itself and even the forms of the media themselves are shaped by large-scale historical patterns. Examining mass media in cities draws attention to the porous nature of the boundaries assumed by these studies, to the ways in which these communities are interpenetrated by social, cultural and economic forces outside them and over which they have only minimal control. The community studies methodology tends to conceal these crucial issues.

Media and Modernization

Anthropological community studies outside the United States were also dealing with these issues. Critiques of the community studies approach had become commonplace by the mid-sixties. Mitchell could have been speaking of the Lynds or any of those following them when he wrote:

> The classical anthropological method takes a unit—a "tribe" or "society" or community—and presents the behavior of its members in terms of a series of interlocking institutions, structures, norms and values. It is not only anthropologists working in urban areas who have found this sort of assumption difficult to maintain, but also those who have been conducting "tribal" studies.... They have found that the effect of groups and institutions not physically present in the tribal area influences the behavior of people in it. The unit of interacting relationships, in other words, is larger than the tribe. (1966: 56)

Such critiques were part of a growing effort to study social structure on larger and larger scales, including as states (Redfield 1941), subnational regions (Bennett 1967) and nations (Steward et al. 1956; Adams 1970). Models for such research varied. Robert Redfield, working in Latin America with folk communities on the orbit of major urban centers, theorized a cultural continuum between "folk" and "urban" societies (1964). Where folk societies were marked by face-to-face interaction, sacredness, and homogeneity, urban societies were marked by anomie, secularization, and social experimentation. Redfield presumed that as individuals moved from folk communities to cities, or as an entire society moved toward a more urbanized culture, there would be a breakdown in cultural traditions. Urbanizing individuals and societies would suffer from cultural disorganization and would have higher incidences of social pathologies such as divorce, alcoholism, crime, and loneliness. Although simplistic and severely handicapped by a neo-evolutionary bias, Redfield's continuum offered an early approach to studying communities in relation to larger units of social organization.

Many anthropologists also found inspiration in Julian Steward's classic two-tier model, which divides society into national and local levels. Descriptions of national structures derived primarily from documentary sources and interviews with political actors are then read against ethnographic studies of local communities (Steward et al. 1956).[10] What was problematic in such studies was theorizing the nature of the links between the two tiers, the paths through which and across which the levels communicated. Certainly mass media were one of these channels of communication, but how exactly? What roles did they play at the various levels where they were produced, distributed, and consumed?

Mediating Traditions

One effort to link the urban/national and folk/local levels involved a new conception of urban/folk relations, based on interrelations between urban centers and folk peripheries. In "The Cultural Role of Cities," Redfield and Milton Singer (1954) described two cultural functions performed by all urban centers, with varying degrees of intensity and elaboration. "Primary urbanization" serves an "orthogenetic" function, in which cadres of literati appropriate widespread "folk" symbols to rationalize, elaborate, and codify a "Great Tradition" for the larger society. Cultural messages emanating from the capitals of classic empires or modern nation-states thus serve to safeguard cultural tradition and produce homogeneity. "Secondary urbanization," by contrast, serves the "heterogenetic" function of introducing and mediating technological and economic change, producing new ideas, cosmologies, and social practices into a society. This approach allowed Redfield and Singer to move beyond the study of folk communities to the larger social domains in which they were embedded.

> Great Traditions get fashioned out of local folk cultures, or Little Traditions, through a process of continuous development by professional literati centered in orthogenetic towns and cities.... in metropolitan centers, ancient and modern, another process—heterogenic transformation—operates to destroy or supersede the great cultural traditions of an indigenous civilization. This transformation is carried on with the help of a new social type of professional intellectuals—the intelligensia—who stand aside the boundaries of the cultural encounter, mediating the alien cultural influences to the natives and interpreting the indigenous culture to the foreigners. (Singer 1960: 106-107)

Singer argued that the dynamics between great traditions and lesser traditions could be studied in three ways: through an examination of "sacred geography" (the co-organization of physical and social space, and the association of the city with external cultural centers), through the study of the professional literati and intelligensia and their respective social organizations, and by the study of "cultural performances" as the most concrete observable units of culture, "the analysis of which might lead to more abstract structures within a comprehensive social system" (1960: 114).[11]

One of Singer's immediate discoveries in applying this model to a study of cultural performances in Madras was that the two processes of primary and secondary urbanization are neither discrete nor discontinuous in everyday life. Rather than being associated with distinct "types" of societies, he found that orthogenetic and heterogenetic processes were operating in Madras simultaneously. Not only did the Brahmin caste end up supplying the bulk of *both* the literati *and* the intelligensia; the same individuals could serve different functions at different times. Singer also saw "rites and ceremonies" as coextensive with the forms of cultural performance expressed through theater, concerts, radio, and film, and saw the linkages between rites and ceremonies as indicating the general patterns of social change.

Singer begins by considering the increasing popular preference for religious devotion (*bhakti yoga*) over the other two primary strands of Hindu practice, ritual observance (*karma yoga*) and the path of knowledge (*jñaña yoga*). He relates the rise of devotional practice as a reaction to, but also an accommodation with, modernity. Certain historical aspects of *bhakti* devotionalism seem to accommodate well to democratization, and the decrease in ritual ties caused by urbanization. He examines the traditional forms of *bhakti* performance—devotional love songs (*bhajans*) and story recitation (from the *Ramayana*, *Mahabharata*, and the *Puranas*)—and then the ways in which these are appropriated and transformed in the mass media.

According to Singer, one characteristic of mass media—its production of a discrete text that can be mechanically reproduced—has crucial consequences, changing how audiences experience cultural performances in several ways. First, identical performances can now be experienced by widespread audiences. Second, media "performances" are capable of repeat showings in a commoditized manner quite apart from the ceremonial and agricultural calendars around which traditional performances were originally organized. Third, these productions are increasingly cut off from the distinctions of caste, sect, language, and sponsorship crucial to traditional performances. Finally, the texts are sent directly from urban production centers to reception technologies in local communities, bypassing the "living cultural network" of traveling performers who engage in mediating performances to meet local desires and expectations. Yet Singer does not restrict himself to mass media as a unique institution in the process of mediating the traditions. He follows the *bhakti* performances through incarnations in many media, including concert music, dramatic plays, dance recitals, and other forms of urban performance.

What Singer ultimately finds in his case study of Madras is that the theoretical continuum of the Great Tradition and Lesser Traditions does not map neatly onto the empirical continuum of urban/village. "Both kinds of traditions are found in villages and in the city in different forms" (Singer 1960: 154-155). Although mass media are urban phenomena in their production, they often exhibit what today might be called "hybridity," which Singer calls a "transcendence" of local folk and ritual forms in a media form associated with the urban. This is particularly true of novels and "social films," written in vernacular language, with dramatic themes of a local flavor (intercaste marriage, innocent villagers traveling to the corrupt metropolis, etc.).

Singer insists, moreover, that although urbanization of media forms has tended to mean secularization in Western societies, this is not necessarily happening in India. Rather than secularization, the mass mediation of popular culture has tended toward popularization and democratization. At the same time, they exhibit a strong selectivity process, contributing to the growth of *bhakti* devotion at the expense of *jñana-marga* and *karma-marga*, which can be less easily adapted to commoditization, rationalization, and urbanization.

Singer's richly layered approach, which views the popularization of tradition as simultaneous with, and involving the same media as, Westernization, which recognizes the role(s) of cultural "brokers" in both processes, and which recognizes mass media as coterminous with other modes of expressive culture, offers many useful insights toward building an anthropology of mass communication. It was weakened, however, by its underlying commitment to a paradigm that posited a necessary dichotomy between urban, Westernized and modern, on the one hand, and village, local, and traditional, on the other. Recasting the dichotomy as a continuum does not solve the underlying epistemological problems posed by this model, especially the habit of seeing societies as entities that can be posited as "moving" along a continuum toward modernity.

The modernization hypothesis that Singer was unable to abandon in his work on mass media—even when his data argued against it and his interpretive models do not require it—was an artifact of Singer's era, perhaps an artifact of the entire history of social theory. Certainly the need to posit (and then explain) a distinction between "primitive" and "modern" runs through the work of the founding fathers of social thought, from Comte to Durkheim, Weber and Marx. Although there is a tradition in anthropology that mitigates against it,[12] dichotomous distinctions between modern and nonmodern societies have always been central to social thought. Ethnographies that examine media almost inevitably tie it specifically to modernity, either as a sign or a vehicle, or both.

Mediating Social Change

One of the first anthropologists to examine media as simultaneously sign and vehicle of modernization was Hortense Powdermaker. Having completed an ethnography of Hollywood (1950), Powdermaker became interested in "the communication of modern Western culture through the mass media" (1966: xiv). To pursue this interest, she traveled to the Rhodesian Copperbelt, a mining community in a British protectorate of Northern Rhodesia. Powdermaker never speaks of "modernization," only of "social change," but she differentiates between "traditional" or "tribal" societies marked by kin-based sociality, collectivity, and ritual control over the world, and "modern" societies marked by individualism and a scientific, technological control over the world. Through their religious, political, and economic dominance, Europeans have wrought tremendous changes on indigenous modes of thought and action, and Powdermaker is interested in the specific processes by which these changes are occurring.

Although she pays careful attention to the political and economic systems of control exerted by the Europeans (mostly British) who administrate the Copperbelt region, her primary interest is in shifts in worldview. The Europeans offered a radically different (in the dichotomous language used by Powdermaker, perhaps even opposite) way of organizing human life. Both traditional and modern activities and beliefs exist side-by-side in Coppertown, and the Africans, individually and collectively, make choices as to what they will accept, what they will reject and what they will modify. But choose they must, Powdermaker says, because what contact with Europeans has brought them is a recognition that there is more than one way to exist in the world. Africans and their ways of life, once taken for granted, are now necessarily objects of their own scrutiny and contemplation.

The mass media—here Powdermaker means radio, films, books, and newspapers—are not the only, or even the primary, media through which these processes of cultural self-examination and change take place. The human Europeans with whom the Africans worked, usually in subordinate positions, represented and expressed the Other in more powerful, personal, and direct ways. The media, by contrast, are impersonal and indirect, she says. Yet because the media are part of leisure time, rather than work time, their consumption is less constrained. They therefore serve not only as a vehicle for social change, but as an *index* of it. Powdermaker thus spends little time analyzing media production or texts, preferring to focus on how and why people consume these media texts and what people make of them.

For Powdermaker, modernity in Coppertown consists of a new economic order combined with a new moral order. Africans came to Coppertown seeking "the jobs, the money, and the material goods which the new economic order offered" (1962: 291). In the township, some traditional activities continued but others were seriously disrupted (the tribe, while important as a social and moral concept, had ceased to be politically meaningful). At the same time, the township made available new leisure activities—radio, movies, classes, social clubs, dance halls, football—which symbolized modernity as a moral order. Participation in these activities symbolized a desire to enter into this new cultural world, and served as a mediator between the old and the new.

Not everyone *wants* to participate in this new world. Only 50 percent of those she surveyed listened to radio, and although 58 percent had at some time gone to the movies, only 39 percent were actively going to movies at the time of her study. Those who chose not to consume Western media were put off by its technological mediation of social activity. To them it seemed "childish to listen to something which is in a box, without seeing the person talking" and to see "the shadows and unreal things which move as human beings in the cinema" (1962: 232).

Central to Powdermaker's work is a theory of play. She saw media as set off from the rest of life, part of the congeries of activities that form leisure time. Nevertheless, drawing on Kroeber (1948), Keesing (1956), and Huizinga (1955), she argues that the play that people engage in during their leisure time does crucial cultural work:

> The functions of leisure are direct and indirect. They may be a preparation for social mobility, not just through knowledge gained in formal courses or classes but also through a sense of participation and identification with the larger modern world. Imagery of self, of human relations, and of the world may be altered by some of the new activities, such as the use of mass media. Other activities may strengthen and even exaggerate traditional roles. In some activities, there may be a blending of old and new imagery and roles.... Leisure may also be the time when a man transcends his limited functions—in the past, as a farmer or herdsman; today as a miner or clerk—and feels part of life as a whole. It may provide an opportunity for affirmation, to be at one with one's self and with the world. (Powdermaker 1966: 226)

Although Powdermaker describes these operations in psychological terms—she speaks, for example, of "ego integration"—her essential argument involves the role of the imagination (c.f. Appadurai 1996), both individually and collectively, in engaging with and making sense of the world. Powdermaker sees much of media consumption as functionally equivalent to rituals of integration that allow people to feel "at one with the world," a phrase she repeats several times.

But media consumption is a ritual that involves a different form of integration than the collective social rituals of the community. "The mass media introduced to Africans another form of reality—a world and peoples beyond their experience" (Powdermaker 1962: 228). Media thus introduces the problem of difference, and makes the self an object of enquiry by presenting others against which it can be considered. The imagination is at play, and it is playing with *difference*, responding to the bifocality that such media introduce. The alienness of the Other in this case is simultaneously attractive and repellent; attractive because of the ways that it is tied to desirable material goods and changes in status, alien and repellent because it is articulated through unfamiliar (and perhaps undesirable) cultural codes.

Interpretation of media accordingly has two features: new images and concepts are interpreted in terms of older concepts and images, and the process of interpretation is itself socially mediated. For example, the Africans in Powdermaker's study seek to understand the moral order of cowboy films in terms of an idiom of kinship, speculating on the ties of blood that might link various characters in a film. They also evaluate films in terms of local moral codes. For example, they approve strongly of the fistfights (a desirable pastime for all young men) while finding the use of guns by humans against other humans to be reprehensible. These efforts at explanation and interpretation are not individual, however; on the contrary, they are social. The Africans in Coppertown rarely experience media consumption as an act of individual interpretation. In films, for example, soundtracks cannot be heard because clusters of viewers are busy negotiating interpretations of what is going on—so loudly, says Powdermaker, that the shouting can be heard for miles. But audiences not only shout, they stand, lean forward, flex their muscles in sympathy with fight scenes, and otherwise interpret the films with their bodies. Powdermaker's analysis of audience interpretation derives not only from interviews but from recording the ongoing dialogues in the theaters.

Powdermaker's work offered an insightful ethnography of media consumption, which tied the meanings of consumption to particular times, places, and peoples. There are many details lacking; I'd like to know the names of the films for which she records audience reactions, and I'd like to see the voices of the Africans interpreting texts more closely embedded in descriptions of the filmgoing and radio-listening experiences of Coppertown. But these are minor points.

The more serious flaws in the project are due to the functionalist theoretical language through which her argument is articulated. Because she sees the work of media play in terms of individual psychology, she has no real theory of how imaginative work gets translated into social action. Abstracting voices from acting subjects, she can offer only a weak sense of media consumption as a practice. Ultimately we are left with a theory of individual psychological integration into a (new) functional system—a typical functionalist approach that privileges the notion of social stability and assumes that hybrid cultural forms are only stages on a path from one stable social system to another.

Development Communication

If functionalist theories tended to predetermine the outcome of media studies, this was even more true with the rise of "development communication," which emerged as a central site for work among applied anthropologists. Early work in development communication sought to yoke mass communications with linear, evolutionary models of social change to create a powerful tool for pursuing goals of economic modernization. The recognition that mass media were simultaneously vehicles and indices of modernity gave way to the question of whether this was a vehicle that could be driven.

Central to the notion of development communication was the conceptualization of social change as a unilineal process of modernization. As it emerged in the decade following the end of the World War II, modernization came to be conceived as a process through which "underdeveloped" countries could be speeded through stages of "development," retracing the steps of the "developed" countries (yet somehow skipping the colonial "stage") at a rate faster than that of the developed nations themselves. In pursuit of their own political agendas, the industrialized nations on both sides of the Cold War were eager to offer both economic and ideological capital for furthering such national development. One of the most widely used models of development was that proposed by Rostow (1960), who offered five-stages of development: traditional society, preconditions for take-off, take-off, drive to maturity, and age of mass consumption. In this model, the traditional society was "hampered by limited production facilities; based on pre-Newtonian notions of science and technology, and constrained by rigid social structure and irrational psychological attitudes" (Rostow 1960: 4-5).

While the state had to work directly, or in partnership with the private sector, to improve production facilities, mass communication was seen as the central tool for educating the masses about science and technology, breaking down traditional social structure so that alternative forms of division of labor could be adopted, and replacing the irrational mode of traditional thought with the rational calculation suitable to mass consumption. Wilbur Schramm explained this by borrowing from Karl Deutsch (1961) the concept of *social mobilization*, "the process in which old social, economic and psychological commitments are broken down and people become available for new patterns of socialization and behavior" (Schramm 1976: 46). In an earlier work (1964), Schramm had explained that "the task of the mass media of information and the 'new media' of education is to speed and ease the long, slow social transformation required for economic development, and, in particular, to speed and smooth the task of mobilizing human resources behind the national effort" (27). This orientation has come to be known as "the dominant paradigm." Pioneered by Daniel Lerner, Ithiel De Sola Pool, and Lucien Pye, as well as Schramm and Rostow, this approach to understanding the relations between mass communication and social change was "simple, linear, deterministic and tinged with optimism" (Melkote 1991). Since it was founded on the belief that the process of development meant transition from the traditional to the modern along a single, common path, with underdeveloped countries emulating the developing countries and developing countries emulating the developed countries, the dominant paradigm led to an approach to communication that was vertical in nature, authority based, top-down, expert-driven, non-negotiable, well-intentioned, and hortatory (Ascroft and Masilela 1994).

The communication and development methods that followed these theories tended to be linear and to focus on what was supposed to happen according to the predictions of the theory, rather than the more ethnographic task of what was actually happening in the communities. The first highly influential model was that of Lasswell (1960), who said communication could be characterized by asking "*Who* says *what* in which *channel* to *whom* with what *effect*?" Although Lasswell's model is broad enough to encompass many kinds of pragmatic approaches to communication, Lasswell tied it to Freudian theory, and some of those adapting his work to development communication transformed it in turn by linking it with behaviorist psychology. A second highly influential model was developed by Shannon and Weaver (1949). Sometimes called the "telephone model," Shannon and Weaver's framework was originally intended for use in the area of information technology, but was used analogously by behavioral and communication scholars. In this model, an information source encodes a message, then sends it via a signal to a receiver, which decodes the message for the destination. The paradigm based on these models came to be called the "hypodermic needle" model (Berlo 1960), the "bullet theory" (Schramm 1971) and the "stimulus-response theory" (DeFleur et al. 1975). The crucial aspect of such theories were that they came to treat audiences as passive message recipients of compelling media messages. The irony was that in doing so, they often assumed an atomized audience, connected to the mass media but not to each other—a condition more closely approximated by the developed countries than those they were labeling as traditional.

The Shannon and Weaver model introduced a number of terms that became central to development communication, including encoding and decoding, sender, receiver, and signal. Above all, it introduced the concept of *noise*. In the model, the signal is always exposed to noise sources between its emergence from the transmitter and its arrival at the receiver. The noise-source concept became a powerful way to explain the failures of development communications projects to achieve the maximum results predicted by the model: traditional cultural beliefs and values distorted or blocked the receipt of messages. Communication theorists drew heavily on early sociologists and anthropologists like Weber (1964), whom they interpreted as arguing that "Oriental" values, ideas, and traditions were incompatible with modernity (Bellah 1965; Rose 1970). Theories and methods were generated to deal with these "obstacles" by seeking to create media that would act directly upon the "personality structure" of the individual media message recipients (McLelland 1967).

Beginning in the mid 1970s, the dominant paradigm came under increasing criticism from both within and without the development communication field. Portes (1976) noted that many models treated Third World countries as if they were tribal societies, ignoring their elaborate bureaucratic structures, complex markets, and formal legal systems. Frank (1969) argued that the development of Third World nations actually created underdevelopment within these countries by widening the gulf between "haves" and "have nots." Anthropologists like Singer (1966, 1972) and Srinivas (1973) questioned Weberian descriptions of Indian religion and the links drawn between Asian values and social change. Other critics also questioned whether value-enactment models that pretended to act directly on the personalities of message recipients took serious account of the sanctions, norms, and other social structural factors present in a society.

These criticisms have led to alternative models of communication and development, which offer more pluralistic views of guided social change. These new models seek broad-based forms of development that take into account the merits of traditional technologies and values, seek to avoid the acceleration of the poverty gap between classes within developing countries, seek to include participation by local communities in policy framing, and stress labor-intensive, low-capital solutions to problems. For example, Melkote (1991), following Wang and Dissanayake (1984) and Hedebro (1982), calls for models of development oriented toward four goals: (1) equity in distribution of information and other benefits of development; (2) active participation of people at the grass roots; (3) independence of local communities to tailor development projects to their objectives; and (4) integration of old and new ideas, the traditional and modern systems, the endogenous and exogenous elements, to constitute a unique blend suited to the needs of each particular community. Mody (1991) offers explicit design strategies using audience research to frame development messages in consonance with local traditions and interests. Such techniques, however, have often offered no more than a sugar-coating to the "bullet." While the operationalization of these goals has generally involved an increased attention to the relation of message content to media consumption habits, so that we see such phenomena as development soap operas (Singhal and Rogers 1989) and family-planning music videos (Coleman 1986), few developing countries have seriously attempted to reduce state monopolies on mass media in order to involve greater localization and "grassroots" participation.

From an analytical perspective, a key problem with the communication and development model is that by predefining goals and outcomes, it conceals much of what actually takes place as new media forms enter into communities. An account of a film program in health and family planning in rural Zaire can serve as an illustration of some of these issues (Carael and Stanbury 1983, 1984).[13] Carried out on the island of Idjwi in Lake Kivu in eastern Zaire, the experiment sought to use films to spread information about hygiene and the advantages of birth control in an agricultural community faced with rapidly expanding population but a deteriorating environment. Creating a series of thirteen films using local actors, the researchers spent two years circulating between twelve sites with mobile projection equipment, showing the health films along with documentaries and "other films."

Since most of the Idjwe had never seen films before, a new mode of literacy had to be created:

> The constraints belonging to cinema became the object of an apprenticeship on the part of the public. In the beginning, some people placed themselves behind the screen and just listened. Others placed themselves too far for hearing. The light of the projector was often cut by a silhouette without that person's awareness. The first showings were very noisy. Certain actors were recognized by the audience and that elicited much emotion. Progressively, under the guidance of the projection team and with the learning process, a public developed, the men in one group, the women in

another, and the children circulating between the two groups. (Carael and
Stanbury 1984: 342)

The films became extremely popular—indeed, so popular that "two villages built a road so that a projection could take place there" (1984:
343). All of the traditional authorities, as well as such modern authorities as the directors of the schools, the nurses and the teachers, "considered that participation in the projection was an obligation.... In the
social code, the films came to occupy an important position" (ibid).

Evaluations of the film project do not explore in detail the place of
these films in the social code, the film projection as a social event, or
film viewing as a new form of interpretive practice. Nor are the anthropologists interested in how the Idjwe understood the films; "meaning"
is here reduced to a single message, which the viewers are presumed to
have either received or failed to receive. The hybridity of interpretation
and consumption that so impressed Powdermaker is not of interest.
Where the anthropologists do express interest in the social practice of
film consumption, it is to search for impediments to proper transmission of the intended messages:

> It appeared that one member of the conjugal pair, and more often the hus-
> band than the wife, attended when the other could not. ...but does com-
> munication between them exist? Many questions regarding sexuality are
> forbidden between husband and wife. This suggests that communication
> within the family is an eventual barrier or could distort a message trans-
> mitted by the media. (Carael and Stanbury 1984: 343)

Cultural practices such as gendered modes of domestic talk, thus
become treated as sources of noise, static that impedes or distorts the
transmitted message.

The appropriation of the transmission model of mass communication
by development studies had significant consequences for anthropologists studying the role of media in social change. The study of social
change became increasingly articulated in instrumental ways. The role of
media as a vehicle and index of social change remains, but in the hands
of many applied anthropologists, it becomes a vehicle to be driven, and
its indexicality, rather than covering a broad spectrum interconnected
with daily work and leisure, is reduced to specific assessments devised to
see if the vehicle has arrived at its intended destination.

National Culture (at a Distance)

Yet another anthropological body of literature on mass media was produced in the 1940s and 50s by a large group of anthropologists of the

"culture-and-personality" school. The impetus for this work came from the Office of Naval Intelligence, which was interested in assessing the cultures of both enemies and allies to better interpret intelligence and to construct propaganda (both that aimed at building civilian morale and that aimed at diminishing enemy morale).[14] Because the war made most of the communities they had studied inaccessible for anthropologists, the question arose as to how to study "culture at a distance" (Mead and Métraux 2000).

One solution was to understand mass media texts as expressive of the national cultures that produced them, in the same ways that rituals and folktales were being studied by anthropologists as expressive of the cultures of smaller-scale societies. These scholars relied on "interviews with exiles and immigrants and symbolic material (books, pictures, films, etc.)" (Gorer 2000: 82) to elicit general cultural patterns. The primary technique was to read novels, newspapers, and essays, view movies, listen to music and radio, and then to discuss these with members of the communities, variously constituted by refugees, immigrants, or even first- or second- generation descendants of immigrants. Anthropologists often worked together in small groups, meeting and discussing the interviews and the ongoing research.

The program was institutionalized first by the Office of Naval Intelligence and later by Columbia University, which, after the war, established a center for Research in Contemporary Cultures (RCC), headed first by Ruth Benedict and later by Margaret Mead and Rhoda Métraux. The personnel included at various times some of the major names in anthropology: Conrad Arensberg, Gregory Bateson, Jane Belo, Ruth Bunzel, William Chen, Francis L.K. Hsu, Rosemary Spiro, and Eric Wolf, among many others. Under a number of names, including the Council for Intercultural Relations and the Institute for Intercultural Studies, this network of scholars produced a lengthy series of publications, among them Erikson 1950; Honigman and van Doerslaer 1955; Mead 2000a; Mead, Gorer, and Rickman 2001; Mead and Métraux 2000; Mead et al. 2001.

The goal of the project was to do for large-scale societies—particularly nations—what many of these same anthropologists had sought to do in smaller-scale societies: generate holistic statements that are in some way applicable to every member of the society being described. "To be fair, the RCC researchers believed—as we no longer do today—that societies do exist in uniform, largely undifferentiated groups characterized by their common overarching patterns of behavior" (Beeman 2000: xxiii). This approach was epitomized in the classic *Patterns of Culture* (1934) by Ruth Benedict, the first director of the RCC project, who sought to describe entire societies under single categorical labels such as "Apollonian" and "Dionysian." What Mead, Gorer, and the others brought to this quest for description of uniform patterns was an explanation for such regularity, which was to be found in common forms of socialization and enculturation.

From the first, the program was organized around the theoretical assumptions of the culture-and-personality school. People's personalities were deemed to be shaped by their cultural environments; cultural environments were, in turn, replicated because of the uniformity of personality among the members of the community. This position was coupled with a belief in the psychodynamic model of personality development. Attempting to repatriate Freudian theories while accepting Malinowski's critique of them (Malinowski 1966), culture and personality scholars assumed that stages of psychosexual development were universal, but that cultural ways for handling these stages vary from society to society. Similarities in childrearing practices led to similarities of personal character.[15] Similarities of personal character could be generalized to larger social units, up to and including the unit in which the War Department was primarily interested in: the nation. It thus became possible to speak of "Alorese personality" (DuBois 1944) or "Soviet character" (Mead 1951) or "Japanese character structure" (Meadow 1944; Gorer 1946) or "Polish personality" (Métraux 2000).

A central technique was the extraction of common *themes*, propositions about what constitutes moral behavior, or about "the valid and enduring goals of human existence" (Wallace 1961: 104), which are shared among members of the social group. Some themes involve what we might now call "master narratives." For example, through the American media there runs the theme that good men[16] (who are hard to find in a chaotic and lawless world) must fight tirelessly against great odds to bring order to the community (Wallace 1961). In various transformations, this theme runs through American Westerns, "private eye" narratives, science fiction, and many other genres, in print, radio drama, theater, film, and television.

Other themes are curious patterns discovered by attending to media cross-culturally. Wolfenstein notes, for example, that while father-son conflict is a theme in many American and British films, in American films the son is almost always vindicated in the end, while in British films, it is the father who always turns out to be right (2000: 296). Such patterns were used by her, and by other anthropologists of the day, in a manner akin to the use psychoanalysts were making of projective tests to understand the personality of the individual. Media "themes" were thus treated as expressions of the collective cultural order of a specified social group. Bateson summarizes the approach:

A painting, a poem, or a dream may give an exceedingly false picture of the real world but insofar as the painter or the dreamer is an artist, insofar as he has complete control of his medium, the artistic product must, of necessity, tell us about the man himself. In the same way a film, insofar as it is an integrated work of art ... must tell us about the psychology of its makers, and tell us perhaps more than they intended to tell.... In the analysis, the film has been treated not merely as an individual's dream or work of art, but also as a myth. We have applied to it the sort of analysis that the anthropologist applies to the mythology of a primitive or modern people (1980: 21).

The notion that culture and personality are fundamentally similar is common to Boasian anthropologists, and probably has its clearest expression in an essay by Edward Sapir, who treats culture as the "personality" of the society and personality as the "culture" of the individual (1985a). Sapir himself recognized that this approach raises the problem of dealing with individual variation within communities, and he was struck by the fact that no one individual knew "the whole culture" (1985b), but he never offered an alternative to treating culture and personality as equivalent constructs.

The RCC scholars carried Sapir's speculations further: by using child socialization and psychological integration as mechanisms to explain the link between culture and personality, they argued that the "basic" personality of the individual and the culture of the group are perfectly congruent, at least for methodological purposes. "Any member of a group, provided that his position within that group is properly specified, is a perfect example of the group-wide pattern on which he is acting as an informant" (Mead 2000: 44). The goal of the cultural analyst is to work from commonalities among diverse types of data to make broad, holistic generalizations that are somehow true for any member of the community.[17] This approach has been criticized for "begging the question" of individual diversity. Critics also questioned the use of "nations" as cultural units and the concept of culture as "patterned."[18]

Mead and her colleagues were quite aware of these problems, and careful reading of their methodological statements reveals that they were prepared to deal with the criticisms at a theoretical level. Mead, for example, discussed the relations between nations as units and the various subcultures that constituted nations (2000: 24). Mead readily acknowledged that the nation was not a natural unit, and even that there were, perhaps, no "natural units" of description. Rather, the unit of description is, in part, an artifact of the method—a realization that later became the basis for the "epistemological crisis" in anthropology described by Ruby (1982), Clifford and Marcus (1986), Marcus and Fischer (1986), Clifford (1988); and others. Mead's argument seems to be that the method is not *necessarily* linked to the nation; it is applicable to units of any scale. Beeman comments that "it is easy to see that the RCC researchers' 'national character' analytic strategy can apply to all sorts of public behavior, discourse, and symbolic expression. Moreover, it can be used for groups of *any* size, including families, clans, ethnic groups, gender groups, socioeconomic classes, or castes.... [T]here is no need to use the nation-state as the minimal unit of analysis to validate the process" (Beeman 2000: xxii).[19] What is at issue for the RCC methodology is the generalizability of the holistic statements that anthropologists abstract from their data. Unfortunately, with the exception of one exemplary work by Bateson (1972), such theoretical issues are relegated to asides and footnotes in most published work. The struggle to find more sophisticated ways to express the links between theory, method, and cultural description was rarely made central in the actual published analyses of the RCC scholars.

This is certainly true of the most famous work to arise out of this project, Ruth Benedict's *Chrysanthemum and the Sword* (1946), a study of Japanese character, which can be read in part as a defense of the then-controversial Marshall Plan.[20] The RCC project produced a large number of published media studies, including studies of Italian films (Wolfenstein 2000), French films (Belo 2000, Gorer 2000) Chinese films (Weakland 1956, 2000), Soviet films (Mead 2000, Schwartz 2000), Nazi films (Bateson 1943, 1980, 2000) and British and American films (Wolfenstein and Leites, 1950), as well as 118 volumes of unpublished papers.[21] It also stimulated a number of scholars to pursue this kind of analysis. Yet the project began to decline shortly after the war, and with it declined anthropological attention to media. By 1966, John Weakland complained in a letter to the *American Anthropologist* that "the study of films, and of national cultures generally, has been badly neglected" (Weakland 1966: 477).

The decline of this approach to mass media seems to have been due to a number of factors. The historical conditions that gave impetus to the project were no more. Although the world was transformed by the war, field sites were again accessible, and resources were available to fund ethnographic studies of the more traditional participant-observation kind. Although funding for some of the Institute for Intercultural Studies projects continued after the war through the American Museum of Natural History, the Rand Corporation, the Office of Naval Research, and the Massachusetts Institute of Technology, the free-floating network that once included 120 anthropologists declined. Perhaps the most significant reason for the decline, however, was that the theoretical model that had informed the work ceased to be accepted by most anthropologists.[22] Ultimately, this model failed for at least three reasons:

1. Many of the arguments were essentially tautological. Much of the work of the RCC scholars seemed to extract the cultural pattern from observed behavior, and then used the cultural pattern to explain observed behavior.

2. Concerns arose over the underlying assumption that mass media expressed general cultural patterns, rather than expressing the ideology of an elite that controlled such centralized means of expression. More broadly, this critique can be extended to the central question of the studies of media production articulated by the Frankfurt, Birmingham, and Glasgow schools of media studies, among others: what are the relations between the media industries and the communities that consume their productions? Bateson's study of the film *Hitlerjunge Quex* has been so criticized. Dante Leite is cited by Neiburg and Goldman (1998) as claiming that "they offer accounts of German national character when in fact they are talking only about Nazis." In fact, Bateson consistently uses the term Nazi in his text. The full version of the essay, which was not published until 1980, makes clear that he saw the film as the product of a Nazi elite appropriating and using psychologically resonant symbols to influence broadly "German" audiences in such a way as to create more Nazis. But even if wrong in this specific case, Leite's point is nonetheless relevant. Many of the studies are less sophisticated than Bateson's. The use of published English translations of Chinese folk stories (some collected from second- and third-generation immigrants to the United States) to analyze "Chinese character" (Heyer 2000), for example, raises a number of problems concerning the relationship between mode of production and cultural expression.

3. The notion of nations as cultural units has been questioned again and again by scholars. The problem of generalizing upward, from a few interviews, a few movies, a few widely distributed behaviors, to a national eidos is problematic. While it is true that recent attention to the nation as a cultural entity resonates with the project, media is now seen more commonly as a vehicle through which the national community is "imagined," both in content and through shared practices of consumption (Anderson 1991), rather than as an expression of a preexisting shared system of "national" themes and knowledge.

Media as Symbolic Systems

The notion that films, television, print, and radio encode key cultural symbols did not disappear with the decline of national culture studies, but continued as a small and marginal interest within the discipline. Symbolism has always been a central interest of anthropology, even when it was treated as subordinate to or attendant on kinship and social structure. That a culture's "utterances" (Malinowski 1922: 24-25) or "ensembles of texts" (Geertz 1973: 193-233) express an underlying shared worldview remains a central premise for most anthropology. Perhaps the earliest major symbolic study of media came from the tireless William Lloyd Warner, whose later work involved explicating the symbolic meanings of particular kinds of texts and performances in American society. His most exhaustive study was an analysis of a popular daytime radio soap opera, *Big Sister* (Warner 1953, 1962; Warner and Henry 1948), for which he and W.E. Henry, a colleague at the University of Chicago's Committee on Human Development, studied seventy listeners using psychological testing, interviews, and surveys of social indicators. Warner argued that the soap opera was, in essence, a secular morality play which expresses the "the feelings and beliefs of its audience by use of idealized symbols of good and evil and of things feared and hoped for" (Warner and Henry 1948: 64). The audience of *Big Sister* was predominantly made up of lower middle-class women economically dependent on their husbands' wages. The world outside the home was largely outside the sphere of action of such a woman, yet it posed a threat to her and her dependent children through possible economic dislocation of her husband. This world also imposes on her a fairly strict moral code, a breach of which would threaten her standing as wife, and hence, her security. In the interviews, many women described the program as being "true to life" and explained aspects of the stories with reference to elements in their own lives, even describing what they imagined the program's characters looked like in terms of their own friends and family.

The symbolic structure of the radio drama relates directly to the social reality perceived by the audience. In *Big Sister*, the "primary theme declares that good and noble women who are wives and mothers are invincible within their own arena of life, the American family. Men, who are superordinate elsewhere, are subordinate and dependent on the wisdom of the wife" (Warner 1962: 264-265). Drama is created by the possibility that this ideal state of affairs can be breached, and the security of the wife and mother threatened, especially by the loss of a husband to another woman, by the loss of a husband's job, or by death. The program "aroused normal anxiety in the women and provided symbolic solutions to reduce the anxiety that had been aroused" (1962: 265).

Warner built on this study to offer his most complete statement of the symbolic functions of media in his 1962 work, *American Life: Dream and Reality*. Here, Warner argued that complex societies like the United States, because of their structural diversity and social complexity, suffer from an ever-increasing differentiation of "specialized symbol systems" which threatens social cohesion. Advances in technology and social practice must be accompanied by "symbolic advancement" if they are not to lead to social disintegration. Along with school and civil religion,[23] the mass media, which "allow tens of millions of people to be one audience and, at a given moment in time, one group—because of a core of common response to the same symbols," have "been of primary and crucial importance for the integration of the diverse secular worlds of modern men into coherence and unity" (Warner 1962: 250). With this emphasis on the role of culture in the psychological integration of individuals into the social system, Warner remains firmly in the same Parsonian functionalist theoretical camp as Powdermaker.

But even as Warner and Powdermaker were writing their final works, studies of symbolic materials were already sharply diverging from the Parsonian tradition. The tendency of sociologists and anthropologists to find over and over again that symbols served only as vehicles of social "integration" into coherent and cohesive social systems was being transformed by new theories and methodologies that searched more broadly for the place of meaning in social action. Ethnomethodology, symbolic interactionism, structuralism, hermeneutics, and social semiotics are very different approaches to analyzing the work of symbols in human action, but all emerged from an increasing concern with understanding not only how institutions functioned to create or undermine social equilibrium, but what the social world *meant* to the people who created it through their everyday lives. The majority of studies of mass communication coming out of anthropology in the 1970s and 1980s were written by symbolic anthropologists. Drawing on the works of Claude Lévi-Strauss, Victor Turner, James Peacock, David Schneider, Mary Douglas, Clifford Geertz, and others,[24] these scholars focused on applying the principles of symbolic anthropology to media texts, treating these texts as symbolic expressions of the cultures that produced them.

Susan Bean's essay "Soap Operas: Sagas of American Kinship" can serve as an exemplar of this sort of analysis. Bean argues that soap operas (in the United States in 1974) offer a repetitive, ritualized, and coherent "expression of the principles on which the American family is based" (Bean 1981b: 173). As Bean elicits it from soap opera plots, this ideal family involves two dyadic relationships: that of husband and wife, and that of parent and child. Each of these relationships presupposes three elements. The husband-wife relationship presupposes a man and woman in love, with marriage as the culmination of love, and sex as its natural expression. The purpose of this dyad is to create families. A family consists of "a man and woman in love and married with a child who is the product of their sexual union" (167). This creates the parent-child relationship, which presupposes three elements: "a blood tie, a social tie and a bond of love" (169). This simple structure suffers from a peculiar tension. Love is the key operator, but in the logic of American kinship as expressed in soap operas, love between man and woman is a mysterious force outside human agency ("people fall in love, they don't jump," writes Bean). People can fall out of love with their spouses but never with their children.

Soap operas generate melodrama by violating one or more of these elements, and transforming dyadic relations into triangles. "[T]he principles on which family life is based are revealed in dramatic dilemmas that violate the ideal order" (Bean 1981b: 173): "A man is married to one woman but in love with another; a child's natural mother and its legal and loving mother are two different women" (174). Soap operas seek resolution of the breach of the ideal "by uniting the several elements in a single relationship: the man marries the woman he loves; the child learns to accept his legal and loving mother as if she were his natural mother" (174). The argument is typically structuralist: the meaning of the soap opera is the logic by which symbols are organized, not the play of symbols themselves.

Bean specifies the nature of the audience; in this case, women make up some 80 percent of the audience. They are attracted to soap operas because in America, "women are the custodians of kinship," and soap operas "are about establishing and maintaining the family in America" (163). Viewing soap operas becomes a ritual process in which fundamental social values are breached, then restored. The differences between one soap opera plot and another are matters of *bricolage*, the continued improvisational play of symbols following the same fundamental cultural logics. Like Bateson and many others, Bean insists that media are like myth. She has, however, new and more complex, methods of mythography.

In line with this, and fundamental to the approach of symbolic anthropologists of the day—particularly when dealing with media— was a failure to address the differentials of power between producers and consumers. Working at the levels of generalization to which their structuralist and culturalist approaches led them, these anthropologists saw producers and consumers as members of the same general cultural community, drawing on the same body of shared symbols to create and to interpret media. While this is true up to a point, it is also true that the play of symbols is constrained by hidden economic relations. The melodramas described by Bean are called "soap operas" because they were sponsored by corporations advertising soap. These corporations exerted enormous influence over the style and content of the programs. The consistent refusal of most American producers to situate television narratives in any real historical context is partly a desire by the sponsors not to offend anyone, for fear the offense would extend to their product.

It is also telling that Bean, a renowned Tamil linguist, should choose for her analysis American soap operas, rather than exploring any of the films, radio songs, fan magazines, or other products of the large and vibrant Tamil media industry. In doing so, she illustrates a trend among anthropologists of the period in treating media as the expressive culture of Western industrialized society and avoiding studies of media in their host communities (unless these were studies of "modernization," as we have seen). Thus Ivan Karp, an expert on African ideological systems, wrote on the Marx Brothers (1981). John L. Caughey, a specialist on the Truk, studied how Americans interact with media figures in their imaginations (1984, 1985). South Asianist Peter Claus offered a structural analysis of *Star Trek* (1982). Conrad Kottak, a South Americanist, turned his analytical lens on *Star Wars* (1982a, 1982b).[25] The venue for such papers was also telling; rather than appearing in reviewed journals, they tended to be published in books aimed at undergraduate courses in anthropology.

Ulf Hannerz summed up the problem as early as 1971: "I have a feeling that anthropologists usually regard mass media research within their discipline as gimmickry. This is a rather unfortunate attitude." (86). Indeed. In the years from 1970-1985, most of the handful of anthropologists who wrote about media outside of a North American or Western European society were themselves transnational scholars whose membership in the societies they studied was deeper than that of participant observation: among them were Pakistan-born anthropologist Akbar Ahmed, who wrote about press coverage of a religious mass suicide in Pakistan (1986) and about Indian films (1991); German-born convert to Hinduism, Agehananda Bharati, who offered an "ethnoscience" of Indian cinema (1977a, 1977b); Indian anthropologist Veena Das, who examined the structure of kinship in Pakistani romance novels (1973), and Indian anthropologist T.N. Madan, who used Hindi, Kannada, Marathi (1987a), and Tamil (1987b) novels (in translation) to explore Hindu concepts of morality and suffering.[26]

Conclusion

In her 1993 summary article on mass media study by anthropologists, Debra Spitulnik wrote, not without justice, that "[t]here is as yet no 'anthropology of mass media'" (293). There had been one, briefly, but it was gone. Community studies and national character studies dwindled, unable to overcome the limitations of their methodological and theoretical assumptions. Anthropological studies of the place of media in social change had been hijacked by the utilitarian theories of the development communication school. For twenty-five years, anthropological output on mass media had been sporadic, and the works that had emerged were disconnected from one another, as well as from the work being done in other disciplines.

A new "anthropology of mass media" was, however, rapidly emerging, taking as its foci the construction of difference, media production outside the industrialized West, and attention to the role of mass media in the construction of identities. This emerging media anthropology is theoretically eclectic, freely borrowing concepts and theoretical language from communication studies, British cultural studies, and literary criticism, as well as from theoretically sympathetic strands of social theory and political science. It builds on the turn in media studies toward audience analysis, but introduces into it the reflexivity that has become increasingly central to ethnography in anthropology. Finally, this new, emergent anthropology of media is engaged with pushing the boundaries of anthropological theory and ethnographic practice as these are challenged by the collapse of people-culture-place isomorphism that has resulted from globalization, and the appearance of new technologies of representation that offer increasingly interactive and interpersonal alternatives to centralized "mass" media.

Notes

1. See, for example, Douglass 1924, 1928; Fry 1924, 1925; Chapin 1979.
2. The only anthropologists actually cited in *Middletown* are W.H.R. Rivers and Clark Wissler.
3. The Lynds emphasize the underlying cultural meaning of this metaphor, arguing that the idea that time is a resource that is "spent" is integral to the Middletowners' "pecuniary society" (1929: 225).

4. For example, a Middletown newspaper in 1890 suggested that two useful questions to add to the census would be "What is your opinion of the evolution theory?" and "Have you read *Robert Elsmere?*"

5. The titles of these films give a good idea of what is meant by the genre "modern society film": *Alimony, Married Flirts, The Daring Years, Sinners in Silk, Women Who Give, The Price She Paid, Name the Man, Rouged Lips, The Queen of Sin*. Middletown's favorite stars of such films, according to interviews with cinema managers, included Norma Talmadge, Gloria Swanson, and Thomas Meighan (Lynd and Lynd 1929: 266).

6. *Middletown* is even worse in establishing a theory of ethnicity. African-Americans, although living in a self-contained ghetto community in Muncie, are almost entirely ignored by the Lynds.

7. Packard (1959) cites community studies of Statesboro, Georgia; Decatur, Illinois; San Jose, California; Wasco, California; Indianapolis, Indiana; Morris, Illinois; Oakland, California; Danielson, Connecticut; Burlington, Vermont; Philadelphia, Pennsylvania; Park Forest, Illinois; New Haven, Connecticut; Lansing, Michigan; Franklin, Indiana; Kansas City, Missouri; Sandusky, Ohio in addition to " the earlier classic studies of Newburyport, Massachusetts, by the W. Lloyd Warner group and the study of Muncie, Indiana, by the Lynds."

8. For critiques of the functionalist paradigm, which held sway in anthropology and sociology from the 1930s through the 1960s, see Abrahamson 1978 and Cohen 1968.

9. On the difference between open and closed systems, see Bertalanffy 1968.

10. For a review and critique of the study of complex societies in anthropology from the 1930s through the 1960s, see Adams 1970.

11. Sara Dickey's critique of Singer for failing—like most other anthropologists—to "examine the power differential between producers, performers and audiences" is thus correct de facto but not de jure. Although Singer chose to study performances, his notion that the literati and intelligensia form specific social networks opens up the possibility for analysis of power relations.

12. As a graduate student, I was told an (possibly apocryphal) anecdote about Sol Tax and the dichotomous distinction between modern and nonmodern societies. Asked after a lecture in which he criticized the term "primitive society" what he would replace it with, Tax supposedly said, "There is no scientific value in having one word for 'oak trees' and another word for 'all the other trees in the forest.'"

13. I use Carael and Stanbury here not because they are a particularly egregious example of this tendency, but rather because they are particularly good at packing a great deal of descriptive information into two relatively brief essays, making it possible for me to make these observations. The issues I describe here arise not from failures on the part of the researchers, but are a natural outcome of the principles around which their research is designed.

14. The application of anthropology to a war effort remains controversial. For interesting discussions of both the ethics and theoretical implications of the RCC anthropological-military nexus, see Mabee 1987, Neiburg and Goldman 1998, and Price 1998.

15. The degree to which the culture and personality school emphasized childrearing is debatable. In methodological statements proponents tended to be more cautious than in their analytical papers. Mead answered one critic by saying, "culture is never derived from child rearing practices, but child rearing practices are a significant factor in cultural transmission and culture change" (1961: 137).

16. The last few decades have seen a regendering of this theme, particularly in science-fiction and private-eye narratives, so that good women are now likewise engaged in fighting the good fight, rather than being onlookers or objects of desire. The theme

itself seems surprisingly unaffected by the replacement of a Sam Spade or Mike Hammer with a Kinsey Milhone or V.I. Warshawski. The insertion of members of other marginalized groups has also been growing, so that we now have African-American, Native American, Chicano, homosexual, and other transformations of what can constitute a "good man" in American society. That the underlying theme stays the same testifies to the continuing power of these cultural configurations.

17. The RCC scholars were never interested in media per se except as it related to other forms of expressive culture and broad behavioral patters. Métraux writes:

     [o]ne is not concerned with the way in which a specific writer develops plot or character or elaborates on a series of themes or uses particular images, nor only with the ways in which themes and images are expressed in paintings or in films, not with the ideal version of the culture as it may be specifically presented in various sorts of materials, but rather with the interrelationship among all of these (2000: 240).

18. For a summary of these criticisms, see Wallace (1954, 1961).

19. Wallace (1961) has an argument against this as well, insisting that the very notion of "pattern" necessarily involves an assumption that what is *shared* by members of a social group is what is important. This, however, is clearly a question of outlook. The RCC scholars were interested in the ways societies produced uniformity, while Wallace was concerned with the social organization of diversity.

20. For contemporary perspective on this book and its lasting influence, see Kent 1999, Fukui 1999 and Modell 1999.

21. These documents are currently housed at the U.S. Library of Congress and the library of Georgetown University in Washington, DC.

22. See Neiburg and Goldman 1998 for an elaborate critique of the ideological under-pinnings of national character and the continuity of these notions in contemporary anthropology.

23. Warner is one of the pioneers in research into the mythologization of the past, the invention of tradition, and the establishment of civic ceremony as central to the cultural construction of national identity (1959, 1962).

24. Of these, Victor Turner and James Peacock are the only two who turned their own attention to media. Turner believed the ritual processes of tribal societies were comparable with film and other "genres of industrial leisure," which "play with the factors of culture, sometimes assembling them in random, grotesque, improbable, surprising, shocking, usually experimental combinations" (1982: 40). Peacock's Weberian theories on the role of media in the evolution of modern society (Peacock and Kirsch 1970; Peacock 1979) seem to have been less influential than his Weberian critique of content analysis approaches to media theories (1969) and particularly his classic *Rites of Modernization* (1968). With "its attention to actors, producers, audiences, texts, and their symbolic, political and economic contexts" (Dickey 1997: 425), this ethnography of Javanese *ludruk* theater is still being held up as an exemplary model for how to do ethnographies of media.

25. Kottak later produced several works on television viewing in Brazil.

26. A notable exception to this pattern is the American symbolic anthropologist William O. Beeman, who wrote about American advertising (1986), but also, and quite seriously, about Iranian media (1982, 1983, 1984).

Chapter 3

MEDIA TEXTS

When people read books, scan newspapers, or watch movies, it is the content—the stories, the news, the spectacles—that usually draws them in and holds their attention. What people articulate of their experiences with the media is bits of information, stories, and dramatic scenes. In everyday social interaction, talk about the news we've read, the movies we've watched, and the TV serials we've viewed greatly exceeds talk about the press, about Hollywood or Bollywood, or about the television industry.[1] It is not surprising, therefore, that the study of content should be at the heart of most media analysis. Perhaps the most fundamental assumption in most studies of mass media across disciplines is the assumption of the importance of the message, or set of messages, embodied in the media text.

Media, as I argued in the first chapter, forms a double circuit. In one path of the circuit, media producers are selecting cultural elements from the pool of public culture, transforming them and returning them through some medium, as texts, to public space. Consumers select from among the myriad media texts in circulation, according to patterned and sometimes institutionalized systems of practice. The text, in this view, is simultaneously a material locus of collective representations—in various configurations—and the central object of exchange between producers and audiences.

Media content is connected to social life in various complex and contradictory ways. Content may be seen as revealing the intentions of powerful senders, usually corporate or state structures. Or, content may be seen as a crystallization of the social relations—political, economic, sexual—existing at the time of its production. It may be assumed to encode a deep structure of ideological or psychological meanings. In any of these views, media content becomes something that must be unpacked and examined.

Interpreting the Text

The central concept in the study of media content is the text. A *text*, as I shall use the term, is any discourse fixed by some mode of representation: writing, magnetic tape, photography, video, or any combination. Text should thus not be understood here as an exclusively linguistic phenomenon but also as a visual and auditory one. Indeed, the most common use of "text" is to refer to written material, which is a visual representation of meaningful sounds.

The essential defining characteristic of text is that it is fixed and coherent, having a beginning and an end, a structure and a topic or referential meaning. A text is *about* something. The word "text" gets its name from this feature of coherence, deriving from the Latin *textus* meaning "something woven together" (Hodge and Kress 1988: 6). This essential cohesiveness allows a text to be transferred from context to context, while still being recognized as the same thing. The Indian film classic *Awara* (1951) meant one thing to the Indian audiences who saw it in theaters at the time of its release; it meant something else to the millions of Russians who saw it again and again, making it the most successful foreign film of that time; it means something else to contemporary Indian audiences, who see it on television through a frame of nostalgia and changing social mores; it means something else to families of Indians abroad, renting it from a video store and showing it to their children as part of a cultural heritage; and it means something yet different to a group of American students in a class on South Asia who know they will have to write a reaction paper on the film. Yet in each event, *Awara* remains essentially the same film.[2]

A more precise semiotic definition would be to say that text refers to a structure of messages or message traces, which has a socially ascribed coherence. The last part of this definition—socially ascribed—perhaps requires some explication. The coherence of a text is never entirely given by the text in itself but depends on cultural codes for its interpretation.[3] Consider an example from art. The Navajo have long practiced what outside observers have called "sand painting." On a flat piece of ground, a Navajo artist will carefully pour different colored sands to create a picture. Such a picture is, by the nature of its medium, impermanent, subject to the winds and the rain; for the Navajo, this impermanence is part of the meaning of the text. Moreover, sand paintings are not meant simply to be viewed; created in the context of healing ceremonies, they are intended to be pressed into the bodies of the ill.

Many visitors to Navajo communities, admiring the pictures, desired more permanent versions they could possess and own. They introduced technologies through which sand could be adhered to a board and treated with chemicals to prevent shifting or damage. This produced an entirely new kind of text, one that featured Navajo iconography but was not a true sand painting according to original Navajo cultural codes (Parezco 1983). For the Navajo, the meaningful "coherence" of the text of a sand painting includes not only the iconography of the images but also includes the dimension of time, the fact that the text will not last. We might say that the text is only completed for the Navajo when it is dissolved. For the tourists who visit the Navajo reservation, the text is complete only when it is *physically* fixed, so that it can be purchased, possessed, and owned.[4] Thus, the rules by which coherence is ascribed to texts are cultural. Just as cultural codes guide us in the aesthetic evaluation of a text, so do they guide us in our understanding of textual coherence, of what makes something a text.

Hermeneutics, the practice of deriving such codes from texts, seeks to make clearer the meanings of a given text by explicating how texts achieve their effects. Paul Ricouer (1981) argues that hermeneutics proceeds in two ways—through *explanation* and through *interpretation*—and that these processes are always in tension with one another. Explanation involves the description and analysis of the elements that make up the text, whereas interpretation involves ascribing significance to those elements. Explanation is essentially akin to linguistics, except that the units of analysis are of a higher (that is, more complex and synthetic) order. One can isolate units and categories of units, show how they are related by proximity, number, and many other characteristics. This process can be quantified.

Elicitation and description by themselves are insufficient. Understanding what theses processes mean to those who encounter particular texts requires us to attempt to understand how these structural elements are related to the cultural codes that people use to shape their encounters with the text, and thus to interpret the text. Interpretation is a selective process by which the interpreter makes decisions as to what elements of the text to pay attention to and which meaning of many possible meanings applies to a particular set of textual elements.[5] Interpretation is necessary because symbols do not have a one-to-one relationship to their referents, as the examples above suggest. This principle of *polysemy* alerts us to the fact that any text will have multiple meanings depending on the cultural codes that are used to interpret it. This principle applies not only between such differentiated groups as the

Navajo and the tourists who come to visit them, but also among and between members of the same societies. Interpretations of texts can thus differ not only across national, ethnic, and language boundaries, but also according to gender, age, education, status, caste, rank, or other social distinctions. Moreover, the different ways we approach and interpret media texts may help to create and maintain those very distinctions. The play of polysemy is itself central to defining the similarities and differences by which groups establish identities.

In the remainder of this chapter, I will discuss six dimensions of textual understanding based on relations of the various elements that give the text its coherence. These include the relations of the elements that constitute the text (structural relations); the relation of the text to other texts (intertextual relations); the relationship of a text to the media by which it is constituted (instrumental relations); the relationship of the text to the participants in the text-act, that is, to the creators and audiences presupposed by the text (social relations); the relations of the text to its subject, or referent (referential relations); and the relations of the content of the text to what is *not* present in it (distinctive relations). Interpretation and explanation proceed by analyzing a text in terms of one or more of these six dimensions.

Structure

Structural analysis seeks to understand the text by examining the relations between the elements that constitute a particular text. It takes as its object not these elements themselves but the *relations* between them, assuming that these elements are, in fact, never things in themselves but only an expression of a relationship. Take, for example, the common practice of draping beautiful women across cars in advertisements. There is no natural or essential relationship between a woman and a car. Looking at a picture of a beautiful woman does not necessarily bring road vehicles to mind, any more than looking at a picture of a car necessarily brings women to mind.[6] It is the juxtaposition of elements, the relationship, that generates meaning in such advertisements.

The structuralist method of looking at text is based on the assumption that all systems of signification operate (at least in part) on the model of language.[7] Languages are "doubly articulated" semiotic systems, organized at every level by two sets of rules: those that are syntagmatic and those that are paradigmatic. At the phonological level, for example, paradigmatic relations determine what sounds out of the total stream of possible sounds are meaningful for a given language, while syntagmatic rules determine how sounds can be combined to create meanings. Both of these systems are arbitrary—that is, there is no necessary or natural connection between any set of sounds and its meaning.

The rules that govern these relations are not always conscious. In natural languages, one set of these sets of rules is called a grammar. Most people cannot articulate the grammar of their own language—they just speak.[8] But linguists working with small discrete bits of language—words and sentences—can extract and describe the rules that apparently underlie speech. In the same way, media representations can be assumed to be produced in accordance with semiotic rules, which both producers and consumers "know" at some level, but may be unable to articulate. A media text, in other words, has an internal "grammar," a code that can be decoded and which is organized by paradigmatic and syntagmatic relations. Structural analysis proceeds on the assumption that cultural codes, like linguistic codes, are doubly articulated into syntagmatic and paradigmatic dimensions. A *paradigm* is a set of signs, and a *syntagm* is a new sign that has been constructed by combining the signs in the paradigm under the guidance of a code. For example, an alphabet is a set of signs, a paradigm. Any word or other meaningful text constructed from them is a syntagm.

Syntagms

Syntagmatic relations are relations of signification organized in time and space. There is nothing free about how syntagms are formed; they are never randomly thrown together, but are constructed using certain rules. In English, at the morphological level, the sound /b/ at the beginning of a word can be followed by only a small set of other morphemes: vowels, /l/, /r/ or /y/. It is impossible for /t/ to follow /b/ at the beginning of a normal word. In Arabic, it is impossible to find three consonants in a row without a vowel to break them up. These kinds of rules constitute syntagmatic structures. The question for media semiotics is, are there comparable combinatory rules at work in media texts?

The answer is yes, particularly if we understand that syntagmatic structures do not constitute unbreakable rules so much as rules and resources that producers and consumers of media can draw on in constructing or interpreting the text. It is possible, for example, to construct syntagms that violate rules for specific performative effects. The name of American horror novelist H.P. Lovecraft's alien deity Cthulu violates several phonological rules of English. The effect is to connote alienness. Yet it follows English rules sufficiently to maintain a kind of plausibility or resonance that is not present in a name like Mxyzptlk (the fifth dimensional imp who sometimes plagues Superman). The former is used in tales of horror, in which some semblance of plausibility must be maintained; the latter is used for broadly humorous tales in which plausibility is abandoned. The ability of authors to gauge the effectiveness of such deviations with audiences is part of their semiotic competence, or "talent."

A collection of syntagms formed from one paradigm can, in turn, become a paradigm. Indeed, this happens in languages. In English and Arabic, the alphabet is the paradigm from which the syntagms of words are formed. In turn, the respective sets of English and Arabic words become the paradigm sets from which English and Arabic sentences are formed. We describe this feature as "double-articulation." The same thing happens in media texts. In the American film *Casablanca*, the words "Here's looking at you, kid," are part of a dialogue sequence, a syntagm. Yet the words *as a unit* have taken on a social currency and have become part of a paradigm set of signature movie lines that can be collected, quoted, and parodied for performative effect in various settings, including other movies. Similar processes have been observed in Egyptian, Indian, and Chinese cinemas, in Zambian radio, and elsewhere.

In larger discourses, the syntagmatic structure includes the way symbolic elements are combined to construct a narrative or other text. The story of a film, the "top-down pyramid" of a news story, or the patterns of rhyme and repetition in a love song on the radio are all syntagmatic structures. But syntagmatic relations are also relations of space: the arrangement of pictures and texts in a photo album, the arrangement of lines in a shape poem, and the arrangement of panels on a comic book or *manga* page are all also expressions of syntagmatic relations.

But even though some structures seem to be widely distributed, there do not seem to be universal syntagmatic structures. Syntagmatic structures must be described, not assumed. Certain syntagmatic structures can define part of the meaning of a genre of text. Lee Drummond, for example, argues that the essential tension of the James Bond movie story is built around a relentless chase. In Bond films—as in many other American adventure flicks—tension derives from the ability of prey to turn on their predators. The tension of the chase is constructed through shifting relations of predator and prey. Most of the Bond films are structured by a double chase: a short but intense initial scene in which Bond is chased, yet overcomes his numerically superior adversaries, and a longer chase, which makes up the central narrative of the film. The two segments are separated and joined by the opening credits and theme song (Drummond 1986, 1996). Even still pictures have syntagmatic structures. In any magazine advertisement, certain pictures, colors, and words dominate, while others are subordinate. The eye follows patterns of viewing and reading that can be guided by the designers of such media.[9]

Paradigms

But if syntagmatic structures arrange elements in meaningful relations in time and space, there is the important question of where these elements come from in the first place. A group of elements that can be inserted into a syntagmatic structure is called a *paradigm set*. Elements in a paradigm set carry meanings apart from their relations to one another in time and space. Part of this meaning derives from *reference*. Signs refer to things in the world or, more accurately, to *ideas* about things in the world (which is why there can be signs that refer to imaginary things like flying carpets or unicorns). But reference does not take us far enough in trying to understanding the meanings of signs. For example, the words "sheep" and *mouton* both refer to the same conceptual animal, but this is not all there is to the meaning of these words. According to Saussure (1983), we produce meaning not only by linking signs together in time and space, but also by doing something which is outside that temporal sequence: we choose a sign from a whole range of alternative signs. Meaning thus derives not only from the sign's referential meaning but also from its relations of similarity and difference to *other* signs. Saussure calls this kind of meaning the value (*valeur*) of a sign. The French *mouton* may have the same referential meaning as the English sheep, but it does not have the same value. The reason is that English has both terms *mutton* and *sheep*, a distinction which is not available in French. Saussure emphasizes that a sign gains its *value* from its relation to other signs.

When a journalist writes, *A leading Iraqi official today denounced the U.N's arms' inspection commission*, she chooses each sign from a range of alternatives. She could also have written:

Deputy Prime Minister Tariq Aziz ...	condemned	...
A top Hussein aide	... reviled	...
Iraq	... refused to cooperate with	...

Each word and word set has a different value and each choice she makes has consequences for what follows. Her choices reflect not only her knowledge of and competence in the relevant linguistic and social codes but also understandings of her audience: beliefs about their knowledge, sympathies, and competences.

When we look at such a range of possibilities, we are examining the paradigmatic relationship between signs. Units within a paradigm differ according to features they have in common or which they lack. Just as /p/ and /b/ are almost the same sound, differing only by one feature (unvoiced/voiced), so the choices available to the journalist differ by specific features. These features include the amount of background knowledge they assume, the degree of sympathy they imply, and so forth. The term *denotation* is frequently used to talk about the referential meaning of a sign, while *connotation* refers to the values a sign carries with it because of its web of associations of similarity and difference.

The value of a sign and its referential meaning are not unrelated, but value may well be the paramount relation. At the most primary level of language, the phonetic, the meaning of sounds derives from their values, their distinctions from one another along some axis. Neither /s/ nor /z/ has a referential meaning. The meaning of the sounds is derived from their similarity and difference from one another; the s/z distinction being one of unvocalized/vocalized. Once you've discovered such a feature (vocalization), you will discover that many other sounds in the language depend on the same characteristic.

Structural analysis assumes that this insight also applies to larger features of discourse. Discourses—myths, sets of images, performances, texts of every sort—are comprised of cultural units that are rendered meaningful not only by their referential value but by their relations of similarity and opposition to other signs within the same discourse.

We can examine the syntagms and paradigms in any medium. Dyer (1989) discusses the selection of a specific photographic sign, a stallion, in a Marlboro ad. The connotations of stallion rely, as Dyer puts it, on the reader's cultural knowledge of a system, a code, which can relate "stallion" to feelings of freedom, wide open prairies, masculinity, virility, wildness, individuality, and so forth. To make a selection of a stallion in confidence that an audience will make these connections requires both a practical knowledge of a cultural code of distinctions and similarities as well as a confidence in the widespread knowledge of that code among consumers. One way to analyze these codes when dealing with media in or of your own society is to use the *commutation test*. This technique involves imagining the consequences to a text if you substituted one element from the paradigm with another. What would happen if one were to substitute for the stallion a pony, a donkey, or a mare? What would the ad lose (or gain) in its persuasive purpose, and why?

Structural Analysis

A complete structural analysis should not stop with either a paradigmatic or syntagmatic analysis but should show how they exist in tension. A classic form of structural analysis was developed by Vladimir Propp in *Morphology of the Folk Tale* (1928). Propp argued that most European folktales have essentially the same structure, consisting of a paradigm of seven "actants" (villain, donor, hero, helper, princess, dispatcher and false hero) who move the story through a set of six stages:

Preparation → Complication → Transference → Struggle → Return → Recognition

Any given folktale narrative is a transformation of this model. Any given actant can be played by two or more characters against all sorts of backdrops, and the action in a particular story may focus on some stages more than others, but the overarching structure stays the same. Propp's system appears to be fundamental to many diverse Western narratives outside the folktale, ranging from movies like *Star Wars* (Kottak 1982a, 1982b) to British news stories about philanthropy to the Third World (Benthall 1993).

Most forms of structural analysis owe their models to anthropologist Claude Lévi-Strauss (1963). Although Lévi-Strauss has argued that the techniques of the structural analysis of myth are not applicable to literate and postliterate societies, few media scholars have agreed with him. Many have been particularly attracted to his insights concerning structural transformation. Lévi-Strauss argued that structures often reproduce themselves in transformed ways, particularly through the use of oppositions and reversals: a young man replaces an old man, a boy replaces a girl, and so forth. The elements differ (in patterned ways) but the underlying structure remains the same. Kottak (1982b) has applied this insight to the analysis of the first two *Star Wars* films, arguing that not only do a series of transformations occur within each movie, but each movie can be shown to involve a series of transformations of the previous films, forming a structural whole. Lee Drummond extends Kottak's argument about *Star Wars* and adds similar observations of *E.T.* and *Poltergeist* (Drummond 1996).

Intertextuality

Texts are defined not only by the relations of their internal elements, but also by their relations to other texts. Texts share elements—symbols, themes, storylines—with other texts in ways that are central to their textual meaning. Knowledge of prior texts serve as guides to both text producers and text consumers. Intertextuality refers to the ways these links in form and content connect a text to other texts. Intertextuality can provide general frameworks for interpretation (genre), but it can also serve as a point of strategic departure from these frameworks to create a form of aesthetic play.

Genre

It is double-articulation, the fact that a unit of meaning assembled from one paradigm by a set of syntagmatic rules can become, as an assem-

blage, a unit in a new paradigm, that opens up the possibility of examining texts in terms of their mutual use of common elements. Meaning,
in other words, inheres in part in the associations of symbols with one
another in a web of *intertextuality*. Any given signifier not only has as
referents the denoted signified but also a set of intertextual connotations whose accessibility to any given media reader/consumer involves
their literacy in an overall intertextual web. Sharing among sets of elements that have become partially fixed create genres.

The term *genre* refers to a norm or expectation that producers and
consumers have about text based on these sets of shared elements.
These elements establish a given text as a token of a generic type on the
basis of sets of resemblances or shared characteristics. As a semiotic
project, genres are interesting because they explain the meanings of
symbols by referring texts to one another. "TV show," "movie," "novel"
are all genres, as are "mystery," "horror," "comedy," and so forth. We
can type the genre of a particular text on the basis of our experience of
other texts of the same type. Genre analysis involves exploring the characteristics that define genres and describing their presence or absence
in particular texts. What constitutes genre classifiers in a given text?
Actors, directors, visual images, types of music, and other elements can
all serve to "type" a particular genre. The same film can be classed
simultaneously as a Western, a John Ford film, a John Wayne film, a
love story, and so on.

Every society has words to label speech genres, and most have
developed—and continue to develop—language for labeling different
categories of media texts.[10] The Mexican *telenovela* and the Arabic
musalsal are both frequently translated into English as "soap opera,"
yet there are identifiable differences as well as similarities between
these three genres. Tabloids in America, weekly newspapers with pictures of Bigfoot, sightings of Elvis, and front-page "revolutionary diet"
headlines are not quite the same thing as the daily newspapers the
British call tabloids, although there are similarities. Walter Armbrust
also uses this principle as a way to examine the differences between
American and Egyptian viewings of the Egyptian film *Terrorism and
Kebab*. Whereas in America the film is packaged for the "art film" market to be read intertextually with and against other films of its genre
("foreign film"), Armbrust suggests that Egyptian viewers will
encounter it as "an 'Adil Imam film," their interpretation conditioned by
their knowledge of the Egyptian comic superstar's prior roles in such
films as *Ragab on a Hot Tin Roof, Shaban Below Zero* and *Ramadan on
the Volcano*, none of which circulated in the art film markets.

What makes this especially interesting is the recognition that genres are not fixed but fluid, that one of the central projects in the analy-

sis of media is examining the play of genre conventions. In this understanding, no text is a perfect token of a genre; rather, every text is a cluster of different generic signifiers. Moreover, texts do not just embody
genre conventions, they may play with them, bend them, or stretch
them; the resulting texts may in turn become conventionalized so as to
produce a new genre or a new way of understanding an old genre.
What Hawkes writes of novels can be applied to all media genres:
"Each new novel is not only generated by the preexisting notions of
what a novel is, but it can also change that notion, and so itself generate a modified one" (1977: 101).

If we assume that these changes are not entirely arbitrary but are
linked to shifts in political-economy and social structure, it allows us to
imagine a social theory of genre, which begins from the principle that

> [g]enres are not static but dynamic entities. Partially closed, defined by inter-
> nal relations of their formal elements, they are also open to the ongoing flow
> of social life, shaped by changing social conventions that they in turn shape.
> What needs study, then, is not genre conceived of as a fixed, archetypal
> mold, stereotypically reproduced over generations, but actual processes of
> genre creation and evolution, which involve discontinuity as much as conti-
> nuity, transformation as well as reproduction. (Traube 1990: 375)

One example in this direction is offered by Mark Pedelty (1999), who
looks at the historical and contemporary significance of Mexico's popular music genre, *Bolero*. Pedelty sees *Bolero* as part of a "ritual complex" of media that mediate between official state versions of modernity
and the realities of everyday life. As *Bolero* texts travel from song to
screen to stage, they carry with them in each incarnation part of the signification of their previous incarnation. Moreover, as the texts travel
from medium to medium, they also travel through time, and the genre
gathers further signifying force as it comes to be framed first as "nostalgic" and then "traditional," even as it continues to be about the contradictions of modernity in Mexican society.

Intertextual Play

A second way of looking at intertextuality is as a kind of symbolic play,
the drawing of iconic, indexical or other connections between texts,
genres, and media to create meaning. In this sense, intertextuality is an
active social process involving the extracting of a sign or set of signs
from one setting (decontextualization) and inserting it (or them) into
another (recontextualization) (Bauman and Briggs 1990; Briggs and
Bauman 1992; Silverstein and Urban 1996). This sort of intertextual
play is sometimes called *bricolage*, Lévi-Strauss's term for the appropriation of preexisting symbolic materials that are ready-to-hand, to create
new configurations.

Intertextual bricolage is intimately bound to such central linguistic concepts as genre, self-reference, plagiarism, parody, irony, and indexicality. As an interpretive practice, intertextual play is communicative insofar as links between the original setting and the recontextualized setting are recognized. Recognition of intertextuality by an audience does not require intent on the part of the producers of a text, although intent may be imputed to them. Likewise, recognition of intertextuality by some audiences does not imply recognition by all, nor does it imply that audiences will make the same intertextual references.

Armbrust (1998a) offers the example of how the casting of John Wayne in *The Searchers* used the actor's historically conditioned screen image to create a particular effect:

> Ford's depiction of frontier brutality with overtones of incest might have been an excellent film with any competent male lead: with John Wayne as the protagonist it was shocking and unforgettable. Why? Because we were seeing not just the grim *Searchers* but also *Stagecoach*, *The Long Voyage Home*, *The Quiet Man*, and *They Were Expendable*.... The overall effect [of these films] was to make John Wayne into an icon of a certain kind of American ideology, an ideology that privileged masculinity, toughness, and honor. Therefore to see him mutilating corpses and lusting after his niece in *The Searchers* added a complex layer of emotion to [the] film.... No other actor could have played the role the same way, or one suspects, as effectively (288).

Conscious strategic use of intertextuality is a powerful tool for media producers to enhance consumption. Product placements, spin-offs, parodic comedies, and commercial tie-ins all depend for their effectiveness on audience recognition of intertextual relations.

Some theorists have argued that an increasing self-conscious use of intertextuality by producers illustrates a coming of age of a medium, particularly television. Increasing use of intertextuality, in this argument, indicates that the medium has reached sufficient semiotic depth that it can become self-referential. The medium has become "postliterate" when its codes of production and consumption have broken free of its moorings to the written word and are built on a foundation of prior texts. Such arguments ignore the history of intertextual play in television. In the United States, television from its earliest days self-consciously parodied itself, particularly in comedies like Sid Caesar's *Your Show of Shows* or the prehistoric versions of contemporary television pop stars caricatured on *The Flintstones*. Intertextuality has also long been a linking mechanism for congeries of American television programs like *The Beverly Hillbillies*, *Petticoat Junction*, *Gomer Pyle USMC*, *Mayberry RFD*, and others, in which characters occasionally strayed across boundaries of one program to visit characters in another. Yet another form of intertextual link common in the early years of American television was created when actors or musicians would appear on these television programs as themselves, as when bluegrass and country musicians would visit the Clampett family at their Beverly Hills estate in *The Beverly Hillbillies*. What's more, the overlap between media genres makes it difficult to tell when a program is parodying itself, its medium, or drawing from other media. When, in the early days of American television, Sid Caesar appeared as an exaggerated stereotype of a gangster on *Your Show of Shows*, was he parodying the gangsters of cinema? Of radio? Of pulp novels? Of television? Certain types of images develop precisely because of the intertextuality that exist *between* media.

Nor is all intertextual play motivated by artistic vision. Commerce may also play a part in the process. Product placement is a commercial form of intertextual play with a long history in the media. From the steaming coffee Mama serves her guests as Maxwell House announced its sponsorship of *I Remember Mama* (Lipsitz 1986) to the use of brand-name products as central plot devices in *Seinfeld* (Andersen 1995), there is an abundance of evidence that creative use of intertextuality in television is intimately connected with the commercial aspects of the medium. The intertextuality between movies and products in the United States is at least as old as the 1932 Marx Brothers film, *Horse-feathers*.[11] This kind of textual play puts fictional characters into a world of commodities much like the world in which many of the viewers live in. Such product placement carries elements of advertisements into the story worlds of films, but it also blurs the distinction between entertainment and advertising.

In recent years, the manufacturers of products have begun to pay for such placements. Robin Andersen (1995) argues that the role of intertextual relations between advertising brands and consumer goods in the United States has become a central element in many media genres, particularly on television. Rather than operating merely as gags and background props, some American television, notably the popular 1990s situation comedy *Seinfeld*, made branded products central to their storylines. In one *Seinfeld* episode, for example, the protagonist, witnessing an operation on a friend, accidentally drops a Junior Mint™ into the open body cavity of the patient. The doctors do not notice the mint and seal it up inside the body. When the patient undergoes a miraculous recovery, doctors call it a miracle and talk of a "higher power," which produces ironic reactions from the Seinfeld regulars (and laughs from the audience). Junior Mints™ are only one of the everyday consumer items that appeared as plot devices in *Seinfeld*; over the years Dockers™ jeans, Sun-Maid Raisins™, Pledge™, Snapple™, Drake's Coffee Cake™, and Chuckles™ candy have all played roles on the program, just as BMW has played a key role in the James Bond films. Andersen observes:

> This new generation of television advertising/programming creates a hybrid narrative of persuasion and entertainment. The product is so thoroughly embedded within the text that it serves as a plot device and, indeed, becomes the main theme of the entire program. No longer a singular positive text, the product now has its ups and downs as well. It begins to acquire the attributes of a character. (1995: 256-257).

Medium

Any text is also defined in part by the medium through which it is expressed. I use the term *medium* here in the same broad sense in which I introduced it in chapter 1; it thus includes speech and writing, print and broadcast, as well as their more specific forms. These include not only mass media such as radio, television, newspapers, billboards, magazines, books, photographs, films, records, and Web pages, but also telephone, letter, fax, e-mail, video-conferencing, computer-based chat systems, public address systems, and *karaoke* machines, among others.

The relationship of a text to its medium is significant for two reasons. First, texts can only exist in the material form of a medium. Since each medium has its own sociotechnical constraints and possibilities, the essential character of the text may be grossly or subtly transformed by recasting it from one medium to another. That is, the material vehicle of a text has implications for how consumers encounter it. Second, the medium used may itself contribute to meaning by framing a text in a particular way. A spoken text is not the same thing as a written text. A hypertext offers a different kind of vehicle for representation than does a movie. The medium through which symbols are expressed is thus always and inevitably a defining characteristic of the text.

Is the Medium the Message?

The notion that the nature of the medium shapes understanding has been explored by a number of scholars. The strongest statement is Marshall McLuhan's famous aphorism "the medium *is* the message," which he seems to have used in different contexts to mean a number of different things.[12] The one that concerns us here is his argument that the nature of a medium shapes the meaning of the texts for which it acts as a sign vehicle. Each medium has its own opportunities and constraints in broadcast and reception based on its technology. Because of these phenomenological differences, technologies of representation shape the meanings of the messages in several ways.

First, different media offer different kinds of constraints. Print media are bound by the technological constraints of printing technologies; films by cinema technologies, and so forth. Transforming a text from one medium to another creates a new and different text because of the technical constraints, of each medium. The reverse of this is that different media offer different kinds of opportunities. Transforming a text from a novel to an audiotape introduces certain constraints but also opens up possibilities: sound effects, music, the use of one reader or multiple actors, and so forth. Transforming a novel into a film introduces certain other constraints, but also opens up a number of visual possibilities.

Third, it is possible that these differences in constraint and possibility shape perception, and thus meaning, in various obvious and subtle ways. Caton (1999) makes an interesting argument of this sort for the film *Lawrence of Arabia*. The film was made using a particular wide-screen technology, Super Panavision. The film was designed to be seen in this technology, in terms of vast panoramas that could not be taken in by the audience's gaze without moving their heads. The intention was that

> [a]t the film's most intense visual moments, the wide screen would allow the frame to virtually disappear, with the result that one felt one's body to be coterminous with, and not outside of or removed from, the action represented on the screen. (Caton 1999: 75)

The failure of the film industry to maintain this technology means that it is now virtually impossible for contemporary viewers to see the original film as intended by its producers and as viewed by its original audiences. Seeing it on a contemporary motion picture screen reduces the size to an appropriate one for the new "megamall" system of film distribution in which theater owners generate profits from showing as many films as possible. Renting the movie at a video store and watching it at home—even on a big-screen TV—is, in some sense, to see a different film than its creators intended.

Entire registers have emerged for talking about particular media in terms of the constraints and possibilities of their technologies of production. The photographic register includes camerawork (lens choice, focus, aperture, exposure, camera position); composition (framing, distance, angle, lighting), film (quality, type, color); developing (exposure, treatments); and printing (paper, size, cropping). Cinematic and televisual registers would include many of these, but also registers linked to movement and time (cuts and fades, editing rate and rhythm, compression, flashbacks, flashforwards, slow motion, etc.) as well as to sound and narrative style.

Sociotechnical Artifacts

In spite of their apparent utility, views that media technologies powerfully frame and define the kinds of messages they contain must be considered cautiously. While media certainly have specific characteristics that shape the way they are used, we must be careful not to overestimate the relationship of media form and cultural meaning. A television news producer once told me that it was ridiculous for social critics to condemn news programs for turning news into morality plays because the television medium *requires* television news to have a narrative construction. Considered strictly as a technology, this is patently untrue. Similar assumptions hold about the need to cut novels down in size to fit the "time constraints" of film. But if there is no constraint on the length of film inherent in the technology itself; the restriction is based on producers' assumptions about audience expectations and on the economics of their industry. These producers are actually speaking about *sociotechnical* constraints (Pfaffenberger 1992)—ideological presumptions about what a technology is and does within a particular social and cultural milieu.

The history of the telephone offers a fine cautionary tale of our tendency to conflate the technological and the social. As originally marketed by Bell and Watson, the telephone was intended not as a two-way communications device but as a unidirectional medium by means of which subscribers could listen to lectures and concerts from the privacy of their homes. If the notion of the telephone as a broadcast medium seems absurd or unsettling, argues Naomi Baron (1999), it is because we have a tendency to regard the modes in which we use media as given by the technologies themselves, rather than as part of a social and cultural context. The evolution of the telephone into a medium for interpersonal communication was a long and convoluted one, and the device continued to be advertised as a reception device until the end of the nineteenth century. The "maturation" of the technology involved additional technical and engineering improvements, but only in conjunction with shifting efforts to market the device under changing social conditions. The telephone was a difficult sell because the market was shaped by political and social contexts often hostile to the new invention. With the telegraph system already in place, most simply couldn't see any use for the telephone. Editorialists railed against its introduction into the home as an invasion of privacy that would allow fast-talking salesmen to invade the sanctity of domestic space. It became primarily a professional tool—police superintendents could be linked by telephone to their stations, government ministers to their offices, so they could be contacted in cases of emergency. The minister couldn't necessarily call the police superintendent, however, because the telephone was not initially marketed as a multiuser device. The relatively low demand for the telephone made switchboards a late development. The widespread expansion of the telephone from business to personal use in the United States began only in the 1890s, nearly twenty years after the telephone first appeared, when rural communities began pooling finances to create regional exchanges (usually operated out of households) with party lines that afforded a virtual sense of community life to far-flung farm families. It was almost thirty more years before shifts in urban communities led to widespread adoption of the telephone in American cities.[13]

The relationship between a text and its medium is thus never a strictly technical relationship, although social uses are often *assumed* to be mandated by technology. People have understandings about how to use communication technologies, which they naturalize as being a necessary component of the technology. When we see communication scholars classifying the telephone under "interpersonal communication" as opposed to "broadcast communication," we need to be conscious that these distinctions are not necessarily given by the technologies themselves but rather by the social contexts of their use. Instead, we should be thinking of "'media cultures' with their own codes and conventions" (Manuel 1993), of the "cultural roles" that media play in a society (Beeman 1982), or of the "ecology of communicative forms" (White 1999) in which each technological medium is seen as existing within a cultural environment that gives it meaning. Underlying these notions is a recognition that media serve different functions at different times in different societies. Moreover, media are *understood* by members of these societies as occupying particular functional positions.

The key issue here is that media mean more to people than that which is given by their technologies. They not only express meanings through the texts for which they act as vehicles, but they themselves are meaningful in ways that go well beyond their technological constraints. Understanding a text in terms of its relations to its medium requires attention to sociotechnical codes that vary from one social system to another. A salesman for computer systems once described to me a laser typesetting system he'd sold to a Nigerian newspaper as a cheaper and more flexible system than their old offprint technology. The grateful clients had sent him copies of the last issue of the paper done using the old system and the first issue of the newspaper using the new system. The differences were remarkable: the new type was crisper, clearer, and much easier to read. The clients believed that the new technology was giving their paper more authority and improving circulation. On the other hand, when the Urdu newspaper *Milap* in New Delhi switched from its old system of handwritten Urdu script to a new, computer-generated font, audience perceptions of the sharper, easier-to-read font were not positive. The editor told me readers thought it looked "cheap" and "modern," and lacked the authoritativeness of the traditional technology. The newspaper had to try out three different Urdu fonts before they found one that looked enough like handwriting to satisfy their readers, and *Milap* continued to use hand calligraphy for headlines.

So the medium *is* the message, but not necessarily in the ways that this statement is normally understood. Media technologies provide constraints and possibilities for the construction of representations, but the meanings of these for consumers of the text often have much more to do with how these media are understood to function in society than with the actual technologies themselves. Once they are established in particular niches in a social ecology of communications, however, it becomes difficult to think of them as anything but what they are used for. Technologies become, in a sense, naturalized.

Reference

The coherence of a text depends in part on the fact that it says something about something. That something about which the text "speaks"—or, more accurately, that which the text represents as its subject—is its *referent*.[14] The referent can be something phenomenologically real—like a tree—or something imaginary, like the living trees in the *Wizard of Oz*—or something whose ontological status is ambiguous, like UFOs.

The distinction is not a simple one. Saussure was careful to clarify that when one uses a word like *tree*, the referent of the sound is not any actual tree in the world but a concept, a part of a cultural code. Saussure assumes the relative autonomy of language in relation to reality; language does not require a word to have a real world referent. This is not to say that trees don't exist but rather that to use language to talk about the phenomenal world requires us to do special work. We must link the categories to objects through additional signs. When I say, "This is a tree," or use a gesture to point to a tree, I am linking semantic categories to the world of experience, a process called *deixis*. The article "this" and the pointing gesture are both deictic signs.

A semiotic language for describing deictic signs was developed by Charles Sanders Peirce, an American semiotician. Peirce said that in addition to arbitrary, conventional modes of signification (which he called symbolic), it was possible to signify something by resembling it. A photograph signifies its subject because it resembles its subject—although one may need to be taught how to recognize such resemblances (Deregowski 1980). This sort of signification is called *iconic*. In addition, Peirce suggested that it was possible to signify something by being connected to it, an *indexical* relationship. Peirce used an example from the novel *Robinson Crusoe*, where Crusoe finds Friday's footprint in the sand and immediately realizes that there is another man on the island with him. The link between the signifying footprint and the signified human is not based on an arbitrary social convention but on the recognition that only humans make human footprints.[15] Causal relations are not the only relations of contiguity that can create such signification; it is also possible for parts to stand for wholes, categories to stand for members, and so forth.

Referential Meaning

Relations of iconicity and indexicality are not at all mutually exclusive. A typical newspaper photograph, for example, is an iconic representation of the event that is being described in the story. At the same time, it is an indexical sign in that a photograph assumes a photographer who snapped the picture. This indexicality becomes an important means by which newspapers construct their authority, which is based on having "been there" so that they can "report it." Deictic reference is thus central to the work of journalism and many other sorts of nonfictional texts. Journalism seeks to describe the world of experience by naming and categorizing people and places. Documentaries seek to provide perspectives on real people and authentic events. Reality TV seeks to capture events as they occur. The image derives its authority from an implied set of relations of production.

Claims that texts make of themselves are the starting place for analyzing referential relations. The reality status accorded to or claimed by a text is sometimes called *modality*. In making sense of a text, its interpreters derive meanings from textual cues to determine the text's plausibility, reliability, objectivity, credibility, truth, accuracy or facticity according to social codes. In Western television journalism, for example, texts make claims to be actual (rather than acted), to be live or to be recorded, and so forth. Some texts are rooted in the assumption that there is a world "out there," which they describe for their readers. Journalism—in its various media incarnations (radio, television, print, Web)—is a genre of text that owes its existence to the assumption that the world can be accurately represented.

The same set of codes used to tell the truth can also be used to lie, of course. In 1992, NBC's *Dateline* aired a segment in which it filmed GM pickup trucks crashing and igniting—apparently confirming contentions by critics that the trucks were hazardous because their gas tanks were external. An investigation by GM led to the discovery that

78	Anthropology & Mass Communication

the news program had attached incendiary devices to the truck to ensure that it would ignite, and had made the fifteen-second fire appear to last much longer through the use of multiple camera angles. American legal codes interpreted this as libelous, and it was characterized in popular discourse as a lie—even though NBC contended their intention had been simply to provide dramatic visuals for the more carefully nuanced spoken narrative that accompanied the segment.

People question the truthfulness of media texts, but they do so according to cultural codes that set up parameters for evaluation. In the United States, most people read news with an eye toward determining whether or not it is "biased"—that is, if the representations of things and events are colored by personal desires and leanings of the reporter. In doing so, they draw upon their experience of the world (and social codes) and of the medium. In India, on the other hand, I found that many newspaper readers assumed in advance that all newspapers were colored by particular social and political leanings and chose their newspapers with this in mind (M. Peterson 1996).

Many modality codes are based on a correspondence theory of truth, which suggests that it is possible to compare propositions with an independent reality external to representational systems. Parenti (1993) offers a classic approach of this sort. The problem with this sort of analysis is that it raises the question of *whose* perspective of reality— *whose* experience of the world—is going to count as the empirical reality against which to evaluate other accounts. The issue is not so much whether things exist in the external world, or even to what extent they can be seen as independent of our modes of apprehending them, as it is one of articulation, of constructing accounts of these things. Is it possible to create a text, in any medium, that is a neutral, unmediated description of the world? Journalists write from experiences of the phenomenal world—observations, interviews, leaked documents. But however unbiased one's reporting is, the articulation of experience in words and images—the text—always remains a construction. Texts are inevitably made, not given or discovered. The reality referenced by the text is never the same reality experienced by the reporter; the reality of the text is constructed in representations.

A text is necessarily a construction, but the choices of how one constructs the account can be very revealing. As we have seen, paradigmatic choices have consequences for the referential reality inscribed in the text. It means something very different to write about "female circumcision" than "female genital mutilation." The choice between "militants," "guerrillas," "freedom fighters," "rebels," "separatists," and "terrorists," is not and cannot be a neutral choice; each and every option has a different set of associated meanings that become part of the reality constructed by the text. Texts become sites of ideological struggle in which different realities are contested.

Referential analysis asks questions about how texts construct believable worlds. Not all texts make claims that these worlds be referentially true, yet they still make referential claims. Fictional narratives—most movies, sitcoms, soap operas, *musalsal*, *telenovelas*, novels, and so forth—do not make claims to be referentially true, but they do still reference a believable *storyworld*. A novel, for example, is known to be false but is written *as if* it were true. People evaluate it on the basis of its ability to allow them to pretend it is true. Advertisements offer referential claims about goods and services, but these are often embedded in a series of symbols that seek to evoke specific emotions, desires, or needs.

Participants

Any text assumes the existence of people, of those who created the text and those who consume it. A book assumes a writer or writers and a reader or set of readers. A movie assumes a group of moviemakers and a public of moviegoers. Choosing a generic set of terms for participants in media acts is therefore difficult. In this book I've tended to use *producers* and *consumers*, to avoid privileging any particular medium. There are problems with these terms, however, which have led a few authors to offer the terms *makers* and *users*. Many other media analysts working with texts use the terms *writers* and *readers* generally for any kind of text, not just written texts. Participants are also sometimes referred to in mass communication studies as *encoders* and *decoders*.

Addressors

Any text, claims Ricouer (1981), assumes an *intent to say*. Someone sought to say something. This someone is generally called the *addressor*, the person who sends the message and has ultimate responsibility for it. The addressor need not be a literal person; it can be a spirit, a device, or an institution. The latter is common in everyday Western media discourse, where it is common to hear people say things like, "the media is really ganging up on Bush." In this case, the whole media industry is treated metonymically as a single entity, the sender of a congeries of messages.

More commonly, the addressor is constructed as an individual. The ascription of authorship to a text is itself a cultural code; not all societies consider authorship a significant aspect of all texts. In Western media, though, it is typical to speak of films as belonging to a director's *oeuvre*, of novels as having authors, of news as having reporters, even advertisements are assumed to be authored by the company that provides the goods or services advertised. Such interpretive practices are but a social convention; media production is generally such an enormously complex, multilayered and collaborative activity that to speak of any single author is problematic. Getting at actual modes of media production and the goals of those involved in them is therefore a task for ethnography.

Getting at authorship as a property of the text is another matter. Texts refer to authors in a number of ways. Authorship can be constructed by certain forms of prose, such as direct address. Authorship markers, such as newspaper bylines, may serve as referential indices to authorship. Note that these referential signs of authorship are rarely as simple as they appear to be. The "person" named as author of a novel, for example, might be the individual named, another individual operating under that name, a group of hired writers operating under that name, the individual named working with any number of unnamed others in the production of texts, and so forth. Small fiction magazines have sometimes employed "house names" to disguise the fact that the same writer has two stories in the same issue. Particularly prolific writers may write a large volume of work under pseudonyms creating, in essence, two separate authorial personalities, often within the same genre (well-known examples include Erle Stanley Gardner's separate ouevre as A.A. Fair, and Stephen King's corpus as Richard Bachman). American science-fiction authors with dwindling sales sometimes use pseudonyms to evade publisher's expectations that their books will not sell (Bacon-Smith 2000: 211). Such strategies work only because authorship is a specific textual property and not merely an indexical relationship to a person.

Authorship serves several functions. The importance of authorship rises as texts become commodified, since authorship is linked to ownership. The relationship is never one-to-one, however, because the named or implied authors are not necessarily the legally recognized owners of the text. Indeed, sometimes the author of the text is deliberately separated from the owners of the text to maintain a distinction between art and commerce, or news as a public trust and news as a commodity. Authorship may also assist a text in establishing authority. A byline on a news story serves not only to establish authorship, but also to fix responsibility for the truth assertions in the text.

Addressees

The participants constructed by a text include not only an authorial persona but also an ideal reader, someone imagined by the addressor and by the text. Roman Jakobson (1960) recommends the term "addressee" to distinguish this textually constructed person from actual recipients, readers, or viewers, who may or may not share any of the characteristics of the imagined consumer to whom the text is addressed. Umberto Eco offers the term *ideal reader* to suggest such a model reader, whose interpretation could be justified in terms of the text. In the 1920s, *National Geographic* magazine ran many advertisements for world cruises. Taking some 121 days and costing $2,000 (at a time when the average American income was $700 per year), the addressees of these ads were members of the leisure class, people who could indulge themselves in such activities. Many other people no doubt read the ads, but the ads are not addressed to them. The term addressee can be extended to include a generalized public of persons presumed to share the same codes, interpretations, and beliefs.

The addressee is distinguished in part by the modes of address used in the text, particularly the point of view a text takes toward its subject matter. Television and film texts in which the camera shows us events as if from a particular participant's visual point of view presumably encourage viewers to identify with that person's way of seeing events, or perhaps invites viewers to feel like eyewitnesses to the events themselves. Third-person "omniscient" narrative may appear more distant from the addressee, constructing the addressee as the recipient of facts and events that appear to speak for themselves. The addressee may be constructed as singular or plural, an individual or part of a group. Subtle textual cues may construct addressees as patrons, pupils, colleagues, or many other roles.

Silence

For everything that is said, there are other things that were not said. For every choice made, there are choices that are not made. For each overt connection, there are disconnections. Every text is as much about silences and absences as it is about representation and presence. We have already described the way that the value of a sign derives from what it is not as much as what it is. This same principle operates at larger levels of discourse, including media texts. Signs of this sort, which are absent from a text, but which nevertheless influence the meaning of the signs actually used, are sometimes called *absent signifiers*.

The Unsaid

One of the most common forms of media analysis is the examination of what is not said in referential discourse. Different cultural codes note different kinds of silences as meaningful. In English, the phrase "conspicuous by their absence" defines one widely shared idea about meaningful silence. The importance of this concept to media in American society is marked by media watchdog institutions, which study media "bias." It is important to remember, though, that the notion of bias is part of a cultural code that assumes there is an unbiased, neutral way to represent. Each of these institutions adopt particular ideological stances. They recognize absences as conspicuous because of their own sensitized positions. Using American notions about journalism as an objective discourse, they define these absences as "biases" and make assumptions about the producers of the absent signifiers.

Silence can also teach us a great deal about the commonsense world imagined by those who produced the text and the audiences they imagined would read it. Much of what is said in any text assumes a silent, "taken-for-granted" set of assumptions. This is the sort of meaningful silence we might categorize as something that "goes without saying." Much of what confuses us in watching foreign media stems from such silences, symbols for which no specific interpretive contexts are offered in the text because, from the producer's point of view, none are needed. One anthropological approach to media has been to offer to "fill in" the unsaid. Painter (1994) offers an excellent account of Japanese television shows in which he fills in the unstated cultural assumptions that make the programs meaningful to Japanese audiences.

The Unspeakable

Some things are unsaid because, within a particular context, they *cannot* be said. Such texts can be described as "unspeakable" (Tyler 1987) or "unsayable" (Wittgenstein 1975). Certain responses to censorship fall into this category. During Indira Ghandi's "emergency" in India (1975-1977), not only was the Indian press heavily censored, but newspapers were not allowed to make any overt reference to the fact that they were censored. Several newspapers responded by withholding news. *National Herald* simply ran blank spaces where stories had been censored. When told by the government that they couldn't do this, the paper ran censored stories without headlines. *Punjab Kesari* stopped running news on its front page, replacing it with movie star pictures and features that belonged to its "magazine" section. *Times of India* occasionally ran government press releases unedited, without bylines. All of these texts used some form of silence, or absence, as a means of signaling that the news had been censored. Here, absence stands for absence; an overt silence speaks out as a metamessage revealing a more important , but less obvious silence.

Not all such censorship is political in the restricted sense. During the 1990s, most medical journals refused to accept research papers offering evidence or opinions that contradicted the HIV/AIDS link, regardless of the credentials of the scientists conducting the research (Hodgkinson 1994). That HIV caused AIDS was accepted as fact by mainstream medicine. To print articles countering this would reduce the prestige of the journal. The same is true of papers concerning evidence for the American Bigfoot or Nepalese Yeti in journals of physical anthropology, or the possibility of extraterrestrial visitation in archaeology journals. Peer review, central to academia's system of production, serves all scientific publications as a means to effectively silence voices that are too far out of the mainstream of opinion in a given field. Most media genres have similar mechanisms in place. Here, absence stands for *presence*, the presences of an agreed set of boundaries of knowledge within a discipline.

Another form of unspeakable silence occurs in many genres of media production in which the text cannot refer to itself because to do so would violate the nature of the text and transform it into something else. In American print journalism, for example, sources and their words are prominently featured, but the actions of journalists, including the questions they ask to elicit those words, are deliberately concealed.[16] Indeed, to include the journalist in the frame of the story is to violate the cultural canons of objectivity. It would not be an exaggeration to say that journalistic authority is built on silence, on the concealment of journalistic presence.

All of these forms of organized silences constitute "disciplinary regimes" of discourse (Foucault 1984b: 60-61), which reproduce themselves as other texts intertextually reproduce the same silences. This is not an inherently bad thing: without some system of authority over distinctions, texts would lose coherence and meaning. Nevertheless, that such regimes are necessary does not mean they are not also loci of power relations and must be recognized as such.

Conclusion

The relations of a text to the elements that comprise it, other texts, its medium, its participants, its references and its silences provides enormous scope for the analysis of media. But even though texts have a real existence in the world, and the elements that comprise the texts can be described and organized, interpreting the meanings of these texts forces analysts to make interpretive judgments. These judgments often involve assumptions not only about the codes by which consumers interpret texts, but also about the nature of meaning in social life. Of crucial interest to scholars relating texts to social life has been the issue of power—the putative power of the text over its consumers and the importance of this power to the structure of modern society. The nature of these assumptions is the subject of the next chapter.

Notes

1. This disparity may not be as great as has generally been assumed. Much more attention to discourse *about* the media and its place in public life, as well as the effects of such discourse on media production and consumption, is required by social scientists.

2. And yet not completely. Subtitling, re-editing, dubbing, and other transformative operations are common practices which certain "inflect" texts for different audiences. I will discuss the ramifications of such inflections in chapters 9 and 10.

3. The notion of cultural codes entered linguistics from information theory primarily through the work of Roman Jakobson (1990). It remains a problematic term (see Alvarez-Cáccamo 2001). Here, I will use *code* to refer to the process that "links related signifieds (meanings, concepts, cultural categories) to signifiers (sign vehicles). Codes are consequently complex and can be analyzed to discover the rules for linking signifieds to signifiers (semantics, the process of semiosis); the relationship among signifiers (both syntactic or combinatory, and paradigmatic or substitutive); the relationship among signifieds (e.g. contrast, inclusion, metaphor); and the relationship between codes." (Bean 1981a).

4. The tourist's desire for a fixed form of Navajo sand painting is not unlike the relationship between speech and writing, in which "writing preserves discourse and makes it an archive available for individual and collective memory" (Ricouer 1981: 147). A similar fleeting vs. fixed dichotomy is central to issues of performativity; Anna Deaere Smith and Doreen Kondo speculate that the general scholarly preference for analyzing film over theater arises because the performativity of theater undermines easy notions of the "fixedness" of the text (Kondo 1996: 330-331).

5. The language of "selection" and "decision" should not imply that interpretation is necessarily a conscious and strategic project. The decisions an interpreter makes are often overdetermined by his or her cultural background, and by the contexts in which the text is encountered. In the case of scholars, the decision about what to pay attention to is often determined by their theoretical position. In other words, as used here "decision" does not necessarily imply a free *choice*.

6. As we will see, however, it is possible for a particular arbitrary set, such as /beautiful woman/ + /car/ to become so sedimented that it becomes a single cultural unit—/beautiful woman and car/ — which can then be combined with other units.

7. The idea that other symbolic languages are like language is a useful assumption but cannot be proved. Sebeok and Danesi (2000) and Bloch (1998) argue against such a model in favor of evidence that cognitive modeling precedes cognition and that articulation of such models by language requires a translation. Drummond (1996) makes a similar argument, insisting that the widespread assumption that language precedes and undergirds myth is mistaken; in fact, mythic models of the world precede language, even though they are socially expressed through language and image. Another objection is that since linguistic models are based on an assump-

tion of a vocal-auditory apparatus, technological mediation should require an adjustment of the model. To my knowledge, only Sol Worth—whose theories we shall discuss in chapter 7—actually built into semiotic theory a recognition that technological mediation may require a modification of our understanding of the units of articulation.

8. Grammar here is used in the linguistic sense to refer to descriptions of the rules by which people actually speak, rather than the scholastic use of grammar to refer to prescriptive rules describing how people are *supposed* to speak.

9. The study of the theories of semiotics and effects held by advertising and other media industries is terribly understudied, in spite of a vast number of professional texts. See Sahlins (1976) and McCreery (2001) for exceptions.

10. Genres tend to multiply and differentiate in a never-ending process of trying to conceptually map the mediascape. John Postill (personal communication) reports that the German magazine *TV Spielfilm* has a huge range of film genres and subgenres in its previews, many of which are creative hybrids of others. A small sample from the 11-24 August 2001 issue includes: *Erotikthriller, Maerchen, Zeitreiseabenteuer,* TV-Drama, *Gaunerkomoedie,* TV-*Kinderdrama, Kinderdrama, Trickmaerchen,* Western, TV-*Krimiabenteuer, Kinderkrimi, Abenteuer, Kostuemdrama, Kinderabenteuer, Aktionkomoedie, Jugendkrimi, Lustspiel, Fantasyromanze, Abenteuerkomoedie, Westerndrama, Klamauk,* US-Thriller, Filmbiz-Satire, *Komoedie,* TV-*Krimi,* TV-*Endzeitdrama,* TV-Thriller, TV-*Dokuthriller, Maedchen-Abenteuer, Krimiromanze,* Sci-Fi-Horror, *Gruselspass, Kifferklamotte, Grossstadtballade,* TV-*Historiendrama, Klamotte, Actionthriller, Doku, Erotikkrimi.*

11. In one scene in *Horsefeathers,* the villainess is floundering in the water, calling on Groucho, who is sitting in a boat, to throw her the life saver. He removes from his pocket a roll of Life Savers™ candies and tosses one to her.

12. In addition to arguing that the medium shapes the nature of the message, McLuhan made three related arguments. First, Mcluhan asserted that using a medium is a meaningful experience in itself regardless of the content one consumes. Second, he postulated that the experience of using particular media changes the perceptual habits of its users. Third, he contended that the real "message" of the media is the impact it has on society through these transformational processes. I will discuss some of these issues in Chapters 9 and 10.

13. On the history of the telephone, see B. Singer 1981, Pool 1983, Fischer 1992, and the papers in Pool et al. 1977. Douglas and Isherwood (1981) discuss how differences in social relations in British and American communities led to a much later development in Britain of the consumer *desire* to own telephones in the home. Baron (1999) argues that the lessons of the evolution of telephone usage can help us understand the emergence and evolution of other "language technologies," such as e-mail. White (1999) examines the relationship of telephone and television as two "niches" in an elaborate communications ecology.

14. It is by no means a necessary condition of a sign that the signifier has a referent. Many signifiers do not have referents. In language, for example, a connective such as "and" is a powerful signifier but it has no referent; its meaning is its function.

15. It is possible, of course, to lie with indexical signs; this is the point of red herrings in mystery novels. But the lie only works *because* of the indexical codes that link sign and referent.

16. For exceptions that make the rule, see Clayman 1990.

Chapter 4

THE POWER OF THE TEXT

That media texts affect us is plain from everyday experience. We can put a novel down to find ourselves momentarily disoriented, shifting from the storyworld of the narrative back to that of everyday experience. We can leave a movie theater feeling exhilarated or wrung out. The music we hear on the radio can invoke enthusiasm, nostalgia, or puzzlement. A news show can induce fear or relieve our anxieties. A key question for nearly all those studying mass communication is whether these shifts in mood and perception are momentary, or whether they have long-lasting effects on our thoughts and actions. To what extent might our consumption of media texts change us, and to whose benefit? Perhaps an even more cogent version of this question is, to what effect might they induce complacency, and to whose benefit?

One of the central distinctions between anthropologists studying media and mass communication scholars has been the understandings these disciplines have had about the relationship between media texts and society. As we saw in chapter 2, until recently, anthropologists who looked at media at all tended to see both media production and consumption as social practices not unlike other social practices, being both reflective of, and constituent of, the communities in which they are produced and consumed. Media texts were often examined as cultural artifacts whose form and content were reflective of the societies in which and for which they were produced. With its attention to the connections between symbols and cultural codes, what was missing from much of this anthropological literature was sustained attention to political economy, class, and hierarchy, that is, to structures of *power*. Mass communication scholars, on the other hand, tended to conceive of media production and consumption as a route of communication from senders to receivers. Many focused on the asynchronous aspect of this system as its defining feature, and theorized about it accordingly. They assumed that unequal control over the means of media production implied symbolic power. Power, in this sense, has generally been defined as the capacity media have to shape viewers beliefs, actions, and aspirations.

This chapter examines text-focused theories of power, analytical positions that theorize about the power that media texts have over their audiences. These theories assume that media messages have effects, but they differ dramatically in their positions about these effects. Theories that suppose a strong, even overwhelming, power of the text over its consumers have always been countered by theories that see textual interpretation as shaped by the consumer's social position, cultural knowledge, and personal biography. In the last two decades, attention has increasingly shifted to theories that position themselves between these two, imagining texts as having real effects, but effects that are mediated by the interpretive practices of the consumer. These positions within media studies have been paralleled by recent anthropological approaches that are bringing new analytical tools to the study of media as myth.

Getting the Message

At the heart of most mass communication studies is an understanding of communication as a transfer of messages from senders to receivers. Applied to the asynchronous nature of mass communication, this becomes a theory of *encoding* and *decoding* texts. Producers of media texts produce these texts according to specific codes; the receivers of messages decode these texts. The primary meaning of a message, in this view, is its content. There are a number of positions one can take with regard to such a model. One can emphasize the power of the encoding process, envisioning passive recipients whose interpretations are shaped by the messages themselves. At the other extreme, one can place primary agency in the decoding process, and treat messages as open texts to which each viewer will bring his or her own viewpoint. Or one can attempt to imagine the text as the site of a negotiation, or struggle, between encoded messages and the decoding process. These viewpoints have been labeled in different ways by different scholars. Here I will refer to them respectively as literalism, idealism, and constructivism.

Literalism

A literalist approach assumes that the meaning of a text is encoded in and determined by the text. Meaning, in this view, is limited to comprehension. This is operationalized as *decoding*; the work of the reader is to extract the correct meaning from the signs with which it was encoded. Such a position is often tied to *intentionality*. It assumes that what is encoded in a text is the meaning the encoder intended to convey. Communication occurs when the decoder correctly understands the intended message; failure to decode the message according to the author's intent yields misunderstanding.

Literalist approaches need not be linked to intention, however. One can also make the assumption that the meaning of a text is given because the text is a transparent vehicle through which reality is represented, a representation that "shows things as they really are." Realist art, objective journalism, scientific description, and naturalist photography all seek to represent a world that is assumed to exist prior to, and independently of, the act of representation. This form of realism involves an *instrumental* view of the medium as a neutral means of representing reality. Realism seeks to naturalize itself, often by concealing the processes involved in producing texts so that mediated representation appears to be a window on reality. Ironically, this concealment (as in the restriction on newspaper reporters to use the pronoun "I" to establish their own position as instruments of representation) is often referred to as "objectivity."

This notion that the material world constitutes a fundamental reality aside from signification is one of many forms of *essentialism*. Essentialism in this sense involves any means of understanding representation that grants a special ontological status to some entity, regarding it as preceding and foundational to the process of signification. God, the material world, feelings, perception, cognition, human nature, society, and technology have all been held at various times and by various people to be "transcendental signifieds" (Derrida 1978) of this sort. Analysts can use such a privileged object as a foundation on which to contrast representation and reality, and to identify subjective and objective ways of knowing. Most measurements of bias, for example, assume some privileged mode of knowing against which we can measure the accuracy of a representation to describe reality.

Idealism

The opposite of a literalist approach is the rejection of any form of reality in favor of a completely semiotic world of codes within codes within codes. Roland Barthes, for example, referred to reality not as a thing in itself but as an "effect" of the sign (Barthes 1986). Reality, in this view, is a construction of the representations made of it. All representations have as their signified other representations, so that the experience of reality is always and everywhere, mediated by signs. Reality in an objective sense is thus both unknown and unknowable.

This epistemological stance regards reality as entirely subjective and constructed in and through our use of signs. Jacques Derrida took as the fundamental principle of his "deconstructionist" philosophy the rejection of the possibility of any transcendent signified. As such, this position offers a powerful stance of radical skepticism and a tool for exposing the social and historical constructedness of apparently "objective" phenomena. Yet such an approach runs into an epistemological problem of its own in that it tends to grant an ontologically privileged status to language as a signifying system. That is, in using language to represent their own arguments about the subjectivity of the world, many of these scholars tend to treat their own writing as capable of representing what *is*, not just their understanding of what is. Other scholars ascribing to idealist positions recognize this problem and make a considerable effort to deconstruct language itself, and reflect ironically on the impossibility of their own efforts to speak outside of representation (Derrida 1978).

Constructivism

A third approach, called *constructionist*, seeks to examine the "social construction of reality" (Berger and Luckman 1966). In this view, *experiences* of physical and social realities are very real, but their representation and articulation is always mediated by preexisting social and cultural codes (learned through previous experiences). In this view, reality has authors. Experiences of reality are remade as we represent them, yet we can seek to understand the social, cultural, and historical conditions of that authorship. Constructivists like Latour (1993) have criticized both literalists and idealists for being reductionistic, arguing that even those who reject the privileging of an object in the world may nonetheless grant this privileged status to some component of their analytical method, especially discourse. Latour also recognizes that many constructivists (mistakenly) grant the same privileging to social practice. Latour argues that constructivism, properly conceived, should seek neither to deny reality outside of signification nor to reduce the subjects of analysis to any particular type of ontologically privileged object (discourse, social practice, objective fact). Rather, constructivism seeks to recognize that all phenomena are "simultaneously real, like nature, narrated, like discourse, and collective, like society" (Latour 1993: 6).

Theories about how people understand the media relate these various positions about the nature of the communicative process to the position of the reader with regard to the text. Essentially, media theorists have assumed either that the meanings readers derive from texts are determined by the text, that the meanings a reader derives from a text are dependent on the imagination and background of the reader, or that meaning is somehow negotiated between the structures of the text and the background and competence of the reader.

The Open Text

One understanding of the role of the reader is as a privileged interpreter who creates the text by reading it. Such an approach is consonant with an idealist notion of representation described above. In this understanding, every text is an "open work" (Eco 1989) to which the reader brings his or her own interpretive codes, competences and experiences. The media text, or message, constitutes the context through which individuals engage in interpretive and imaginative work (or play, if you will).

This sort of approach can be attractive for anthropologists, who often find themselves viewing films with friends in host communities, friends who have radically different ways of interpreting films. I once discussed a film entitled *Oasis of the Zombies*, about undead Nazis guarding a treasure from European treasure hunters, with Ayman, an Egyptian student. Whereas I saw it as a trashy foreign horror rip-off that combined then-popular zombie flicks with Orientalist themes, Ayman read the film as an allegory of the thousands of land mines left behind in the Sahara desert by the Germans, Italians, and British after World War II. Like the zombies of the film, these land mines claim a few Bedouin lives each year and guard the "treasure" of the land. My own interpretation was conditioned by having seen the film many years before, on TV, in a dubbed version, and by the fact that at the time we were discussing the film, I had been lecturing for two years on Orientalist themes in American and European films. Ayman's interpretation was conditioned by the fact that he saw the film in the original Spanish, while vacationing with friends in Spain, and by the fact that while he was in Spain, Egypt had unusually heavy rains, which had exposed many long-buried land mines, bringing this dormant issue back into the Egyptian media (which he accessed while in Spain through the Internet). Such idiosyncratic readings, shaped by different knowledges, different viewing experiences and immediate social contexts, offer support for an open work theory.

What's more, discussions with others about media texts can alter one's own subsequent interpretive frames. Thus Marc Augé writes of hopelessly trying to explain to American and French diplomats, discussing the "contamination" of French culture by American media, that such ways of understanding the circulation of media (which assumes that films somehow carry the culture of their producers) became irrelevant to him once he had watched the U.S. television comedy *Bewitched* on the Ivory Coast. There, while the stories were understood as fictional, both in-laws and witches are equally real referents, and the possibility that one's in-law may be a chaotic witch is not implausible. Augé's notions of high and low culture, and the way he viewed television, were by his account altered through these sorts of experiences (Augé 1986). Through the accumulation of viewing occurrences, as part of more general individual life experience, people develop individual modes of understanding and articulating their readings of media texts. These constitute *idiocodes*, distinctive ways in which interpretation is performed by specific individuals. Yet just as in sociolinguistics the existence of idiolects, individual patterns of speech, does not mean that languages are not socially and culturally patterned, so the existence of individual interpretive frames should not lead us to assume that such idiocodes are not organized in patterned ways. Similarities of life experiences can be expected to lead to commonalities in interpretive codes.

One popular mass communications theory that makes use of the notion of relatively free text consumers is a "gratifications" model, which seeks to understand the texts in light of consumer pleasures and uses. Rooted in functionalist psychology, this approach assumes that the media offer solutions to certain psychological and social needs created by the contexts in which people live. Early formulations (Katz et al. 1974) assumed rationality and conscious choice by media consumers as well as a market structure through which media circulate. In this view, people make choices from an array of available texts about what media to consume to meet particular needs and desires; media arise to meet the needs and desires of audiences, and they collapse when they can no longer serve their function or when something new comes along that better serves that function.

Later research sought to rectify some of the problems with the theory, particularly its failure in most work to distinguish between goals (gratifications sought) and outcomes (gratifications received). (Palmgreen and Rayburn 1985; Rosengren Palmgreen and Wenner 1985). McQuail has offered the following definition for uses and gratifications research as reflecting current trends:

(1) Personal social circumstances and psychological dispositions together influence both (2) general habits of media use and also (3) beliefs and expectations about the benefits offered by media, which shape (4) specific acts of media choice and consumption, followed by (5) assessments of the value of the experience (with consequences for further media use) and possibly (6) applications of benefits acquired in other areas of experience and social activity. (1994: 319)

This reformulation of a much-cited definition by Katz (Katz et al. 1974) reflects the more central role given in recent years to socially learned knowledge in shaping understandings of media and evaluating the success of media in meeting needs and desires. At the same time, it reflects the actor-centered, voluntaristic, and functionalist approach of gratifications theory. At its core, gratifications theory seems to offer a theorized restatement of the kinds of things American media consumers are likely to point to as assertions of "common sense" in response to claims of media power: "nobody's forcing you to watch. If people don't like it, they can turn it off." Since common sense is culture-specific, anthropologists have reason to be cautious of theoretical models that too closely approximate the cultural logics of Western societies.

Even those scholars most clearly associated with the independent role of the reader have long recognized that there are limits to the interpretive freedom of individuals. Eco, for example (1979: 40), argues that we can distinguish between interpretive *work* ("the free interpretative choices elicited by a purposeful strategy of openness") and interpretive *play* ("the freedom taken by a reader with a text assumed as a mere stimulus"). For those who choose to do interpretive work, the text itself establishes an effective boundary on the decoder's practices. "A text is a placed where the irreducible polysemy of symbols is in fact reduced because in a text symbols are anchored to their context" (Eco 1990: 21). Eco describes as "closed" those texts that show a strong tendency to encourage a particular interpretation, in contrast to more "open" texts which invite alternate or multiple readings. Eco further argues that while mass media texts *tend* to be "closed texts," the fact that they are broadcast to heterogeneous audiences means that multiple and diverse decodings of such texts are unavoidable.

The Dominating Text

The opposite of the free interpreter is the notion of the reader whose sense of reality—and hence behavior—is determined by the messages of the text. In this view, the meaning of the text is given by its form and content. The reader is a relatively passive decoder of the text, whose messages shape his or her values, norms, and actions.

Direct effects

The most complete notion of this sort is often referred to as the "direct effects" model of the text. In many early studies of mass communication, scholars never questioned that the mass media affected people in some direct, linear fashion. The project was to map the chain of influence as it moved from senders to receivers. Although a good deal of audience research was conducted, the clear majority of this work was in the form of *content analysis*, in which recurring elements in the form or content of texts were categorized and counted. Many of these quantitative studies were built around notions of the psychological power of redundancy. The assumption was that although receivers of media messages may interpret individual messages idiosyncratically, the sheer quantity of certain images or messages would nonetheless tend to affect mass behavior. The most convincing arguments of this sort come from studies of media and violence, although even here there is considerable argument over what the mechanisms are and to what extent media influence on violent behavior correlates with such social conditions as family life, social class, ethnic stigmas, the availability of weapons, and so forth. The problem with these studies is not only that they assume viewing has uniform effects, but that they assume that concepts such as "violence" have a priori referents that can be quantified. Such studies often ignore the contexts that make one kind of violent action heroic and another cruel.[1]

Direct effects assumptions have also not proven convincing where they have been used in development communications, as described in chapter 2. Early development theories like those of Rostow (1960) argued that certain cultural formations ("pre-Newtonian notions of science ... rigid social structure and irrational psychological attitudes" 1960: 4-5) stood in the way of more "rational" Western modes of thinking that were needed for Third World nations to become industrial capitalist countries. Linking the transmission model of communication to behaviorist psychology, communication theorists produce the model of direct effects that has come to be called "the hypodermic model" (Berlo 1960), the "magic bullet theory" (Schramm 1971), and the "dominant paradigm" (Melkote 1991). Failures of actual efforts to induce direct effects on the behavior of mass audiences in Third World nations led some scholars to add the concept of "noise" to the model. In this sense, non-Western cultures were not only incompatible with modernity but their cultural traditions served as powerful "noise" sources that distorted or blocked the intended messages. Contemporary attention to local definitions of progress have led to a decline in direct effects approaches to development media.

Ideology and Hegemony

While theories of direct effects have fallen out of favor, the idea of the reader who is dominated by the text has by no means been abandoned. A good deal of media theory is allied with a Marxian approach that stresses the role of *ideology*, the function of symbols to maintain the existing power structure. For those adopting a literalist stance, ideology constitutes a political distortion—whether or not so intended—of a neutral reality. Understanding the consumption of media texts to be fundamentally ideological is particularly associated with the "Frankfurt school," including such scholars as Max Horkheimer, Theodor Adorno, Louis Althusser, and others. In this theory, the mass media are part of a "culture industry" that appropriates symbols and reconfigures them into messages whose form and content subject consumers to this ideology. For Althusser, ideology was a system of representation that functioned to induce in the subject an imaginary relation to what Althusser took to be the "real" conditions of existence, which are conditions of domination, subordination, and alienation.

The ideological effectiveness of media texts lies in the fact that they are transparent; that is, we have become so used to the familiar conventions of our everyday use of media that we fail to recognize the fact that these are representations. When people refuse to recognize their own manipulation but instead resort to statements such as, "It's just entertainment," "It's based on a true story," or "pictures don't lie" they treat the medium as an instrument that expresses feelings or reflects the real world, and they minimize its materiality and textuality. Ideology relies on our common sense to tell us that television journalism or photography or narrative offers us a window on the world.

Used in this way, *common sense* represents the most widespread cultural and social understandings of the world in a given social community. Common sense consists of those familiar assumptions and values that are taken for granted by most members of the culture, and seem self-evidently natural and normal. Common sense is ideologically powerful since it consists of assumptions that seem to go without saying and appear not to need to be deciphered or demystified. That common sense is never entirely coherent only adds to its effectiveness, as the object of ideology is to suppress obvious contradictions and incoherences in common sense when these might seem to contradict the interests of dominant classes. Common sense is but one form of *naturalization*, the ultimate goal of ideology: to make the *status quo* seem not cultural but natural, not historically contingent but inevitable. Once conceived of as natural, taken-for-granted, and inevitable, cultural forms can be called hegemonic. *Hegemony* is a term coined by the Italian Marxist writer Antonio Gramsci to describe the complicity of people in their own domination through their belief in symbols that relegate them to subordinated statuses. A hegemony is a lived system of meanings and values that constitutes a sense of reality for most people in a given society—not a bad definition of culture. But the term "hegemony" is intended to draw our attention to the fact that such a system of meanings is never neutral; it always at the same time consists of the lived dominance and subordination of particular groups of peoples.

The Frankfurt school saw consumers of mass media as subjects whose identities are constituted by the texts they consume. Through a process of "interpellation" (Althusser 1972), consumers are constituted as subjects by the text. This process occurs as individuals consuming the media are forced to adopt (or are "interpellated into") a subject-position that is structured into the text and its codes. When individuals encounter in the media elements of their own identity—their sense of gender, ethnicity, sexuality, age, caste, and so forth—presented in powerful and compelling ways, they begin to measure themselves against the screen images. For some influential theorists, such as Emile Benveniste (1971), human subjects have no existence except in those specific moments when we articulate ourselves (to ourselves and others) through discourse. In this view, the media powerfully shapes our subjectivity by presenting possible selves to us in a way that engages us in this process of self-articulation. The psychological semiologist Jacques Lacan (1968) argues that media images present us with Others who reflect back possible selves against which we measure ourselves: "I am a woman—why isn't my body image like that woman's?" "I am a man—why am I not capable of the feats of that man?" Lacan calls the realm in which this construction of the self takes place, "the imaginary." Insofar as the mass media are taken to be reflections of everyday reality, their power to compel or constrain our self-conceptions becomes ever greater. The relationship between sets of texts and the negotiation of identity is often conceptualized in terms of discourse.

Discourse and Hegemony

The concept of *discourse* has become central in contemporary media studies. In linguistics, discourse refers to units of actual communication. Any coherent talk or writing—coherent in the sense that is has both content and structure—constitutes discourse. More recently, discourse has come to be understood not as a unit of communication but as a range of ideas or body of knowledge about some topic that is articulated in actual instances of communication, especially fixed texts. This discourse, itself relatively coherent and structured, can be uncovered by analyzing texts that are instances of it.

Interest in this concept of discourse has been primarily shaped by the work of Michel Foucault. Foucault's focus on discourse and power begins with the recognition that there is an intimate relationship between a topic and the way representations of that topic are organized. Foucault emphasizes that semiotic codes and their meanings do not stand outside society and history; rather, they are always subject to the historical and social contexts of the time and to prevailing power relationships and conflicts. Discourse encodes relations of difference, distinction, and power that are relevant in a particular historical moment. A cultural system is composed of multiple discourses, each constituting a limited range of ways of articulating its topic and, by that very limitation, defining what is possible and not possible to say. Thus, there are the discourses of, say, radio and television news, the discourses of medicine, science, academia, and so on. In any given community there is a constant ideological struggle between many discourses. Discourse is a locus of power as different discourses struggle for ascendancy. Some discourses become hegemonic by becoming taken for granted, naturalized, and essentialized. Other discourses vie with these in an effort to open up new ways of articulating and expressing social relations. Discourse, says Foucault, "can be both an instrument and an effect of power" (1978: 101).

Foucault's approach to discourse has been extremely useful for those looking for a way to link media texts to power structures. Scholars use Foucault's language to talk about how symbols are marshaled to maintain existing social structures. Like other theorists of ideology, Foucaultian scholars are particularly interested in explicating those discourses which are so taken for granted that people accept them as realities rather than representations. Such discourses are hegemonic by virtue of their naturalization as common sense. Building on these notions, a body of work has emerged that combines a Marxian interest in political economy and a concern with human emancipation with attention to cultural representation and ideology. Gender, sexuality, subordination, and race have emerged as central issues in this work. Scholars have tended to focus again and again on certain discourses that are linked to these key issues and are instantiated in a wide variety of texts. These discourses have labels: patriarchal discourse, enlightenment discourse, development discourse, Orientalist discourse, nationalist discourse, and so forth. A description of "Orientalism" will serve here as an example of how such approaches work.

Orientalism is a term used to describe "a body of knowledge produced by texts and institutional practices, responsible for generating

authoritative and essentializing statements about the Orient, characterized by a mutually supporting relationship between power and knowledge" (Prakash 1990: 384). This concept of Orientalism was initially
established and explored by Edward Said in a series of books including
Orientalism (1978), *The Question of Palestine* (1980), and *Covering
Islam* (1981), as well as in numerous articles. The key notion in Orientalism is that the whole idea of the Orient is a construction by European
and American writers over centuries. "The Orient" in this sense is an
idea that allows writers to group together a vast number of peoples
across time and space and to write about them. The Orient, therefore,
isn't about any "real" place; it is an imagined (and imaginary) place
projected onto real geographic and social locations. Western writers
construct "the West" by constituting an opposite, a mirror image which
is everything the West is not. Western writings about the Orient are thus
always more about the emergent self-identity of the West than they are
about actual places in the Middle East or Asia.

As a result, Orientalist discourses change over time as Western concerns change. Compare, for example, the two American films *The Sheik*
(1924) and *Not Without My Daughter* (1991). Both are marked by
stereotypy and Western projections of otherness, but they produce very
different representations of the Middle East. In *The Sheik*, the Arab
world is a sensual place where women's ownership by men paradoxically allows them to freely express their sensuality and sexuality—just
the sorts of things the American "new women" at that time were trying
to exert with their bobbed hair, knee-length dresses, cigarette-smoking,
and increasingly sexually explicit literature (including the novel on
which the film was based). Women are dominated by men, but they in
turn transform this domination into love through their sexuality.[2] Men
and women of the flapper era borrowed the terms "sheik" and "sheba"
from Orientalist films to socially articulate their identities as different
from those men and women employing older models of self and sexuality. In *Not Without My Daughter*, women are repressed and controlled
by men in exactly the opposite way—they are covered and desexual-
ized, rendered powerless—opposites, again, of the American woman
(portrayed by Sally Fields in this film), but not opposites that are to be
taken as models. In an America where women possess a version of the
sexual freedom fantasized about by their predecessors, the imagined
Orient now serves as a cautionary tale about the danger of giving up
that freedom to a man.

Said's idea of Orientalism is tied to a specific theory of power. In
writing about the Orient as it has, the West has continually created a
world it is justified in dominating. Orientalism is never *just* a style of
writing, it becomes a form of knowledge, an account of the reality of

this world. It becomes hegemonic. Orientalism has been particularly interesting to scholars as a system of knowledge that cuts across national, social, and cultural boundaries. Part of the reason for this is historical. Orientalist discourses justified colonialism. At the same time, colonialism reproduced, reinforced, transformed, and spread Orientalist discourses. In the process, Orientalism entered into the writing practices of colonized peoples. The colonized frequently reproduced Western discourses, characterizing themselves as constituted by "Oriental" cultures. This is true both of those who sought to resist Western dominance by emulating it (saying, in effect, we can become modern by becoming Western) and of those who sought to reject it by insisting on the value of "our Oriental culture." By entering into the debate on these terms, these writers reproduce the very power structure they are seeking to resist.

This has led many to make strong statements about the dominating and hegemonic power of discourses such as Orientalism. In "Can the Subaltern Speak?" (1988), Gyan Chakravorty Spivak has argued that colonial discourses make it impossible for members of subordinated groups to mount any real resistance since they can do so only on the terms of the dominant society. That is, if the colonized "other" cannot express his or her own interests except by using the very discourses through which colonization takes place (law courts, parliamentary speeches), does not the other cease to speak as colonized and to speak instead as a colonizer? This is an important question. It is closely related to the more general problem of all representation: how can anyone or anything (whether Oriental, woman, black, etc.) be spoken of without reinscribing the dominant discourses that define people, places, and actions as members of dominant and subordinate orders?

This argument, which certainly has force, suggests that powerful discourses like Orientalism are irresistible. Like Spivak's, Said's work often seems to suggest the inescapability and irresistibility of Orientalism: one cannot write about the Middle East without participating in reproducing a power structure. This seems especially true when Said turns his critical gaze on journalism, as one of the principle contemporary producers of Orientalist discourse (1981).

Resistance

Even theories that assume the primacy of the ideological structures encoded in the text allow for the possibility of aberrant and resistant readings. *Aberrant readings* occur when the consumer of the text applies to their interpretive practice codes which are at variance with those most obviously encoded in the text. An allegorical reading like my student's interpretation of *Oasis of the Zombies* would be considered an aberrant reading. But there is also room for deliberate, even systematic, resistance in this body of theories—if there weren't, there could be no scholarship, since the scholars would be as dominated by the structures of the text as are the rest of the text's consumers. Indeed, the purpose of most scholarship of this sort is precisely to expose these texts as manipulative practices so that the readers of the analyses can learn to read resistantly.

The goal of resistant reading is to dismantle the rhetorical structures of the text to expose the fact that texts do not necessarily mean what they seem to say. One of the most sophisticated strategies for constructing oppositional readings is *deconstruction*. In its widest sense, deconstruction is a form of cultural criticism that seeks to demonstrate how signifying practices construct, rather than simply represent social reality, and how ideology works to make such practices seem transparent. In the work of Derrida, deconstruction is a practice of locating textual contradictions in such rhetorical features as metaphors, allusions, footnotes, discontinuities, and so forth. In exposing these contradictions, deconstructionists seek to show what is missing from the text, and to demonstrate that all key concepts depend for their power on unstated or hidden oppositions. I wish to point out, however, that such deconstruction is not the privileged domain of semioticians. It occurs in everyday practices. Such common statements as "Boy, the media are really ganging up on Bush" effectively serve to deconstruct the usual notion of media "objectivity" by reminding hearers that representations are constructed by groups of persons with agendas.

Another type of resistant reading is *defamiliarization*: revealing the socially coded basis of taken-for-granted phenomena by making the familiar strange. Defamiliarization is central to the anthropological enterprise, since anthropologists seek to juxtapose the different logics, codes, and practices of different communities. Most theorists writing from within the notion of the dominant text tend to write as though one requires an education in media analysis to successfully defamiliarize media and to construct alternative and resistant readings. Indeed, the purpose of much scholarship in this area is to offer readers just such an education. But such processes are also a part of everyday life. It shakes up our own sense of viewing practices when we realize that it is possible to view "the bed-hopping world of 'Knots Landing' and 'Falcon Crest' as documentary" (Armbrust 1996a: 128), or to understand the computer dating service portrayed in a sitcom as a form of prostitution (Abu-Hashish and Peterson 1999). This kind of strategy occurs not only between but within societies too, in parodies and ironies, in calls by high-school textbooks to have students read advertisements as "modern poetry," and so forth.

Struggling with the Text

That resistant readings are not only possible but naturally occurring in social life points to the fact that there are limits to the power of a text over its consumers. In this regard, it is useful to return to the writings of Michel Foucault, from whom Said and other scholars derive many of their theories of discourse and power. Foucault argued that "discourse transmits and produces power; it reinforces it, but *also undermines and exposes it, renders it fragile and makes it possible to thwart it*" (1978: 101, emphasis added).

This notion that dominant discourses are always pregnant with contradictions and ambiguities that can be exploited to produce resistant, against-the-grain readings has been offered by a number of scholars seeking to understand discourse, both both within and outside the media. The Frankfurt school, the central forum for Marxist theory in North America, had always paid lip service to the principle of "dialectical criticism." Derived from Marx, this approach assumes that while any cultural artifact—any actual manifestation of expressive culture— inevitably reproduces the ideologically dominant positions in society, it must also inevitably reflect some of the contradictions that are latent in that society. In other words, just as every social system contains within it the seeds of its own transformation, so every artifact of expressive culture must contain structures that reflect these latent transformations.

Dialectical criticism, then, involves the effort to read expressive culture by tacking back and forth between a manifest representation of reality that reflects and reproduces the status quo, and alternative representations that reflect latent possible representations of reality.[3] Yet dialectical criticism is never easy, as Adorno, Horkheimer, and other members of the Frankfurt school discovered. With the possible exception of Walter Benjamin, the members of the circle tended to lean in their own work toward analyses that assumed the complete domination of the text over the imaginations of the audience, producing "enthusiastic obedience to the rhythm of the iron system" (Horkheimer and Adorno 1994).

Another theory of resistance is offered by "hybridity" theories, of which Homi Bhabha (1990, 1994) is perhaps the best known spokesman. Hybridity theories argue that while works of expressive culture necessarily employ dominant discourses, these discourses are always transformed (or "deformed" or "contaminated") by the specificities of production (and, by extension, consumption). As culture producers engage in various forms of mimicry, appropriation, resistance, and accommodation, what is produced is a new, hybrid discourse, neither the pure voice of the dominating social position nor the pure voice of the resistant "other." Bhabha then takes a further step, arguing that *all* texts—including analyses of media by scholars—are inevitably hybrid. Texts that set out to describe resistance *do* inevitably reinscribe dominant discourses (as Said implies), but never completely, just as they never completely deconstruct and subvert them. In hybridity theory, no reading is ever completely resistant nor completely dominant.

Yet a third strand of theory that seeks to open up interpretation while holding on to theories of power is that inspired by the "dialogical" and "translinguistic" notions of text that have arisen out of the rediscovery in the 1980s of the work of Mikhail Bakhtin (1984). Bakhtin's work has been influential in literary criticism, linguistics, and some anthropology; perhaps the best known proponent of this approach in film criticism is Robert Stam (1989). Stam defines the meaning of film as part of a dialogical process "between the text and *all its others*: author, intertext, real and imagined addressees, and the communicative context" (1989: 187, emphasis in original). In practice, though, Stam prefers avant-garde open texts in which the "aberrant readings" are already built into the text, rather than the more difficult task of assessing the play of interpretation in the popular mass media consumed by most people around the world.

All of these approaches to text—dialectic, dialogical, and hybridity—represent converging trends across disciplines and theoretical approaches to criticism that seek to open up opportunities for analyzing multiplicity of meaning, and particularly resistance to dominant discourse. Many scholars use these forms of criticism to make assumptions about resistance by audiences. Much of this work builds on James Scott's analysis of "everyday resistance" (1985). Scott argues that strong notions of hegemony and false consciousness, such as those suggested by theories of dominating readings are simply wrong. Scott argues, based on his own ethnographic research, that people in dominated positions within hierarchical structures are not particularly mystified by the dominant culture into accepting their own domination; they recognize and articulate theories about their own exploitation that are more or less sound. Rather, the power mobilized by dominant groups in modern societies is so great (particularly monopolization of the use of force) that members of the underclass recognize the futility of the kinds of radical resistance that Marxian scholarship seems to expect of them. Instead, Scott argues, members of the underclass engage in a stream of regular practices of resistance in the workplace, the home, and in public rituals like weddings.

Scott's notions of everyday resistance are useful and can be easily documented in everyday life. The question of how effective such strategies are is another issue. Some scholars argued that focusing on such resistance simply offers media analysts a way to avoid looking at the very real patterns of dominance toward which these acts were ineffective. Recent critics have charged that many accounts of resistance have been insufficiently contextualized, resulting in the political sanitization of struggles over domination and subordination (Ortner 1995) and that the study of resistance has become merely an academic fashion, in which scholars are now seeing resistance everywhere, where they once saw domination (Maddox 1997).

Hybridity, dialogical, and dialectical theories can be brought to bear on this dilemma by viewing the text as the site of a struggle between different and competing discourses to which consumers bring their own interpretive skills, knowledge of codes, intertextual awareness, and so forth. Meaning in this sense is negotiated between the unique reader and the structures of the text. Most analysts discover in the text an "inscribed reader," an intended audience who will give the text its own "preferred reading," but attempt to recognize alternative readings that might be constructed by readers who modify, ignore, or reject the preferred reading according to their own interpretive practices.

The question that arises is, of course, how does one determine the range of possible readings? How do we choose how to construct diverse readings? For sociologically-minded scholars, the obvious answer was to assume some sort of correlation with social position. One of the most influential statements concerning the connection of readings to social positions is Stuart Hall's division of "types of readings" into dominated, negotiated, and resistant (1977). Hall's model recognizes the importance of active interpretation by readers, but within the limits of relevant codes and social contexts.

Hall's theory remains based on the idea of a preferred reading, which reflects the dominant ideology of society at the time of the text's production, but also recognizes the dialectical contradictions of the text.[4] The *preferred reading* is the crystallization of the social formations in existence at the time of its production (complete with their contradictions) and therefore not necessarily the result of any conscious intention on the part of the producer(s). When the consumer of a text fully shares the ideological position encoded in the text, he or she accepts and reproduces the preferred reading. The meaning of the text appears "natural" and "transparent." In such a "dominated reading," texts are read uncritically and the status quo is accepted as natural.

A *negotiated reading* broadly accepts the preferred reading and the dominant group's definitions of the status quo, but resists and modifies it in ways which reflect the consumer's social positions, experiences, and interests, including reserving the right to negotiate more equitable rights within the existing social order. Radical or oppositional systems of meaning arise out of struggles by marginalized and oppressed groups. This system produces *resistant readings*, readings that recognize but cut across the grain of the preferred reading to express and articulate the interests of oppressed groups. There is also an implied place in the model for aberrant readings, readings that do not recognize the preferred reading at all.

One of the problems with this model comes from the very notion of a preferred reading. As used by many scholars, this seems to reproduce the literalist notion that there are meanings which are in some way "built into" the form and content of the text. Hall himself has explicitly rejected this textual determinism, yet in his writings on television news, Hall writes as if the dominant ideology is inherent in the mode of production, through overcoding and redundancy, thus reifying the medium in the same way textual determinists reify the text. There are methodological problems here as well; for example, having introduced the possibility of reader agency, it is not at all clear how a scholar can determine the preferred meaning of a text except through intuition.[5]

In the end, theories about the power that texts have over us depend on assumptions about how texts are "read." But reading is no simple act. If "the activity of reading [consists of] detours, drifts across the page, metamorphoses and anamorphoses of the text produced by the traveling eye, imaginary or meditative flights taking off from a few words, overlappings of spaces on the militarily organized surfaces of the text, and ephemeral dances" (de Certeau 1984: 170), then the attribution of power to texts, and the understanding of power through textual exegesis becomes increasingly problematic. One way out of this is to imagine alternative ways to approach media texts than as works to be "read." One such alternative model involves treating media as myth.

Notes

1. See Peacock (1969) for a Weberian critique of some of the assumptions made by direct effects studies concerning the process by which symbols affect humans. See Allison (2001) for an interesting anthropological critique of the assumptions scholars make about what "violence" *means*.

2. *The Sheik* and *Son of the Sheik,* and the novels by E.M. Hull on which they are based, can be read as extended rape fantasies
3. On the Frankfurt school and its dialectic theories, see Jay 1973 and Buck-Morss 1977. For one approach to dialectical criticism, see Adorno 1973.
4. Hall originally used the term "preferred reading" in relation to television news and current affairs programs but the term—not originally his—has been applied by others to many kinds of media texts.
5. It might be possible to pose this as an empirical problem—to use audience research, treating the most common reading as the preferred reading. It is not clear, however, that this would fit well with Hall's underlying assumptions about the culture industry.

Chapter 5

MEDIA AS MYTH

Anthropological studies of media, as we saw in chapter 2, have not been accustomed to dealing with power in the same ways as the media and culture theories described in the previous chapter. For one thing, until recently, anthropology tended not to problematize the broader political systems that their own work often helped to shore up—colonialism, for example, or the centralized state power implied by many models of development. Furthermore, anthropologists' models of power were derived from the study of non-state societies, so they often expected to find consensus rather than coercion. The absence of mechanisms of overt coercion in many of the societies they studied made anthropologists look at how power was organized by consensus—people disciplining their own behavior because they believe it is the right way to behave. Beliefs about the rightness of behaviors were assumed to be part of a shared set of values broadly distributed across society rather than a hegemonic system for maintaining the power of a particular segment or class of the populace. Only more recently have some anthropologists come to argue that these consensual, egalitarian societies can be construed as patriarchies and gerontocracies (Gledhill 1994).

Another central problem for anthropologists regarding issues of power and hierarchy is how to see organized systems of oppression where they are not articulated as such by one's hosts. To define a section of a community as oppressed against people's own expressed notions about their lives is to step outside the anthropological commitment to cultural relativism and take a stance outside "the native's point of view," a stance from which the anthropologist can describe how things *really* are, as opposed to the way the community sees them. This is a typical Marxian approach, but one that places the anthropologist in an unfortunate epistemological position above his or her host community. Work by Alverson (1978), Nash (1979), Rosen (1984), and others all raised crucial issues for political anthropology concerning the importance of the ways peoples creatively engage with, and interpret, systems that appear "objectively" unfair, brutal, or exploitative. To reduce the revolutionary creative potential of such cultural expression to "ideological domination" would be a betrayal of anthropology's commitment to respect the worldviews of those they study.

One way for anthropology to proceed is to examine the social subordination that members of the society themselves identify, and to analyze media discourses in ways that connect these to other forms of discourse, while complicating and undercutting commonsense theorization. Applied to media analysis, such an effort involves treating media as *myth*, as a conceptual tool that allows people to make sense of the world by mobilizing symbols for the construction of identities, boundaries, and cosmologies.

Yet simply labeling media as myth hardly resolves the problem. The definition of what is to be called "myth" and how myth is to be analyzed and related to society remains a fundamental problem for anthropology. Debates in anthropology over the extent to which the meanings of myth are inherent in narratives or situated in their moments of performance, the degree to which they are authoritative or constitute resources for creative interpretation, mirror, to some extent, the kinds of debates described in the preceding chapter. The most powerful tool for the analysis of myth, the structural analysis of Lévi-Strauss (1963), has itself both been widely appropriated by media analysts and deeply criticized within the discipline for its assumptions of the boundedness of cultural systems and its failure to deal with context. Structuralism has given way to a series of poststructuralist approaches to text, discourse, and myth, that seek to hold to the fundamental insights of structuralism while opening up to a world in which the easy assumptions of the isomorphism of culture, people, and place are no longer viable.

Poststructural Mythologies

An example of both the strengths and weaknesses of this poststructural shift in media analysis can be found in Denis Duclos's exploration of America's "culture of violence" which he calls *The Werewolf Complex* (1998). Duclos explores and draws parallels between three types of discourses of "heinous acts": (1) discourse about serial killers, primarily as expressed in the many popular books about them; (2) horror fiction and film; and (3) Germanic mythology. Duclos begins by showing us that discourses about serial killers (a multimillion-dollar publishing industry whose production characteristics Duclos does not explore) shy away from the utter pessimism that lies in the words they quote from serial killers themselves. Attention to the actual words of serial killers betrays an underlying nihilism of worldview, an abyss of meaninglessness that is painful to face. The writers of books about serial killers therefore do not face it. Instead, Duclos argues, in their psychological and sociological explanations for why individuals become killers, American authors romanticize these killers in the act of writing about them. This romanticism is carried even further in the horror fiction and film fantasies consumed by millions of Americans; while the films and fictional representations vie with each other to push the envelope of excessive representations ever further, they continue to mask the nihilism that gives rise to these horrors.

How are we to understand the existential despair, the meaninglessness of serial killer discourse? To look into the face of this abyss, Duclos turns to pre-Christian Germanic mythologies, especially to tales of Odin and Loki, and to tales of berserkers, werewolves and vampires, which he contrasts with the "Latin" mythologies expressed in classical and Catholic texts. Although Duclos rejects a Jungian theory of archetypes, his notion of an underlying historical cultural code stretching back in various forms to antiquity is at least as credulity-stretching as the idea of a collective consciousness burbling up in odd places. The core of his argument seems to be that Indo-European mythopoesis poses certain questions of its descendants, not the least of which is the struggle between our animal nature (evil) and our tendency toward a civil society (good). In the Mediterranean transformations of this mythic complex, the answer is to have good encompass bad through an appeal to transcendant principles of reason and justice, as in the *Oresteia*, or in the later (Catholic) Christian theodicy, which made the devil a mere component of God's overarching plan for human salvation. The Nordic answer to this transformation is starker, he argues, so nihilistic as to be almost unbearable. The battle between order and chaos is unending. Ragnarok is always just around the corner. What is more, the very strength the gods have to keep the forces of chaos at bay draws from their own dark side: to defeat the giants, the gods must frequently rely on deceit, theft, and betrayal—the very characteristics that define giants as evil. The deep structures of these Germanic myths have preserved themselves in Calvinist theology, and recent historical and social changes (about which Duclos says little) have allowed them to emerge in a transformed state in contemporary America.

This, then, becomes the core of Duclos's argument: that underlying the American discourses of serial killer books and horrific texts is an

American view of human nature that sees man's animal side or dark side as a source of strength that must not be cast aside. We all have a Hyde to our Jekyll, and neither side can survive without the other. In times of normalcy, our dark side must be suppressed; it is dangerous to our social worlds. But in times of stress or danger, we must draw on our dark side to survive. This fundamental American belief about the duality of self, which Duclos traces through a series of texts from books about serial killers to the film *Deliverance* (1972) to werewolf comics, is "a cultural answer" to the question of why America, for all its prosperity, is one of the most violent nations in the world.

Duclos's thesis is both fascinating and frustrating. Insofar as he is trying to define and describe a pattern—a myth—that expresses itself through multiple American discourses, Duclos succeeds admirably. That there is a strong cultural predilection expressed in American media not only to construct the self as a moral duality, but as an irresolvable duality whose good and evil sides are mutually necessary, seems unarguable. Any consumer of U.S. media ought to be able to multiply Duclos's examples infinitely in genres ranging from horror novels to westerns to *Star Trek*.[1] Yet does the reality of this pattern credibly link the psychology of serial killers to the structural contradictions elaborated by Germanic mythology?

The chief difficulty of Duclos's project is that in setting out to offer a cultural solution to a social problem, he evades the social, dismissing any attempt to relate the cultural pattern to violent action. Serial killing is here treated as an "elementary form" of the culture of violence, a site in which this semiotic structure can be seen in a particularly pure form. The presumption seems to be that given the existence of the werewolf complex, Americans are more likely to turn to violence as a solution to various different social problems than are members of cultural systems with different ways of constructing moral identities. The nature of the social categories that produce occasions for violence are not relevant to this argument.

Yet even if we accept the possibility of transhistoric cultural structures, some attention to the particular sociohistoric situation that has allowed this berserker pattern to emerge in the contemporary United States seems warranted. Duclos himself cannot help but bring the social back in. He makes reference to social structure here and there, as when he suggests that state surveillance and discipline increases the tensions that lead to violence, which in turn justify greater surveillance and discipline in a schismogenic pattern. Such scraps are treated as commonsensical rather than being grounded in any empirical observations. Like many explanations whose validity is determined by the coherence of its rational model, this postulation remains ultimately more provocative than convincing.

Meanwhile, Back in the Dreamtime ...

A very different argument, also building on the work of Lévi-Strauss, is offered by Lee Drummond's *American Dreamtime* (1996). Drummond defines myths as "fantastic, bizarre stories that propose solutions to fundamental questions about human existence" (1984: 1). He suggests that the success of blockbuster movies, particularly those that lead to multiple sequels, generate widespread fandom, and induce people to return to watch the movies again and again, is rooted in their ability, shared with other kinds of myths, to "confront and attempt to solve elemental dilemmas of human existence" (1984: 2). Drummond rejects theories of myth (and film) that see these as processes of mystification generated by the economic order in favor of an assumption that mythic thought is a primary precondition for sociocultural reality, a "framework of conceptual relations, a set of possibilities [that] must be in place before a living being can have what we would call a human experience" (1984: 2).

But Drummond's semiotics is not that of "the structural study of myth" (Lévi-Strauss 1963). For one thing, Drummond rejects the primacy of language in favor of the primacy of myth. Overturning Barthe's (1973) definition of myth as a secondary language system, Drummond argues that our perception of things-in-the world in terms of symbolic categories *precedes* our naming them.

Drawing on his own theoretical work conceptualizing culture as a complex of semiotic "intersystems," (1980), Drummond wants to argue for a topological theory of culture. This imagining of culture as an n-dimensional space has been suggested before, notably by Edmund Leach (1961) and James Fernandez (1986), but Drummond carries it further by merging it with Victor Turner's concepts of liminality and antistructure, and borrowing metaphors from Creole linguistics (Bickerton 1975) and quantum physics.[2] This topological metaphor envisions culture as *semiospace*, "a quality space of 'n' dimensions or continua" (Fernandez 1986: 13). These dimensions are cultural categories articulated as binary oppositions but better expressed as continua, of which the binary pairs are only the polar extremities. Drummond likens this semiospace to the Aboriginal concept of the Dreamtime, the time and space outside of time and space, where myths happen. Films, like other myths, are not texts to be interpreted according to codes; rather they are movements across vectors within semiospace to be *experienced* and made part of our lives. This involves a rejection of the whole concept of semiosis as a hermeneutic process. Media experiences *are* semiotic, as are life experiences, but textual exegesis is not necessarily the best method of explicating them. Rather than a process of decoding, semiosis here consists of making sense of experience as it happens, both consciously and unconsciously.

At the heart of Drummond's argument is the notion that liminality is not a condition that occurs only when we are in a state of transition "betwixt and between" stable cultural structures. The liminal, as first described in Arnold van Gennep's classic *Rites of Passage* (1960) and later expanded on by Victor Turner (1969, 1974a, 1974b), is the state we inhabit when we are between states. Drummond insists that we are *always* in a liminal state, that humans are always betwixt and between various possible states of being. As we move through physical and social space, we also move across the vectors of semiospace, making sense of our experiences as we go. But we can—and do—also visit semiospace imaginatively. For example, we can, at any point, remember and reinterpret our prior social and physical experiences. More to the point, we can have experiences in semiospace without corresponding social and physical experiences. This is where expressive culture fits in.

For Drummond, movie theaters are the "temples of the Dreamtime" (1996: 20). When we view a movie, regardless of the preposterousness of the plots, we become travelers in the topography of semiospace. This experience allows us to sort through central dilemmas of our lives (the most central of which is "who/what are we?") by experiencing various virtual worlds in which the cultural categories central to our lives are twisted into powerful new (and old) configurations. The astonishing popularity of certain films has little to do with their poetics (social or aesthetic), but rather is a result of the power of their particular play of forms across semiospace.[3]

Drummond applies his own model to the study of several American motion pictures: the James Bond cycle, the *Stars Wars* cycle, *Jaws*, and *E.T.* (although he touches on more than one hundred others in the process). His analysis of these films is built around three axes of semiospace:

$$
\begin{array}{ccc}
\text{Us} & \longleftrightarrow & \text{Them} \\
\text{Animal} & \longleftrightarrow & \text{Machine} \\
\text{Life} & \longleftrightarrow & \text{Death.}
\end{array}
$$
[4]

Each of the films or film genres Drummond examines articulates a particular configuration of symbols along these axes. By unpacking these configurations, Drummond believes that movies can tell us something about our culture, our identities, and about humanity itself.

The Evasion of the Social

In spite of Drummond's emphasis on how we construct our identities from experiencing semiosis rather than interpreting texts, his actual analytical procedures involve such standard semiotic concepts as syntagm, paradigm, and genre. In his analysis of James Bond, for example, Drummond begins by mapping out the genre itself, circumscribing the films and demonstrating how they are unlike the novels and cannot be understood as simple projections of Cold War ideology (1986, 1996). He continues by analyzing Bond films in terms of their syntagmatic structure: they are chase movies but they are also movies in which the roles of predator and prey keep unexpectedly reversing. His mapping of Bond on the culture continuum makes Bond a mediating figure between cultural oppositions—a paradigmatic analysis. He concludes that Bond is an embodiment of "the master of machines," a widespread contemporary mythic figure who serves as a necessary counterpart to the "master of animals" identified by folklorists and mythologists. Using small, personalized gadgets, Bond takes on villains who seem to operate multinational corporations of villainy. His tools, however, are supplied to him by the state—itself not very different in type from the villainous bureaucracies he battles. Bond's ability to be both of and against the system, to master small personalized machines and use them to mount resistance against users of huge, murderous machines, and his ability to both operate as part of a system while flaunting his own individuality, offers a compelling myth for audiences who find their lives increasingly bounded by state and corporate bureaucracies and permeated by machines of every sort and kind.

Drummond's theory holds out multiple possibilities for an anthropology of interpretation. That the interpretive uses people make of movies become part of a process of defining themselves, in relation to others, by positioning themselves in a semiotic space is a useful model, if not pathbreaking. This framework follows from Fernandez's notion that a metaphor is a movement of pronouns in such a space (1986). The semiospace consists of multiple categories; but our selves and our experiences are inchoate, ambiguous, unbounded. We give shape to the inchoate by naming it, and in doing so, we move our pronouns— I, you, they, it—along the continua of semiospace, constructing our identities as we do so. Drummond is extending Fernandez's position by arguing that *all* thinking is metaphorical and that metaphorical thinking precedes metaphorical expression and performance. As myths, metaphors are two-dimensional movements within and across semiospace. As myths, movies are multidimensional configurations within and across semiospace.

More challenging to mainstream semiotics of film is Drummond's insistence on film consumption as *experience*. Drummond is arguing that all of our experiences are continually being mapped in semiospace. Myths are not texts, they are virtual experiences, opportunities to experience vectors of semiospace that are socially and physically different from the experiences of everyday life, yet play with the same symbols. Bond offers a powerful virtual experience for the worker in the office, who has an employee identification number much longer than 007, who is trying to balance individuality with the constraints of the system, who is proud of his personal skill with his computer but would also sometimes like to put a bullet through it.

There is much in Drummond's mythic analysis that remains unclear, however. One objection might be that it needs to address the phenomenology of the viewing experience. Drummond speaks of theaters as temples of the Dreamtime. Does this make our videotape players and DVDs "shrines" of the Dreamtime? Is our experience of the Dreamtime the same in the temple and the shrine? In someone else's shrine? Another issue involves Drummond's inadequate bounding of his topic. Are all films mythic, or just the supergrossers? Is Bond the same kind of mythic experience for the Nigerian itinerant laborer in Lagos as for the American teenager in Topeka? What shall we make of films that do not appear mythic in the ways he has described, that do not pull in audiences by the millions throughout the world? Are they somehow fundamentally different kinds of experiences? Equally important, how does this experiential understanding of movies spill out into the world of everyday life?

In one of his rare semiethnographic sequences (Drummond prefers to write about virtual people rather than observed audiences) Drummond describes children in a bookstore buying *Star Wars* figurine bookmarks. The question is raised, What do these bookmarks mean to the children? What cultural worlds do they conjure? Are the virtual worlds of *Star Wars* T-shirts, bookmarks, toys, and so forth the same virtual worlds conjured by the movie? If not, what is their relationship? How far does a cultural analysis of the film cycle take us, really, in understanding the semiotic web spun by children out of films, apparel, and toys? Drummond partly answers the question by arguing that we are an artifactual species: the *Star Wars* films are *about* artifacts (droids, spacecraft, lightsabers, Death Stars), and they spin off into more artifacts. They are virtual states of the same mythic complex, different from movies and yet somehow the same. Commoditization—whatever its social effects in furthering the logic of late capitalism—allows children to move from consumers of one form of expressive culture, movies, to producers of another: play. What is lacking in Drummond's work is any way to examine this movement across social space and its consequences in the cultural dimension.

Drummond's invocation of the nature of the human species as part of his incomplete answer to these questions points to the fact that he is concerned with developing an *anthropology* of movies in the broadest sense, that is, a theory of what it means to be human. He has chosen to focus on three semiotic dimensions he sees as essential to this. He sees these axes as primordial, as part of humankind's evolutionarily programmed nature. We are the animal that knows it will die, that kills and knows it has killed. We are the prey who learned to make machines so that we could turn on our predators. We are the predators who learned how to domesticate our prey and make them part of our social worlds. We are the species that bands together not out of instinct but out of culture—by creating distinctions between ourselves and others.

But are the dimensions suggested by these characteristics—animal/ machine, life/death, us/them—all there is to human semiospace? We are a species split into males and females who (at least until very recently) must mate to provide offspring for the continuation of the species. Should gender be one of these axes? Should sexuality? We are a species marked by phenotypic differences. Should race be included? Is it sufficient to subsume all these distinctions under a single us/them continuum? The evolutionary biology metaphor in which Drummond ultimately roots his analysis may be more troublesome than it is useful.

Finally, Drummond offers only cursory attention to the political economy of film production, distribution, and consumption. Where he speaks of it at all, he treats media representations as modern versions of "folk" expression: "we—not Ian Fleming, Sean Connery or Harry Saltzman, but the collective *we* of a distinctively human, myth-making Dreamtime intelligence—have called James Bond into being" (Drummond 1996: 153). There is some attention to individual artists—Drummond invokes Spielberg and Lucas occasionally as mythopoeic agents—but elsewhere he speaks of the great respect due "the unheralded screenwriters who reworked the novel into a script, and for the directors, actors and technicians who gave the script life" (136). The people who give form and substance to the Dreamtime are collective and anonymous, as are the audiences. As with structural analysis generally, Drummond would have us attend to the bricolage, not the bricoleurs.

These criticisms point in a particular direction: to the exclusion of the social from the cultural analysis of media as myths. If there is a primary, mythic interpretive dimension to media, so there is also an important series of social dimensions that not only may serve as interpretive filters, but may also serve as constraints on the mythic process.

Toward a Sociology of Spectatorship

In arguing that mythic analyses of media like those of Duclos and Drummond abandon the social, I am not attempting to (re)constitute a simple-minded dichotomy between a cultural world of symbolic forms and a social world of concrete action. The social world is itself always symbolically constructed, and cultural forms only find expression in social action, including speech. Rather, I am suggesting that in focusing on such "universal" axes as life and death, animal and artifact, and us and them, media analysts who have focused on myth have sometimes overlooked the power of more detailed attention to the social. A mythic hero may indeed mediate between life and death, but at the same time, he may occupy social roles: husband, father, lover, son, farmer, or warrior. His enactment of these roles and ways in which these roles are constituted by similarity and difference with other characters in other roles constitute a crucial function of the myth to articulate social categories.

Consider Drummond's failure to attend to portrayals of gender roles in his analysis of the Bond films. The master of machines in these films is also a master of women, and in much the same manner—they are objects he uses with superlative skill in pursuit of his missions. To do so, he must use his own body as a kind of sexual machine (Kemnitzer 1977). The individual Bond film to which Drummond pays the most attention, *The Spy Who Loved Me* (1977), is particularly interesting in this regard as it introduces a woman as a rival secret agent, possessed of skills rivaling Bond's. The byplay between Bond and his female rival becomes a key subtext in which the reversible predator-prey syntagm, which Drummond argues organizes all the films in the series, also takes place along the axis of gender. This becomes even more interesting when we connect the film to its historical context: after a series of diminishing box-office returns from the three previous Bond films, *The Spy Who Loved Me* was the movie that "saved" the Bond series from extinction. Could the structural transformation of Bond's lover from passive to active—thus allowing the reversible predator-prey war of the sexes—have triggered part of the audience response to the film? Is it possible to connect such shifts in gender representation to other, corresponding changes in gender roles in American society?

There is certainly no theoretical need to exclude the social dimension from mythic analysis. In addition to the Lévi-Straussian understanding of myth as tendering solutions to problems of human existence there has long been a Malinowskian understanding of myth as a "social charter." Malinowski's famous example is that of the origin myths of Trobriand Islanders (1944). Members of every lineage can tell the story of their clan origin by referring to the place where their founding ancestress and her brother emerged from the depths of the earth at the dawn of time with the set of crafts, skills, and spells they would hand down to their clan. These myths explained the origins of the clans and also justified the kin structure that designated a woman and her brother as the central family unit.

In Trobriand society, clans are also ranked relative to one another, and this ranking is explained and justified by yet another myth. In this myth, the totemic animals emerged from the earth in a particular order (first the dog, then the pig, and so forth), reflecting the hierarchical ranking of the clans. Malinowski points out that when social systems change, so do their explanatory myths. According to Malinowski, when the pig clan over time came to politically eclipse the dog clan, the myth was transformed to explain the relationship. Rather than change the order in which totemic animals emerged from the earth, Trobrianders added a new myth to the cycle, an account of how the dog ate food that was taboo, thus giving up the purity that would allow it to claim first rank. In a sense, this system preserves both truth and historic precedence. The dog clan was historically primary and came to lose its status; the myth explains the dog as emerging in the primary position but losing it to his own error.

This linking of the logic of the text to the logic of social domains is crucial to many anthropological understandings of myth, and needs to be included in understandings of media as myth. One way some anthropologists have begun to read media texts is to seek to link the potential polysemy of a given text to specific historic social positions. In doing so, anthropological approaches to media begin to merge with those of media studies. Stuart Hall's work, with its emphasis on links between social position and textual exegesis, offers a starting place for theorizing ways that texts can be linked to readers. Hall's tripartite categories are not particularly interesting if we understand them as types of readings related to concrete groups of people. But the model becomes more interesting if we understand Hall to be postulating *positions* that various kinds of interpreters of media *can* occupy depending on various kinds of class positions. In other words, dominant, negotiated, and resistant readings don't define groups but rather describe *virtual* experiences different media consumers might have as a result of their life trajectories.

Read this way, Hall's work opens up the possibility of a theory of spectatorship. Using such a theory, analysts attempt to construct readings of texts that show us various positions of spectatorship that consumers can occupy. These positions are categorical, not empirical. They are rational models that link together various symbols and formal features along key semiotic axes. They suggest possible trajectories of interpretations according to such social categories as class, race, sexuality, and subalternity. This has become central to much work in contemporary cultural studies that sees viewer identification as shifting among characters as films progress (Clover 1992; Shaviro 1993; Rubey 1997; Allison 2001). In her study of American slasher films, for example, Carol Clover argues that viewers enjoy both (and simultaneously) the slasher's pursuit and slaying of the girls *and* the successful fighting back by the "final girl." The virtual worlds into which media consumers enter allow the dissolution of fixed identities and the exploration of multiple possible identities across boundaries that cannot be transgressed in the real world of social consequences.[5] Myths and media, in other words, allow for experiences the real world can't provide.

One anthropologist whose work has been exemplary in its explorations of positions of spectatorship is Elizabeth Traube. In a series of works (1990, 1991, 1992, 1993), Traube has sought to construct readings of American films that link textual features to shifts in political economy and the corresponding shifts in gender, labor, and family structure. In her most cited work, "Secrets of Success in Postmodern Society," she examines four films of the Reagan era as "part of the making of the new middle classes" (1989: 273). Traube argues (in a manner consonant with Clover's work) that there is no single middle-class "structure of feeling" but rather "a number of interrelated currents, which the culture industry partially absorbs, packages and returns to the public in various configurations" (279). Three of the films she looks at offer such a new configuration of the trickster, an independent hero whose ability to play with impressions and manipulate others produces success. The fourth, which offers a version of youthful success based on a less autonomous version of the young hero was notably less successful. Indeed, she points out, the more omnipotent the hero is in his antiauthoritarian maneuvers, the more successful the film. Traube argues that these levels of success reflect the audience's selective acceptance of the ideologies being served them—part of the process by which the collective "we" calls into being Dreamtime manifestations such as Bond.

Note that Traube combines structuralist notions of myth with a more Malinowskian perspective. The "young corporate employees of today and tomorrow" (1989: 273) are entertained by the story of the films, but the logic of the storyworld that underlies the antics of plot and character offers them models of behavior appropriate to the emerging society of late capitalism. The films offer "class education for the elite, a narrative pedagogy that celebrates a socially useful, seductively antiauthoritarian style" (1989: 284) based on the qualifications of success in corporate bureaucracies: "adeptness at inconsistency, alertness to expedience, agility in avoiding blame, finesse in handling people, disarming charm, sophisticated taste, and, most essential of all, the ability to control and manipulate one's public face" (Traube 1990: 377). These films are a transformation of the American trickster genre whose roots are in *Tom Sawyer*. The contemporary films rest, however, on a special kind of "trick": "comic resistance to authority has been steadily drained of oppositional content, and used to legitimate the dominant order" (1990: 376)

Traube's semiotic analysis of the text tacks back and forth between the producers and the consumers of these films. In doing so, she offers us a theory of media that positions both audiences and producers in relation to the text. While restricting herself to a semiotic analysis, the analysis is informed by an understanding of media texts as embedded in a cultural circuit. Neither a manipulative, ideological force imposed on audiences from above nor an authentic cultural expression of shared values and collective representations, Traube builds on Hall (1977, 1982) to posit a dialectical struggle within the circulation of cultural forms similar to the one I have suggested in chapter 1: "Popular desires and discontents are selectively recognized by the culture industry, actively reshaped and disguised, and returned to audiences in their new textualized forms" (Traube 1990: 376-377).

While Traube offers only one reading of the texts, her work suggests the possibility of a move to a more plural way of analyzing media texts. In response to a critique of her work that found it lacking in attention to "native" understandings of texts (Moffatt 1990), Traube argues that "[a]ny commercially successful cultural commodity constructs multiple though not unlimited positions from which it can be meaningfully viewed" (1990: 377). Understandings of films can be expected to vary according to class position, gender, and ethnicity, among other social positions. This observation allows us to repatriate the Foucault-inspired discourse analysis described above. In this view, audiences are not constructed by hegemonic discourses encoded in the text; rather, texts are sites of intersection and struggle between discourses. Audiences approach texts with ambivalence or enthusiasm according to how their own life trajectories have prepared them to experience and interpret various kinds of symbolic configurations, and audience members are capable of simultaneously experiencing several positions of spectatorship.

Traube's suggestion here opens the possibility for an anthropology of spectatorship that uses the discursive features of the text in conjunction with observations about the political and social context of the period(s) in which the text was produced and consumed to construct a set of spectator positions. These positions vary along lines of social cleavage and cultural distinction. Such a position combines discursive theories with an understanding of social fields akin to that of Pierre

Bourdieu—it assumes the intersection between cultural tastes and specific social formations.[6]

At the same time, this approach resonates with Clifford Geertz's call
for a semiotic anthropology that maps the bounded but infinite possibilities of interpretation of symbols in specified cultural contexts. In a
famous passage, Geertz borrows a metaphor from philosopher Gilbert
Ryles (1984) in which he describes the play of meaning and ambiguity
among people winking at a party. The man with a twitch, the man
winking at a friend to alert him to a joke, the man winking at a woman,
the woman winking back, the man winking as a mockery of the man
with the twitch—all these winkings and blinkings are physiologically
the same act, yet they are differently interpretable. Geertz writes that an
analysis of such a situation seeks to expose "a stratified hierarchy of
meaningful structures in terms of which twitches, winks, fake-winks,
parodies, rehearsals of parodies are produced, perceived, and interpreted, and without which they would not ... exist" (Geertz 1973: 7).

In the same way, a theory of spectatorship sets off to establish a
stratified hierarchy of interpretive positions that one might take toward
a text. Rather than giving *a* reading, such a theory of spectatorship
would attempt to delineate the range of meaningful readings for a given
context—presumably a historically situated community. These readings
would be related to class positions, gender, and other points of social distinction relevant in that community. These readings would not be
expected to be able to be mapped to social groups, but rather express the
bounded yet vast play of identities possible through a text or set of texts.

Steven Caton offers one of the clearest examples thus far of what
such an approach might look like. In *Lawrence of Arabia: A Film's
Anthropology* (1999), Caton offers a series of different readings of the
same film. A reading for Caton is "largely a construction by a film analyst of the way in which a film *might* be apprehended from a particular
spectator position. The most one can claim is that the construction is
plausible, given what one knows about specific audience reactions,
what spectators have said about the film in interviews, what the historical practices of film viewing might be at any given period and so
forth" (1999: 20).

Caton begins by exploring code and context. The semiotic structure
of the text is explored in a chapter that situates it within the other work
of its director and two writers. In the first three chapters he explores the
political economy of transnational movies, features of the epic genre,
the syntagmatic and paradigmatic tensions of the story's narrative, the
artistic biographies of the primary artists of the film, and the link
between technologies and the phenomenology of viewing. In the second half of the book, Caton offers three more readings of the film, view-

ing it as an allegory of cross-cultural encounters, as an Orientalist film that nonetheless engages in a critique of colonialism, and as a film without women yet one that is deeply marked by gendered representations and tropes of sexuality.

Caton uses documentary material to contextualize the film: autobiographies, interviews, advertisements, memoirs, reviews, histories, and social commentaries. While these constitute readings of the texts, they are not data of the same type. Reviews, magazine and newspaper articles, posters and memoirs are all themselves media performances of a particular type. Caton moves beyond documentary evidence and auto/ethnography only briefly, toward the end, when he discusses the reactions of three sets of teenage "focus groups" discussing their viewing of the film as part of an educational series, and offers a brief account of student discussions in a course he taught on the film.

Conclusion

This is, perhaps, as far as textual analysis can take us: a set of plausible readings of a text as it might be apprehended from different spectator positions. Semiotics, particularly in its modern concerns with hegemony, hybridity, ambiguity, and dialectic, is a powerful tool for analyzing the text. Yet it is not enough. Social meaning cannot be entirely reconstituted from the text.

To say this is not to reject textualist approaches. Although the formal features of texts—binary oppositions, tropes, intertextualities, and so forth—cannot in themselves validate particular meanings, the close reading of texts is likely to remain significant to the anthropology of media. Texts *do* have formal features. These features are partly the result of the social actions of producers and they are selectively appropriated and interpreted by audiences. Meaning can never be reduced entirely to producer intentionality or to audience autonomy but must recognize the place of the text as the site of an interpretive struggle. Some form of social poetics, rooted in semiotic analysis, is necessary if we wish to understand the media.

The analytical turns described in this and the preceding chapters approach media texts from a variety of directions that can build on one another. The mythic level examines media texts as sites in which the boundaries of cultural categories are probed, disrupted and reconstituted. This mythic process becomes epic when, as in many popular narrative media, the creation or destruction of boundaries is the act of larger-than-life heroes. Media offers us a virtuality in which we can meditate on experiences that are not our own, mythic experiences that allow us greater scope than ever for imaginative play and bricolage. The work of the bricoleur is never free, however. Like Malinowski's pig and dog clans, there are historic and social cleavages that play a part in the process of mythopoesis. Any media text has multiple positions corresponding to social positions available in the society and the distribution of codes and interpretive competence among the people inhabiting them.

What we have at this point is a theory of spectatorship without spectators. Recognizing that media create virtual experiences, textual analysis can at best offer us the possibility of exploring some of the possible experiences people might have. In the end, however, theories that make a priori assumptions about what happens to people *in general* when they encounter texts are simply insufficient. Far from interpellating individuals into controlled and controlling structures, the sheer multiplicity of images and growing number of contexts in which media consumption takes place may transform the nature of human experiences. Abu-Lughod captures this well in writing of an Egyptian villager, Zeinab, for whom "[t]elevision is an extraordinary technology for breaching boundaries and intensifying and multiplying encounters among life worlds, sensibilities and ideas" (1997: 21). For Zeinab, as for all of us, texts provide a vast cultural reservoir from which we can and do draw symbolic materials for making sense of our selves and our situations. To explore the meanings of media requires us to turn from the analysis of texts to the lives of actual consumers, to the contexts of their encounters with media texts, and to the contexts in which they put to work the symbols they draw from the media. It requires an intimate method of exploring spectatorship in its social and cultural contexts. In the next chapter, I argue that ethnography is the best means to accomplish this goal.

Notes

1. In class discussions of Duclos's work, someone nearly always points to a text not cited by Duclos: an episode of *Star Trek* in which Captain Kirk is literally separated by technology into good and evil halves. Even in this fairly utopian future, much of what makes Kirk a fine Starship officer depends on his dark half. As an exclusively moral and reasoning man, Kirk is portrayed as weak, ineffective, and unable to make decisions.
2. Drummond's evolving thoughts on these matters can be traced through a series of papers. An earlier model involved imagining binary oppositions not as sets of para-

digmatic distinctions à la structural linguistics but as polarities in a continuum. Culture is thus a series of continua that can be named by binary oppositions but which have room for multiple interstitial gradations. Drummond describes these in this earlier work as "totemisms" in the Lévi-Straussian (1973) sense of classificatory systems: a totemism of animals, a totemism of machines, and so forth.

3. Drummond's focus on popularity revolves around the notion of extraordinary behavior according to the general cultural codes of the society—in this case, the United States. The fact that there are some movies that viewers in the tens of thousands will stand in lines for hours to see, while most movies do not produce such behavior, requires explanation.

4. We follow Drummond's use of arrows here as a way of distinguishing his continua from the conception of binary oppositions.

5. Media scholars sometimes mark this distinction as between the "reel" world and the "real" world.

6. Bourdieu uses the term "class" but in a broader sense than either Marx or Weber. For Bourdieu, "class" refers to any form of social distinction that has consequences for the relative positions of power that people have within a defined social field.

Chapter 6

THE ETHNOGRAPHY OF AUDIENCES

Every few miles, it seemed, they passed the same huge poster on roadside hoardings, a photographic depiction of a rippling expanse of purple silk in which there was a single slit, as if the material had been slashed with a razor. There were no words in the advertisement except for the Government Health Warning about smoking. This ubiquitous image flashing past at regular intervals both irritated and intrigued Robyn and she began to do her semiotic stuff on the deep structure hidden beneath its bland surface.

It was in the first instance, a kind of riddle. To decode it you had to know that there was a brand of cigarettes called Silk Cut. The poster was the iconic representation of a missing name, a rebus. But the icon was also a metaphor. The shimmering silk with its voluptuous curves and sensuous texture obviously symbolised the female body. And the elliptical slit with a lighter colour showing through was still more obviously a vagina. The advert thus appealed to both sensual and sadistic impulses, the desire to mutilate as well as penetrate the female body.

Vic Wilcox spluttered with outraged derision as she expounded this interpretation. He smoked a different brand, himself, but it was as if he felt his whole philosophy of life was threatened by Robyn's analysis of the advert. "You must have a twisted mind to see all that in - it's a perfectly harmless bit of cloth."

"What's the point of it then?" Robyn challenged him. "Why use cloth to advertise cigarettes?"

"Well, that's the name of them, isn't it? Silk Cut. It's just a picture of the name. Nothing more or less."

"Well suppose they used a picture of a roll of silk cut in half—would that do just as well?"

"I suppose so. Yes, why not?"

"Because it would look like a penis cut in half, that's why."

He forced a laugh to cover his embarrassment. "Why can't you people look at these things, you know, as they are, take them for as they are?"

"What people are you referring to?"

Notes for this section begin on page 159.

"Highbrows. Intellectuals. You're always looking for the hidden meaning in things. Why? A cigarette is a cigarette. A piece of silk is a piece of silk. Why not leave it at that?"

"When they're represented they acquire additional meanings," said Robyn. "Signs are never innocent. Semiotics teaches us that."

"Semi-what?"

"Semiotics, the study of signs."

"It teaches us to have dirty minds, if you ask me."

Meaning and interpretation never take place in a social vacuum. In this excerpt from David Lodge's novel *Nice Work* (1988), Robyn's interpretive operations on the text are clearly akin to those discussed in chapter 3 of this book. Yet Vic's are also. Although he claims a literalist insistence that things are what they appear to be, he recognizes some of the iconic and indexical aspects of the ad. Iconically, the ad is a rebus, a visual onomatopoeia of the product name. Through this iconic invocation, the ad serves to index the absent product. Rather than presenting a viewer like Vic with an image of the product, the ad forces Vic to do the work of making the connection. In enticing viewers to fill in the absent signifier, the ad seeks to make a stronger connection between the viewer and the product than would an ad that does more of the interpretive work for the viewer (O'Barr 1994: 8-10).

While Vic's reading of the ad *as* ad recognizes the ideology of the market—the desire of manufacturers to get their names before audiences to encourage consumption, Robyn finds an equally obvious but more disturbing ideology in the metaphoric connotations of the ad. The iconic resemblance of the slit cloth to female genitalia, combined with the metonymic relationship between the slit and the razor that made such a cut appeal not simply to the playful imagination but to dark, suppressed, even unconscious desires. These desires are socially shaped by the patriarchal structures of the society, which advertisements of this sort play off, and in doing so, reinforce.

One important thing suggested by this scene is that the codes people employ to interpret texts, though deriving from widely distributed cultural formations, differ according to social position. In the language of the previous chapter, Vic and Robyn inhabit different positions of spectatorship. In the novel, Vic is Rummidge University's plant manager, an unashamed Thatcherite who fully embraces the consumerist ideology—"his philosophy of life"—underlying the advertisement. Robyn's interpretation of the advertisement is driven by her own liberal politics, her gender, and her position as a professor of literary criticism at Rummidge who engages in this sort of "semiotic stuff" as an everyday part of her academic work. One of the purposes of audience ethnography is to examine actual situated discourse by informants in order to unpack the codes that shape their interpretations of a text, rather than attempting to analyze the codes entirely from the structure of the text, as Robyn does. Robyn, as a member of the cultural system whose texts she is analyzing, has her own situated knowledge of its codes and structures to draw on. For anthropologists positioned as insiders/outsiders studying communities they are in but not of, the need to derive codes through ethnographic methods is essential, as is recognizing and describing the situated nature of these codes, their unequal distribution across levels of society.

But the brief scene between Robyn and Vic reveals something else as well. Interpretation is never just a matter of social positioning. Interpretation is always motivated. It is a social *act*, a performance by particular persons in particular situations. Robyn's attention to the ads is triggered by their regular recurrence along the side of the road but also by her position as passenger, able to give them more attention than she might as driver. Vic's own attention is drawn to the ads by Robyn's comments. His own articulation of the meaning of the ads is not "just" an interpretation; it is also a reaction to Robyn's analysis, driven at least in part by a distaste for the sexualized nature of her interpretation and his desire to distinguish himself from her, and from the category of "intellectuals" into which he casts her. Semiosis is never just a matter of norms of interpretation at play in the inner world of cognition but also a matter of performance, of social interaction. What's more, the norms of interpretation can themselves become a matter for debate, as when Vic and Robyn shift their argument from being about the meaning of the ad to being about practices of interpreting it. Public debates about media and how to interpret them are not only public discourses that serve to frame the interpretation of news, they are also invoked to accomplish pragmatic ends in the messy everyday situations in which interpretation takes place (Wilk 1995). The question of whether semiotics is an authoritative analytical practice that reveals the lack of innocence of the ad or is itself a problematic, "dirty" practice is thus mobilized here by Vic as a strategic move in an ongoing argument over different social positions.

Media ethnography attempts to tease out all these levels of analysis through observation of and engagement with the everyday situations in which media are consumed and the practices by which media are interpreted. Media ethnography seeks to understand the ways in which people encounter media texts and how this shapes their reception of them. People not only use cultural codes to interpret texts but also to shape the nature of their encounter with the text. One of the problems with so much of the semiotic language we've been using—"reading," "interpretation"—is that it implies a Western model of the literary act, in which a solitary reader silently and individually engages with a text. What is needed is a broader approach that seeks to examine how texts connect with the everyday lives of their consumers. Such a shift from the analysis of texts to the analysis of audiences brings with it a key question: How do we place the audience at the center of meaning making?

The Shift to Ethnography

The turn to ethnography in media studies—a shift from the less intimate, positivistic modes of research that marked both functionalist and gratifications approaches to more contextual studies—came in the early 1980s and was exemplified in seminal works by David Morley (1980, 1986) and Janice Radway (1983, 1984a, 1984b).[1] Morley began by recognizing that, in Britain, television viewing is primarily a domestic practice: it is done in the home, and in the context of the family. Although previous studies had recognized this, they tended to treat family viewing as a backdrop against which the individual consumers were affected by and pursued pleasure through viewing. Morley insisted on foregrounding the family. He interviewed people in their homes, and interviewed families together, rather than separately, in order to catch something of the interactive flow of their discourse.[2]

Morley's effort to focus on the family allowed him to study the ways that television viewing as a *practice* interacts with other social dynamics of family life, particularly those of domination and subordination. Morley found that a vast number of issues raised in the interviews—"power and control over programme choice; viewing style; planned and unplanned viewing; amounts of viewing; television related talk; use of video; 'solo' viewing and guilty pleasures; programme type preference; channel preference; national vs. local news programming; and comedy preferences"—reflect and reconstruct widely distributed patriarchal gender patterns. Men may not always hold the remote, control the program choice and silence fellow members of the family audience (although they often did), but in all of the eighteen families interviewed, masculine control was a key issue around which family constructions of viewing circulated.

But media consumption can engage power in other ways as well. Janice Radway found that American women used romance novels as a means of resisting domestic systems of power. In a series of interviews with forty-four women in "Smithton," Radway was able to admirably link text and context in a single coherent analytical framework. As texts, romance novels offer narratives in which an intelligent, independent woman overcomes a series of emotional and physical obstacles to win the love of a man who has likewise been transformed during the course of the novel into someone who can care for and nurture her. Women escape into this world in which they are nurtured from a domestic reality in which they are called on to selflessly care and nurture for others. Radway writes that "The romantic fantasy is ... not a fantasy about discovering a uniquely interesting life partner, but a ritual in which one is to be cared for, loved and validated in a particular way" (1984a: 83).

The real strength of Radway's study is her recognition that rituals are not only symbolic displays, virtual worlds of the sort described in the previous chapter, but are actual pragmatic and performative events. The *act* of reading for many of the women in her study provided an escape from the constant activities of domestic labor.

> Because husband and children are told "this is my time, my space, now leave me alone" they are expected to respect the signal of the book and to avoid interrupting. Book reading allows the woman to free herself from her duties and responsibilities and provides a "space" or "time" within which she can attend to her own interests and needs. (Radway 1984a: 64)

These studies by Radway, Morley, and others initiated a crucial turn away from seeking the objective meanings of the text to an understanding of how acts of media consumption and interpretation are understood by those who engage in them. It is a shift from a *textual* semiotics to a *social* semiotics that opens the way for an increasing ethnographic engagement with situations and acts of media interpretation. In the years since these pioneering studies, "ethnography" has thus become a central theme in media studies.

But what is meant by ethnography for these scholars? Both Radway and Morley largely limit their contact with the people about whom they write to interviews.[3] Much of what seems to be called "ethnographic" elsewhere in media literature appears to imply an effort to "read" an audience the way one "reads" a text (c.f. Fiske 1987: 272), a practice derived from the structuralist studies of Dick Hebdige (1979) rather than the methods normally associated with anthropological fieldwork. Hirsch (1989) argues that scholars in media and cultural studies often understand ethnography only as a general method of data collection, a gloss for "qualitative research"; they thus fail to recognize that ethnographies are themselves *produced* by particular practices. More comprehensively, Nightingale (1993) argues that although many of the research *techniques* of media ethnography (participant observation, group interview, solicited writing, fan letters, informal discussions, censuses, etc.) are broadly speaking, ethnographic, the research *strategy* is not. Reading several canonical works in cultural studies against the definition of ethnography from Marcus and Fischer (1986), she argues that ethnography in media studies lacks (1) attention to cultural difference, (2) close observation, (3) commitment to recording, (4) provision of descriptive detail, and (5) attention to the contiguity of what is being described to broader aspects of social process, which are expected by anthropology. In particular, she decries the lack of reflexive engagement with the voices of one's hosts, and the failure of media ethnographies to seek the production of a dialogical text, particularly where that might lead to a lack of closure. She argues that the insistence on closure by many "ethnographers" constitutes what Rosaldo (1986: 82) called the "false ethnographic authority of polyphony" in which presentation of interviewee's voices masks the ways in which they have been appropriated and marshaled to support the author's point of view.[4] Nightingale concludes:

> It is time to look again at anthropology, and at ethnographic research techniques, to re-evaluate their use in cultural studies audience research both as a heritage and as a future direction. (1993: 175)

Sites of Reception

For ethnography, a central problem in audience studies lies in the very notion of "audience." The idea that the dispersed groups and individuals who encounter a particular text somehow constitute an "audience" for it in any particular or meaningful way is highly problematic. Pluralizing the term—it is common now to write and speak of "audiences" and "publics"—resolves part of the theoretical problem posed by the notion of mass audience, but fails to address the methodological issues. Indeed, if anything, it increases them. Imagining a single "mass audience" was useful for media scholars because it allowed for techniques of random sampling. Abandoning the now theoretically bankrupt notion of a single mass audience created by the text forces us to ask exactly where we are to locate media consumers. The usual ethnographic answer is to seek people in *places*—communities, events, sites—where they are engaged in meaningful action. This involves a shift from texts and their imagined spectatorships and from interviews in which people tell stories about their own media practices to the presence of ethnographers in the living rooms, viewing halls, movie theaters, dormitory common rooms, drive-ins, movieplexes, peep booths, bars, coffee shops; and countless other venues where media consumption actually takes place. Such a shift allows us to put the "analytical focus on a marked activity ... well defined in time and space" (Armbrust 1998b: 414).

In this section, I will examine the ethnographic analysis of reception as *event*, a set of situated acts that can be described and contextualized.

While any event has multiple dimensions, I offer here a general rubric of key dimensions to which ethnographers engaged in this kind of work have paid fruitful attention: *technologies, settings, situations, ends, participants, actions* and *activities, patterns of interpretation and interaction,* and *genres.*[5] Each event, described in terms of the intersections of these elements, constitutes not a sample but a case study; from an accumulation of case studies of various degrees of similarity, description at larger levels of generalization can be offered.

Technologies

To look at sites of media reception is to examine social interaction with and around technologies. Site analysis raises a number of questions about technologies, including: How do the technologies of the medium shape the viewing experience? What sorts of literacies do technologies give rise to? How do the costs of technologies intersect with preexisting distributions of wealth and status? "The very force and impact ... of any medium changes significantly as it is moved from one context to another ... a theater, the living room, the bedroom, the beach, a rock concert.... That is, the text is located, not only intertextually, but in a range of apparatuses as well, defined technologically but also by other social relations and activities" (Grossberg 1987: 34). Media technologies, then, must be attended to in at least four dimensions: their specific technical constraints insofar as these can be determined; their functions within modes of production; their signification as material objects; and their signification as communication modalities.

By the *constraints* of a medium, I mean the technology's specific form and functional features. Large cabinet radios are less mobile than transistor radios; motion picture films are physically heavy and require expensive, unequally distributed projection systems, while videotapes are lightweight, inexpensive and utilize less costly, more widely distributed viewing equipment. Radios can be shared with people outside the house by turning up the volume, but televisions must be positioned at windows. These constraints tie in directly to local modes of production: wet cell batteries in the early days of British radio being carefully carried to specialty shops for recharging by girls who didn't want to get acid on their clothes (Moores 1993: 79), televisions in Gurupa, Brazil, purchased by those families who can afford not only the set, but can mobilize a workforce to transport the television down the river and construct a wooden tower for its antenna (Pace 1993). Thus do markets, government regulations, and technological knowledge intersect with local distributions of wealth and organization of labor.

As material objects, media technologies have specific meanings. Pfaffenberger (1992) argues that "the standard view" that technologies have primary instrumental functions (which meet "needs") and secondary social functions (which adapt artifacts to cultural and social uses) is itself a cultural construct that promotes a particular modernist ideology. He argues rather for an understanding of technological artifacts as parts of specific "sociotechnical systems" that "produce meanings as well as goods." Spitulnik (1998a, 2000) offers excellent accounts of the sociotechnical realities of media reception in Zambia, beginning with the fact that radios are marked by scarcity, since "[t]he price of a basic radio is beyond the reach of most people unless great sacrifices are made" (Spitulnik 2000: 1). Batteries alone can cost the equivalent of a week's supply of food for a large family, and while many urban middle-class families have electricity, they cannot afford the more expensive radios with A/C power capacities. Class position is thus a powerful determinant in media consumption.

Radios in Zambia circulate in time with the rhythms of everyday life, moving from the house to the workplace to the stoop to the sitting/dining room to the bedroom during the course of a day. Nonportable radios will have their volume adjusted up or down to allow them to be heard as people move from site to site. Radios that are issued by government ministries circulate from work to home each day. This circulation also occurs along routes that move across social boundaries. An urban employee visiting a village will bring his radio with him, where it will shift from a personal possession to a community possession that circulates through the community quite apart from its owner, marking status and being passed around as "part of a more general relation of exchange and reciprocity that exists and is constantly renewed between those involved" (Spitulnik 2000: 11). Radios are thus not only mobile but *mobilized*, such that "[r]adio users, sharers, carriers, and deniers play off the significance of radio-as-prestige commodity, within a wider set of social relation involving kinship obligations, gender relations, generational differences, socioeconomic status, urban-rural tensions, and so on" (14)

Physical Setting

Media technologies are located, and media texts are thus encountered, in particular physical spaces. Physical spaces, like technologies, operate both at levels of constraint and of signification. One of my students in Cairo described to me the viewing of American movies on video by Sudanese refugees in Cairo as primarily a social event in which food, drinks, and conversation abound. Although videos, televisions, and VCRs are scarce commodities among the refugee community, and some members would prefer attentive viewing to socializing, the cramped quarters of the flats—themselves an index of the refugees' lack of employment papers and steady incomes—preclude any spatial splitting of the event into social and viewing components.

Built space is never strictly a matter of physical constraint, of course; lived spaces are always shaped by cosmologies, and living in those spaces in turn shapes our cultural understanding.[6] The integration of media technologies into social space can thus affect the ways spaces signify. Lyons, for example, describes the integration of a twenty-inch television set into the mud brick house of a Benin chief, directly opposite the household shrine "dedicated to the 'trinity' of the Holy Aruosa Church" (Lyons 1990: 429). For Lyons, this signifies not only that television has become as significant an influence in the lives of the chief and his family as are the traditional rituals, but also the degree to which television is integrated into, rather than replacing, other forms of Nigerian culture. Finally, technologies can transform space by the ways in which they are integrated into the activities that take place there—as, for example, in Spitulnik's example of the movement of radio or the adjusting of volume, to follow activities in and around the physical spaces of the home.

Kent (1985) offers an example that integrates all three of these dimensions based on participant observation of families of different ethnicities—Navajo, Spanish-American, and Euro-American—in the American Southwest. Television signifies differently in these communities. For the Navajo, television is a choice, and the decision to own one signifies a particular stance toward Westernized modernity and class mobility. In Euro-American homes, television is taken for granted; it is a necessity whose lack would be significant. Kent found that the integration of television into the home did not affect the cultural coding of space—the lack of sex-specific monofunctional spaces among Navajo, for example, and the large number of such spaces among Euro-Americans. It did, however, radically affect the range and organization of activity, since people tended to conduct household work around the television. In every home with a television, television viewing was the dominant evening and night activity. Moreover,

> [t]elevision viewing reduced the diversity of activities. Navajo families of varying degrees of traditionality who had no television, for example, performed a large array of activities—family discussions, butchering, weaving baskets and blankets, making quirts and inexpensive necklaces, playing with young children, talking, grooming horses and so on. The contrast with the activities of the ... family with the television ... is striking. Moreover, television has reduced the number of loci at which activities occurred, since the set was usually located in the living room and most activities revolved around it. (Kent 1985: 124)

Finally, media reception sites can be seen as shaping the cultural space of the larger geographies and topographies in which they are set.

Singer's suggestion that the mediation of new cultural forms can be studied by an examination of "sacred geography" (the co-organization of physical and social space) is perhaps best realized in a study by Brian Larkin (1998) of the place of movie theaters in the cultural topography of Kano, Nigeria. Movie theaters operate as landmarks, physical traces of the history of colonial rule and urbanism, sites of political and economic conflict, places of rumor and opportunities for control and containment of potentially uncontrollable transnational technologies. Attention to physical setting as intertwined systems of constraints, systems of signification, and locations of activities is crucial for ethnographic understanding of the ways people encounter media.

Situation

Situations are defined, and often multiply defined, by participants in ways that are related to, but by no means determined by, physical settings. Examining the social definition of the situation involves at least two intertwined concepts, the social definitions of the setting itself and the social definitions of the activities taking place there. In communities in Nigeria (Lyons 1990), India (Hartmann, Patil, and Dighe 1989), and elsewhere in the world there are or have been public viewing centers with televisions provided by the government or purchased by local community agencies. Watching TV in such centers is conceived differently than watching TV in homes. Where both possibilities exist, but opportunities are differentially distributed, settings intersect with local issues of status, wealth, class, and other distinctions to create a range of possible meanings.

In societies where people are segregated by gender, class, caste or other social distinctions, definitions of social settings mark and reproduce these distinctions. "Going to the movies" for women in Lemu on the Kenya coast means attending on Wednesday, "Ladies' Night," when men are forbidden, and women can drop their headcoverings and chat with one another throughout the film and during the intermission (Fuglesang 1994: 5). Watching videos, by contrast, refers to domestic viewing with members of one's own family. Likewise moviegoing and domestic video watching in 1990s Kathmandu, are fundamentally different activities that mark class distinctions, such that one "Nepali film producer lamented, 'Classy people don't go to the theatre anymore'" (Liechty 1998: 96). "Situation" in this rubric thus refers not only to conceptualizations of situation as space but also to conceptualizations of situation in relation to activities. "One rarely just listens to the radio, watches TV, or even goes to the movies—one is studying, dating, driving somewhere else, partying, etc." writes Lawrence Grossberg (1987: 34).

Ends

Closely related to the conception of setting as a site of activities is the issue of the goals toward which a reception event is organized. People enter into media reception activities with goals in mind: to be entertained, to learn something, to be distracted, to avoid other activities, to relax, to bring friends together, to have something to occupy their minds while they are doing other tasks, and so forth. Ends may be immediate or they may involve imagined social futures, as when someone goes to a popular new movie in order to be able to talk about it with peers. Ends also organize activities. Obviously, watching a video in a university media lab for a course assignment creates a different kind of experience than watching a video at home with family, not only because of the different significations of space but also because of the ends toward which the activities are aimed and the supplementary activities (taking notes vs. making popcorn) that may be associated with them.

Following Hymes (1977) it is useful to distinguish between *ends* in the sense of stated or implied goals and actual *outcomes* as defined by participants and by observers after the fact. Indeed, we often know what a viewer's or listener's ends were only by their comments on the outcomes: disappointment, satisfaction, surprise, boredom. It is not only subjective experiences but, through these, social relations that can be transformed by viewing. One woman who had left her rural American home after receiving a scholarship from a prestigious east coast university, told me of returning with her new husband, a fellow graduate student of that university who also came from the rural Midwest. At her sister's house:

> we were watching videos. My sister liked old black-and-white movies, maybe because they're cleaner than modern films, and she's a biblical Christian. So they asked us to pick a film and we picked *Citizen Kane*, which we both love. They'd never seen it. And when it was over, we were saying, "wasn't that a great movie?" and I could see that they had been bored and confused by the film, and I suddenly realized, "I'm not like them anymore." And I could see in my sister's face that she thought so, too.

In such cases, outcomes are quite different from, perhaps even opposite of, the ends toward which the activity was pursued.

Participants

Ends and significations do not exist as properties of an event without people to pursue and interpret them. What kinds of people engage in this kind of film reception? How do social categories such as class, caste, ethnicity, religious community or family position organize participation in this kind of event? Work in the sociology of media since Morley has confirmed and expanded his observations of the ways that family television viewing replicates domestic power structures. But work is lacking on the ways media consumption outside the home and in other kinds of contexts reflects and reconstructs—or resists—social relations. How, for example, does media viewing construct sociality among nonromantic, nonfamily groups—friends, acquaintances, colleagues, classmates? How are these socialities maintained, and when and how are they dissolved?

Liechty (1998) offers a useful account of changing class distinctions in Kathmandu as they relate to cinema and video viewing practices. In "the 1960s and 70s, Kathmandu's cinema halls hosted the full gamut of local society from rickshaw pullers to top government officials." Members of the upper class dressed up to attend films, drove to the theater in cars, purchased expensive tickets for seats in the balcony, and maintained a dignified silence throughout the presentation. Lower class Nepalis sat in the lower section, whistling and clapping their approval at various points in the film. Liechty comments:

> During these decades, Kathmandu's cinema halls were like microcosms of the local class universe. Upper and lower classes occupied high and low spaces in the theater where ... even while upholding class difference, the cinema hall was ... a place where all of local society shared a common consumer space, and a common consumer object. (1998: 93)

Actions and Activities

An ethnography of reception involves attention to the sequence of acts that participants engage in as part of the viewing process. Ideally, this includes not only general description of cheering or whispering, but insofar as possible, detailed description of the physical and verbal actions that take place in any media event. The forms of domestic power relations (and resistance to them) that interested Morley and Radway, for example, are constituted, reproduced, and resisted in myriad simple actions. Powdermaker (1962) reports having assistants scattered through the boisterous audiences of films in Coppertown recording what was being said around them. Yet it is not only talk, but sequences of actions that are important. If the activity is a "date," how is the moviegoing structured into the activity? If there are choices, who decides which movie will be viewed? Media consumption often settles itself into sets of ritualistic behaviors associated with certain definitions of a situation—what Armbrust (1998b: 413) calls "habits of spectatorship." As part of this, attention should also be given to transitions between activities, including the transitions between other activities and media consumption. Such description should also include attention to activities being pursued concurrent with reception: sewing, cooking, conversing, doing homework, eating, and so forth, and the apparent effects these have on engagement and disengagement with the media text (Lembo 2000).

Patterns of Interaction and Interpretation

From an accumulation of details of reception practices, it is possible to build up an account of the general patterns governing various kinds of media consumption behavior. By combining interviews with observation, it is possible to come to conclusions about both the *patterns of interaction* by which participants determine what kinds of actions are considered appropriate or out of place, and also *patterns of interpretation* that govern how assessments of media are to be articulated.

The description and analysis of *patterns of interaction* is the key to understanding how sociality is constructed or expressed in situations of media consumption, an understudied phenomenon. Richard Pace describes how in Gurupa, Brazil, "[d]uring soccer games and nightly *novellas* (Brazilian soap operas) the televisions were aligned with windows to face outward into the street, where large crowds could gather to catch glimpses of the program" (Pace 1993:191). When Pace himself stopped watching television because of the poor reception, he was accused of shutting himself up in his house and selfishly refusing to share with the community.

The assumption that the normative ideal for media consumption is sitting quietly so that one can "concentrate" is an ethnocentric one.[7] A number of accounts suggest that there is a wide range of behaviors that can be normative in a given context of movie viewing. Thus we read of crying, clapping and shouting in Nepal (Liechty 1998: 102); cat calls, running commentary, cheering, and booing in Iran (Naficy 1993: 41); shouting, jumping, and imitative movement in colonial Rhodesia (Powdermaker 1962: 258); shouting, clapping, whistling, and booing in India (Thomas 1985: 128-130); and so forth. With regard to Nepal, Liechty argues the following from informant interviews:

> For the often rural-born, poor, working class patrons of Hindi films the "satisfaction" and "enjoyment" of cinema going derives largely from the experience of shared emotions, of laughing, crying, and shouting in the company of hundreds of others who you know, in that instant, perfectly share your own strong feelings of pathos, fear, joy and anger. The real satisfaction of cinema lies in affirming one another's understandings and experiences of pleasure. (1998: 102)

The study of *patterns of interpretation* involves discovering typical ways by which people articulate the meanings of texts. Here the goal isn't so much to understand individual, or even collective, subjectivities, as it is to understand what and how members of communities believe it is appropriate to speak about various forms of media consumption. This is a significant issue, because in most societies the vocabulary for interpretation is weakest in those very forms of media that are most popular. "Popular" cultural forms are frequently dismissed as vulgar and unimportant not only by intelligensia but by the majority of consumers as well. Armbrust discusses Egyptians' tendency to say of certain forms of popular music or film, "it has no meaning," in spite of the fact that they can discuss the meaning at length (Armbrust 1996a). Similarly, in the United States, for consumers to give to science-fiction television the kind of devoted critical attention that is acceptable for a genre such as Opera (or even "classic" cinema), is to position oneself as needing to "get a life" (Jenkins 1992: 9-49). Dutch fans of *Dallas* find it difficult to describe their own pleasure because the norms of interpretation available to them foreclose the possibility of such media being acceptable (Alasuutari 1992).

In spite of the denigration of popular media as worthless, people do evolve common ways of speaking about their media consumption. In many societies, interpretive discourse centers around issues of reference: the degree to which a text is "realistic" or "true to life." Liechty describes how in Nepal, middle-class women viewers expect films to be both "realistic" and "practical for the self, and capable of instilling a proper sense of morality in others" (Liechty 1998: 109).[8] Lembo has generated an elaborate model not only of how American televison viewers interpret plausibility, but of ways in which implausibility is evaluated and explained (Lembo 2000). Yang (1994) discusses "habitual modes of film interpretation" that allow discussions of film to deflect state discourse by reading films "past them, against the grain, or by taking off on tangents from them" (116).

One of the most complete explorations of patterns of interpretation is offered for Banjarese audiences in south Kalimantan province, Indonesia, by Caldarola, who discusses six patterns of interpretation through which television viewing becomes an act of "*negotiation* in which mass media form and content are reconciled with the values, norms, and ideologies of Banjarese culture" (1992a: 34). In addition to assigning truth values, Banjarese audiences jointly narrate the filmed action, "providing a parallel to that which is presented in visual form on the screen" (34). They also actively seek to interpret programs through local values, assuming that media stories' messages are ultimately prosocial narratives offering lessons that can be applied to the problems of real life. Finally, Banjarese audiences tend to uncritically accept media sources, and to interpret television using an orthodox Islamic framework that opposes *akal* (rationality) to *hawa nafsa* (animal instinct). Caldarola goes on to argue that all six patterns "derive from symbolic conventions related to the precursor modes of expressive culture" (28).

Genres

In chapter 3, we examined genre as a feature of any given text's intertextuality, but it is important to also recognize genre as a social category. Culler defines genre in a socially useful way as "a norm or expectation to guide the reader in his encounter with the text" (1975: 126). Every community has a vocabulary for talking about categories of media. As Culler's definition suggests, local taxonomies of media intersect with other dimensions of cultural life such as gender, age, and class. The American dichotomy of "guy movies" and "chickflicks" guides selection of films and appreciation of them. Submission by a date to watch a film from the category assigned to the other gender can be a gesture of affection or an acquiescence to dominance, or ambiguously, both. Liechty finds a similar gendered dichotomy in Nepal between young, middle-class women who watch Hindi films on video and their husbands who dismiss all contemporary Hindi films as "unreal" in favor of American films (Liechty 1998).

Yet it is not only identities and subjectivities that are correlated in complex ways with gender; genre is often tied to the nature of reception sites. In Cairo, theaters that show Indian films and Chinese "Kung Fu" movies are in the bottommost tier of a local hierarchy and are not visited by women, who must watch such films at home on video or at the Indian Cultural Center, if at all. The original timing of afternoon soap operas in the United States, both on radio (Warner and Henry 1948) and on television (Bean 1981b), was tied to patterns of women's domestic labor. Indeed, as cable and satellite broadcasting have vastly expanded available programming, so that we have entire channels devoted to specific genres, there is a corresponding increase in the degree of social and commercial work these genres must accomplish (c.f. Richardson and Meinhof 1999).

As new genres emerge, they create new spaces for meaning. Not all societies are as persistant as Caldarola's Banjarese about interpreting new kinds of texts in terms of preexisting expressive forms. New kinds of media, as Das (1995) argues for soap operas in India, may open up new possibilities of discourse, such as personal confession. New media genres can also spin off into yet newer media genres, as in the way Muslim Hausa authors created a genre of popular literature, *littafan soy-ayya*, by adopting themes and problems from Hindi films and recontextualizing them into Nigerian society. New identities emerging as a result of transnational flows of people, may also produce new genres of media to mark them, such as Muslim hip-hop in Berlin (Soysal 1999), or the Rai music among the Franco-Maghribi communities in France, whose content expresses new anxieties about hybridized identities and, simultaneously, inserts itself into preexisting taxonomies of genre to trouble the keepers of "pure" culture (Gross, McMurray, and Swedenburg 1992).

Positioned Spectators and Acts of Interpretation

Together, these eight categories comprise a useful heuristic for the analysis of sites of media reception. The goal in analyzing such sites is not so much to produce detailed case studies by themselves, although these are valuable, but to move from ethnographic studies of specifics to descriptions of general cultural ecologies of media reception. A few excellent examples have been produced, notably Liechty (1998) for cinema and video viewing in Nepal, Armbrust (1998b) for movie theater-going in Cairo, and Pace (1993) for television viewing in Gurupa. But these are but a few examples of the tremendous number of overlapping sites and occasions for media consumption that remain to be described. Such work will help to challenge in two ways the large number of European and American studies that take the domesticity of viewing as a given. First, it exposes the number of ways media consumption may take place outside the home, and emphasizes that these are themselves historically situated sites in a vaster mediascape. Second, it opens up our understandings of domesticity by introducing multiple forms of constructing "family" and "domestic" activity (Lyons 1990).

Studying the sites of reception tends to shift our attention to the functions of media consumption rather than its interpretation; the ways in which sociality is constructed, family power is enacted or resisted, new forms of social behavior are tried out. Content affects such issues, but in the examples we have seen, specific content often seems less important than generic content. It is genres of films that are important in cinema-going in Cairo; the relative hierarchy among theaters is determined in part by the kinds of films shown and the extent to which these are deemed acceptable for women to view. Likewise, it is not specific telenovelas that have altered the temporal organization of events in Gurupa, but the fact that telenovelas are a 9 p.m. staple that all who have access to televisions feel compelled to watch.

Yet the social actors in these sites of reception *do* engage with specific texts, and this engagement involves pleasure, persuasion, interpretation and other acts of consciousness. The analysis of sites of reception is useful not only for its capacity to open our eyes to social dimensions of media use that go beyond engagement with the text, but also offer us the capacity to *situate* acts of interpretation. Ethnography, that is, offers us an opportunity to return to the text-based theory of spectatorship described in the previous chapter, and expand on it to produce a theory of spectatorship that involves actual spectators. This possibility derives from shifting our focus from texts to engagements with texts by situated social actors.

Ethnography need not reject dialectical, dialogical, and hybrid approaches to the text. Bakhtin, Habermas and Bhabha are all correct: interpretation of texts *is* polyphonic, dialogic, dialectical, and hybrid. Ethnography examines these qualities through a change of focus from the text to acts of interpretation by persons in situations. The interpretive act is at once situated in a particular moment in time and space, embedded in a web of social relations and is engaged with the invariant but polyvalent structures of the text.

Media texts and the situations of their reception conjointly open up imaginative possibilities through their play of symbols. Interpretation occurs at the intersection of mass-produced forms of representation, situated practices, and imagination. Turning to the interpretive acts of individual consumers thus changes our analytical focus to what happens to people within sites of consumption as they imaginatively engage with texts, to how people individually, as well as collectively, define both identities and selves. It brings us to issues of pleasure, subjectivity, and identity.

Pursuing Pleasure

Ethnography invites us to look at pleasure as socially constituted. The very existence of "blockbusters" and "bestsellers" demonstrates the possibility of a single text bringing pleasure to millions—something that cannot be reduced to a psychological epiphenomenon. Needs, desires, yearnings, nostalgias, and escapes are not given by the structures of texts; rather, they are socially constituted. Ethnographic research seeks to reflexively engage with peoples' discourse about media to learn about their pleasures.

At the same time, it must be admitted that pleasure is difficult to engage ethnographically. Media consumers often have only a minimal register for discussing their own pleasures. Those with whom ethnographers watch television are often perplexed by questions posed to them about taste and pleasure, particularly when such questions are asked of "popular," "vulgar," and "meaningless" forms of entertainment, about which such questions are not supposed to be asked. Articulation of pleasure, if sought directly through questionnaires or surveys, is often concealed behind broad and unrevealing terms such as "fun," "cool," or "exciting." People's own modes of articulation may even deny that their motivations involve pleasure, as when some of my American students have insisted that seeking to escape the stress of schoolwork by "vegging out" in front of the television was not pleasure. Yet vegging out—the "veg-" prefix is borrowed from the word "veg-etable"—is a nice example of a local taxonomic category of pleasure. In American society, where sitting in front of the television when there are other things to do is condemned as a waste of time that makes one a "couch potato," vegging out allows actors to reconstitute "being a veg-etable" as an empowering choice, an intentional and temporary vegeta-tive state one escapes into as a means to relax, reduce stress, and get away from one's troubles. Vegging out involves escape but specifies that one is escaping to nowhere, that an avoidance of critical mental activ-ity is precisely what is sought. The claim to be vegging out thus accepts the general American public discourse of television as a wasteland—the "waste" in particular involving a waste of time—and simultaneously challenges it by claiming, in essence, that one has a *right* to do nothing if one has been working too hard. Americans who say they spent an evening "vegging out" are likely to follow the statement with an expla-nation of why they are *entitled* to veg out—a litany of stresses or labors—and sometimes also assertions to confirm that the world they escaped to was indeed a place that involved minimal mental activity: "There was absolutely nothing on worth watching," or "It was practi-cally all commercials, nothing could hold my interest because it was always being interrupted. I hardly ever watch TV, I hadn't realized how many commercials there are." This latter comment also positions the activity as a rare one for this person, emphasizing the strategic nature of vegging out as a life choice, and hence acceptable within American understandings of choice.[9]

Although the elicitation of folk categories of pleasure has not yet been widely carried out, there have been considerable efforts made to describe pleasure in analytical terms. It is possible to use these to con-struct a preliminary typology of pleasures as logical categories. *Sexual* pleasures involve erotic imaginative play and have perhaps been the most extensively theorized forms of pleasure in academic literature (Mulvey 1989; L. Williams 1989; Clover 1992). The pleasure of know-ing things, *epistephilia*, goes beyond news, and is a staple of many dis-courses of media consumption, in upper Egypt (Abu-Lughod 1998a), Indonesia (Caldarola 1992a) and Los Angeles (Naficy 1993), to name just a few places. Epistephilia has many dimensions, ranging from the enjoyment of a community in knowing things about the world beyond its boundaries, to the need to "keep up" with what others know, to the personal satisfaction of knowing more than someone else. *Aesthetic* pleasures occur when the form of a text fulfills expectations based on aesthetic codes (Hymes 1984). *Ludic* pleasures derive from our surprise, shock, and stimulation when texts violate our aesthetic expectations by breaking or exceeding them (Beeman 1982). *Escapism* (Radway 1984b), as we have seen, becomes of keen social interest when we delve into the questions of what one is escaping *from* and what imagined social worlds one is escaping *to*. *Moral* pleasures (Caldarola 1992a) arise from finding in texts moral "life lessons" that apply to one's self and others. *Trangressive* pleasures occur when a text exceeds social norms to engage the viewers' imaginations on the level of fantasy or ambiguity. *Phatic* pleasures occur when one imagines the texts as offering resources for forthcoming social interactions. *Imaginary sociality* (Caughey 1984) refers to the pleasures derived from establishing imaginary social relationships with media figures, whether characters, the actors who play them, or other public figures frequently in the media. *Nostalgia* is the pleasure that arises from the recapture of real or imagined past experiences.

Such a typology—and it could be extended—is of use only as a heuristic device, since pleasure is a fluid and ambiguous thing, and consumers can find multiple pleasures (and displeasures) in a single text or viewing experience. The possibility that viewers can find pleasure *and* displeasure in the same texts was originally theorized in a seminal article by Laura Mulvey (1989) as a paradox in which women (and, by extension, others in subordinated or marginalized social positions) find themselves experiencing pleasures from the narrative pattern of a text even while recognizing that the meaning of the text is threatening to them. Mulvey argued that this situation encourages women's complicit or dominated readings of a text—they must either deny pleasure or deny meaning. If they choose the latter, they become complicit in the hegemony of the text. This argument assumes, of course, that individual subjects construct only a single reading of a text. What's more, it assumes that there must be logical consistency within this reading. Ethnographic work on audiences does not, I think, bear this out. Mulvey later modified her original position (1981), and a series of works by other film and television scholars in the late 1980s and early 1990s have extended this retheorization. These new theories recognize the possibility that, for example, feminist scholars (and other viewers) could enjoy some aspects of Hitchcock films (Modleski 1988), pornography (L. Williams 1989) or horror movies (Clover 1992), even while recognizing and criticizing the ways that the texts construct women as subjects. In a similar vein, Caton (1999) discusses his deep "fascination" with and "enthusiasm" for *Lawrence of Arabia*, even while recognizing its imperialist tone.

Selves and Subjectivities

To deal with this multiplicity of pleasures and displeasures, we need to open up the concept of self from a coherent inner "core" that inhabits various roles and identities, and which can be interpellated into a particular subject position—dominated, negotiated or resistant—and replace this with a more fluid notion of selfhood. The self is increasingly described in dialogic terms, an inchoate voice engaged with memory and immediate experience. That this self is engaged in dialogues with discourses that go beyond the immediacy of reception is evident from the fact that so many ethnographies that describe displeasure do so in terms of *guilt*. The pleasures of viewing the distant desirable worlds of the West struggle with nationalist discourses about the dangers of media pollution (Wilk 1995); the pleasures of escape struggle with demands to be productive (Lynd and Lynd 1929); the enjoyment of the "popular" struggles with exhortations to aspire to "higher" pursuits (Alasuutari 1992).

> "When you listen to people talking about their viewing habits and about their favorite TV programmes, their discourses on the subject of television, it immediately strikes you how profoundly moral this issue is. There are very few programmes that people will freely and plainly admit they like to watch; with the exception of perhaps the evening news, people seem to feel a need to explain, defend and justify their viewing habits." (Alasuutari 1992: 561)

These problems of pleasure and guilt, shame and entertainment, simultaneously experienced by the acting subject, force us to consider the issue of subjectivity, and whether media consumption is "a contested space in which subjectivities are constituted" (Mankekar 1993: 471).

Subjectivity refers to that personal and unique realm in which each of us experiences the world. Subjectivity is experience and reflection completely apart from articulation. It is the space within which selves are constituted. As such, it is the realm within which one encounters mediated experiences and makes sense of them. For many scholars, it is the key to media domination, as subjectivity is made subject through experiences of reading, listening, and viewing. A central question in philosophy, psychology and anthropology is the degree to which human subjectivity can be said to be "free." Jean Paul Sartre (1963, 1970) makes a strong distinction between his own position, that subjectivity is absolute freedom, and the extreme sociological position of Marx, in which subjectivity is entirely shaped by external social, political and economic realities. In between are positions like those of Heidegger, which suppose that subjectivity can only operate through the pre-given categories of language, or that of Levi-Strauss, who argues that there are pre-given categories of cultural thought that operate at the level of subjectivity.

In the previous chapter, I examined the notion of an analysis of "subject positions" which juxtaposes various possible readings of media texts on the basis of social distinctions of class, ethnicity, gender, and other categories. The shift to ethnography suggests that neither the virtual readings nor the human subjects are as coherent as this theory of spectatorship supposed. The creation of a theory of spectatorship that pays attention to actual spectators involves a shift to a messy reality in which texts are polysemic, and human subjectivities are multiple and shifting. In the interpretive act, selves and textual meanings mutually constitute one another.

Getting to the constitution of subjectivity is a task that requires careful attention to the sites of reception as well as to the form and moments of articulation of self in discourse. Early efforts in this direction often overemphasized one or the other. One such effort was *Reading National Geographic* by Catherine Lutz and Jane Collins (Lutz and Collins 1993), which sought to integrate semiotic and audience analyses. Lutz and Collins asked fifty-five white Americans of various sexes, classes, and age cohorts to look at a set of randomly selected photographs of non-Western people from the magazine *National Geographic*, and to say what they saw as "going on" in the pictures. They were also asked a series of open-ended questions about their preferences for the photos, their ideas on cultural difference, and about the magazine itself. The authors found that people often spoke, even within a single interview, in several voices, expressing multiple, overlapping and sometimes contradictory positions. Sometimes they would express mutually contradictory ideas with equal force and without any suggestion of irony. Other times people expressed different interpretations in more experimental or ambivalent ways. A master narrative emerges from this polyphony, in which non-Western peoples are conceived as exotic others representing earlier forms of human development in an evolutionary paradigm.

The study, while in many ways excellent, is flawed in two significant ways. First, the project decontextualizes the photographs, treating them outside the contexts of consumption of the magazine. A more serious objection concerns the quasi-experimental nature of the study. Rather than allowing the audiences' voices to guide their semiotic analysis of the texts, Lutz and Collins's own readings of the photographs produce the analytical categories used to code reader responses to the photographs.

There have been subsequent studies which reverse this sequence, allowing the words of those interviewed to guide subsequent analyses of the programs (H. Lyons1990). Alternatively, one may eschew formal interviews altogether in favor of actively viewing with one's subjects. An exemplary work in this vein is Purnima Mankekar's *Screening Culture, Viewing* Politics (1999), which is a study of Indian women and families watching television programs that turn symbols of family and gender into narratives of nation.

The intimate ethnography of viewing that makes up the bulk of Mankekar's book is sandwiched between two chapters that lay out the social, political, and economic context of television in India. Closely tied to discourses of development, Indian national television (*Doordarshan*) was envisioned as a medium through which the nation could be drawn together through the sharing of images, news, and narratives. Unsurprisingly, then, nearly all television programs (Mankekar focuses on ten), whether melodramas, historicals, or mythologicals, present strongly nationalist sentiments in varyingly overt and covert ways. What is of particular interest to Mankekar is the use of the family as a key trope through which national sentiments are expressed. The family is a powerful evocative symbol in India, and television producers are keenly aware of this. Yet the family is not just a symbol to be evoked; it is also a crucible of experience, sometimes nurturing, sometimes deeply painful, and representations of family on television inevitably invoke reflections on the intensely personal and subjective experiences of family, which in turn shape the ways in which people interpret discourses on nationhood.

But the very fact that such reflections *are* deeply personal renders them all the more difficult to readily articulate. The articulations gathered by Mankekar are the products of her own engagement with these women in everyday settings—not only watching television but returning to the home for tea or to help in the preparation of meals. Mankekar's ethnography takes place through growing relationships with women viewers and their families at various degrees of intimacy. She is keenly reflexive about her own place in each family, and records the degrees of openness or suspicion—about her Westerness, her Hinduism, her education, her class position—expressed by her hosts through gestures, eye contact, and tone of voice. Her understanding of how her informants understand her helps contextualize each discussion of television programs and the articulation of selves they evoke.

The specific settings in which viewing takes place—mostly flats in two different middle- and lower middle-class neighborhoods in Delhi—are described in detail, down to the shining steel cutlery that adorns one of the kitchens. This is never gratuitous—the shabbiness of the clothing, the investment in books, the placement and size of the television—are all indicators of income, of aspirations, of sacrifices, and of

indulgences. The members of the families and the details of their relations to one another are also described, and in a few cases we come to
know them so well that subsequent revelations that come as a shock to
Mankekar come as a shock to the reader as well. An example is the drift
of discussion from the attempted disrobing of Draupadi by her in-laws
in the TV serial *Mahabharata*, to the sexual vulnerability of Indian
women, to the revelation that the husband of one of the viewers, whose
considerable economic sacrifices on behalf of his children have been
likely to evoke reader admiration, was complicit in a series of sexual
assaults on his wife by his father (1999: 127).

Such revelations, which occur "when, as invariably happened in
our conversations, we turned from talking about the serial to discussing
our own lives" (Mankekar 1999: 128), are not meant to be "qualitative
data" in the fixed sense sometimes used by ethnographers of media (see
Hirsch 1989). They are particular articulations of subject positions in
specific moments by speakers reflecting on powerful narrative images.
For Mankekar, "consciousness is a space where forces of class, gender,
race, ethnicity, age group, household position and nation intersect" to
create subject positions (Mankekar 1999: 17). What makes Mankekar's
own ethnography as gripping as any of the television melodramas
whose stories she recounts is her ability to keep before us the fact that
what social scientists often aseptically describe as falling under such
rubrics are, for the men and women studied, *lived experiences*. The
often emotionally moving virtual experiences of television are always
being read against another set of virtual experiences, those of memory.
Interpellation by hegemonic discourses of nation take place within and
across this process. And it is an endless process, in which women are
continually working and reworking their understandings not only of
television and nation, but of their own experiences.

This meeting ground of text and lived experience within situated
moments produces a polyphony of voices. Mankekar does not attempt
to simply line up the readings and place them side by side because "the
lack of closure in women viewers' interpretations is inescapable" (1999:
225). Neither does Mankekar attempt to bring closure by marshaling
these voices to create an *ur*-reading of the text. Rather, as a "feminist
critic of the Indian state" she seeks to deploy her ethnography critically
to "create possibilities for counternarratives that can potentially subvert" nationalist discourses, particularly those of fundamentalist Hinduism, by "insisting on the fundamentally 'incomplete' nature of
hegemonic discourses underscored by moments of rupture" (225). In
this way she attempts to construct her own critical readings of media
texts without either appropriating her informants' discourses or reducing them to examples of categorical types.

Articulating Identity

Ethnography, of course, even one as intimate as Mankekar's, offers no more direct access to human subjectivity than any other methodology; people's articulations of their inner states are always shaped by their immediate situation, including their understanding of the ethnographer's relationship to them. "Rapport," in the sense it is used by many anthropologists, refers to little more than the fact that the ethnographer now understands enough of the cultural codes so as not to get hopelessly lost every time he or she enters a new situation. It is certainly no magical entrée into the mysteries of what people "really" think. Indeed, there is considerable evidence that most people are not sure of what they "really" think about anything in any given situation until they articulate it. The shift to a sense of the plurality of the self is thus sensible for ethnographers on purely methodological grounds. Mankekar's study of subjectivities opens up silences and finds voices for them. She sees and hears women defer to their husbands' opinions in situations of television viewing, and puts these moments of silence against voiced opinions in later discussions where husbands are not present. In doing so, she juxtaposes two issues I want to tease apart here: subjectivities and identities.

If we regard subjectivity as the realm of absolute experience, we must also recognize that this experience is inchoate. Experience is made coherent and meaningful insofar as it is articulated through language or other systems of signification. Articulation involves the mobilization of cultural categories to articulate a particular identity or set of identities. Insofar as the cultural construction of person is public, I speak of *identities*. Insofar as this construction is part of the internal, private play of the imagination, I speak of *selves*. Selves and identities thus exist insofar as they are professed and performed from moment to moment through discourse and other forms of meaningful action. Media create reference sites from which symbols, texts, and other resources for the articulation of identities and selves may be drawn.

A number of people have explored this use of media in the articulation of social identity. Donham describes the role of media in the construction of new identities for male-male sexuality in South Africa. In Soweto, the idea of *skesana* as a woman in a man's body and *stabane*, a hermaphrodite, already exist as local cultural categories families use to construct the identities of selves and sons whose sexual desires are for men rather than women. More recently, upper class men literate in European languages and with access to the Internet are able to construct new identities as "gay" and "homosexual." In doing so, they are not only constructing new mediated identities but are learning a pattern of how to use media in identity construction, one long known in the

West, where "coming out" stories have often implicated the media, with "accounts of trips to the public library, furtive searches through dictionaries, or secret readings of novels" (Donham 1998: 15-16). The concepts of "gay" and "coming out" intersect with, confront, and contradict local notions of nation and identity.

Donham's essay emphasizes the ways that identities are constructed by media in relation to other kinds of cultural resources. Narratives of nation, ethnicity, gender and sexuality, class, and modernity are by no means exclusive provinces of the media. JoEllen Fisherkeller (1997) makes an even more focused argument for the ways media intersect with other cultural systems in identity construction among middle-school students in New York. Adolescents make use of television shows, and particularly specific characters, in creating and reinforcing their identities. But they do not construct their identities from television alone. The students she profiles come to understand social power, gender, and racial and ethnic categories by weighing what they learn from television against what they are learning from a set of other social fields equally crucial in their lives: homes, neighborhoods, peer groups, and schools. She argues that the manner in which youths learn from television is a complex process in which "guiding motivations" from peer, institutional, and family cultures help them define social futures, which are further refined and reimagined through television.[10]

One of the most complete studies to look at the intersection of media consumption and other social fields is Marie Gillespie's (1995) study of young people in the South Asian community of Southall in London. Gillespie examines the ways specific genres of television texts—soap operas, news, advertising—address young people as different kinds of audiences: "News addresses young people as citizens, soaps address them as social actors, ads address them as consumers. They collectively respond to these genres in distinctive ways as participants in a peer group culture in the process of redefining itself with and against its significant others" (1995: 26). Gillespie's "peer group culture" in fact includes all the same social fields identified by Fisherkeller. Further, the sites of reception themselves become key locations where genre, social field and practice come together to construct identity. For example, young people are called on by the traditions of their South Asian diasporic community to defer to adults. Their bilingual positions, however, encourage monolingual parents to call on them to translate and mediate television news. To talk about news with one's parents is to assume an adult identity. This is true both because of the content of news as a media discourse that is "important," rather than mere entertainment, and because of the instructional relationship it put children into with regard to their parents.

Media reception takes place in specific situations that shape the experience of consumption. These situations provide spaces for the articulation of identities, and if this articulation draws on the reservoir of symbolic materials made available through the media, it also takes place in tension with other social domains, other spaces in which identities are being articulated.

But media audiences are not only concerned with the use of media to make sense of the world and one's place in it, or to offer resources for the management of individual identity. On the contrary, the same media resources people exploit to construct identities can be exploited to construct complex social worlds that connect people in a bewildering variety of ways. Through the media, people construct themselves as kinds of persons, and these constructions can form the basis of many forms of sociality.

Media Socialities

Audiences of mass media do not exist a priori. They are actively constructed through careful programming decisions and marketing strategies, as well as transnational flows of information, capital and commodities, and in some cases, the agendas of the nation-state. (Mankekar 1999: 54).

That media serve as resources for the construction of identities is no news to media producers, who organize entire campaigns around efforts to construct advertising (Pedelty 1998), television (Andersen 1995), and magazines (Liechty 1995; Urciuoli 1998) that carefully craft model ethnic, gendered, or other identities to meet consumer desires. Producers appropriate identities and desires, transform them into particular representations, then return them in objectified, usually commodified forms. In doing so, they seek to construct audiences who will imagine others like themselves who likewise are consuming these images. Such audiences are only categories of identity. They exist as discursive constructs, not as socially interacting communities.

Yet media consumers need not remain isolated from others who share their taste in media representation. The mining of the media repertoire for symbols with which to constitute identity includes public display of one's taste. For the new child at school clad in his Pokémon shirt to enter a strange classroom and see a fellow student wearing a similar shirt is to indicate a kinship. Perhaps the simplest form of media sociality, then, is the *discursive community*, an imagined community (Anderson 1991) whose existence is evidenced through an ability to employ certain media concepts in various forms of social discourse. Youth cultures, in particular, seem to be formed worldwide by their ability to share certain mass mediated codes.[11] Knowledge of such codes and the ability to mobilize them can be a key part of being "accepted" by peer groups. People who dwell in media-saturated societies are expected to know about an extensive series of mediated figures beyond their face-to-face social experiences: athletes, musicians, actors, talk-show hosts, politicians, fictional characters, cartoon figures, and so forth. In many societies, familiarity with such figures and an ability to converse with others about their diets, drugs, diseases, sexual escapades, divorces, and legal disputes is required for competent participation in many conversations (Caughey 1984). Because these codes are mediated by mass producers, they are particularly mutable, and keeping up with shifts and changes in "what's hot and what's not" is a central part of sociality in many media and commodity-saturated communities.[12] Such shared codes may involve not only discourse about media, but also acquisition of commodities—toys, albums, posters, T-shirts and so forth, varying with age and community.

The imaginative play of children who interact with or imaginatively become the heroes they admire on television, in films, books, and comics, does not end with adulthood, although its articulations are often more carefully banished to the realm of the individual imagination. John L. Caughey (1984, 1985, 1994, 1995) has been engaged for more than a decade in examining the ways people engage in *imaginary social relations* with media figures. The fact that such figures are not phenomenologically present to the ethnographer's gaze does not dismiss their importance, any more than the inability of anthropologists to experience spirit beings (Hallowell 1960) or wild pig reflections (Schieffelin 1976) reduces the importance of social relations with them in Ojibwa or Kaluli society. Caughey suggests at least six categories of social relations with media figures: imaginary social relationships with media figures, parasocial relations (pseudointeractions) with media figures as part of media reception,[13] identification with media figures, dreams about (and hence, experiences of) interactions with media figures, modeling the behavior of media figures, and face-to-face social interactions built around knowledge of and talk about media figures. Caughey is particularly interested in the psychological aspects of the first five of these categories, with the ways in which these relationships play a role in selfhood (1984, 1985) and with the way in which imaginary social relations as revealed in interviews are modeled on cultural conventions of face-to-face sociability (1989).

As Caughey states, a crucial first step is to determine which media figures are the "significant others" for various social identities. But Caughey's practice of having people make lists and describe how they feel about these figures can at best be a preliminary step; more important is an ethnographic examination of the ways social identities and actions, including talk, are organized around these media figures in everyday life. "Modeling" the words and actions of media figures can be seen in this context not only as part of a psychological process of self formation, as Caughey does, but also as one of several forms of social and cultural capital which, because of their highly commoditized nature, are closely linked to economic capital and, hence, to class.[14]

Mediated Communities

Once brought into being by some commonality of virtual experience, or taste in genre, actor(s) or text, audiences show a remarkable capacity to turn from virtual into genuine socialities: discursive communities, networks, sodalities, corporate groups, exile nations, and odd hybrids of any and all of these. Among the most ethnographically accessible of groups organized by media are diasporic, minority, and transnational communities.

One of the oldest such uses of media in America is to create a sense of homogeneity among diasporic communities. Many immigrant communities in the United States, for example, have long had newspapers that circulated among members of the specific community. Often these are in the language of the community, or are bilingual, and they may reprint articles from newspapers and magazines from the country of origin. In the United States, such media serve to construct a sense of community; not only through shared discourses of identity based on descent or other myths of origin, but also through advertising local businesses owned by members of the community. In so doing, these media reproduce the consumerist ideology of the host country, and insofar as it becomes a part of the identities of media consumers, create the hyphenated Americans predicted by the myth of the melting pot. Exile, immigrant, and minority media are no longer limited to newspapers, but are increasingly supplemented, and in some cases replaced, by television, radio, and other media.

Rarely can diasporic media be said to *create* a community; media producers generally construct audience identities on the basis of groups that already exist in disparate and stratified segments; media products circulate through and among these in patterns that may reflect internal differences, but also often attempt to supersede them. Drawing on Naficy (1993) we can suggest a set of distinctions between *ethnic media*, produced in the host country by and for long established minority populations, *transnational media*, fed primarily by imported media products from the countries of origin, and *exilic media*, produced by exiles living in the host country "as a response to and in parallel with their own transitional and provisional status" (63). Such categories are flexible, overlapping, and incomplete, but they offer a useful starting place for thinking about such phenomena.

One of the most complete ethnographies of a diasporic community is Hamid Naficy's study of the Iranian exile community in Los Angeles (1993). The exile community—numbering between 80,000 and 120,000 when he wrote about it, is dispersed throughout Los Angeles, so although there are areas of concentration, they do not form a "little Persia" or "Irantown." Although many members of the community interact at certain festivals and events, internal differences of religion, languages, and reason for exile serve as points of cleavage that prevent the community from forming a coherent social group. What marks the community, rather, is the sense of being exiles, forced migrants from a place to which they cannot return because it no longer exists. In spite of their education and class positions—well above those of many other American diasporic communities—their liminality is keenly felt. Iranian television in Los Angeles explores this liminality through evocations of nostalgia, fetishization of images, music and language, and essentialist narratives of origin. At the same time, the programs are subject to extreme market pressures, and their air times are fluid and unreliable because television stations catering to minority broadcasting shift schedules in response to the highest bidder. This "televisual ebb and flow is an index of the fluidity of life in exile" (1993: 64).

Naficy argues that exilic television is not only an instrument of exilic identification but that structural features that permeate the diverse programs "organize the symbolic, ideological, and social milieu of exiles in such a way as to encourage incorporation into the dominant universe of American consumer capitalism" (1993: 65). Naficy contends that this mediated rite of passage from liminality to new identity as an Iranian-American is caused by the needs of producers in a market-driven climate to professionalize, avoid controversy, and sell lots of ads. But the mode of production may not be the real driving force for this process. Shryock (2000) makes a similar claim for a federally funded program in "Arab Detroit" that operates outside the strictures of the ad market. The ACCESS public arts program, he says, "is part of a coordinated national strategy addressed to a perennial American concern: how best to manufacture new citizens who can participate smoothly in America's public institutions, markets and politics" (Shryock 2000: 58). This suggests that both entrepreneurial and public-sector media respond to larger cultural imperatives.

But media does not only create a sense of community and syncretism among preexisting "imagined" communities; they may also create interactive communities where none existed. Media form the basis for a number of different kinds of social networks, ranging from ritual communities to discussion groups to fan clubs. *Ritual communities* are those which come together to engage in specific forms of ritual performance around a media text or intertext, such as those Americans who engage in interactive public performances with the text of *The Rocky Horror Picture Show* (Hoberman and Rosenbaum 1981: Locke 1999) and those Indians who have made pilgrimages to the temple to Kushboo in Trichirappalli, Tamil Nadu.[15] Media discussion groups are often described in the West under the more general rubric of fan communities (Camille Bacon-Smith 1992, 2000), but they can, in fact, take many forms. Yang (1994) describes the rise of film-discussion and film review-writing groups in China as a site where state domination of cinema production intersects with rising interest in social transformations in the light of recent political and economic reforms.[16]

In addition to media ritual and small group face-to-face interactions, the increasing availability of small-scale media production facilities—particularly mimeograph, photocopying, e-mail, fax, and websites—have allowed the creation of networks of people brought together by common interest in particular texts or genres. Such interactive communities range from loose affiliations, such as women who frequent specialty bookstores and subscribe to their newsletters (Radway 1984b) to dedicated usenet groups (Clerc 1996).

Fan Cultures

Consumers who build social affiliations around media texts are *fans*, and fan behavior has come in for a great deal of ethnographic attention. One reason is that fans create a great deal of discourse about their own media consumption. Fans thus offer an accessible way to study how patterns of media consumption change as long time media consumers make personal and social investments in media texts and intertexts.[17] Long time consumers develop a *metatext* (Jenkins 1992), consisting of a detailed knowledge of the history, themes, and running jokes associated with a television show, movie series, media figure, or other intertext. The metatext is thus a more orderly version of the kinds of imaginary social relations discussed above. In an ongoing television serial, for example, regular viewers' will accumulate knowledge of character relationships, as well as the whole narrative history of the storyworld of the show. Some fan metatexts may also include knowledge of the production history of the program (casting changes and changes in writers or producers). For such viewers, no narrative is ever contained in a single film or television episode because they are always already relating it to the others they've seen. Fans record their metatexts in a variety of media, and they exchange them. In the process, they create social relationships.

Fan viewing should not, however, be taken as an "elementary form" of audience behavior, as some ethnography of media seems to treat it. As Nightingale (1993: 166) says, "Fans, by definition, always read sympathetically." Even more to the point, the intensity with which fans read media texts is not necessarily representative of the more casual engagements of most media consumers. For fans, the metatext often grows beyond the canon of films, television programs, radio shows, albums, and so forth as they begin filling in gaps or speculating about problems left unresolved by a particular text. In the process, fans tend to seek out others who are equally willing to invest time, energy, and money in thinking seriously about media texts. The sharing of such speculative discourses through fan clubs, fanzines, chat rooms, and websites creates a basis for sociality.

Fan communities engage with, and are engaged by, the producers of the texts around which their activities are based. A number of commercial (fan magazines, official websites) and non- or semicommercial (unofficial websites, newsletters, fanzines) resources help fans develop such metatexts. In major movie production centers, like Hollywood, Bombay, and Tamil Nadu, official websites and fan sites are increasingly created before movies are released, offering material that can be formed into a metatext in advance of the actual screening. Thus, not only fannish vehicles, such as *Star Wars* but also films like *Titanic* can build enormous prior interest. This prior material builds incipient fans because anticipation is created through a metatext generated by the advance knowledge accumulated from the official site (and related fan sites). If the film lives up to expectations, this subsequently enhances the pleasure of the viewers in the same way that the metatexts generated by fans' viewing do. In this way, among many others, the culture industry seeks to orchestrate consumer pleasures.

But fans are by no means under the control of producers. Fan activity may be intensive and sympathetic, but it is not necessarily marked by *uncritical* acceptance of media texts. On the contrary, fans are far more likely to be able to discuss their own pleasures in sophisticated and often critical ways, which may be one reason why fan ethnography has been booming among literary critics and folklorists. Susan Clerc offers a nice example of how debates over gender, for example, play out in an on-line discussion about the X-files. She argues that fans are

> aware of how gender is played out in the series and discuss both the quantity and quality of times each partner rescues the other. When it seemed as if Scully was being rescued more than Mulder during a sequence of episodes, there were complaints in the on-line groups. Several other fans replied with an episode-by-episode list of who had rescued whom and who had been portrayed as victim. Further discussion turned

to the quality of those scenes: Was Scully shown as a victim for longer periods of time, or dealing with her attackers in a less effective manner? (Clerc 1996: 47)

Such debates amount to an on going, collective textual analysis of each show, one that is itself negotiated socially through a technological medium. Fans not only consume media—they often also produce it.

As such forms of sociality grow and move beyond informal discussions and gatherings (physical or virtual) they may become corporate social groups, involving shared resources. Although most studies of organized fan communities are about the United States or, to a lesser degree, Europe, studies from India and Japan demonstrate how diverse and complex the links are that relate fan cultures to the larger society, the forms their sociality takes, and the nature of the relations between fans and media producers.

As described in Sara Dickey's *Cinema and the Urban Poor in South India* (1993), Tamil Nadu is home to a large and thriving fan culture—there are thousands, perhaps even tens of thousands, of such clubs in Madurai alone. Membership is made up primarily of lower-to middle-class and lower- to middle-caste men.[18] Clubs often form networks connecting them to other city, regional, state, national, and even international levels of organization. Clubs are organized around specific stars, particularly male stars, and membership in a club devoted to one star precludes membership in any others. Each star has a distinctive image, which extends from the filmic intertext (and many Indian film stars have an extremely large corpus for fans to draw on) into an imagined social persona of goodness and generosity. Fan club members often refer to their star as "teacher," "elder brother," or "god." Comparisons of behavior toward film star images and *bhakti* (religious devotion) are unavoidable.

Fan club activities are an extension of a more general film culture in Tamil Nadu. Among the poor of Madurai, moviegoers see in films "images of themselves; they see the real problems of their daily lives and the ideal image of their moral selves. Films objectify (some of) the anxieties of their lives and then dissolve them, in part through the glorification of the character of the poor and in part through promises of a life of luxury" (Dickey 1993: 175). Stars play a key role in these images, portraying the virtuous poor, whether suffering for their moral purity or rewarded for it. Stars are immensely wealthy individuals who come to stand for the poor themselves through their intertextual relations to their films and the characters they play in them.

Fans are quite aware of the gulf that separates them from the upper class and of the denigration in which motion pictures are held as "vulgar." Their devotion to the star serves as a way to construct identities that confirm their sense of themselves as morally superior to those above them. They accomplish this in part by extending the image of the star as generous and as a defender of the poor to the fan clubs devoted to him. Although most activities are recreational, nearly all fan clubs profess that they are engaged in "good deeds" and "social services" varying from "civic services, such as notifying authorities of fires or policing neighborhoods, to disaster relief, to donations of food, clothing and other items to the poor" (Dickey 1993: 159). Service to the poor is seen as essential to a club's purpose of "promoting and supporting" the star, but it also allows lower-class fans to occupy the position of givers rather than receivers of alms.

Since the political party in control of the national government has a monopoly on the airwaves, in the 1960s opposition parties began to recruit actors, who already possessed widespread public heroic images.[19] The movement of movie stars into politics is strongly abetted by their relationship with fan clubs. While their film images provide them with the charisma (Weber 1964) required for mass appeal, fan clubs provide both a grassroots network within the star's party and, through civic activities, operationalization of the star's generosity and public interest. At the same time, the fan clubs allow fans to construct moral and social identities that distinguish them from the rest of the urban poor by making them givers of aid rather than receivers, and embedding their own self-narratives within a larger political narrative of the star's devotion to "the people."

Fan activity in the United States is a very different kind of social activity, a site for creating and playing with distinctive modes of action. Focusing particularly on the role of women in fan activity, Camille Bacon-Smith (1994, 1999) describes American science-fiction fandom as the construction of a particular community in which people can emphasize particular dimensions of self, and construct alternative identities from those offered by the society around them. American fans are using their intensive interest in texts to construct a *subculture*, a group which sets itself off from the mainstream by particular markers of difference. The nature of difference is not marked as much by alternative codes of dress, linguistic register, or other forms of public display—although some of these exist in variously distributed ways—as it does in an elaboration of metatexts through a number of expressive genres peculiar to the subculture. These genres include buttons, fanzines, datazines, filksongs, gen-zines, costumes, jewelry, fan art, letterzines, songtapes, and more.[20]

Many of these media serve to establish identity not only by marking one as a fan but also by expressing nuanced registers of identity based on taste in genre and on degrees of esoteric knowledge of the intertext. This kind of marking becomes particularly important when fans leave the intimacy of their own small "circle" to enter the more public arena of fan conventions. Buttons with slogans on them, for example, "signal competence in the manipulation of the codes of the community and act as cues by which participants with equal levels of competence may recognize each other in the public sphere of the convention" (Bacon-Smith 1992: 163).

The relationships between fan clubs and media industries are often complex. Fans serve as core constituencies and consumers, and the cultivation of fan organizations is in the interest of most media producers. Much fan activity is therefore supported and reinforced by commercial or state media industries. Fans are not always uncritical supporters, however. It was a fan write-in campaign that saved *Star Trek* from being canceled its first season—the billions of dollars Paramount has made on the franchise since then therefore owes a tremendous amount to the fan community. Yet the very devotion of fans to a star, text, or genre can lead to aggressive criticism and to efforts to resist changes in direction proposed by producers. The relations between fans and the producers of the texts seem to be linked to other forms of sociality that are transformed in the realm of fandom. These relations are culturally mediated.

Yano (1997) argues that charisma-based fan clubs in Japan, devoted to musicians and other stars, are understood there as modern forms of *amae*, dyadic dependencies, in which one partner demonstrates socially valued traits of loyalty and dedication by supporting and promoting the other. Star-fan relations thus join more traditional *amae* such as husband-wife, child-mother, master-servant, and samurai-attendant. That such relations are commercially created and ritually manipulated by media industries is not necessarily seen as negative in a society where the molding of desire by the media is seen as "not so different from shaping a tree by pruning. Through pruning one acquires greater harmony with one's surroundings, and thereby greater beauty" (Yano 1997: 337).

Similar appropriations of fan culture by the culture industry are found in MTV, where, for example, Madonna fans were invited to produce their own videos for her song "True Blue." A selection of these videos were then played in a twenty-four-hour marathon (Fiske 1987). In spite of such examples, American fan communities generally seem to be both more transgressive in their appropriations and considerably more resistant to industry "pruning" than those fan communities described by Dickey and Yano. Fans in the United States appropriate characters and settings, and use these as the bases for their own stories, which allow fans to explore meanings that go beyond, or add to, source texts controlled by producers. In doing so, fan clubs, film discussion groups, and other fan communities can produce a superfluity of meaning that goes beyond what is intended by media producers. The corporations that produce the media texts appropriated by fans may feel called on to contain these meanings and limit them to fit their own visions.

In America, particularly, where fans appropriate elements from mass mediated texts and turn them into new forms of media texts, the tension between producers and fan cultures is strong. Jenkins (1992) calls such fan appropriations "poaching"—nicely capturing an analogy of serfs attempting to illegally obtain sustenance from lands set aside by the feudal lords for their own use. In creating fan fiction and other expressive genres, fans are appropriating elements of source texts that producers insist do not "belong" to them. The blurring of the boundaries between producers and consumers can be troubling for producers and they may attempt to police meaning to reconstitute this boundary.

One of the most persistent and troublesome fan genres for American television and film producers is that called "slash" by the fan community. The term refers to homoerotic stories that explore the nature of the male friendships expressed in American and British film and television series. Primarily written by women, slash "allows for a more thorough exploration of issues of intimacy, power, commitment, partnership, competition and attraction" apparent in the scripted actions of programs as well as in the nuances of specific performances (Jenkins 1992: 202). In *Star Trek*, for example, "Kirk consistently renounces romantic ties that might interfere with his professional duties, while he has just as persistently been prepared to disobey orders and put his job at risk to protect his 'friend'" Spock (Jenkins 1992: 203). Fans use "Kirk/Spock" stories to find ways to articulate the nature of this self-giving relationship, often in sexually explicit ways.

The sexuality of characters from media narratives, however, is usually closely guarded by the producers of the texts from which the characters originated. Mikulak describes the legal threats that occurred when Warner Brothers discovered fan sites that included sexualized versions of their "Tiny Toons" characters, and the effects of these threats on the fan community. While few in the fan community supported the "pornography" as such, toon fans on the Internet were deeply split over the issue of whether to allow Warner Brothers to police their various personal expressions of affinity for the source texts. This account of a split fan culture fits with accounts from other fan communities. For example, although practitioners of slash (and some other forms of fan genres) may argue that "Slash is a wonderfully subversive voice whispering or shouting around the edges and into the cracks of mainstream culture" that "abounds in unconventional thinking" and is "fraught with danger for the status quo" because of its "successful defiance of social norms," slash authors often find themselves pariahs within their own subculture. Fanzines that see themselves as heterogenous find that once they begin accepting slash, people stop sending them other genres. The productive genres described by Bacon-Smith thus not only fit into a specific and resistant domain against mainstream cultural capital (Fiske 1987; Dickey 1993), but they construct their own distributions of cultural capital within their communities. That some of the most valued forms of cultural capital tend to correlate the most strongly with the versions of the texts promulgated by producers is a powerful tool in exerting control over the fan community.

Fan appropriations of texts and the legal responses of media producers involves the state in regulating media consumers' behavior. Fan appropriations are often treated indulgently by producers when they take place within a range of meaningfulness acceptable to the media producers. When they exceed this range, these appropriations become transgressions and producers seek the intervention of the courts or the state as regulators of consumers' actions. Because most studies of fandom have taken place in democratic countries, little is known about more direct state involvement in fan activity. A rare exception is Yang, who describes how members of grassroots fan clubs in mainland China must declare themselves as members to various state agencies, thus reducing the degree to which nationalist films are likely to be discussed in resistant ways; nonetheless, discussants' tendencies to veer away from the state and the statist meanings of texts toward alternative interpretations is itself a potentially resistant or subversive form of civil action (Yang 1994).

Conclusion

The role of mass media in forming socialities—even fan socialities—is by no means limited to those centered around media consumption and production activities. As vehicles for the distribution of collective representations, media can combine with other artifacts that offer resources for the creation of meaning. Nobuhiro (1998) describes a simple example of this in his account of the "cult" surrounding the racehorse Oguricap in Japan. Oguricap's initial popularity arose on the racecourse, and as stories, photographs, and accounts of "the grey monster" emerged, they attracted large numbers of women to the previously all-male environs of the racecourse. The cult of Oguricap exploded after a nationally televised race (the majority of women fans of the horse in fact never saw him on the racetrack). Retired after this, his last and most successful race, Oguricap's history was read as a powerful symbolic narrative of the unknown (Oguricap had no distinguished pedigree) succeeding against the odds, then suffering defeat (he was hurt after one race) and cruelty (his new owners ran him before he was completely recovered), only to triumph in his final and greatest challenge. After the final race, Oguricap was commodified as a stuffed doll, which became extremely popular. Secondary appropriations of both the doll and the horse followed, not only into other forms of media such as *manga*, but in everyday conversation and narrative accounts of self, especially by women. The cult of Oguricap is an example of the ways in which mass mediation is never only about texts and their interpretation; it is always also about the social practices by which people appropriate media texts to accomplish the work and meaning of everyday life.

The example in this chapter emphasizes how the shift to ethnography moves us from a notion of the power of text to a notion of *interpretive practice*. Interpretive practices involve the reception and interpretation of media texts, but they suggest that the relationship between texts and identities and subjectivities is more complex, and more socially mediated, than many textualist theories would imply. The shift to an ethnography of media consumption reveals the roles that situations, socially organized norms of interpretation, and intertextuality can play in the construction of individual subjectivity, as well as individual and group social identities.

Perhaps even more disruptive to textualist theories of media representation is the inescapability of the connections between other social practices and the practices of media interpretation, such that everyday sociality comes to shape as well as be shaped by media. Nowhere is this more obviously true than in the case of fan cultures, whose practices emphasize the fact that consuming media is not the same thing as consuming culture; on the contrary, culture is always and everywhere a generative process. Recognizing this fact opens up new possibilities not only for the study of consumption, but for the study of production; it asks us to consider the ways in which the activities of media production produce not only texts but persons. Media culture involves more than the text—it constitutes social worlds of work, worlds of meaning that center around the creation of media but are never determined by it. It is to this phenomenon that we turn in the next chapter.

Notes

1. Other major studies that figure in this shift include Brunsdon and Morley 1978, Hobson 1982, Ang 1985, Tulloch and Moran 1986, and Buckingham 1987.

2. Morley found it difficult to keep children engaged, and after the first few interviews, began interviewing children separately from their parents. He later regretted this decision, saying it "had the regrettable effect of shifting the focus of analysis, so that the children's views and comments ... are much more marginal to the analysis than I would have wished" (Morley 1986: 174).

3. Radway later came to espouse a more involved approach to audience ethnography, whichseeks to pay attention to the ways in which "media are integrated and implicated within [daily life]" (1988: 366). See also Radway (1991).

4. This criticism is by no means only directed from anthropology to cultural studies. The question of how to (and whether to) construct more dialogic and polyphonic ethnographies was an issue in anthropology well before Rosaldo, and continues to be strongly debated.

5. I am, of course, indebted for the general outline of this rubric to Hymes 1977 and Bauman 1977.

6. For a classic analysis of the ways built space is ordered by cosmology, see Bourdieu 1979.

7. This assumption is tied, of course, to the textualist metaphors that academics use to write about media (many of which I am using in this book), particularly notions of "reading" media as "texts." Yet increasingly, in the anthropology of literacy, the idea that reading is a solitary, individual activity is also coming to be recognized as ethnocentric (Street 1984, 1991).

8. Their husbands, on the other hand, dismiss these same films as utterly unrealistic.

9. Individual performances of this discourse are always strategic, of course; their articulation is shaped by the speakers' understanding of the speech event in which they take place.

10. Compare Fisherkeller's argument to Powdermaker's recognition that it is in social encounters and relations in the home and workspace that traditional or modern identities are primarily forged; media consumption merely provides a more visible and public access to the process.

11. The classic statement on this is Hebdige 1979. For an overview of the diversity and similarity of such communities around the world, see the papers in Amit-Talai and Wulff 1995.

12. In media-saturated societies like the United States, "keeping up" is not necessarily a complex activity. In the vignette about the *Mighty Morphin Power Rangers* that opened the first chapter, it is interesting to note how little the two girls had to know to participate. In this case, the girls told me they had seen fewer than a half-dozen episodes of the show, whereas for the boys, viewing was a weekday afternoon ritual. The girls were helped by the fact that the structure of the program is extremely redundant. Because of its repetitive structure, children who have seen very few episodes are nonetheless able to draw on the few they've seen to engage in discourse about the program. Likewise, the extension of expensive popular commodities, like action figures, into increasingly cheaper and more widely distributed iterations, including McDonald's Happy Meal toys, makes acquisition of the required commodities easier, although it also introduces subtle distinctions of taste and authenticity that become increasingly complex as one moves up the age grades.

13. Parasocial interaction refers to the practice of having actors and other mediated persons speak "directly" to the audience, mimicking the style and mannerisms of face-to-face interaction.

14. But never in simple or straightforward ways. For example, in the late 1990s, when the "Spice Girls" rock band was part of the requisite code for American girls from elementary through junior high school, I observed how the ability to mimic the accents of Scary, Ginger, Posh, Baby, Sporty, and Sweety enabled a girl with few Spice Girl-related commodities to transcend class boundaries and to position herself prominently in group activities among girls who owned far more CDs, cassette tapes, posters, stickers, notebooks and book covers, washable tattoos, pen sets, videos, and so forth.

15. I first read about the temple to the Indian film star Kushboo when it was built in 1992. I was in India at the time, but I was unable to visit it. Every Kushboo fan website I've seen mentions it, but none offer photographs or details. I have been told that other temples to other movie stars exist, but I've been unable to locate any literature on this practice. One expatriate Indian woman in her late teens (the age Dickey identifies as the narrow niche during which women can engage in fan activity) told me in 2001 about visiting several movie star shrines—including that of Kushboo—during her visits home to Tamil Nadu.

16. Some of Yang's later work (1997) examines the ways the politicized nature of this setting—groups arising from the grassroots, but whose members must register with the state—affects subjectivities.

17. I use *intertext* here in a way that extends the meaning given in chapter 3. In addition to genre and intertextual bricolage, intertext here refers to media figures such as movie stars and music stars, persons known not through a single text but multiple texts, whose images come to take on a particular character in the imaginations of fans.

18. Almost all organized fan activity in India is male, although women are certainly avid consumers of fan materials. A few small and separate women's clubs do exist, but women inevitably abandon them by the time of their marriage.

19. M.G. Ramachandran, N.T. Rama Rao, Jayalitha, Shivaji, Amitabh Bachchan, Sunil Dutt, and Vyjyanthimala are among the major Indian stars who have entered politics.

20. See Bacon-Smith (1992) for a lengthy glossary of these and other fan terms.

Chapter 7

❧

THE ETHNOGRAPHY OF MEDIA PRODUCTION

L ike consumption, media production is fundamentally a social and cultural act, involving not only the creation of media texts but also the generation of identities, interpretations, subjectivities, statuses, and meanings among the persons engaged in media production. When television producers imagine audiences who will enjoy viewing their new programs, they imagine others like and unlike themselves, (re)constructing their own identities in the process of constructing the imagined audience. When film directors see themselves as authors, they imagine something of themselves in the films they direct. Journalists who go out to "get the story" are engaged in the same kinds of interpretive practices as any other social actor; they are making sense of what is going on in terms of the signifying repertoire available to them, while also being part of a system of production whose economies and policies prefer some articulations over others. Media production is a form of work, and work has long been recognized in social theory as one of the crucial domains where social structure, collective identities, and selfhood intersect. That media producers are at work in the fields of symbols does not necessarily make their labor a special case.

That media production is a cultural practice like any other has not always been fully appreciated in studies of media producers. Analysts often seek to demystify production, deliberately rejecting the "native's point of view" to show readers "what is *really* going on." This has been particularly true of studies of American journalism, in which popular notions of "objectivity" and editorial independence are belied by attention to actual processes of production. Production culture has thus often been treated in a narrow sense as sets of organizational constraints and institutional practices that determine particular kinds of contents. Unfortunately, this approach usually either ignores the pleasures, beliefs, and everyday meaning-making by social actors engaged in media production, or treats them as secondary or irrelevant. Underlying this approach is a tendency to equate media with culture, and to assume that the production of media texts *is* the production of culture.[1]

What I wish to argue in this chapter is that media producers are never only engaged in the production of media texts; they are also always engaged in producing themselves as social persons in relation to others. Media production always and everywhere involves epistemologies, heuristics, competences, and aesthetics, as well as social organizations, hierarchies, rituals, and technologies, and all of these together constitute the worlds in which these producers live and work. These worlds are at the same time linked to larger cultural formations. Just as ethnographies of media consumption have needed to move beyond reception to the creative spaces where people integrate media texts into their lives, so ethnographies of production must recognize the fundamental relationship between the production of texts, the construction of identity, and the connections between production cultures and the larger cultural worlds in which they are embedded.

As we saw in the previous chapter, meaning is never simply found in a text; rather, it is socially negotiated and struggled over. Meaning lies between texts and their consumers (and, as we saw in the discussion of fan culture, between consumers and producers). In this chapter I aim to extend this argument to the relations between texts and their producers.

The ethnography of production must therefore proceed on several levels. First, it must examine producers' engagements with the technologies of production, particularly the ways in which ownership and control over the means of media production are organized. Second, it must examine the ways that media production consists of myriad practices taking place within specific fields in which statuses, identities, pleasures, and knowledges, as well as money, are at stake. Third, it is necessary to recognize the interpretive practices that producers bring to their task, and the ways these are derivative of larger cultural discourses. Finally, it is necessary to attend to the fact that producers are themselves also consumers, and the roles played by consumption in producers' entextualization practices.

Centering Analysis

At the heart of any ethnographic study of media production is a key question: who *speaks* through the mass media? Who is addressing audiences and to what extent are their views and intentions encoded into the texts? Our answers will always be partly determined by the theoretical positions that frame our studies. The study of media production is always embedded in assumptions about the relation of mass media to the larger society. If texts have fixed meanings that dominate consumers, the fixed meanings must be assumed to reflect the worlds of those who produce the texts. And if, on the other hand, texts are hybrid and dialogical, the study of production promises to reveal to us how such social contradictions come to be crystallized in texts. In theory, investigation could discover the extent to which producers are, in fact, part of a hegemonic "culture industry" or whether media producers fall under the more general cross-cultural rubric of *communication specialists*, "super-salesmen, politicians, orators, actors, folk artists, writers, comedians, journalists," and others "who depend on their performance skills to achieve success and fulfillment in life. The most successful of these communication specialists know ... how to exploit the ideational shapes of their culture successfully in order to generate powerful, effective communication" (Beeman 1982: xv).

To sort out these approaches, some mass communication theorists have found it useful to differentiate between *mediacentric* analyses, which emphasize institutional influences on content, and *sociocentric* analyses, which emphasize the ways media draw on widely shared cultural symbols and norms in shaping their content (McQuail 1994: 186-187). Most sociological studies of media production have tended to be mediacentric, emphasizing the significance of organizational influences on content. In part this is a result of their focus: the vast majority of these studies have emphasized news production (Tuchman 1972, 1978a, 1978b; Rosenblum 1979; Fishman 1980; Gans 1980; Gitlin 1983), seeking to juxtapose such processes as selectivity and gatekeeping with the widespread belief in Western liberal societies that news will offer an objective picture of reality through which persons can contribute, as informed citizens, to a democratic society. Investigators taking such a position are interested in the ways legal regulations, media ownership, political process, organizational structure, professional roles and routines, and categories of identity (class, ethnicity, gender, caste) organize and constrain media production. In the process, attention to the agency of the individual communicative actor is often lost. Artists, actors, writers, directors, producers and others are reduced to mere agents and vehicles of the institutional structure, acting out predetermined roles.

Sociocentric analysis, by contrast, calls on investigators to look at media producers as social actors who have special competences in the manipulation of symbols. They are seen as very much *of* their society, analogous to bards (Lord 1960), griots (Hoffman 2000) and ritual specialists (V. Turner 1967) who draw on shared cultural symbols, utilizing language and image to achieve rhetorical and poetical ends. These are the filmmakers of Drummond's media Dreamtime, acting not as agents for a power elite but as agents for the collective "we" of society (1996). This approach derives largely from anthropology's desire to follow Malinowski's admonition to "grasp the native's point of view, his relation to life, to realize *his* vision of *his* world" (1953: 25).

Mediacentric and sociocentric modes of analysis, however, might better be seen as representing two poles of a theoretical continuum, both ends of which effectively deny agency to the social actors who produce media texts. By agency, I mean the human capacity to act. That is, they ignore the creative capacity of social actors to make decisions and carry them out. Emphasizing the degree to which media producers are driven by social forces and constrained by institutional forces, they tend ignore the degree to which people acquiesce to or resist such forces. What are emerging are more actor-centered approaches that see media production as a form of cultural production like any other, in which agents act according to their cultural values within a defined social field. While producing media texts for public consumption, they simultaneously elaborate codes and aesthetics and, given a sufficiently complex social system, can generate entire subcultures of communication specialties, each with its own ways of speaking, shared knowledges, and key institutions. The ethnography of media production is an emergent effort to bridge mediacentric and sociocentric perspectives, to talk about the agency of media producers within a cultural system while still recognizing their embeddedness in larger structures of power. This involves a shift to seeing the work of media producers as a situated and strategic activity in which performers draw on specific competences and on knowledge of both the specific situation of production and the cultural system more generally. To make this shift, we need to tease out the difficult problems of authorship and authority, and to recognize and resist our desire to reify production in terms of essentially ethnocentric notions of "authored" texts.

Authorship and Authority

In chapter 3, I discussed Foucault's concept of the "author-function" of the text, and suggested that ethnography can show us something of how texts are "really" authored, as opposed to how authorship is signified by elements in the text. In saying this, I do not want to create a false dichotomy between authorship as an empirical practice that we can observe and authorship as a concept encoded in a text. Authorship is an *idea* that tells us how a society's members believe mediated texts come into existence. These ideas influence actual media production, although not necessarily in direct ways. Ethnography can make clear the extent to which the *concept* of authorship can organize relations of control over the text while simultaneously masking them. At the same time, ethnography can seek to clarify the extent to which authorship is central to individual subjectivities within media institutions.

Authorship is not an inevitability. That texts have authors is a simple and obvious fact that becomes enormously complicated the moment it is examined closely. Media production involves complex networks of technicians working with symbols and technologies to produce its texts. In American journalism, for example, texts are negotiated between sources, reporters, and editors. Once they are written, they are copyedited and headlined by specialists (with or without input by the reporter). Layout is negotiated by other text specialists and selections may be highlighted as pull-quotes to draw reader interest or the article may be cut for space—operations considered to have nothing to do with the journalist. Adjacent text, including supplementary material ("sidebars"), may be added using material by other reporters or from wire services. Photograph choices, layout, and captioning are likewise all in the hands of specialists. The texts actually seen by the reader of a newspaper are thus very much a group effort, despite the bylines that ascribes authorship to particular individuals.[2] Media production proceeds by allocating authorial roles and assigning meaning to these roles, both in terms of their relative importance to the text and their relations to one another in a system of social and productive relations.

The fact that media are produced by myriad workers, all of whom can be seen as contributing to the final text, does not make media a special case. Authorship is an increasingly widespread research problematic in a variety of disciplines. Even as contemporary literary critics have been trying to dislodge Romantic notions of authorship in the wake of the rediscovery of the work of Bakhtin, Medvedev, Volosinov, and Vygotsky,[3] anthropologists and folklorists following Bauman (1977, 1986) and others have begun to question old notions of authorless "folk" texts by turning from texts to performances (and hence to the performer) of texts. Several things are at issue in this shift, in particular the question of the uniqueness and specificity of any text that can be understood by others. Any text that can be comprehended by others is necessarily a reworking of a socially given signifying system. Bakhtin argues that there is necessarily a plurality of voice in *any* text, however much a society may have conventions that ascribe to it an author.[4] Production becomes here a process of *entextualization*, the practices by which a particular set of symbols and technologies is employed to make a socially recognizable, meaningful text. Bakhtin's argument becomes even more useful when we extend it to media production, where large numbers of individuals are engaged in the technologically mediated activities that generate texts.

The issue of how a particular system ascribes authorship to a text is crucial because authorship is always about *authority*. I want to suggest that we need to recognize authorship as a cultural construction through which claims to authority are variously established, contested, over-turned, and reproduced. Media production proceeds by allocating authorial roles and assigning meanings to these roles, both in terms of their (ascribed) relative importance to the text and their relations to one another in a system of social and productive relations. In any media production system, the struggle over textual production is a struggle over authority, and vice versa. Relations of media production are generally organized around issues of who in the production system counts as an author and who does not. Certain roles in the process of entextualization are established by custom, law, regulation, and practice as forms of authorship, while other roles and practices of production are relegated to secondary positions and cut off from the authority and responsibility presupposed by authorship. This network of authorship, authority, and responsibility can be mapped and related to specific control over technologies and other resources.

The ethnography of production needs to tease out the centralizing forces of authority—the lineage, the law, the state, the interests of capital—that seek to fix the meaning of the text not only *in* the text but through institutional modes of authority. Media production involves, in various forms and to various degrees, continual efforts to turn dialogue into monologue, to fix the meanings of signifiers or constrain the contexts in which they circulate or limit the nature of practices of interpretation. Often they are quite successful and generate a sense of closure among the communities for which they are intended, although as we saw in the previous chapter such closure is never complete and may be missing altogether when texts are distributed outside the communities at whom they were aimed.

The crucial point is that authorship confers the authority to authorize, which in capitalist systems of media production, means *ownership*. Although cultural symbols circulate throughout the public sphere and become part of everyday subjectivities, the notion that these texts are authored allows those entitled as authors to invoke social institutions to attempt to fix meaning, control circulation and curtail appropriation. As Rosemary Coombe writes, speaking of the control that media producers continue to exert over texts after they enter circulation, "despite the fact that a lot of us cried when Bambi's mother died in that fire, that for some of us it's the closest thing we have to a shared cultural memory of childhood, and that we may well share a socialization in which our own mothers were grateful to be able to echo Thumper's words of wisdom … in other words, notwithstanding his role in a collective cultural heritage, Thumper must be authorized" (1998: 42). Disney can exert its rights of authorship over nearly any use of its characters for any purpose, even the painted versions of them on the wall of a nursery. Indeed, corporations like Disney feel they *must* exert this authority; otherwise authorship become could become diffuse and public, costing them their exclusive economic rights over the characters. What is taking place here is the extension of the author-function of the text (Foucault 1984a) to institutions, including manufacturers, publishers—even corporations whose sole purpose is to manage images.

Coombe argues that the "ownership" of texts is particularly crucial in capitalism, and is expressed through complex legal systems that infer ownership and control over specific signs and their uses through institutions such as the trademark and the copyright. In capitalist systems, such notions of ownership can be conceived as constituting an effort to reduce consumers to roles of passive consumption, to control the extent to which consumers use symbols as part of the generative production of culture. Trademarks and copyrights become "assets" that can be marketed apart from the goods to which the marks are originally designated. The astonishing ubiquity of the Nike "swoosh," a trademark for athletic shoes, becoming a symbol that the corporation markets in clothing, stickers, jewelry, and countless other forms, is a good example of this (Goldman 1998). Although the swoosh originated as a mark by which consumers could identify authentic Nike athletic shoes, it has accumulated additional derivative and secondary meanings that enable it to be independently licensed as a separate entity. Although these additional meanings are public, the principle of authorship allows the corporation to lay claim to them and to prosecute improper uses by members of the public.

In the United States, Coca-Cola has been particularly successful at not only protecting its trademark, but establishing the principle that decontextualizations and recontextualizations of any owned symbol, whether performed by fans, cultural critics, educators, non profit organizations, or others, could constitute a dilution of the symbol's value to its authorized owner, and hence, must be protected by law.[5] The role that consumers play in generating such secondary meanings is concealed and mystified by a cultural logic which ascribes both ownership and intent to authors. In America and other societies where the meaning of a text is conceived as the intent of the author, secondary meanings can, by logical extension, also be confidently ascribed to that author. Authors thus come to be institutionally authorized to control not only denotations but connotations of their texts, provided they have the social, political or economic power to police public displays of these texts.[6]

Issues concerning authority over entextualization are by no means limited to capitalism. As Eric Michaels (1994) tells us, the Aboriginal people of Australia have a sophisticated system for the production, ownership, and distribution of sacred knowledge. Aboriginal texts are in the form of songs, stories, dances, and artistic designs whose entextualization is limited to certain people based on "their positions in the kinship network, their relationship to certain tracts of land, and their interest and skill in ceremonies where these media are performed and taught" (Michaels 1994: 5). Unlike trademarks, whose value depends on their ubiquity, the value of these media depends on their secrecy, and their circulation and the contexts of their entextualization are extremely restricted. Many other distinctions organize the system of production of these Aboriginal media, including gender and class, rhetorical stance, and taboos on representation of the dead, and land rights to areas in which stories are set.

Modes of Media Production

The need of social scientists to attend to authorship to locate authority and agency was driven home to me in 1988 when I attended meetings of the Center for Anthropology and Journalism in Washington, D.C.[7] Speakers were often anthropologists who wanted a forum in which to discuss how "the media" constructed accounts that naturalized, universalized, and essentialized—and hence distorted—the various peoples and communities these scholars studied. In their discussions, these anthropologists almost inevitably performed the same operations on the media that they criticized the media for performing on their host communities: they reduced a congeries of organizations, technologies, genres, legal and political structures, and systems of knowledge to a single, unified, institutionalized, and naturalized author ("the media") on whom responsibility for misrepresentation could be fixed.

In part because Marxian work is concerned with such issues of reification,[8] the Marxian concept of "mode of production" is a useful starting place for teasing out some of these issues. In Marx's work, mode of production is often used to define sweeping, "epochs in the economic formation of society" such as "Asiatic, ancient, feudal, and modern bourgeois" (Marx and Engels 1968: 182-183). Here I will use *mode of production* in a more practical, empirical sense, as it has been used by economic anthropologists and human ecologists studying productive activity among diverse communities.[9] In this restricted sense, a mode of production refers to the specific range of activities that simultaneously produces material goods and social relations in a defined social context. A mode of production consists of both the *means of production*, that is, the technologies, skills, and resources necessary for production, and of *relations of production*, which include not only the sociotechnical roles of the production situation such as directors, actors, writers, musicians, producers, and so forth, but also the ways these are distributed along lines of social distinction such as gender, age, education, class, caste, ethnicity, and so on. Means and relations of production are linked by forms of knowledge that include understandings about how social roles are attained, how skills are to be evaluated, what the essential nature of the product is, what constitutes success, and so forth. Any media text is thus seen as the product of a social order that is rooted in a particular, historically contingent political economy, and this particular political economy is linked to specific technologies which require capital to be created and skills to be put to use.

Some such notion of mode of production is necessary for any effort at cross-cultural analysis of mass media. Relations between the state, production centers, foreign funding sources and markets can be extremely complex. There is a world of difference between the market-oriented "studio system" of early Hollywood and the state-private-foreign hybrid system of contemporary China. Hollywood's mode of production was marked by a studio system that operated by means of a division of labor between sets of professionals whose roles were demarcated by contracts and the rules of powerful professional organizations (Powdermaker 1950). China operates between a state- sponsored film production system and a system of *auteurs* who seek foreign funding, and then negotiate with the state to produce films which may not be shown within China but circulate primarily in external markets (Yang 1993). Several different modes of production may coexist in parallel, at different scales of operation and toward different ends. Diawara (1994) describes the ways in which foreign capital, national boundaries and lack of wide distributive markets creates an auteur cinema in Africa whose films are watched primarily by diasporic and foreign audiences in search of multiculturalism, but not by the majority of African cinemagoers.

Different modes of production can operate in different ways even within national boundaries. The production of public television in the United States not only differs from commercial television, but television production within the Public Broadcasting System (Dornfeld 1998) differs also dramatically from public access, ethnic and minority television production (Naficy 1993; Shryock 2000). Ownership of media technologies, technical know-how and distribution of authority differ considerably in all of these cases, and are rarely stable but subject to change with changing economies and shifting political understandings *of* economies (Chopyak 1987; Öncü 1995).

Means of Production

An ethnography of production must inevitably engage with the media technologies precisely because media messages *are* mediated, and this mediation is accomplished through technologies. An argument can be (and has been) made that technology is *the* determinant feature of any social system.[10] Because of the scale and cost of many production technologies, centralized control over the means of production—whether wielded by the state or the corporation or some amalgam of the two— often appears inevitable. The power of the media to be dominating or affirmative might thus be seen as a consequence of the mode of production rather than the social organization of authorship. Cinema, radio, and television have tended to be one-way, monopolistic, and homogenizing, in part because the nature of their technology seems to lend itself to centralized control.

One of the most nuanced analyses to take this kind of position is Peter Manuel's 1993 study of cassette culture in India. Drawing on Enzenberger (1970), Manuel contrasts repressive *old media* with emancipatory *new media*—videotape, fax machines, personal computers, and cassette tapes. Whereas "old" mass media construct an inevitable separation between a small body of senders and a mass of anonymous receivers, these new media allow each consumer to also be a potential "producer."[11] This allows not only for increased feedback and interaction between senders and receivers, but also for decentralized programming and collective production. Such media are emancipatory in that they are resistant to monopoly and conducive to grassroots control and to diversity of content.[12]

Manuel argues that, historically, control of the means of production by five international recording companies was a key determinant of variety, responsiveness and creativity within the world music industry. The rise of cassette technology transformed the international music industry from its domination by the "big five" because its low production costs allowed niche groups access to recording technologies and also made possible large-scale pirating of music. This transformation can be seen as emancipatory insofar as it contributes to the "goals of local identity reassertion" and contributes to efforts to "revitalize community values, enhance local sociopolitical participation, offer greater diversity and richness of media content, and, in general, address the needs of small-scale communities, interest groups and taste cultures"

(Manuel 1993: 4). Conversely, the breakdown of centralized control over the mass media and the localization of content also allows the media to be used to "exacerbate antagonisms, weaken desirable forms of intergroup solidarity, and promote reactionary beliefs and oppressive practices by backward minorities" (1993: 4). The rise of a cassette culture in north India in the 1970s gives Manuel a place to examine both processes in detail.

The decentralization of media production that Manuel finds in India poses a crucial problem for the ethnographer. As early as 1950, media ethnographers found their task complicated by the fluidity of boundaries in sites of production. Powdermaker complained that Hollywood lacked the perfect isomorphism of people, place, and culture that were assumed by the functionalist methods she had learned from Malinowski, and which allowed her to study the village-dwelling people of the Micronesian island of Lesu as a bounded and coherent social system (Powdermaker 1950, 1966). As an ethnographic site, "Hollywood" was as much a cultural construction as any of the films made there. Yet even as a symbol, Hollywood is bound together into cohesive networks of people living and working within an area of a few hundred square miles.[13] Studies of new media require a reconsideration of the idea of a field site. One solution proposed has been the use of a "multi-sited" ethnography "designed around chains, paths, threads, conjunctions or juxtapositions of locations in which the ethnographer establishes some form of literal, physical presence, with an explicit, posited logic of association or connection among sites that in fact defines the argument of the ethnography" (Marcus 1998: 90). The ethnography produced can be literally multisited in that it describes several sites and the social relations and exchanges that link them. But it may also produce a kind of "hyper-sited" ethnography in that the place it describes is abstracted from the ethnographer's visits to multiple sites. In a sense, of course, this is true of any ethnography; the traditional village culture is, after all, abstracted from interviews and observations that took place within multiple sites where the ethnographer established his or her physical presence. But the problem is certainly made more obvious and urgent by the decentralization of reception common to mass media and by the decentralization of production associated with the new media. Thus, rather than a centralized locus of production like Hollywood, Manuel describes sets of semi-independent producers in multiple locations creating networks of artists and distributors. Binding these multiple networks is a decentralized cassette culture with its own codes and conventions that organizes production and consumption of music in north India.

Until the early 1970s, the Indian recording industry was dominated by India's powerful film industry. Recorded music accordingly took on much of the character of this largely escapist genre. Film and film music were controlled by an oligarchistic monopoly. This film music monopoly dominating the recording industry diminished many folk genres of musical performance and transformed others. Cassette technology came to India a decade or so behind much of the rest of the world, but boomed once it arrived. Initially, cassettes opened the way to music piracy—the production of cheap, local reproductions of both Indian film music and foreign music without payment of copyright fees. This was followed by collaborative production efforts and, finally, the emergence of localized music industries on several scales. In many cases, music piracy seems to have generated the capital that allowed cassette producers to expand into local markets with recordings of local performers of local musical styles and, eventually, to build large recording companies.[14]

Manuel examines the intersections of technology, economies, and genres in a series of accounts that illustrate the ways cassettes became vehicles for religious and traditional music, describing at the same time the way that the spread of cassette music often occurred at the expense of live performance. Picking up on Milton Singer's (1966, 1972) argument that mass media in India incorporates religious symbols, supplementing and sometimes replacing traditional modes of religious transmission such as ritual performance or personal relationship to a guru, Manuel points out that cassette technologies mean that such transitions are no longer obliged by the economies of scale of the old media to serve inevitably as homogenizing processes.[15]

As in other areas of the world, cassettes in India are not limited to music and the entertainment market but have also proven to be inexpensive and largely uncensorable media for sociopolitical expression. Women's movements, electoral campaigns, and regional and sectarian movements have all made use of cassettes for the production and dissemination of their messages.[16] This process is enhanced in India by a media culture in which melody is typically subordinated to the meanings of the words. Creating new songs out of old is thus not a form of postmodern play but part of a long-standing musical tradition involving different notions of authorship and ownership. Cassettes enable, reinforce, and transform the scale of this musical tradition.

Manuel's assessment of the Indian situation ultimately asks us to reconsider the relationship between technologies and social formations, to think beyond such simple dichotomies of "emancipatory" and "repressive." Transmission technologies may lead to monopolistic and monolithic production systems marked by homogenization, deculturation, and the creation of a mass audience that is easily manipulated by power structures, but they may also (and simultaneously) be linked to the building of consensus and shared values, the unification of diverse peoples, prosocial behavior, and mobilization toward shared goals. Conversely, the multicentric systems of production of the new media may promote pluralism, emancipation from state ideological oppression, and empower forms of political and social resistance to structures of power. At the same time, they open new possibilities for social fragmentation, hate-mongering, and factionalism. To examine the means of production is not, therefore, a deterministic activity. The technological forms of media both open up new possibilities *and* create new constraints. They may also introduce new metaphors for understanding sociotechnical relations. These media clearly do have the capacity to be transformative, but only in relation to existing social formations.

Relations of Production

Contemporary ethnographers of modes of media production are thus less likely to be attracted by technological or economic determinism than by the countervailing Marxian emphasis on human praxis—the notion that social actors are to be treated neither as passive objects pushed around by social and historical forces nor as free agents unconstrained by the world around them.[17] Relations of production are never simply given by the means of production; they are always active, practical activities geared toward human needs. The idea that social roles are determined by technologies—that a camera requires a trained cameraman, for example, and that such a role is distinct from a scenarist or a director—is itself a cultural myth that serves ideological functions, one of the most crucial being to mask the extent to which media production is a site of struggle. Struggles over means and relations of production are never merely technological; they involve issues of authorship, authority, and ownership. Indeed, the whole question of ownership of means of production is, in the production of media texts, intricately interwoven with notions of authorship and authority.

Social relations in media production are organized around *sociotechnical roles*. The production of any form of media involves a distribution of activities along various functional lines, involving differential access to, knowledge of, and control over the technologies of production. American television has its executive producers, producers, directors, actors, network executives, advertisers, cameramen, and so forth. Indian newspapers have their proprietors, editors, subeditors, senior editors, reporters, chief reporters, correspondents, special correspondents, *mofussil* ("provincial") correspondents, copytasters, *katibs* ("calligraphers"), photographers, ad salesman, advertising managers, and so forth. These roles offer a useful map of the political economy of production.

The map is not the territory, however. Roles describe functions and the lines of authority that connect them in an ideal-typical way, but actual circumstances alter from situation to situation, and they change over time. The relationship between means of production and relations of production is recursive. Changes in technology affect the organization of productive relations but not always in obvious or direct ways; the adaptation of new technologies is always itself mediated by preexisting social relations.

In India, for example, the subeditor was originally charged with editing and writing headlines for news stories for the page or pages for which he or she was responsible. With the rise of computer typesetting, many newspapers began to require subeditors to produce the layout of the pages for which they were responsible, on the grounds that they knew best how to cut stories to fit available space. While the computer made it possible for one man to do the job of two, the pressure of getting headlines and layouts arranged by deadline forced many subeditors to pay less attention to the editing aspect of their work. In turn, many newspapers that once carefully edited every article, came to increasingly rely on reporters to get the story written "right" the first time, even though reporters are under pressure to writing rapidly and meet deadlines. The result is a widely recognized failure of newspapers to meet former standards of English usage. Rather than recognizing the role of these changing sociotechnical relations, many editors and members of the public connect the decline in text style to a failure of the educational system to produce competent writers.

The first ethnography of media production, Hortense Powdermaker's *Hollywood: The Dream Factory* (1950) recognized the centrality of these sociotechnical roles of authorship. The book is accordingly organized around a set of key social roles in the production process, which together constitute a social system. Powdermaker's definition of a *social system* as "a complex coordinated network of mutually adapted patterns and ideas which control or influence the activities of its members" (1950: 3) sounds deterministic, but her actual ethnographic study of this system moves back and forth between "the system of production" and "the individuals who most influence movies" (9-10) to highlight their recursivity. For Powdermaker, an understanding of the society of movie makers is not to be found only in "a study of the locus of power and its exercise," but also "in the taboos which circumscribe all production, in the values as represented in goals, in historical and economic factors, and in the introduction of new technology and new ideas with resulting conflicts between old and new" (10).

The metaphor of the assembly line invoked by the book's title is crucial to Powdermaker's analysis of the social field in which movies are produced. The book explores sequentially "the manufacture of dreams" by examining the series of occupational roles that are involved in movie production—executive producers ("front office men"), producers, writers, directors, and actors—and discusses the way that each of these occupies a position in a social field marked by tensions between art and commerce.[18] Each position has its own tasks in the manufacture of commodified fantasies, and each of these is, in turn, marked by its own tensions, all of which seem to be transformations of an overarching symbolic opposition between art and commerce. Relations between the five key roles Powdermaker examines are marked by conflict, and because of this, the films produced are the results of struggles rather than cooperation and negotiation.

The ethnography recognizes the extent to which the situation she finds in the 1940s is the result of changing technologies, markets, and products. Powdermaker makes an effort to show how the current system arose as a result of shifts in technology and political economy. The role of the front office men arose from that of the professional showmen who made their fortunes at the dawn of the film industry when people would pay simply for the novelty of moving pictures. Writers and directors became necessary as audience tastes grew more sophisticated and as film stories grew more complex. Producers, as intermediaries between directors and front office men, emerged when silent movies gave way to more expensive and technologically complex sound pictures, which required someone to oversee the connections between technical and aesthetic production.

The particular production structure that Powdermaker found in Hollywood was undergirded by an economic system that combined astonishingly high wages with an almost feudal contract system. This permitted the people controlling budgets—front office men and producers—to exert disproportionate control over motion picture content, even when they could establish little or no reasonable ground for their judgments. Indeed, most of Powdermaker's interviews included tales in which her informants described the arbitrariness of decisions during the production process. Yet all those involved in the production process also have various modes of resistance or negotiation. The end result is that while power and agency operate at various levels and in various ways, no one individual has any real authorial control over films. These tensions are articulated by participants through a discourse that explains people and their actions in terms of commitments to "art" or "commerce." At the same time, status, wealth, and continued employment in Hollywood are determined by the success of the films, a success that cannot be explained or predetermined by any knowledge possessed by the filmmakers. The people of Hollywood handle the complexity and uncertainty of their world by attributing successes and failures to "the breaks," which Powdermaker describes as a form of "magical thinking" à la Malinowski (1953).

The weakest part of Powdermaker's argument is her linking of the social structure of movie production to movie content. She reduces social agency to the imposition of "personalities" or "individual egos" on filmmaking through a process of arbitrary decision making. Her argument is that in the absence of any generally accepted artistic or technical theory for determining what audiences want and how to give it to them, movie-making simply becomes a series of personality conflicts in which people occupying various social positions vis-à-vis one another seek to exert their own wills at the expense of others. Powdermaker writes:

> In the usual Hollywood production of movies, the quality of the movie is much less important than the assertion of the ego of any individual. When the executive insists on cutting a picture so that the motivation of the leading characters is lost, when he refuses to pay any attention to a director's idea about casting, when the star demands that her footage be increased and that of a minor character cut, when the producer dominates a writer or writers, insisting on carrying out his own ideas, good or bad, when the director refuses to listen to suggestions of a gifted actor about his role, when talented people are fired because they threaten the power of someone higher up—then, of course, it is the movie which goes to pot. (1950: 296)

Contemporary readers are likely to find Powdermaker's psychologism clumsy and not very convincing. Her profiles of individuals inhabiting various positions in the production process are useful in illustrating the different strategies that people employ in adapting to the social organization she has described, but the pseudonyms she ascribes to them— "Mr. Big Shot," "Mr. Kowtow," "Miss Successful," "Mr. Intelligent," and so forth—make ridiculous stereotypes of what are actually sometimes fairly nuanced composite character descriptions.[19]

Powdermaker concludes by attempting to situate her analysis within a larger social framework. Arguing that the United States is a land in which many different ideologies compete for hegemony, she claims that

> Hollywood represents totalitarianism. Its basis is economic rather than political but its philosophy is similar to that of the totalitarian state. In Hollywood, the concept of man as a passive creature to be manipulated extends to those who work for the studios, to personal and social relationships, to the audiences in the theaters and to the characters in the movies. The basic freedom of being able to choose between alternatives is absent. The gifted people who have the capacity for choice cannot exercise it; the executives who technically have the freedom of choice do not actually have it, because they usually lack the knowledge and imagination necessary for making such a choice. Much behavior is compulsive, springing from fears, hidden and open. The careful planning and good judgment of the exceptional people have been already described and are in dramatic contrast to the hysterical behavior of the others. (Powdermaker 1950: 327)

Many successful members of the Hollywood production system imagine their audiences "as suckers whose emotional needs and anxieties can be exploited for profit" (329).[20] As a result, the ideology of totalitarianism "is not limited to human relationships in Hollywood, but is reflected in many movies. Life, success or misfortune is usually portrayed as caused by luck or an accident. Only rarely does a movie show the process of becoming successful or the process of disintegration" as a result of life choices (328-329).

Powdermaker is thus arguing that Hollywood, as a production community, is an overelaboration of social trends present elsewhere in America in less fully articulated forms. In turn, the film industry generates via movies story worlds that express and elaborate on its own internal social system. Insofar as people accept and internalize the worldview of the movies—which Powdermaker does not see as an automatic process[21]—the country may come more and more to resemble Hollywood. While this is far too simple a chain of causality to be convincing, it does draws attention to the fact that modes of production are cultures or subcultures that constitute part—but only part—of the lifeworlds of those who work in them. Technological roles are never merely enacted; they are struggled over, negotiated, and reimagined. These struggles employ various cultural conceptualizations (such as authorship) in carrying out these struggles over identity.

The Field of Production

Studies of modes of production reveal that media producers work within a complex network of relations between various institutions and agencies that have various kinds and degrees of power over aspects of media production. A second method of ethnography of media production involves focusing on this network as an ongoing construction of the social actors working in it: a field of production. Such a field has its own autonomous logic, and its own signifying systems according to which producers ascribe values to things in the field. These fields are sites of struggles not only over the meaning of the text but many other things: money, status, pleasure, fantasy, identity, authority, and so forth. Pierre Bourdieu describes the objects of struggle in a field of cultural production as capital: economic, social, linguistic, and symbolic. The positions of various social actors in the field is determined by the kinds of capital they possess. Struggles occur as "the occupants of these positions seek, individually or collectively, to safeguard or improve their position and to impose the principle of hierarchization most favorable to their own products" (Bourdieu and Wacquant 1992: 101). This "imposition" involves the ability of some agent or agents to dominate the field by defining what will count as valuable within a given field (particularly, as I argued above, what shall count as authorship). That is, by controlling what counts as valuable, dominant social agents can induce others to struggle over rewards within a system that already favors their position. Once established, such a dominant position becomes *orthodox*; it is the system of values according to which people measure their own success and competence, and against which people rebel. Establishing one's own position as orthodox is not the endgame, however; domination is always incomplete. Defining an orthodox position never completely suppresses the heterodox positions that various agents seek to promote as a new orthodoxy.

Media producers, as social actors in the field, find that certain kinds of actions (those established as orthodox) are valued and rewarded while others are unrewarded or censured. Through this, they build up a sense of habits and predispositions toward certain kinds of actions and against others. While actors often take note of their own positions and attempt to strategize about what actions will best serve them, more often they act according to their life experience, that is, to the internalized and largely unconscious sense of how things are, which they have acquired through their life experience. The field of production is thus constituted by their habitual actions, even as their habitual actions constitute the field as a meaningful place, with sense and value enough to make worthwhile the investment of one's energies.

One advantage of such an approach (whether or not we adopt Bourdieu's particular language for it) is that it allows us to look at social actors not simply as *occupying* specific roles but as *struggling* over them, even as they struggle over creating a text. When a director in Hollywood, for example, seeks to assert his control over writers and actors, he does so by invoking not only his own hierarchical position but his personal track record of success, claims about how things are supposed to be done, and claims about what audiences want (often referring to other films that are similar and dissimilar to the one currently in production). The director's success or failure in marshaling such symbolic, cultural, and social resources has effects not only for his or her future work, but for those of other directors working with these writers and actors. Social actors can also operate collectively, as in a guild for example.

Studying the social field demands the ethnographer's presence in everyday practices of media production. Observing the kinds of authority marshaled during particular moments of struggle gives the ethnographer a knowledge of the kinds of capital valued in the field; observing the successes and failures of various forms of capital gives the ethnographer an understanding of the relative weight of these various forms of capital and of the relations of authority and subordination that run between the various positions in the field.

Any field of media production is thus organized around two domains that mutually construct one another. At one level, there is the primary domain of media production that brings together the social actors into the particular network and set of relations required to construct texts. At a second level is the set of issues at stake in the field for the actors *as* persons (as opposed to roles in the productive system): wealth, status, power, pleasure, identity. Linking these two domains is a complex web of signification involving not only technical skills and knowledge, but ethics (what interpretation/representation is *right?*), aesthetics (what interpretation/representation is *correct?*), and audience (what interpretation/representation do consumers *need* or *desire?*).

Recognizing that there is a web of signification defining the values that will count in a particular field is important. Values and meanings never merely serve to rationalize and justify relations of production; they also crosscut them, creating opportunities to challenge, redefine, and argue about how things out to be done. The concept of the social field gives us a metaphor for talking about the network of social relations in which media production takes place. It lets us turn our attention from the specificities of roles as functions within the organization of media production and to ask what *else* goes on within, around, and through the relations between men and women occupying these roles. The goal is to be able to describe the ways in which authority and power are negotiated as actors pursue their own ends within a particular social configuration. This involves neither reducing the structure to modes of production by exposing how things are "really" done (according to a set of values already held by the analyst) nor reducing the structure to a set of roles and functions in the ideational world described by media producers themselves. A description of the "fields" of media production should describe the sets of values that bound the field. It is through and around such sets of values that relations of production, and particularly relations of power and authority, are negotiated.

Central to this kind of analysis is the recognition that media production is always a site of struggle over what the meaning of the text is to be and, further, that this struggle is, for participants, never only about the text but always also about power, status, wealth, and identity. Relations of production are roles in a system of text production, but these roles are always occupied by people engaged in struggles over salaries, authority, promotion, self-worth, recognition, and power. These struggles are articulated through systems of values—appeals to aesthetics, ethics, rules, tastes, and so forth. Descriptions of fields of media production are descriptions of the systems in which agents engage in contestation and negotiation over authorship and audience in order to simultaneously construct texts and identities.

One exemplary work that deals with struggles over identity in a field of media production is Mark Pedelty's ethnographic account of war correspondents in El Salvador, *War Stories* (1995). The impetus for his project is similar to that of many sociological studies of the press: to discover why accounts of the world produced by a supposedly free press are overdetermined in ways that privilege the U.S. state and American corporations. This question is raised again and again in many different settings by social scientists studying the press because in American media culture, the press is mythologized as a key democratic institution, providing information and attention that allows Americans to consciously assent or dissent to their government's uses of their collective power. The press is celebrated in public discourse, fiction, movies, and other collective representations as "the Fourth estate," whose role is to watchdog the three branches of government. The media's broad powers to intrude into the private lives of citizens are partly rooted in this conception. Against this public mythos, Pedelty argues that in coverage of foreign affairs, there is little question that the news media tend to generate a single orthodox perspective on events; in El Salvador this monological perspective is the attribution of the nation's ills to an endemic and naturalized "culture of violence."

Pedelty argues that this overdetermination of content cannot be reduced to censorship if this is understood simply in terms of a dominating institutional structure. Instead, he favors an approach that allows us to see how agents subordinate themselves so as to produce these patterned accounts of violence. He describes a press corps in El Salvador as a field of social action organized by six "disciplinary apparatuses" (1995: 5): patterns of military control and organized violence, the hierarchical social organization of the press corps, relations with news sources, production culture (myths and rituals), discourse patterns, and the organizational structures of news media. Pedelty's term "disciplinary apparatuses" represents a fusion of Foucaultian and Marxian notions of power. From Foucault he borrows the recognition that power is essentially productive (of pleasure, of knowledge, of discourse) rather than simply repressive. In this view, social actors discipline themselves in order to produce valued goods and services (such as media texts) and to simultaneously produce the rewards—pay, promotion, notoriety, identity, fantasy—that derive from their action. Power "needs to be considered as a productive network which runs through the whole social body" (Foucault 1984b: 60), and thus produces disciplinary regimes. At the same time, Pedelty recognizes that while networks of power may run through the social body, in any given field of production there are powerful institutional forces at work that act as agents through which disciplinary practices operate to overdetermine particular knowledges and discourses. Pedelty thus links the notion of discipline with Louis Althusser's notion of "industrial state apparatuses" (Althusser 1972) in an effort to emphasize the extent to which "the 'social body' contains nodal centers, hierarchies of control and specialization" (Pedelty 1995: 6). Such apparatuses authorize and legitimate productive practices, both those of the texts and those of the awards that accrue from them.[22]

As Bourdieu says, to understand what a journalist writes, it is necessary to understand his or her place in the journalistic field: the status of the newspaper for which the journalist writes (and hence the authority with which he or she speaks and asks questions), the journalist's specific competence in the writing technologies privileged within the field, the position of the journalist within the sets of roles within the newspaper, and the history of the journalist's prior relations with the social actors he or she is constituting as sources (1998). Pedelty offers a careful delineation of these sets of relations through ethnographic fieldwork among war correspondents in El Salvador. The journalist exists in a hierarchy based on the overall prestige of the newspaper for which he or she works, a position that affects relations with military officials who control movements, and elite sources who control the quotes that are essential to newswriting. One's competence as a writer is determined by how well one can discipline one's self to the constraints of a highly specific journalistic form. This form, with its emphasis on authoritative voices, mimetic language (particularly quotation), and the need for "balance" requires journalists to establish and maintain particular kinds of relationships with sources. Ultimately, to successfully produce "objective" news that is acceptable to editors back home requires journalists to establish and maintain the cooperation of a series of authorities.

Pedelty is particularly effective at capturing the sense with which the cultural identities of American journalists are bound up with organized systems of authority. For the journalists he covered, *being* a war correspondent involved a certain epic identity accompanied by a particularly high status within journalism. But being a war correspondent requires employment, and employment requires a journalist to file stories acceptable to an editor—that is, meeting formal standards of newsworthiness, objectivity, and timeliness. The pleasure, fantasy, and status that come with one's identity as an independent, tough-minded investigator of abuses of power thus depend on one's authorization by (and subordination to) an organization with bureaucratized routines and practices, and hierarchies of gatekeepers.

In addition to the ongoing discipline produced by interactions with institutional gatekeepers, American journalists arrive in El Salvador already disciplined in one sense: they have learned the appropriate ways of constructing news stories according to American discursive structures of balance, objectivity, and fairness. This journalistic practice can be turned against reporters by bureaucratic systems: the embassy can control access to elite sources whose comments are necessary to a balanced story; the military can delay safe-conduct passes or confiscate film and equipment for violation of arbitrary and mutable regulations (and thus reduce the authority the reporter derives from being where the news happens). Since the American style of "objective journalism" denies journalists the opportunity to describe the conditions of their information gathering, no trace of these manipulations appears in most final stories.

What is particularly compelling about Pedelty's approach is that war correspondents, as social actors, are not reduced by a putative process of socialization through the beliefs and rituals of journalistic practice into mere vehicles that provide "officials a place to elaborate interpretive webs as part of a negotiating and signaling process" (Schudson 1987). On the contrary, they are active agents who, with various degrees of resistance, cynicism, or acquiescence, submit themselves to a system that allows them to do work they find compelling and satisfying, a system that authorizes and validates their identities as members of a select breed of cosmopolitan adventurers.

A key problem in the social description of media production involves the description of those social fields that overlap and intersect with the primary fields of media production. In Pedelty's ethnography, for example, "the editors" are ever-present agents of discipline with whom reporters routinely interact by phone, fax, and telex, but they are far from El Salvador and from Pedelty's field site, and we see them only through the accounts of the reporters in El Salvador. While their decisions have tremendous consequences for the correspondents back in El Salvador, and Pedelty does a solid job of representing how they act as agents of discipline on reporters, these editors make decisions based on their own positions within fields organized by *different* sets of disciplinary apparatuses, which are not apparent to us. Even more crucial to Pedelty's ethnography is the work of the United States State Department. In El Salvador, the embassy exerts enormous pressure on reporters, since "balanced" reporting requires quotations from them. The disciplinary apparatuses through which their actions can be understood remain largely unexplored, and embassy staff are reduced to mere agents of their own institutions.

This is a problem because media production thus takes place not only within *a* social field but within a constellation of fields that can be described together as comprising "media worlds," on the model of Howard S. Becker's "art worlds" (1976, 1982, 1990, 1996). Becker defines an "art world" as a structure of cooperative activities necessary for "art" to happen. All art works, he says,

> involve the cooperation of everyone whose activity has anything to do with the end result. That includes the people who make materials, instruments, and tools; the people who create the financial arrangements that make the work possible; the people who see to distributing the works that are made; the people who produced the tradition of forms, genres, and styles the artist works with and against; and the audience. For symphonic music, the list of cooperating people might include composers, players, conductors, instrument makers and repairers, copyists, managers and fundraisers, designers of symphony halls, music publishers, booking agents, and audiences of various kinds. For contemporary painting, an equivalent list would include painters, makers and purveyors of canvases, paints, and similar materials, collectors, art historians, critics, curators, dealers, managers and agents, such auxiliary personnel as, say, lithographic printers, and so on. (Becker 1990: 69)

Work is needed to explore ethnographically the ways in which such support industries serve as integral parts of the mode of production and sites where relations of production are forged and reforged. Historical studies of media since the mid 1990s have increasingly been looking at labor, class, and subsidiary industries,[23] as has some recent work in anthropology, sociology and cultural studies. The merchandizing of media figures (Simensky, Bryer, and Wilkof 1999), the role of international distribution of film in local economies (Vitalis 2000), the flow of international capital in movie funding (Caton 1999), the policing of trademarks (Coombe 1998), the creation of image industries (like Elvis impersonators), the evolution of satellite TV "routes" (Price 1999), and similar institutions and activities supporting and enabling media production are attracting the attention of anthropologists and mass communication scholars. These fields overlap, support, and make possible the media industries, while existing as derivative industries and subcultural systems in themselves.

Many of these subsidiary and support industries may act as interpretive intermediaries—"cultural brokers"—serving as a crucial part of the interpretive process. Japanese film and television producers coming to Egypt for location shooting employ local professionals who scout locations, find local talent, arrange for translators, and find food and lodging for production crews. In performing these tasks, these agencies mediate the experiences that Japanese writers, directors, actors and producers have in Egypt, and so influence the ways that Egypt is represented.[24] Similar observations can be made of lawyers, publicity agents, translators, franchisers, marketers, and others whose work provides part of the context within which production proceeds. Linking the fields that form "worlds" of media production will prove a complex but necessary step in media ethnography, whether it proceeds through multi-sided ethnography or through theorists linking and synthesizing the work of several ethnographers.

Laboring in the Fields

There is a third approach to the analysis of media production: the detailed description of the acts through which media texts are negotiated. This project is not dissimilar to the preceding one, but its focus shifts. Rather than focusing on the structure of the field and the nature of the disciplinary apparatuses by which agency is organized and ordered, this approach involves focusing on agency in the immediate situation. Such an approach allows us to examine creativity and interpretation as they are played out in both the social and textual dimensions. This framework focuses on interpretive practice: media producers interpret the social world during the act of representing it, and they do this by interpreting the social contexts through which they apprehend the world they are representing. It is out of these interpretive practices that the regularities perceived by media sociology as structures emerge. This approach assumes that interpretive creativity is not random but both constituted by and constitutive of social heuristics and cultural epistemologies. By social heuristics, I mean routines, procedures, and concepts that are part of the professional knowledge of the media producer, and which assist him or her in the process of interpreting the world so that it can be represented. By cultural epistemologies, I mean specific ways of knowing things associated with particular practices. What American journalists call objectivity, for example, is a cultural way of knowing, a set of assumptions about what constitutes valid knowledge and how such knowledge is to be obtained. Epistemologies and heuristics are crucial aspects of a media producer's professional competence.

Competence and Biography

Close attention to individual agency in the production process leads us to the complex problems of competence and biography. Competence here refers to the capacity of social actors to use their cultural knowledge in appropriate and effective ways. Competence is a tricky issue for social science, and especially for anthropology, which seeks not only to emphasize social rather than individual aspects of cultural action but also aims to be relativistic in its approach. Yet competence is a crucial issue in fields of production. First, there are local codes of competence that need to be teased out. Second, within fields of production, there are hierarchical rankings of actors based on how others in the field evaluate their competence according to these codes. Third, there are institutional authorities that help determine these hierarchies. Finally, there are the strategies by which people demonstrate their competence and hence alter or reproduce their positions in the field.

Competences are tied to biography, which refers not only to the unique life trajectory of an individual, but to the ways these trajectories are articulated as narratives. Successes and failures, by whatever standards these are measured, are remembered by participants in the social field and employed as evidence of competence. Creating a biography that will be known to audiences, agents, casting directors, and others is part of one's cultural capital in many fields of media production, which is why billing, bylines, and other markers of authorship are worth struggling over. At the same time, actors have genuine skills and talents which they bring to bear on the production of media texts, and which often provide them with a very real sense of accomplishment. Biography thus yields two levels of data. On the one hand, there are the actual skills, talents, and techniques learned and used by particular actors in the course of their life trajectories; on the other, there is the way these life trajectories, in the narrative form of biographies or biographical anecdotes, are marshaled as capital.

Although anthropology has long made use of the life history as a form of data, it has usually been treated as a form of case study (e.g. Shostak 1981) or as a resource from which more formal data can be derived (Agar and Hobbs 1985). Although either of these approaches could be useful in the study of production, to serve as a description of agency in media production, such an effort would need to tie the life history to the agent's movements across changing fields of production while avoiding the pitfall of tying meaning to intentionality. A starting place for such an effort is offered by Merleau-Ponty's phenomenological account of the interplay between Cézanne's art, his life history and his changing perceptions of the world (Merleau-Ponty 1977). Merleau-Ponty's strength is in seeing Cézanne's work and the "accidents" of his life history, as mutually constitutive. What is missing from Merleau-Ponty's analysis is a recognition that such "accidents" are shaped by larger social and cultural forces (Dolgin, Kemnitzer, and Schneider 1977). The closest thing to this sort of social biography is perhaps one of Caton's multiple "readings" of *Lawrence of Arabia*, in which he examines the tensions between the life trajectories—both personal and professional—of the writers and director and the specific mode of production, especially its international scope, in terms of the text produced (1999: 63-99). Yet another (somewhat less theorized) model might be

Virginia Danielson's 1997 social biography of the Egyptian singer Umm Kulthum, in which the accumulation of skills and knowledge and the social construction of a public biography are presented as recursive processes taking place within a shifting field of public tastes, entertainment technologies, and social life.

Interpretive Practice

More fully realized are studies that use ethnography of the situations of production to explore the interpretive practices of agents as they negotiate authorship and representation. By *interpretive practice*, I mean "the ways that routine procedures, cultural categories and social positions come together in particular 'instances' of interpretation" (Beeman and Peterson 2001). Media producers are always engaged in practices of interpretation that precede and order their practices of representation. The selection of what will or will not be included in a media representation, and how a particular representation will be entextualized, whether as a narrative film, a news article, or a comic book, is an interpretive task. So is the process of deciding what an audience wants, desires, or needs, and what effect a particular text should have on an audience. By focusing on the particular activities engaged in by a defined set of agents to produce specific texts, ethnographers seek to examine practice in media production without either reducing it to a structural epiphenomenon or reifying it as monological, authoritative and transparent.

As a methodology, the analysis of interpretive practice builds on recent work involving intersections between discourse analysis (Bauman and Briggs 1990; Silverstein and Urban 1996), the ethnography of communication (Hymes 1977), performance studies (Bauman 1977, 1986), and social poetics (Herzfeld 1997), all of which begin from the description and analysis of concrete situations (with particular attention to the details of language) to understand larger social and cultural processes. This way of analyzing media turns our attention from the structures that organize action to the contingency that is always present in media production and the specific momentary, negotiated processes by which agency is employed to challenge, change or reproduce structure. This approach seeks to talk about media producers as cultural actors like anyone else, but without evading issues of power and domination.

Interpretive practice focuses on situations rather than on the social field as a whole, in the certainty that much will be revealed in the details of interaction. As described by Beeman and Peterson (2001), interpretive practice rests on four points:

1.   it involves the assumption that interpreters exist within an operational epistemology and heuristic action framework;

2. it requires that we see interpreters in active interaction with the community in which they operate at several levels of social involvement;

3. it assumes that interpreters have practical, pragmatic, and even perlocutionary goals in the exercise of their interpretations; and

4. finally, it assumes that their interpretive work is susceptible to the social forces within which it is contextualized—economic, political, and cultural.

Operational Frameworks

Media production involves making authoritative representations— about the world, about audiences, about how things are—and the truth- fulness or reasonableness of these representations rests both on the cultural epistemologies that producers share with other members of their wider social worlds and on the authoritative procedures for con- structing representation that can turn the contingency and ambiguity of the production process into predictable routines and believable frame- works. In their account of United States newspaper accounts of legal and illegal immigrants, Coutin and Chock (1995) argue against seeing journalists simply as nodes of institutional structures in favor of view- ing them as social actors like any others: like any American faced with ambiguity and contradiction, they draw on widely distributed American systems of knowledge to figure out what's going on. Faced with a new law that disrupts the widely shared American dichotomy between legal and illegal immigrants, journalists locate and construct a new dichotomy—between illegal immigrants deserving of United States citi- zenship and those undeserving—and make this the basis of their repre- sentation. Culture is understood here as widely distributed systems of symbols through which people make sense of the world in order to ori- ent themselves, construct identities, and communicate with others. Media producers necessarily draw on these same symbolic systems in order for the representations they create to be meaningful.

Focusing primarily on the representations themselves, Coutin and Chock are unable to examine the situated actions through which jour- nalists engage in this kind of cultural mediation—the kinds of heuristics and logics specific to journalists that organize their practices and allow them to perform these tasks as symbolic mediators. Unlike "ordinary" social actors, media producers never only interpret the world but must always do so in ways that allow them to represent it. In this view, media producers are like the epic singers described by Lord (1960) as per- forming patterned acts of creation. Engaged in ongoing, improvisatory production of texts, they draw on a professional knowledge of narrative patterns, tropes, frames, and formulas to construct and reconstruct accounts for particular kinds of audiences. The cultural epistemologies they draw on exist in tension with the heuristics, routines, and habitual practices by which they commit interpretation to representation. In describing how AIDS became a story in India in 1992, I paid attention to the ways Indian journalists struggled to fit the new story into their standard frames for writing about the world. After a brief period of experimentation, journalists found ways to frame the story in familiar ways. Underlying this analysis is the notion that widely distributed systems of knowledge that media producers, as members of a society, share with others, exist in a dynamic relationship with sets of heuristics for handling the contingency, ambiguity, and unpredictability of media production (M. Peterson 1998).

Because of this, epistemological and heuristic frameworks often serve not only to organize interpretive action but also often to mystify the interpretive process as it happens. In American political journalism, off-the-record discourse allows a space in which the meaning of events can be negotiated between reporters and their sources in a concealed manner. Since off-the-record discourse is "unwriteable," sources can offer reporters tips, assessments, flattery, suggestions, and directives without fear that their words will be reproduced. The absence of quotation in off-the-record discourse thus enables dialogism and negotiation while concealing the extent to which journalistic practices are co-constructed between journalists and sources. The concealment of the extent to which journalism's discovery procedures are negotiated is necessitated by *objectivity*, which is simultaneously an epistemological and an operational concept. As the former, it is part of American common sense, a "folk epistemology, conceiving of 'the truth' as being singular, unequivocal, and semantically transparent once it has been identified" (Briggs 1986). The notion of objectivity insists that there is "a world of objects out there apart from experience of them, a world of things that are real and can be known, as opposed to things which are merely believed or felt. News stories are factual insofar as they accurately map the object-world to which they refer" (M. Peterson 2001: 208). This is operationalized by objectivity as "a personal stance toward the world of objects. To know the object world, one must put aside one's own feelings, beliefs and interests so that one can 'see things' objectively in order to produce factual accounts" (M. Peterson 2001: 208). Together, these form a logic that can be applied to a multitude of situations, generating a variety of activities and meanings but which requires journalists to conceal from their accounts the extent to which these meanings are socially negotiated.

Other genres of media draw on other kinds of heuristics. For producers of narrative films and television shows, what the audience *wants* often becomes crucially important, and struggles are likely to take place over who gets to define the audience (and hence the text). Although the mapping of demographics to frameworks of reception is a dubious practice sociologically, from the perspective of media producers, whose wealth, status, and knowledge are on the line, it greatly reduces anxieties. Painter (1996) demonstrates how the general cultural understanding that there are fairly coherent kinds of people becomes operationalized into written guidelines describing audience types. At Japan's ZTV, professional women seek to degender themselves so as to fit smoothly within the seniority system; certainly they don't position themselves as (and thus speak for) the *shufu* ("housewives") who make up the primary audience. Instead, the research department constructed a set of six categories of housewives, from "broad-minded, almighty housewife" to "tranquil and prudent housewife," based on degrees of assertiveness in society and in the domestic sphere. Such heuristic devices combine with other assumptions (many of them extremely denigrating) that producers have about their audiences to produce particular telerepresentations of gender.

Social Involvement

The fact that media production involves co-narrative and dialogic elements leads to attention to the ways in which interpretive and representational practices are embedded in broader social activities. Journalists, advertising executives, filmmakers, and other media producers are all deeply engaged throughout the production process in all manner of other social activities. Like Coutin and Chock's journalists, they are engaged in making sense of the world in general, and the sense they make of it affects their creation of representations of it. Davila describes the ways in which the actors in Puerto Rico's popular *El Kiosko Budweiser* drew on their own working-class urban backgrounds to construct characters who are widely recognizable types. The actors further exploit local social issues to create carnivalesque portrayals, criticisms, and reversals of "the dynamics of contemporary Puerto Rican society" (Davila 1998: 465). Her focus on the improvisatory nature of the show, and the roles of the actors in the production process allows her to describe the program not as offering a single unitary message but rather an "amalgam" of meanings.

Several studies have sought to describe the ways in which the relationship between fields of production and the other social fields with which they are interconnected can be complex and recursive. In a study of "Western" and "Eastern" identities among German journalists, Dominic Boyer examines how everyday social knowledge, the professional knowledge of the field of media production, and the knowledge entextualized in the representations they produce "co-elaborate one another" (2001: 460). Easterners are conceived as particular kinds of people whose writing is shaped by their origin in the former communist state of East Germany. Critical writing by Easterners about German economics and politics are dismissed as sour grapes or ingratitude, while positive writing about these subjects is dismissed as a learned submissiveness to authority. Unable to stake out positions in these most prestigious genres of writing, Easterners tend to move into cultural and social writing, reproducing a belief that these are the kinds of things Easterners are best at. Westerners' experiences of this in the newsroom confirms for them the validity of their own beliefs about the differences between Westerners and Easterners, and hence authorizes them to continue to write authoritatively about the essential characteristics of East and West.

This process is repeated in many sites of media production, centered around distinctions of gender, age, race, and other salient categories. In this view, the same recursive process by which media and other forms of professional knowledge create social/cultural identities in public culture occurs in the microlevel of the media workplace. Media producers enact culturally constructed distinctions between categories of person, essentializing in their everyday professional practice the same categories they reproduce in the texts they write. Thus society at large and the microsociety of media producers come to mirror one another.

Ends and Goals

Media production, then, clearly involves the same kinds of noisy, demanding, contestation and negotiation found in other forms of social interaction. The social actors engaged by and with interpretive practices enter into this dialogic activity from different social positions and with different practical goals. They seek, within the constraints of their knowledge and practical competence, to articulate, entertain, order, persuade, authorize, educate, inform, and limit possible interpretations in pursuit of their own practical ends. The resulting contestations and cooperations reveal asymmetries among participants seeking mastery over the entextualization process.

These goals are not easily predictable. They do not always derive from positions in the field of media production but may arise from other positions in other, intersecting fields or from other parts of an actor's life history, as in the editor of a Washington, DC-based newspaper whose instructions to a reporter were fed less by the immediate contingencies of the story than by state political implications, structures in which his family had political interests (M. Peterson 2001). Tad Ballew

(2001) explores the complexity of goals and outcomes in a many-layered account of Chinese television producers' efforts to construct a commercial for their program, which had not yet aired. The program sought to bring classical Chinese opera to the rural masses. Members of the production staff sought to position it through advertisements showing "rural" people claiming to greatly enjoy the program. The persons they enlist in their project—a vice-chairman of a worker's association, factory workers, laborers in a rice field—all have goals of their own, ranging from *guanxi* (networking) to publicity-seeking to cash, which cross and intersect with the motivations of producers who desire to use these participants as representatives of "rurals".

Understanding goals and intentions thus requires us to distinguish between primary and secondary levels. At the primary level, media producers seek to entertain, educate, persuade, enlighten, amuse, inform, and so forth through their texts. Struggle at the primary level is both over the goals themselves—"is our purpose to educate or to entertain?"—and also over the ways in which these goals are to be operationalized. At the secondary level, we need to see media producers as social actors whose work in a field of media production does not bar them from the same goals as actors in other social fields: raising status, increasing wealth, affirming identity, fulfilling fantasies, pursuing pleasure, and so forth. Struggles at the primary level are always at least partially shaped by struggles at the secondary level, although these struggles are rarely glimpsed in the texts produced. Indeed, in industrialized media production, the masking of pursuits at the secondary level is a standard part of the work.

Economic, Political and Cultural Contexts

All of the interpretative practices described here occur within complexes of overlapping social fields, of which the most ubiquitous are the market and the state. The focus of interpretive practice on agency does not by any means presuppose resistance to power, or suggest that the dynamics of quotidian creative action is not subject to political, economic, or other social and cultural constraints. Indeed, many of those I've cited above emphasized the extent to which the apparent contingency, contestation, and negotiation produce or reproduce structures of power. Thus the ways that off-the-record discourse is employed by sources favors "professional sources" like trained press officers over other sorts of actors, even while concealing their place in the production process (M. Peterson 2001). Davila emphasizes that while *El Kiosko Budweiser* "provides a space for social criticism and reversals of hierarchy" it does so "always within the dominant parameters sustaining colonial Puerto Rican society" (1998). And Ballew (2001) emphasizes that the representation of "rural" China by the Rural Channel take place in the context of a post-Mao, post-Communist proliferation of meanings and identities, especially regarding such entities as "rural," "urban," "modern," and "backward."

Perhaps the most complete ethnography of media production to attempt to include these many levels is Barry Dornfeld's *Producing Public Television, Producing Public Culture* (1998), which examines the negotiation of authorship in the production of a documentary series for America's Public Broadcasting System (PBS). Dornfeld was a researcher and production assistant for the seven-part documentary series, *Childhood*. As such, he had intimate access to the workings of the highest level of production work. Hierarchy at PBS is complicated by the fact that the system is a fairly loose affiliation of stations, and that production usually involves "co-production" between several different production companies, in this case WNET New York, Channel Four/London and Antelope Films, with different goals and different financial and technical commitments to the project. Authorial negotiations take place within a hierarchical social organization, but one constituted less by organizational mandates than by specific competences (tied to professional biographies) and differential control over limited budgets.

One of the most interesting insights in Dornfeld's ethnography is that there are several loci of negotiation. Prominent among these is the context of "poetics" in which understandings of the documentary genre and specifically of the documentary series for which PBS is known, are defined and redefined. Content gets negotiated as producers and directors employ various forms of authority, from appeals to budgetary limitations, to epistemologies of objectivity, to traditions of representation, to aesthetics, to personal experience. Linking many of these are discourses about audience needs and desires. Producers refer again and again to audiences to justify particular creative or technical choices. Yet the relationships between the producers and these audiences is likewise a point of negotiation; since PBS audiences are supposed at once to be both educated and entertained, producers shift positions back and forth between suggesting what audiences will want to see and what they should see.

Dornfeld makes us privy to several sets of negotiations, and summarizes other sets of decisions for us. These reveal the ways in which processes of media production are intertwined with larger cultural discourses about selves and others, which become reproduced in various ways. Because the series *Childhood* sought to compare and contrast human development across boundaries of time and space, producers inevitably draw on not only the production cultures described above but on their personal conceptions of history, or culture, of biology and the ways these are entailed in difference and universality. These understandings of how the world works necessarily intersect with and inform the more specifically professional poetic, aesthetic, and technical discourses.

None of these negotiations take place apart from social, political, and economic considerations. Running as a backdrop throughout the production are a series of tensions about the way this program will fit into the shifting position of PBS in American society. *Childhood* was produced at a time when the idea of public-supported broadcasting was under increasing fire from politicians and for-profit competitors creating a perceived "need" for PBS to broaden its audience. Meanwhile, the unprecedented success of the PBS series *The Civil War* created a new benchmark for PBS against which future productions such as *Childhood* were measured, culminating in a kind of "blockbuster" mentality (Dornfeld 1998: 178). The commitment to education became increasingly tempered by a commitment to capturing unusually large (for PBS) percentages of the Nielsen ratings. Success or failure as so measured becomes part of the professional biographies of the producers, from whence derives the social and economic capital for future projects.

Conclusion

The three approaches to the ethnography of media production described in this chapter—focusing, respectively, on the mode of production, field of production, and interpretive practice—are not exclusive but complementary ways of looking at similar phenomena. There is a similarity in the general point of view and in the type of questions asked, which transcends even theoretical language and temporal distance.

Any media text derives from a process of *entextualization*, the creative reworking of elements from a signifying repertoire and their "fixation" in a new text. The studies of media production that I have examined here all recognize a certain common set of issues:

1. Production of media texts involves the coordinated work of multiple actors, each possessed of different biographies, skills and competences.
2. Authorship is a cultural principle through which these congeries of practices are interpreted. The concept of authorship allows those involved in media production to assign, and struggle over, authority, ownership and control over the text.
3. The distribution of authorship roles in any system of production is unequal. These inequalities of authorial power

constitute a social field in which media production is negotiated.

4. The social relations of production are embedded in, and constitutive of, a set of sociotechnical relations. These involve actual constraints placed on action by the medium but also, and more empirically apparent, beliefs about the nature of technology and how it organizes relations of production.

5. These beliefs, which are often mystifications or naturalizations of cultural processes, constitute a general operational epistemology, and heuristic action framework, for media producers.

6. Media producers are members of communities and hence engaged in active interaction with the community in which they operate at several levels of social involvement. They are not only writers, directors, journalists, editors, and cameramen; they are also spouses, parents, friends, shoppers, television viewers, newspaper readers, and so forth. Their membership in multiple social groups and their possession of other cultural identities has important consequences for their interpretive work.

7. Media production is goal oriented. Media producers have practical, pragmatic, and perlocutionary goals that direct and organize much of their work. These goals exist at primary and secondary levels. At the primary level, media producers seek to entertain, educate, persuade, enlighten, amuse, inform, or otherwise affect audiences through their texts. But as social actors working in a field of media production, their goals also include such personal pursuits as raising status, increasing wealth, affirming identity, fulfilling fantasies, and pursuing pleasure. Goals at the primary level are always shaped by struggles at the secondary level, although these struggles are rarely glimpsed in the texts produced.

8. These goals can be arrested, contradicted, affirmed, or redirected by the social forces within which media production is contextualized, forces that are economic, political and cultural.

The organization of productive roles is never a simple technological distribution but always also a profoundly moral one. By *moral*, I mean that arguments about work become arguments about identity that revolve around values, around issues of what is correct and incorrect, right and wrong, just and unjust, ethical and unethical. These values link the field of production to larger cultural domains, but they take on new inflections within media cultures. That technical (and technological) languages are moral and evaluative is not a new observation.[25] Productive activity in media is a social activity, and as such, involves pleasures, statuses, and emotions, as well as capital, skill, and technology. Media production involves sets of contested values, which constitute the boundaries of overlapping social fields in which various forms of economic, social, symbolic action take place.

One of the strengths of ethnography is its ability to capture the uniqueness of cultural systems, and the moral language that underlies the technical, whether at the level of the total mode of production, the community of media production or the situational level. The set of metaphors employed by the ethnographers described in this chapter—manufacture, networking, discipline, negotiation—each arise out of the specificity of a particular field of media production. Powdermaker's Hollywood is not Manuel's Indian cassette culture nor Pedelty's El Salvadoran press corps nor Dornfeld's American Public Broadcasting System. The tropes and interpretive techniques employed by each ethnographer differ from the others because of the historical and cultural differences in contexts of media production, and also from the nature of the ethnographic encounter.

At the same time, ethnography involves limitations as a means of studying production. Powdermaker examines only those participants in the field to whom local knowledge ascribes authority over the creative process. In doing so, she is unable to see degrees of resistance, transformation, or conformity among the many participants in the field of media production whose work is not authorized as authorship. Dornfeld similarly focuses on producers at the expense of the cameramen, consultants, sound technicians, site directors, and so forth, not because these aren't important, but because he had no access to them. Pedelty focuses on journalists to the exclusion of their editors because these latter are dispersed in time and space from the site of his fieldwork. An anthropology that attends to the connections between the multiple sites and overlapping fields within which media production takes place—the ethnography of "media worlds"—is yet to emerge.

Notes

1. This equation of media and culture is widespread, not only in empirical studies of production but in theoretical works that see culture as something consumed. The early work of Habermas (1985), for example, is guilty of this error and it fundamentally undermines some of his formulations of the circulation of discourse in the public sphere.

2. A number of sociolinguistic studies of news have shown the extent to which bylined news stories are authored not only by the reporter, but by a complex web of reporters, editors, copyeditors, publishers, subeditors, and technicians interacting in institutionally patterned ways (Bell 1991, 1994, 1998, Bell and Garrett 1998, Cotter 1999, 2000, M. Peterson 2001, Van Dijk 1985, 1988, 1991). Even that Western cultural archetype of individual authorship, the poet, can be show to be part of a system of production; a classic case is the editorial transformations of Emily Dickinson's poetry in their original publications and the effects of this on the meanings of the poems (C. Miller 1987).

3. See Bakhtin 1981, 1984, 1986, Medvedev and Bakhtin 1992, Volosinov 1973, 1976. Bakhtin's notions about the complications of authorship are exemplified in questions about his own authorship; many scholars take for granted that he is the author of the works published under the names of V. Volosinov and Pavel Medvedev. See Clark and Holquist 1984.

4. In the "translinguistics" of Bakhtin, any text is *always* a token of a generic type, and hence is simultaneously a communal utterance as well as an individual's utterance. Bakhtinian sociological linguistics emerges as an effort to comprehend "the mystery of the one and the many" (Holquist 1986). It seeks its answers in the ways texts "temporarily crystallize a network of relations between or among interlocutors— their respective power and status, their presumed purposes in communicating, their characterization of the subject of discourse, and their relation to other conversations" (Morson 1986).

5. On Coca-Cola, see Pendergrast 1993. For a fascinating cultural analysis of the legal issues involved in trademarks and authorship in the United States and Canada, see Coombe (1996, 1997, 1998).

6. When local entrepreneurs use inexpensive technologies of reproduction to construct less expensive versions of texts for alternative markets, this is illegal in societies with copyright laws because it violates principles of authority as ownership. Duplicates of tapes, books, and computer programs are said to be "pirated," a deliberate use of a term for the illegal seizure of persons and property.

7. The Center for Anthropology and Journalism was founded (and largely funded) by Randolph Fillmore, the first press officer of the American Anthropological Association in 1986. The CAJ sought to increase dialogue between anthropologists and journalists and to create a space for anthropological perspectives in the mass media.

8. The term "reification" derives from the Latin *res*, or "thing," and means literally "to make a thing of." It is not Marx's term but Lukácz's (1968), although the notion derives from Marx's discussion of commodity fetishism (1967: 72) and his extension of fetishization from objects to practices, particularly in his discussion of how labor, a social practice, becomes a commodity, a thing, under the circumstances of capitalism (1967: 168).

9. It may still be possible to ethnographically explore such epochal modes of production as capitalism, but as Daniel Miller (1994, 1997) argues, it will have to be done by means of examining the many "capitalisms" that exist in specific situations, times, and places.

10. The position that technologies drive the system of production is consonant with some Marxist writings that seem to imply technological determinism: "In acquiring new forces of production, men change their mode of production, their way of earning a living; they change all their social relations. The hand mill will give you a society with the feudal lord, the steam mill a society with the industrial capitalist" (Marx 1963: 92). Here I want to take a less determinant position and simply emphasize that technologies and social roles have recursive relations to one another.

11. I insert quotations here because the cooperative nature of some new media, such as cassettes and the World Wide Web, require considerable negotiation to link producers and consumers. This suggests that the terms producer and consumer may be inadequate to properly describe these positions in the new and evolving communication circuit.

12. Compare Manuel's analysis to Ithiel de Sola Pool's "technologies of freedom" (de Sola Pool 1983).

13. Fifty years later Hollywood's boundaries have expanded to encompass much of the networked world, including producers and directors in New York and London, increasingly international location shooting, screenwriting by Internet, and so forth. The ethnography of this symbolic place thus becomes even more challenging.

14. Until the revision of copyright laws in 1984, India used a modified version of the old British colonial law, written before electronic reproduction was invented. It is thus not at all clear that such "piracy" was in fact illegal at the time.

15. For ethnographically and historically detailed expansions on Singer's insight, see the essays collected in Babb and Wadley 1995. The idea that new media make it possible not only to create alternative but resistant sources of transmission of religious symbols is also explored in the work of Jon Anderson (1995, 1999) and some of the papers in Eickelman and Anderson 1999.

16. See Beeman (1984), Abu-Lughod (1989) and Sreberny-Mohammadi and Mohammadi (1994) for other studies of cassettes transforming previous modes of media production and consumption in the Middle East, and thus creating new spaces for cultural expression.

17. A classic statement is Marx's famous quote from "The 18th Brumaire of Louis Bonaparte": "Men make their own history, but they do not make it just as they please; they do not make it under circumstances chosen by themselves, but under circumstances directly encountered from the past" (Marx 1963: 15).

18. Powdermaker's choice of roles to pay attention to replicates her informants' own understandings of "authorship," in which technical roles—everyone from the cinematographer to the grips—are relegated to a secondary creative status. They are viewed as technicians of the apparatus by which the authors do their work.

19. I will not here speak of the distraction of her frequent comparisons between Hollywood and "primitive" or "stone age" man. These cross-cultural comparisons were inserted, Powdermaker complained in her autobiography, strictly in response to demands by her publisher and she regretted them.

20. The papers of Hollywood professionals, now often archived for their historical value, offer countless examples to support Powdermaker's contentions about Hollywood producers' contentions about its audiences. My favorite is the remark by Universal Studios executive Al Lichtman in a 1953 letter to Walter Wanger that his studio makes "tits and sand" movies (*Arabian Nights*-inspired fantasy adventure films) for "morons who like that sort of thing." The letter, cited in Bernstein and Studlar (1997) is in the Walter F. Wanger collection at the University of Wisconsin.

21. Powdermaker asserts that the degree to which people internalize films of these sorts have much to do with processes of alienation, anxiety, and objectification associated with the transition of the United States to a consumer society.

22. Pedelty does not use Bourdieu's language but his approach is similar. In practice, he follows Bourdieu's formula for "mapping" a social field: first, description of the relations of power between institutions in the field; second, description of the objective structure of relations among the positions in the field; and third, description of the practices (particularly habitual and unreflective practices) of the agents who occupy these various positions.

23. See, for example, the papers in Hardt and Brennan (1995), and much of the work published in the journal *Media History* (published since 1994).

24. I am indebted to Charlotte Crouch for this example.

25. For example, see Perin 1977 for a useful account of how the bureaucratic language of land use by federal agencies is, in fact, a moral and value-laden language that depends on several key assumptions about cultural identities in America.

Chapter 8

COTTAGE CULTURE INDUSTRIES

In 1966, Sol Worth, a professor at Annenberg School of Communication at the University of Pennsylvania accompanied anthropologist John Adair to Pine Springs, Arizona, a Navajo community. There they taught six Navajo how to use 16mm movie cameras and asked them to each make a film. They deliberately sought to avoid teaching them any of the visual aesthetics typically associated with conventional American film production: when and how to use close-ups, editing for continuity, and so forth. The goal was to see what kind of films the Navajo would make if left to their own imaginations, and particularly to test whether there were visual and narrative aesthetics unique to the Navajo that the new medium would reveal. The results were fascinating: not only did the Navajo films suggest differences in the ways the world is visually and spatially organized, but traditional modes of Navajo oral story-telling were transferred into the new visual medium. The study influenced a generation of scholars in a number of different disciplines with its conclusion that far from the medium being the message, the medium could be flexibly adapted and used by non-Western peoples to tell stories in their own ways.

In the decades since Worth and Adair carried out their experiments, the increasingly flexible tools of mass communication and mediated representation have spread beyond the control of state industries and the near-monopolies of Hollywood, Bollywood, and other industrial production centers. Media production has been appropriated, adapted and, in some cases, embraced by countless communities around the globe.[1] These communities do not form a "culture industry" as described by the scholars of the Frankfurt school, or if they do, they are "cottage culture industries," existing parallel to state and private monopolistic culture industries and engaging in various forms of competition with and contestation of state and corporate dream factories. An anthropological theory of media production, one that refuses "to be deceived by the significance of scale" (Herzfeld 2001: 295) should be able to handle these smaller situations of production as handily as those of the institutionalized state and corporate media "dream factories" examined in chapter 6, and with the most of the same conceptual and methodological tools. The purpose of this chapter is to examine the lessons learned from ethnographies of the dream factories and news industries and ask whether they can, in fact, be applied as well to the small-scale productions of indigenous peoples, alternate cinemas, ritual videotape industries, and other cottage culture industries.

From the Native's Point of View

At the core of the Worth and Adair project with the Navajo was a semiotic theory about visual communication based on the notion that film is a kind of language, one that reflects underlying cultural norms of visual perception. Worth used the terms "edeme" and "cademe" to refer to what are called "shots" in the normal register of filmmaking (1966: 331-334). A *cademe* is the shot as it emerges from a camera. An *edeme* is a shot as it is actually used in a film. In making such a distinction, Worth is suggesting an approach that is quite different from most other semiotic systems of analysis that impose the rules of linguistics on non linguistic forms of semiosis. Worth's semiotic is a system that adapts analysis of media to the specific ways in which meaningful units— "utterances" in Worth's linguistic analogy—are mediated by technologies. Worth's approach is an important one because it suggests that studying film poetics from the view of production—which involves knowing how many cademes are being produced, how they are selected and transformed into edemes, by whom and with what rationales—is different than studying finished film texts, in which one has only edemes to work with.[2] Worth's approach is one of the few semiotic methods of media analysis that introduces *mediation*—that is, the ways media technologies alter the processes by which meaningful "utterances" are produced, into analysis. The employment of cademes and edemes is also interesting because they are empirical units whose boundaries are remarkably clear, which is more than one can say of Lévi-Strauss's *mythemes*, or David Schneider's *cultural units*.[3]

Worth's approach assumes a double-articulation, but one that is quite different from that of the structuralist semiotics described in chapter 3. Worth and Adair were interested first in what shots filmmakers chose to film, and second, in the ways these shots were put together. They assume that using images sequentially to create meaning is universal but that the rules by which people join images is cultural. "If one image follows another in sequence, there should be some connection between them. But the logic that connects them may differ" (Worth and Adair 1970). This leads them to a study of cultural codes, whose analysis they group into four areas:

> (1) the narrative "style" of the films, related to the mythic forms and symbols of the culture; (2) the syntactic organization and sequencing of events and units of "eventing"; (3) the cultural, perceptual and cognitive taboos influencing either semantic or syntactic organization and structure; and (4) the relation between verbal language structure and visual "language" structure. (Worth and Adair 1970: 23)

Analytically, these are many of the same questions semiotic analysis asks of media texts. Methodologically, however, this approach differs considerably from those examined in chapters 3 and 4, because Worth and Adair assume that the best way to go about such an analysis is to observe the producers at work and to ask them questions about why they construct meanings in the ways they do. Their method assumes further that if the logics by which producers join edemes into longer films is a cultural logic, rather than an idiosyncratic authorial system for making narrative, similar patterns will be seen in more than one of the films made by members of the community, and audiences within the community will accept these sequencing styles without undue comment.

As anticipated by this theory, the organization of the films produced by the Navajo filmmakers suggested a different logic for organizing visual information. For example, the Navajo frequently violated the normal rule of Hollywood filmmaking that editing and sequencing should seek to conceal joints so that the audience sees a continuous unit of action. In one film, a boy is filmed walking to a tree. As he passes behind the tree, the film is edited so that he suddenly appears on the other side. In another film, a man is on his knees, picking roots, and then suddenly appears walking down the road holding the roots in his hand. Navajo filmmaker Maxine Tsosie, when asked by Worth whether this sudden jump wouldn't confuse an audience, replied, "But everybody will know that if he's walking in this shot that comes last, he must have gotten up between the time he was sitting and the time he's walking." Navajo viewing the finished films seemed to agree with her. This indicated to Worth and Adair a distinction between two different codes of visual representation.

The work of Worth and Adair draws our attention to indigenous aesthetics of representation. They believed not only that different societies have different systems of representation but that these are related to common behavioral patterns and to more fundamental issues of worldview.[4] Thus a Navajo behavioral rule of avoiding looking people directly in the face manifests itself in an avoidance of close-ups of faces. The Navajo concern with harmony and balance is demonstrated not only in the insistence that the film class be balanced in numbers of men and women, but in aesthetic attention to telling "whole" stories, even where that means filming people doing actions they do not normally perform in everyday life.

Worth and Adair discovered that these films revealed not only codes of visual perception but also some of the ways aesthetic assumptions about traditional media could serve as grounds for building aesthetics for new media. Indigenous theories of representation for traditional media, such as the rules for oral storytelling, sometimes structured the ways in which these new media were used to create their stories. Although the Pine Ridge Navajo walked as little as possible, preferring always to ride horses or pickup trucks, the characters in their films are frequently shown walking as a means to bridge each scene. This follows a standard pattern of narrative construction in Navajo verbal performance, in which walking is used to move a story from scene to scene. Likewise, in constructing "documentaries" of weaving and silver-smithing, the filmmakers felt it necessary to "show the beginning" by filming people making and dying wool, and gathering silver ore, even though Navajo craftsmen do not, in fact, engage in these activities. The videos thus reveal not only "ways of seeing" but links between ways of seeing and "ways of speaking," that is, ways that certain kinds of experience are to be represented. Ultimately, Worth and Adair sought to demonstrate that different communities may establish very different relationships between signs, concepts, and sociality.

The notion of indigenous aesthetics tied to larger cultural patterns resonates strongly with the work of the earlier National Culture studies, particularly such studies as Bateson's "Morale and National Character," in which the author argues that propaganda aimed at building morale or demoralizing troops will achieve its intended effects only if specially tailored to fundamentally different systems of signification. Images and texts that would be deeply demoralizing to Germans might well seem ridiculous to Britons or Americans, and vice versa (Bateson 1972b). What sets Worth and Adair's approach apart from national culture studies on this point is their insistence on paying attention to the contexts in which these codes are entextualized. Far from seeing encoding only as an unconscious cognitive activity, Worth and Adair attempt to draw attention to its sociality. Indigenous aesthetics never only express internalized ways of seeing; they also always call attention to the social relations that these ways of seeing express and through which they are expressed. Worth and Adair argued that any study of indigenous aesthetics therefore required close attention to the social organization of production. In their own work, for example, they sought to create a sociological balance in their experiment by having people who were tokens of particular types (following the positivist logic of "controlling for variables": an artist, a politician, a craftsman, a woman, etc.). The Navajo, for their part, required a harmonious balance between natural forces such as male and female, and insisted that the group have three women and three men. Worth and Adair paid particular attention to the ways the filmmakers used kinship and other social and political networks to get their films made, and the social and political repercussions of filmmaking, as when one filmmaker was required to give up film he took of a ritual that went awry or pay a fine of six sheep.

In spite of this effort toward striking a balance between code and context, critics are correct in complaining that the study remains heavily focused on filmmaking as an expression of a culturally shaped cognition. The very structure of the experiment, in which new media are introduced into a community that has not previously used them in order to see if such an elementary form of usage will reveal a particular visual code assumes a particular kind of distinction between code and context. It assumes that such codes are learned, internalized, and subsequently expressed (and hence reproduced). An alternative would be to consider all media to be socially negotiated in contexts, to see the tension between code and context as one in which context produces code and text simultaneously as social action. Such a view, which is more consonant with the contemporary turn to performance in anthropological linguistics than the older Bloomfieldian linguistic approach of Worth, would recognize the value of Worth and Adair's experiment in demonstrating the reality of indigenous aesthetics while at the same time emphasizing that their results are shaped by the nature of the experiment in which people who are for the most part uninterested in the technologies are paid to be taught how to make films for their own consumption but primarily for the consumption of others.

Michaels and Kelly (1984) offer an exemplary effort in building on Worth and Adair's effort to study the contexts through which indigenous aesthetics are produced, this time in a naturalistic rather than experimental setting. In their account, George Jupurrula, a Warlpiri filmmaker, sought to make a narrative film about the Coniston massacre, in which Australian constables killed eighteen Aborigines in retaliation for the death of a white prospector at Aborigine hands. A local prohibition on the mention of the names of the dead until a grandchild generation has appeared had made Aboriginal accounts scarce, but in the early 1980s the prohibition ended.

Yet even though Jupurrula was an eyewitness to the massacre, and related not only to several of those who died but even to the killers of the prospector, *and* to the woman over whom the prospector and the Aborigines had fought, he does not, under Aboriginal custom, have the rights to tell the story. To make the film, he gathered together as part of the production process all those who had story rights. Among the Warlpiri, authority over the ceremonial performance of stories is divided between people classed as *Kirda*, who have the right to perform stories, and those categorized as *Kurdungulu*, who have the right to know stories and act as witnesses to ensure they are properly told. *Kirda* rights are passed through fathers, while *Kurdungulu* rights are passed through mothers. In addition, the events are related, both historically and mnemonically, to features of landscape, over the representation of which various people have inherited rights. In summary:

> the "creation" of a videotape by directorial design was interpreted by Jupurrula to require that the entire taping event be organized consistent[ly] with the rules for story performance in the more formal and ceremonial terms of Aboriginal traditions. This meant that an entire set of aboriginal relations had to be observed and respected, requiring an assemblage of nearly thirty people to participate in the recording of a single person's story. And these people had to stand in specified relationships to the story, the storyteller, and the land on which all this was being done. Only certain people, *Kirda*, could be on camera. To be filmed was associated with participation ... and [was] therefore compromising of the *Kurdungurlu* role. The director/cameraman himself had to be *Kurdungulu* to the *Kirda* of the story he was taping. (Michaels and Kelly 1984: 32)

The authors emphasize that this by no means represents a standard procedure for Warlpiri videotape-making. Rather, it emphasizes the generative and emergent nature of productive activity, the ways in which a filmmaker draws on cultural forms to produce a videotape that others in the community would regard as authentic in spite of the novelty of the medium. Other solutions are possible, and other accounts of the Warlpiri demonstrate that other modes of relation have been employed in production (Ginsburg 1991; Michaels 1994). Far from the medium imposing certain types of roles on communities, these accounts demonstrate that, "given the opportunity, Aboriginal people will, in fact explore the potential of new media technology to serve their objectives and yet to fit into appropriate cultural requirements" (Michaels and Kelly 1984: 33) and illustrates Worth's point that "new technologies of communication need not be used only in the ways of the technological societies that introduced them" (1972a: 353).[5]

Indigenous Media

Worth and Adair's study begins and ends with the words of Sam Yazee, a Navajo elder who, when the experiment was first proposed to the community, asked whether the project would harm the sheep. Assured it would not, he asked whether it would help the sheep. When the visitors admitted it would not, he asked, "Then why make films?" Yazee's question points up the artificiality of Worth and Adair's experiment and raises the question of how we are to understand media in communities that *do* choose to make films, operate radio stations, broadcast television, or produce videotapes. Who or what does such media production help? Who or what does it harm? Such questions turn our attention from the elicitation of indigenous codes to the study of media production. But to answer such questions, production must be studied in ways that extend beyond the immediacies of who holds the camera and how they negotiate with kin to get a movie made; we must turn to the larger social, economic, and political contexts in which such relations are embedded.

For decades, mass media has been increasingly pervading the lives of indigenous peoples. Such media threaten indigenous ways of life, but they also offer new opportunities. Media can be simultaneously recognized by members of a community as an opportunity to connect with larger worlds while at the same time seen as potentially "destroying a whole generation" (Wilk 1995). Eric Michaels was building on Worth and Adair's work when he worked with the Warlpiri people of the Central Desert of Australia to develop their own local, low-power television (Michaels 1994). But there was a crucial difference. Whereas Worth and Adair introduced filmmaking into a largely indifferent and occasionally resistant Navajo community to test their own theories about culture and visualization, the Aborigines with whom Michaels worked were eager to become television producers. To a large extent, they sought to use indigenous production as a form of cultural assertion against the alternative cultural forms being imposed on the community through a newly launched Australian communications satellite. As Sam Yazee's remarks imply, the appropriation of new media technologies takes place in a context in which these tools have come to be seen as somehow valuable in pursuing local objectives. "When other forms are no longer effective, indigenous media offers a possible means—social, cultural, political— for reproducing and transforming cultural identity among people who have experienced massive political, geographic and economic disruption" (Ginsburg 1994b: 94). Media technologies hold out particular strategies or possibilities for the communication of cultural knowledge in order to achieve various kinds of social and political goals.

The shift from the experimental procedures of Worth and Adair to more naturalistic ethnography among people who have already begun to use new media, involves a shift of attention from cognition to sociality. Faye Ginsburg coined the term *indigenous media* to refer to "that work produced by indigenous peoples, sometimes called the 'Fourth World,' whose societies have been dominated by encompassing states, such as the United States, Canada and Australia" (1991: 107).[6] Such groups include Aboriginal Australians, Native Americans, Amazonian natives, Saami, Maori, the Quechua and Mayan of Central America, the Ainu, and perhaps such groups as the Welsh, Walloons, Catalans, and Basques.

Indigenous media, of course, is "indigenous" only in relation to something else. This is thus an inherently political definition, involving relationships of power predicated on the mutual recognition of difference. Indigenous media production always exists in a dialogical relationship with other media industries. The various forms of indigenous production usually make up only a tiny percentage of the media circulating in indigenous communities. This fact calls our attention not to indigenous aesthetics as isolates or variables, but rather to indigenous aesthetic codes and contexts of production as responses to shifting relations with the encompassing state.

Socially, most overt indigenous concerns involve using media to create community cohesion through the fixing of texts and through sharing of information. The notion that literacy can help fix cultural knowledge, and hence circulate traditional cultural information across time and space, is part of a long-standing argument in anthropology. The anthropological literature is replete with tales, both authenticated and apocryphal, of communities describing their traditional customs with reference to a book that turns out to have been written by an earlier anthropologist, or sometimes even to have been an early work of the anthropologist asking the questions. Nor has it been uncommon for indigenes to collaborate with colonial institutions such as newspapers to record lengthy cultural materials (e.g. Charlot 1998). Film, audiotape, and now videotape, offer extraordinary new possibilities for such textual fixation. No longer do image, sound, and action have to be translated into words before being preserved; all three sensory domains can be captured as they occur. The fixing of texts may include recording politicians' words, creating a community library of ritual performances from which future generations can draw, the recording of traditional stories and genealogies in their oral form, or the creation of new narrative texts, like the story of the Coniston massacre whose production was described above.

Yet however much intracultural use of media is intended to be conservative, indigenous media production is always assertive as well. The use of video by indigenous peoples is never only a social act of conserving identity through fixing it; it is always also a political act of asserting identity, of using video to create a political presence. This is particularly true of indigenous peoples whose lack of technology has been one of the marks by which they are seen to be "other" by members of the dominant societies around them. Defining indigenous peoples as technologically unsophisticated in the face of empirical evidence to the contrary is an old game. At the dawn of documentary film, we have Robert Flaherty's personal accounts of the ease with which his Ikivimuit informants and assistants took up film technologies, and became sophisticated users of them (Rotha and Wright 1980). Yet what he chose to show on film in his classic *Nanook of the North* was the Eskimo hunter supposedly startled by an encounter with a gramophone. Similarly, Worth, Adair, and Chalfen all reported the skepticism that met their accounts of how quickly and easily the Navajo learned to use film equipment. Among peoples whose identities are defined by their lack of technological forms of mediation, therefore, political assertion need not be based only on the content of the media production; it is significant to many publics simply to see that such people have video-tape machines at all. In the Rodney King incident in the United States, the content of the video was the political issue; the possession of a video camera by an American passerby was scarcely remarked on at all in public discourse. The possession of video cameras by Kayapo Indians of the Brazilian rainforests, on the other hand, cannot seem to go unremarked (T. Turner 1991, 1992).

It is certainly not unknown for indigenes themselves to accept that technology is one of the conditions of alterity that divides them from the encompassing society—and to accept the hierarchies such recognition of difference may imply. Where this has happened, some indigenes may themselves also be impressed by the mediation of their traditions through television or other media technologies. To see one's own traditions and languages objectified and represented in the same media as those of the dominant society can be empowering. Dozens of Native American radio stations exist throughout the United States and Canada, often as parts of efforts to maintain the indigenous language and offer a continuity with oral traditions alongside the many other radio stations that fill the airwaves (Smith and Brigham 1992). Similarly, one of the earliest indigenous television production facilities, the Inuit Broadcasting Corporation in Canada, has been the subject of a number of studies that have made strong claims for its ability to empower Inuit peoples by presenting even a small number of television broadcasts in their own languages and about their own practices amid twenty channels of state and commercial media broadcast from Canada and the United States

(Brisebois 1983; Valaskakis and Wilson 1983; Coldevin and Wilson 1985; Roth and Valaskakis 1989; Bergman 1996).

Yet the adoption of media production by indigenous peoples raises serious issues about the extent to which such practices are destructive to indigenous ways of life. Peter Crawford asked the question "Is a Kayapo with a camera still a Kayapo?" (1995: 16). James Faris argues that engagement in media production merely emphasizes the degree to which indigenous peoples are bit players in the world system:

> The Kayapo and others of the Third World do not join the global village as equal participants, as just more folks with their video cameras. They enter it already situated by the West, which gives them little room to be anything more than what the West will allow. Technology notwithstanding, they will enter only on our terms, unless they forcibly exclude us, prohibit our entry into their lives, eliminate our visits, our technologies and our help, refuse to allow us to see their videotapes, and show them only to themselves. (1992: 176).

For James F. Weiner, even this degree of isolationism is insufficient, because he believes that the technologies of media production are themselves destructive of indigenous modes of thought and expression. In contrast to the assumptions of Worth and Adair, he argues that since "Western foundations of representation, visualism, and subjectivity ... are integral to the filmic media themselves—as we must agree they are if we are to accept that they are cultural products through and through—and that they could be opposed to and even subversive of non-Western modes of knowledge and its acquisition, revelation, and articulation" (Weiner 1997: 198). He argues that peoples like the Foi, whose modalities of behavior avoid self-expression—stolidness and silence constituting appropriate behavior—might thus be radically transformed by technologies of self-expression.[7]

While Faris and Weiner raise interesting points, they are to some extent irrelevant. The Kayapo cannot forcibly exclude the rest of the world, and while they can refuse "Western" technologies of production, the technologies of consumption are already making inroads. The transformation of indigenous societies by the capitalist world system is an accomplished and ongoing fact. Worth and Adair's experiments took place "before the hogans got their satellite dishes" (Halleck and Magnan 1993: 156), and any contemporary media production work is going to be influenced by the (usually state-sponsored) mediated discourses already flowing into indigenous communities in a flood.[8] The choice is thus not between pristine and authentic indigenous cultures, on the one hand, and societies adulterating themselves through the use of media production technologies on the other; it is a question of whether there will be five hours a week of Inuktitut broadcasting of Inuit life amid some twenty channels worth of satellite broadcasting, or three hours a week of Aboriginal content in Aboriginal languages out of 70 hours of airtime on the Central Desert "footprint" of the Australian satellite television network. Faris and Weiner are perhaps best read not so much as a solid critique of the theoretical literature on indigenous media than as a corrective for the celebratory tone of much of this work—a reminder that in the Faustian bargain (as Ginsberg characterizes indigenous media), it's the devil who ultimately wins.

At another level, though, the whole question of authentic expression of cultural identity may itself be an ethnocentric one.[9] As Jay Ruby points out, there is a double standard at work in that most critics fail to discuss how John Huston expresses his identity as an Irish-American through his films, yet films by indigenous producers or "ethnic" filmmakers like Spike Lee are routinely assessed as artifacts of their ethnic cultures (Ruby 1991b). Crawford's question as to whether a Kayapo with a camera is still a Kayapo received a partial answer from the words of Mokuka, a Kayapo filmmaker, who told a European audience, "Just because I use a white man's camera, I don't dress in the white man's clothes" (Crawford 1995: 19). But this raises as many questions as it answers: What about indigenes who *do* "dress in the white man's clothes"? What about indigenes trained to make films or use video-cameras in government schools?[10] What about indigenous producers whose thoughts about native content are shaped by the need to sell advertising in order to support the indigenous newspaper or radio or television station? When does the native cease to be a native? And who gets to decide?

While recognizing that very real processes of cultural adulteration and dissolution have been and are taking place because of transnational political-economic processes (always mediated through the agency of those nation-states with jurisdiction over indigenes), it is perhaps more useful for an anthropology of media to focus on how authenticity and authority play out in the social negotiation of production than to attempt to enter into the debate on who and what is legitimately authentic and authoritative. The notion that I am promoting here, that what is "indigenous" derives from the social negotiation of production, not some inherent and essential "culture," is also articulated by some indigenous media producers. Hopi videographer Victor Masayesva, Jr., says, "A Native filmmaker has the accountability built into him. Accountability as an individual, as a clan, as a tribal, as a family member. The white man doesn't have that. That's the single big distinction," (cited in Leuthold 1998: 1). What makes an indigenous production, in other words, is the style through which indigenous people imagine their audiences. Such a definition works whether the producers are creating their text for intracultural distribution among fellow members of a community, or intercultural circulation, to express Native identities to others. In the former case, one is responsible for filming a ritual or practice in ways the majority will see as correct, while in the latter, for correctly presenting to "them" the "us" we want them to know. In either case, not everyone is going to agree, and technical and artistic and economic issues are going to be negotiated. The question of who is to count as a native and who gets to decide their legitimacy to speak as such, brings us back to the central issue by which Ginsburg defined indigenous media: the tension between power and difference. It is here that the ethnography of indigenous media links up with the studies of corporate and state-sponsored media described in the last chapter: media production is to a large extent about the negotiation of authorship.

Authorship in indigenous media involves the *assertion* of identity, primarily through the creation of texts for wide circulation, and the *conservation* of identity by the fixing of texts that, in oral media of performance, would vanish once spoken. Production—the authoring of these representations—turns on two key issues: authenticity and authority. By *authenticity*, I mean the construction of representations that somehow assert the identity of a community, an "us" that is different from some "them" or set of "thems," particularly that of the dominant culture of the encompassing state which threatens to absorb them. By *authority*, I mean that those creating media texts must be able to credibly speak of and for the community that they claim to represent. This twin process of authorship proceeds through the creation of hybrid representations that combine a traditional "way of seeing" and "way of speaking" with a borrowed "technology of spectatorship" (T. Turner 1991). Note that this approach to technology assumes that it is neither a completely neutral device (as Worth and Adair maintained) nor a hegemonic apparatus (as Weiner assumes) but rather "a creative tool in the service of a new signifying practice" (T. Turner 1991: 93).

Such hybrid creativity is indeed a kind of "Faustian contract" (Ginsburg 1991) or "double-edged sword" (Jhappan 1990) since the need to employ expressive aspects of indigenous peoples' cultural heritage in strategic ways toward political ends may in fact threaten to pervert the living traditions to which they are committed. But this is not a new problem; on the contrary, it has been a part of indigenous encounters with media industries since the nineteenth century. Joanna Cohen Scherer tells us the story of Sarah Winemucca, who drew from her own heritage and from Western imagery to construct for herself a public image as an "Indian princess." Her success on the American lecture circuit proved inadequate to build a political base from which to fight for Native American rights, however, since the very image that she constructed to gain popular attention made it difficult for her to be taken seriously as a political actor (Scherer 1988). Less than one hundred years later, we can see a similar process in the description by Gail Landsman of the Mohawk political resistance at Ganienkah between 1974 and 1986. Recognizing that their struggle to preserve local autonomy was being caricatured in the press as an "Indian uprising," leaders of the community sought to shift media tropes to more sympathetic stereotypes. They successfully built media support by reframing themselves as Indians struggling to maintain their "traditions." Eventually, however, the realities of their goals (such as the development of a local aquafarming industry) became difficult to fit within the sympathetic but essentialist stereotypes of the press, and the community was largely forced to abandon its quest for sympathetic media representation in order to maintain its original political program (Landsman 1987, 1988).

The difference, of course, between Sarah Winnemucca or the Ganienkah Indians and the Warlpiri (Michaels 1994), Kayapo (T. Turner 1991, 1992a, 1992b), Waipai (Gallois and Carelli 1993-94; Aufderheide 1995), Inuit (Roth and Valaskakis 1989), Mapuche (Colle 1992), Navajo (L.C. Peterson 1997; Pack 2000), and other contemporary indigenous peoples is the extent of indigenous control they seek to exert over the technologies by which their cultural traditions are mediated, and the ways they seek to exert this control. Winnemucca and the Mohawk people of Ganienkah were up against media industries with which they could at best seek to negotiate; the Kayapo and Warlpiri and others are attempting to position themselves as producers whose work can maintain cultural continuity even as it mediates social change. The nature of the ways that these engagements take place is complex and needs to be empirically examined. Ginsburg (1991) suggests a continuum of indigenous production practices. At one end is small-scale production like that of the Kayapo or Warlpiri, which focus on productions by a few key producers primarily (but not entirely) for distribution within the local community. At the other end are state-local partnership ventures like Imparja, an Australian "regional commercial television service" run by Aborigines, the Inuit Broadcasting Corporation in Canada, or Navajo radio in the United States. Struggling to keep their licenses, all of these ventures have found themselves facing shifting political priorities and government budgets, efforts to balance (or compromise) indigenous goals with the need to sell advertising, and the need to employ many, sometimes predominantly non-native technicians. Imparja, for example, has been notoriously insistent that the programs it airs be of "broadcast quality"—a non-native criterion that excludes much Aboriginal content not produced by the station itself (Ginsburg 1991).

The mediation of hybridity in these systems, large or small, does not take place in a manner unfamiliar to us from our examination of the media industries in the last chapter. Again we see that authorship of media texts is multiple and that the distribution of authorship roles in community systems of production are unequal. The social field in which media production takes place involves negotiation between various actors with different access to, knowledge of, and authority over media production equipment. The social relations around and through which production is negotiated involve sociotechnical relations, but often in ways quite different from those that mark industrial media production—the need for cameraman and actor to stand in a particular kin relation to one another, for example.

Beliefs about the nature of representational technologies and how they organize relations of production become more apparent to ethnographers when means and relations of production are linked through different cultural codes. Insofar as these media are actually "new," that is, recently acquired by the communities hosting ethnographers, it may become possible to watch a development of general operational epistemologies and heuristics for action. At present, because media producers in these communities are often not professionalized, and the nature of their professionalization is not fixed, producers draw on preexisting kinship patterns and ways of storytelling, adapting them to fit with the new technologies. These producers are members of the communities in which they work and operate in their communities at several levels of social involvement. They are often important political actors whose control over media technologies serves to enhance their status and authority. Others are sophisticated culture brokers familiar at once with local traditions and those of the dominant society, and engaged in active mediation between these different worlds.

As with industrial modes of production, indigenous media production is goal-oriented. At the primary level, media producers seek to preserve cultural materials, to create new venues for the transmission of intergenerational materials, to improve contact and communication between groups, to advertise and sell local crafts. But as social actors working in a field of media production, their goals also involve such pursuits as raising status, controlling resources, affirming personal, familial, and political identities, and so forth. These goals can, in turn, be arrested, contradicted, affirmed, or redirected by the larger social forces within which media production is contextualized—forces that are economic, political, and cultural. For the Aborigines of the Central Desert, the stroke of a bureaucrat's pen could end Imparja's license and transfer it to another corporation, one without active Aboriginal control. For the Kayapo, a shift in international environmental fads—a reduction in interest in the fate of the Amazonian rainforests, with which they have aligned their own aspirations for autonomy—could greatly reduce their political effectiveness in negotiating with the encompassing state.

Activist Imagery and the Activist Imaginary

Yet there is an irony at work here. The political effectiveness of indigenes in shaping the forces that control their local media production can itself be influenced through that media production. Indigenous media production can become a tool through which local political participation with and against the encompassing state is enhanced, and it can be a means by which local communities, aligning themselves with larger issues, attract attention from political forces beyond the dominant state, as in the Kayapo efforts to align themselves with larger Green organizations interested in saving the Brazilian rainforests and, hence, the traditional habitation of the Kayapo. This was made particularly evident by the role of media—state, international, and indigenous—in the mass demonstration organized by the Kayapo and other Amazonian communities to stop construction of a hydroelectric dam at Altamira (T. Turner 1992b).

Indigenous media, which is political by definition, as we have seen, thus forms a special case among many other kinds of media engagements in which a variety of marginalized subjects become involved in creating their own representational systems as a counter to dominant media industries. The technologies of media production are everywhere being appropriated by actors outside state media and the dream factories—individuals, communities, NGOs, unions, social movements. In 1986, for example, during a general strike in Brazil, many local union groups documented events on videotape and shipped the tapes to the national union's Workers' TV project (*TV dos Trabalhadores*). Although initially surprised by the unexpected flood of tapes, Workers' TV members edited the tapes into a single videotape, which was then distributed through an interunion confederation (Aufderheide 1993). Brazilian television, which is primarily interested in "selling the ideology of consumption to those who can afford it" (Oliveira 1991: 212), tends to downplay labor activity; the videotape production and distribution system allowed labor workers to bypass spotty press coverage and build a sense of national community.

Shifts in media technology are increasingly making production technologies available to communities outside industrial production centers. People are using these media to attempt to gain greater control over their social and cultural futures through what George Marcus has called

"the activist imaginary" (1996). This activist imaginary in media production includes alternative television by people in the United States
with AIDS (Juhasz 1995); media services through which Tibetan Bud-
dhist activists seek to speak to and through the world's press services
(McLagen 1996); the production of alternative media in the United
States to construct alternatives to dominant ideological (Pedelty 1993)
or cosmological (Toumey 1994) positions; union laborers using grassroots distribution of videos to counter government claims (Aufderheide
1993); rival political parties in India using cassette tapes to spread election messages in the face of ruling-party control of electronic media
(Manuel 1993); efforts of political dissidents in foreign countries to use
cassettes, faxes, and other "small media" to build revolutionary movements at home in Iran (Beeman 1984; Sreberny-Mohammadi and
Mohammadi 1994) or Saudi Arabia, and Quechua revolutionaries smug-
gling texts and images to computer users who upload them to websites
abroad to pursue international attention (Castells 1997; Cleaver 1998).

Much of this activist imaginary depends on *media ideologies*, that
is, on folk theories (often promulgated by media scholars) about the
effects of media. For those who believe in the power of the media to
directly affect those who see and hear its messages, centralized control
of the media is inherently dominating and decentralization of control is
inherently liberating. Widespread assumptions about the value of publicity for activism has led many activists to see media, not only as a
means but also as an end, while for others it is but one strategy among
many. Nor are activists and their opponents the only ones making such
assumptions; cultural notions about the inherent effects of media on
society tend to lead much of the literature describing activist use of
media in unduly celebratory or pessimistic terms.

Cottage Culture Industries

While useful for extending our analytical imagination beyond the con-
fines of our assumptions about media production based on mass media
in the West, labeling technological media by marginalized ethnic communities within nation-states with some such label as "indigenous
media" is not really very useful in defining a coherent category of media
production that differs substantively from other forms of production.
The label "activist media," which categorizes genres according to the
intentions of producers, isn't very useful either. In either case, what
seems straightforward when looking at certain examples becomes
murky and ambiguous as our scrutiny takes us inevitably to border
zones, such as the ethnic, minority, and indigenous television produced

in the United States, with various degrees of state and private involvement. Indigenous films, activist media, independent filmmaking, home movies, and other such terms all simply point to a key aspect of contemporary media production: the technologies of production are not monopolies of states and capital-intensive corporate entities but involve a wide variety of networks, communities, and social groups, which coexist alongside and define themselves dialogically against, state and private dream factories.

An emphasis on the intentions of media producers can also obscure the ways that contemporary media gets made not just as a result of local ways of seeing but as a result of emergent social relations of production between locals and others engaged with them in media production. Describing a project to create a film based on the legends of the Yup'ik, the native people of Nelson Island, Alaska, Ann Fienup-Riordan described how independent filmmaking, though differently organized economically and politically than Hollywood films, may nonetheless express key sets of Western values and aesthetics even while seeking to make films that differ from those of mainstream movies. In making a film based on the Yup'ik heroic tale cycle of Apanuugpak, the filmmaker chose to highlight what he regarded as universal truths over local cosmologies. In the process, the filmmaker did not so much reconstruct an indigenous "way of seeing" as to take as ahistorical and essential a recently invented tradition that seeks to project into myths a set of contemporary understandings about relations to the land that are quite different from those which pertained in the era in which the myths originated. In this double move, the filmmaker invented "a trope for the condition of modern man based on a tradition of nonownership and an absence of territorial concepts that the people of Nelson Island have themselves invented to validate their contemporary relationship to the land" (Fienup-Riordan 1988: 452). The script ultimately generated (and apparently never made) was a result of contingent and shifting relations between the filmmaker and the Nelson Islanders.

Media production, then, cannot be so neatly divided between the self-representation of indigenous peoples seeking to assert and conserve their identities and the representations manufactured by the monopolistic culture industries of the state and the multinational corporation. There are many other kinds of media production.

In Ghana, for instance, recent years have seen the emergence of low-budget video features that exist parallel to both the state-sponsored national cinema films imported from Europe, Hong Kong, India, and the United States. Many of the filmmakers have their roots in a traveling melodramatic theater tradition, particularly producers of the most popular genre: horror films. The melodramatic narratives and symbolism of good and evil derive heavily from these traditions. By 1999, some two hundred of these films had been made, with more being produced at the rate of thirty to forty per year. The videos are screened for low fees in small bars, open-air cinemas, and video theaters, and their presence is advertised by lurid hand-painted panels. Such fare "offers a highly appreciated alternative to the boring national TV programmes and foreign films" (Wendl 1999: np; c.f. Meyer 1999).

The flexibility of video allows its appropriation and adaptation into multiple settings toward a number of different ends. In Benin City, Nigeria, for example, videotaping the ritual performances of Ohens in urban shrines has become a common practice (Gore 1998). Ohens are priests of public shrines among Edo peoples who recognize the personal relationships of some individuals with spirits or deities. The Ohen builds up a regular clientele through the development of a community centered on his or her particular shrine. Song, dance, and music are keys to ritual worship, and the Ohen is possessed by deities while dancing to music associated with them. Videotaping Ohen performances has become increasingly popular since 1990, to the point that the status of an Ohen and his shrine suffer if his performances are not routinely videotaped. Video operators are hired, but they are also usually socially connected to the shrine. The video production is funded by the shrine's community, budgeted into event planning. But video ownership lies with the Ohen, as owner of the shrine.

Shrine performance videos have their own style, but it should not necessarily be seen as shaped by an indigenous aesthetic code of visual representation in Worth's meaning, because the Edo are quite familiar with the film codes of Hollywood and Hong Kong. Rather, the particular aesthetic of shrine videos arises out of local relations of production and the purposes for which it is made. Shrine videos are not intended so much as records of events to be viewed later as they are "almost mandatory assertions of the importance of the individuals participating" (Gore 1998: 79). The main characteristics of shrine videos are their documentation of the numbers of participants, with special attention to eminent visitors, and their emphasis on real-time filming. "The more that the event is recorded in real time (this is often a 14-day affair in the case of annual festivals), the more prestige and status are asserted" (Gore 1998: 79). Quantity is thus a central part of the video aesthetic, testifying to the importance of the event. Editing the video and eliding the interludes and lulls, necessary by both Hollywood and Hong Kong aesthetics, would invalidate the meaning of this *kind* of video for the Edo.

Similar integrations of media technologies into traditional practices are easy to find. In Egypt, no middle- or upper-class wedding is complete without a professionally made videotape. Private companies specializing in wedding videos abound in Cairo, and they bring to weddings sophisticated multicamera systems and portable editing boards operated by professional directors. When the bride and groom are presented by their fathers to the families and friends gathered to receive and applaud them, the ability of the well-wishers to see the married couple is often obscured by the cameramen backing slowly in front of the couple, keeping them carefully in their viewfinders. The cameramen become a part of the wedding, and just as the videotapes will be edited into seamless entertainment, so participants edit their own attention, stretching a bit to catch a glimpse over or around the cameraman, but doing so uncomplainingly, working their own participation in the wedding around that of the cameramen.

Rituals, as anthropologists have long maintained, are places where we "show ourselves to ourselves" (Geertz 1973) in ways that are both reflective and reflexive of society. But rituals can never be reduced to their communicative function. Rituals *do* things, and what they do, for the most part, is produce persons. This being so, what does the mediation of media do to these rituals? If weddings produce married persons, what are we to make of video technologies that obscure the presentation of the new couple to the community to better produce an elegant, carefully edited record of the presentation? The ways in which media technologies enter intimately into everyday life, allowing people to represent themselves for themselves, is something that demands increased ethnographic attention.

Piccini contrasts documentary filmmakers who seek to examine the ancient Celtic past to explore how people once lived (Piccini 1996), with the practices of tourists with their handheld cameras. "Go to any heritage site or 'living history museum' ... and you will find people filming. What they are filming is all about who they are in relation to their ideas about the past and who they may once have been" (Piccini 1997).

Tourism, not only of the past but of the present, is a key site in which to examine media technologies. Issues of authenticity and authorship are not limited to indigenous or activist media but can include any contact between two groups in which one becomes the object of mediated scrutiny by the other. The never-made film about Apanuugpak has this much in common with the tourist videos that Piccini mentions: the desire to comprehend the self by representing the other (even if these representations are never meant to be seen). Piccini is drawing our attention to the intimacy of this kind of production. It is not only that people use video technology to record the past and the other; it is that they employ them in such a way as to integrate them into the ongoing visual record that they are constructing of their lives, a record that may never be watched in its entirety, and whose meanings thus extend beyond the visual. The outcome of many family videos is volume after volume of cassettes that will never be watched. Media production here becomes a ritual process that constructs the family.

There are many other media production activities that need to be examined. The video security systems in banks and shopping malls, ham radio, live webcast cameras, pornographic interactive webcasts, and many others. The development of low-format, (relatively) inexpensive media technologies has placed the capacities for image making and sound recording in the hands of a wide variety of families, groups and entrepreneurial companies quite apart from the state and corporate culture industries. The tools once monopolized by these media industries are no longer monopolies. The rise of cable and satellite technologies, as well as webcasting, are creating new distribution routes parallel to those controlled by media distribution monopolies as faxes, cassette technology, and mp3 Internet files have already done on a small scale. Yet the integration of these technologies into everyday life remains a key locus for ethnographic attention. It is not only the Kayapo and the Yuendumu and the Warlpiri and the Navajo who generate new hybrid social formations in and through the use of new media technologies; private security companies conducting surveillance on customers, the middle-class Egyptian bride and groom, the Nigerian shrine community, and the Welsh tourists are all doing likewise.

Communities and Industries

The purpose of this chapter is not to draw a sharp line between state and monopolistic private media production, on the one hand, and what I'm calling "cottage culture industries" on the other. Rather, my hope is to draw attention to the fact that corporate- and state-controlled dream factories are not the whole of the production industry. Home movies, national cinemas, video horror movies, pornographic webcasting, indigenous television, film, and radio all involve different technologies and social relations, yet they all coexist in parallel with one another. Moreover, I want to suggest that it is in the interest of media studies to blur these distinctions rather than seek to clarify them, because the discoveries of those who study small media may be productively extended into studies of more industrialized media industries.

Deliberately blurring the boundaries between categories of media production may sound like academic heresy, but it is empirically sound. Camille Bacon-Smith (2000) offers an exemplary study of media production in which the boundaries between passionate consumers and producers are permeable and crossed back and forth with great frequency. Fans, as we saw in chapter 5, are not only consumers but producers of texts; their passionate engagement with their material leads them to produce short stories and novels for publication and distribution through fanzines, fan websites, and other media. The boundaries between these fan culture industries and the professional industries are frequently crossed. Fans become not only authors of science-fiction novels, screenplays, and short stories, but genre book buyers for bookstore chains, editors of magazines, book editors for publishing houses, role-playing game writers, illustrators, and so on. Such professionals remain not only consumers of the kinds of media they now professionally produce, but fans who continue (albeit often in transformed ways) to participate in fan culture. It is not too much to say that science-fiction fans and authors occupy the same aesthetic culture in Sol Worth's sense. Bacon-Smith thus offers us an inverse of Manuel's observation. Not only do new technologies create opportunities for new producers to enter (and construct) fields of production with different degrees of capital but they allow, under some conditions, for an increased engagement between producers and consumers such that the distinctions between them are not only blurred, but the crossing-over creates strategies of action within the field, creative reactions to changes in modes of production. This blurring of distinctions in an American media industry, where these distinctions are conceived as hard and fast, suggests the profitability of examining these issues elsewhere.

Bacon-Smith's study may be a special case within the American mediascape, but it opens up the possibility of empirically exploring the roles of multiple and competing aesthetics tied to subcultural communities of taste not only in terms of consumption but production. At the same time, Bacon-Smith's study demonstrates that such overlaps are always incomplete. The mysterious world of movies and television is an example for the science-fiction industry. Fans find themselves at once captured by the possibilities of movies and television, and at the same time frustrated by the alternative cultural worlds inhabited by producers, and their imperviousness to fans.

Descriptions of cottage culture industries suggest that the worlds of the culture industry and other forms of media production are issues of scale, not kind, and that the anthropological study of production need not be seen only as an ethnography of producers but as the ethnographic study of the ways in which media production technologies are incorporated into and positioned within the social relations of communities. It urges us to consider ways to describe media worlds that encompass parallel modes of media production, that link consumers and producers, and that see mediation as part of a complex of systems for cultural expression and social formation.

Notes

1. In addition to those works reviewed in this chapter, a useful review of the literature on this topic is offered by Richard Chalfen in his afterword to the revised edition of *Through Navajo Eyes* (Worth and Adair 1997: 275-341).

2. In early work, Worth did privilege the edeme as the "basic unit ... since this is the unit that, when combined in sequence, seems to produce the larger unit that we call a film" (1966: 332). By the time of *Through Navajo Eyes* (1972) Worth and Adair were talking of the inextricability of code and context in understanding the making of films within a community. During the same period, Worth shifted from speaking of visual "grammars" to filmic "codes." These shifts seem to have been in part a response to the shift in academic linguistics from Bloomfieldian to Chomskyan definitions of grammar. Chomsky's notion of a contextless linguistics of ideal speaker-hearers does not suit Worth's theories at all.

3. Of course, as Bloch (1998) argues, the whole point of ethnography as an intimate form of research is that it allows the researcher to learn the key symbols of the host culture, even where these are not clearly embodied in language.

4. For a similar anthropological approach to visual communication, see Bateson (1972b).

5. In its original context, this statement is intended as an ethical issue: the responsibility of the anthropologist to inform their host communities that new media need not carry with them the cultural forms in which they are enmeshed in Western societies. In fact, recent work in "indigenous media" suggests that many indigenous communities have less need of being taught this than do media scholars who jump to the conclusion that media technologies are inherently destructive of indigenous cultures (e.g. the debate in *Current Anthropology* 38, No. 2 [1997]: 197-235).

6. On the concept of "indigenous media" and its relations both to mass media and to documentary (including ethnographic) filmmaking, see also Ginsburg 1993a, 1993b, 1994a, 1994b, 1994c, 2002a, 2002b.

7. Weiner's notion that things that are "cultural products through and through" carry with them totalizing modes of thought is a difficult thesis to maintain, however. This view seems be based on the assumption that social facts remain such even when uprooted and transplanted. Here, the medium is not only the message but an entire cosmology. This kind of argument can be made on a logical basis, if one accepts certain theoretical assumptions about culture, but it is difficult to demonstrate empirically.

8. As early as the late 1970s, Gary Granzberg and his colleagues reported on the appropriation of television characters into Cree tales (Granzberg, Steinbring, and Hamer 1977; Granzberg and Steinbring 1980; Granzberg 1982). As contemporary Cree grow up having listened to these orally-mediated narratives, are they less Cree than their predecessors? Nor are the discourses that infiltrate contemporary practices incessantly negative. Indigenes are hardly immune to adopting positive cultural stereotypes from these larger discourses. Even as anthropologists, archaeologists, and historians decry films from *Nanook of the North* to *Dancing with Wolves* for their inaccuracies, many native peoples admire them for arousing interest and instilling pride in the old ways among youth. Adoption of the "noble savage" and "environmental Indian" (Krech 1999) stereotypes—whether from genuine belief or in pursuit of strategic goals, or some combination of the two—can be a powerful form of cultural assertion (Landsman 1987).

9. The arguments about authenticity in and around indigenous media production are summarized well by Pack (2000).

10. Sol Worth seemed to feel that they were not producing films *as* "natives" once they learned to make films according to Western codes of representation. Worth reviewed a documentary made by Mohawk Indians trained and equipped under a Canadian National Film Board program, calling it "a perfect example of the professional white liberal film made in 'consultation' with Indians" (1972b: 1030).

Chapter 9

MAPPING THE MEDIASCAPE

I ran into Shanker as I was getting off the bus that took me from my flat in South Delhi to Connaught Place, where he worked. I had come up to see him. He greeted me with a *"Ram Ram"* and we proceeded toward his shop, where it had been agreed that I could interview him in between the press of business. We passed a newsstand and paused as Shanker considered the large display of newspapers. Apart from the dozen or so foreign papers aimed at the tourists who throng the heart of Delhi, there are more than forty daily newspapers in the metropolis.[1] Choosing among this abundance of newspapers involves organizing them along a system of gradations that takes into account language, political affiliations, and ties to place. Language distinctions include not only the fundamental differences between English, Hindi, Urdu, and Punjabi, but differences in the registers of those languages. The Sanskritized Hindi of *Nav Bharat Times* is admired by many, but rejected by others as pompous and artificial. Newspaper buyers pay attention not only to which party a newspaper may support, but to whether it is a party mouthpiece or a critical organ in which different factions of the party display their conflicts, or one of many shades in between. Newspapers also invoke locales: *Times of India*, for example, published editions in six different cities but in each of these cities it was linked to Bombay in the popular imagination, just as *Statesman* was linked to Calcutta, *Hindustan Times* to Delhi and the *Hindu* to Madras.

Shanker was not trying to make a choice, however; he was waiting for the stand's owner to see him. When he did, they exchanged a greeting, and the man handed Shanker his morning copy of *Punjab Kesari*. No money changed hands; later the newsstand owner would send a boy over to get some *paan*[2] from Shanker. Newspaper in hand, we hurried together to his *paan* shop. Like many of my Indian hosts, Shanker made a distinction between those newspapers he "takes" and those he merely buys. The newspapers one takes must be chosen carefully because they enter into the texture of daily life. They become identified with you. *Nav Bharat Times* is brought to Shanker's home by a local bicycle delivery man, with whom he might share a few words if he is up early enough. The newspaper is conservative, and above reproach in its language, so it can be read by Shanker's wife and children. The "chaste" Hindi is difficult and will help his older children learn proper language. It is the newspaper that Shanker reads each morning over tea and chapattis before he comes to his shop.

Even if *Nav Bharat Times*'s editorial stance and style changed suddenly, Shanker might still continue to take it. "Taking" implies a commitment to the newspaper, perhaps even a compulsion. Indian readers are fond of referring to their "habit" of taking certain newspapers. One man who had moved from Calcutta to Delhi to take a job selling milk, said that although he also now read the *Hindustan Times*, he could not give up the *Statesman* because it was his habit. An insurance agent in Delhi told me, "a man would divorce his wife before he would give up his newspaper."

The *paan* shop was already open, in the charge of Vijay, Shanker's young nephew, who hurries off to get us steaming glasses of sweet, milky tea. Shanker always complained of being a poor man, but he did a lively business all day, not only in *paan* but in sodas, chocolate bars, and bottled water for the tourists. In the late morning, Ram came by and offered Shanker a copy of *Dainik Jagran*. Ram had a station outside the post office, where he helped tourists package things to ship abroad. The two men chatted for a bit. They were old friends, part of a group of four men who trade talk and newspapers in a cycle during the long fourteen-hour workday. By common agreement, I gradually moved from one man to the next, interviewing each in his respective place of business, and listening to him talk about the news with his friends.

As I talked with these men, I was struck by the degree to which their ways of interpreting the texts involved assumptions about who is producing the news and why. Rather than treating the newspaper as a window on the world, they seemed to treat it as a knowledgeable acquaintance—or even a friend—whose understandings of things has to be judged on the basis of your knowledge of his or her character. Again and again, they imagined reasons why the newspaper says what it says. Ram suggested that the fatality and injury figures from recent communal riots were being underreported to keep the stories from sparking further riots. Shanker argued that each crisis was reported to divert people's attention from the last, none of them ever being solved. Padam said that many journalists mean well, but they are at the mercy of their employers, who naturally want newspapers to reflect their own interests. Of course, he added, it all depends on whether or not a newspaper is "sincere."

I have heard this term before from other newspaper readers. Most newspaper readers understand the Indian press to be free from government censorship—unlike television news—but this does not mean a newspaper will use its freedom in the public interest. Sincere newspapers are trustworthy, but not in the sense of being reliably accurate. Any newspaper may not tell you all the complete truth, but sincere newspapers tell the news with an eye to the public good, while other newspapers may lie to you as part of a government plot or to further the interests of their proprietors. Completely insincere papers are contemptuously referred to as *raddi*, wastepaper. The insult is subtle, because in a sense, all newspapers are *raddi* once their news value is gone—the material component of the newspaper is sold by weight as a recyclable good. To refer to a current newspaper as *raddi* is to imply that it has no news value to begin with.

For Shanker and his friends, reading the newspaper is not a cognitive act of interpretation, a decoding or an interpellation into a world of discourse. Rather, it is a set of practices in which the acts of selecting, buying, interpreting, talking about, and getting rid of the newspaper are all mutually implicated. They are conscious of the newspaper as one medium among a web of other media. They are aware of differences in kinds of newspapers and in registers of language that index social distinctions. They have an understanding of the news as a construction by political forces of which they believe they have some understanding. Reading the news thus involves a whole complex of knowledges and practices that link the fields of production and the fields of consumption, other media genres, the news stories themselves, and the medium as a material object.

As I suggested in chapter 7, such a complex can be described as comprising a "media world," on the model of Becker's "art worlds" (Becker 1976, 1982, 1990). Becker defines an "art world" as a structure of cooperative activities necessary for "art" to happen. Shanker and his friends, newspaper producers (publishers, reporters, editors, press operators, and the rest), newspaper delivery people, newsstand operators, the men on bicycles who collect *raddi*, and the rest occupy a "news world" of this sort. This news world is one of several such worlds, and these are, in turn, interconnected (as shown in the ways Shanker talks of television news as opposed to the press).

The notion of the "media world" as a complete whole that encompasses all the activities associated with some medium is useful, but imprecise. It draws our attention to the importance of thinking of all these activities as constituting some kind of interconnected whole, but it offers us no clear way to imagine the connections. Moreover, it offers us limited scope to imagine the connections between each of these worlds. Some scholars have begun to use the term *communication ecology* as a more precise way to imagine this interconnected whole. The term implies a continuum of forms of communication, each with its own technologies, standards, assumptions, and connections to other forms (J. Anderson 1999: 46). "A communications ecology places a technological medium within the cultural environment which gives it meaning and authority" (White 1999: 164). Each of these cultural environments, like the "news world" described above, is a niche in the fluid network that comprises a communications ecology. A constellation of such networks (operating across national and other boundaries) can be said to constitute a *mediascape*, combining both "the distribution of the … capabilities to produce and disseminate information (newspapers, magazines, television stations, and film production studios), which are now available to a growing number of private and public interests throughout the world" and "the images of the world created by these media" (Appadurai 1996: 35).

So far, this book has examined the ways of analyzing media texts, the social organization of production and the situated practices of media consumption and interpretation. Mapping communications ecologies and the larger mediascape involves examining connections between these domains. In this chapter, I will examine ways of mapping mediascapes on ever grander scales. This approach involves looking at

1. the interrelationship between producers, consumers, and the texts they exchange;
2. the patterned relations of producers, consumers, texts and technologies conceived as media worlds defined by *media literacies*, complex units having to do with interpretive practices in relationship to technologies, situations, persons, and communities;
3. the connections between these media worlds, conceived as relations of intertextuality and indexicality; and
4. the relations of these interconnected media systems to other social systems, conceived of as spectacle and as ritual, or social drama.

Connections and Disconnections

Aarti, a young reporter for an English daily in Delhi, had mixed feelings about covering the Second International Conference on AIDS in Asia and the Pacific. "No one I know has AIDS," she told me. "No one I know knows anyone with AIDS. I think the same will be true of the people who are reading my stories." At the same time, she had a sense that the story could be important: it was the local part of a global story, a story that allowed India to be seen as part of a global "war" against AIDS. Yet she feared it might be a potentially sensitive story. "Sensitive" means that she must pay attention to what she writes because "many of these people [newspaper readers] ... aren't critical in their thinking."

Shanker is not the reader Aarti imagines. In Aarti's world, *paan-wallahs* are illiterate and backward, not well-read or capable of sophisticated discussions of politics. Yet there are connections. Shanker, too, imagines other audiences, less sophisticated than himself, who believe whatever they read. And Shanker agrees with Aarti that the AIDS story is an international one, although he is more cynical. He argues that the whole conference is a front, an effort by the government to bring foreign money into India.

Perhaps the most straightforward way to examine the connections and disconnections between the social fields of producers and the interpretations of actual consumers is to combine an ethnography of audiences with an ethnography of the sites of media production or, failing that, interviewing people on both sides of the apparent gulf. Several anthropologists have combined ethnographies of consumption with interviews of producers to juxtapose the stated intentions of the producers with the situated interpretations of those with whom they have watched television or films. Here I will summarize some of the material from a series of works in which Lila Abu-Lughod (1993a, 1993b, 1993c, 1995a, 1995b, 1997,1998a, 1998b) has explored the ways in which the intentions of media producers, shaped by a particular social matrix, are not necessarily at all in line with the interpretations of media texts by consumers.

In Egypt, where Abu-Lughod did her fieldwork, nearly all media production takes place in Cairo, the nation's capital, with the exception of some work in urban Alexandria and some shooting in hired studios in the Gulf states. Within this urban milieu, deeply shaped by the political discourse of print journalism, many television writers, directors and producers are deemed daring for their social criticism, their willingness to make dramas that confront social issues. But, as Abu-Lughod points out, the social issues they confront are social issues as they see them from their own positions in the social field. In addition to the very real political and economic straits created by the possibility of government censorship, writers of serials are constrained by their own participation in particular kinds of shared discourses about nationhood— shared, that is, among other educated urban Egyptians. This discourse is inflected for them by their own positions as media producers, in a milieu in which television is justified as an educational medium. The role of this medium is defined, in turn, by an understanding of education as part of a national process of development, of turning "backward" people into "modern" people.

The audiences imagined by the television writers are always less complex and more clearly bordered than the real people who watch their serials. One famous writer produced a serial about aging women in a retirement community who studied, learned new careers and, in the climax of the program, one even took a husband at age sixty. Abu-Lughod contrasts the sincere desires of the writer to combat what she saw as a universal problem by showing that aging women need not just wait to die, but have lives to live, with talk about the show by women in a south Egyptian village. Many of these women were widows or had absentee husbands, and hence were heads of household. They managed farms, put their children through school, and performed their religious obligations. Some might be interested in learning to read and write to better negotiate with the state bureaucracies or to read the Quran, but having put their children through school, many are all too aware that Egypt's educational system produces far more secondary school and even college degrees than the labor market can absorb.[3]

Even when producers create programs aimed directly at rural markets, they cannot easily step outside their own preconceptions of their audiences. The author of one serial on a rural community even lived in such a community for a time to gather local color. Yet her script could not move outside the fundamental notion that such populations are backward, and that the mission of television is to educate them. Members of audiences in the rural communities with whom Abu-Lughod watched episodes of the serials tended to dismiss these serials as being about them but, like Powdermaker's southerners, were willing to believe they could be about other villages, maybe even those nearby.

Abu-Lughod's work confirms that media texts cannot create their own contexts for interpretation. Mapping this series of disjunctures, however, does more than offer further empirical evidence for understanding consumption as a polyvalent and negotiated process; it suggests a kind of unified plurality of voices, interpretations, and practices. For Abu-Lughod, Dickey, Mankekar, and other contemporary anthropologists, media viewers are not constituted as a community by the act of consumption; rather, they consume within communities of which they are already a part. Access to mass media technologies, the time and place of acts of consumption, norms of interpretation, social discourse about the text, and about the media generally, are all mediated by the communities in which people live.

Yet what is crucial here is the possibility that these disconnections and connections are patterned. The circulation of media texts, and the representational content of those texts, link the social fields of production with the social fields of consumption, and they do so in culturally ordered ways. Media producers seek to create socially relevant content, and to do so they draw on widely shared cultural patterns, yet they do so from within the constraints of their own positions. Rural and lower-class urban audiences may not learn from television the lessons that the cosmopolitan, upper-class urban producers expect them to learn, but they do feel that they learn things; indeed, the two groups share a conception of television as a medium of education.

Media Literacies

Finding patterns in the connections and disconnections created by mass media requires us to extend our ethnographic attention from a focus on the text (including production as the making of texts and consumption as the interpretation of texts), and to turn our attention to some of the extratextual aspects of media often ignored or treated as secondary in media analysis. Although we have seen some examples in chapters 6 and 8, in this section I wish to move such interpenetration to the center and ask how the increasing ubiquity of media forms and technologies in people's lives shapes the creation of social meaning. A survey of the ways that media have meanings in our lives outside of the immediate contexts of production and consumption, would include discourses about media, the meanings attached to the physical objects of media production and consumption, and the extension of media practices into other domains of life.

Public discourses about various forms of media may serve as frameworks for media consumption, but there is no necessity that this should happen. One anthropologist in South Asia told me she was in the Maldives the day television arrived and that the response of the community was to lock their doors for the first time ever. Although there was a widespread belief that television would bring violence and crime in its wake, this belief had no discernible effect on television, nor, as far as she could tell, on the interpretation of specific texts. Discourse about television as a source of corruption from beyond was not linked to actual consumption but served different kinds of social functions. This seems to be consonant with Richard Wilk's observations of moral discourse about television in Belize, in which talk about television has relatively little to do with actual viewing but serves instead as a means of contrasting past and present, local and foreign, and traditional and modern in moral terms. Talk about television absorbs existing class, gender, and ethnic distinctions and re-represents them as being about television:

> I suggest that television has become a social, cultural and political issue that is integrating with ongoing discourse, and is being used by existing groups to further their own positions and agendas. In the process, "television talk" subtly transforms that discourse. It creates new coalitions of common interest. It changes the content and terms of social debate, moving them away from the economic and political and towards the cultural. (Wilk 1995: 244)

Moreover, television in Belize offers a common set of discursive "packages" (Öncü 1995) with which to talk about social change. Broadcasting texts from abroad, it objectifies the local by offering it something against which to contrast itself, creating the possibility for moral discourses about culture. Such discourses have very real effects on society: "Paradoxically, television imperialism may do more to create a national culture and national consciousness in Belize than forty years of nationalist politics and eleven years of independence" (Wilk 1995: 244).

The media also exist among us as physical objects. Although the ethnography of media consumption pays attention to the physical dimension of media artifacts, it usually assesses them as part of a framework for the interpretation of the text. In fact, televisions, radios, CD players, cassette tapes, newspapers, and myriad others are a part of our lives quite apart from our use of them in acts of interpretation. They have uses and values of their own. In Cairo, CD-ROMs offering free internet access are given away in shops and restaurants in affluent neighborhoods. These are often salvaged by taxi drivers who hang them in their cabs, their mirrored surfaces perfect for repelling the evil eye. In India, old newspapers, robbed of their value by the simple passage of time, spawn an entire recycling industry, employing collectors on bicycles, dealers with concrete-block storage units, and employees engaged in the mechanical process of tearing and pasting newspapers into bags that will be filled with roasted peanuts or kernels and peddled on the street.

John Postill offers a thorough exploration of the values of televisions among the Saribas Iban of Sarawak. These include their *market* value, subject to rapid depreciation; their value as *exchange* goods; their value as *status* markers; their *utilitarian* value as sources of information and entertainment; their *moral* value as devices that allow Iban to contrast their local custom (*adat*) with the televised lifestyles and morals of other, more powerful ethnic groups; their *aesthetic* value, as objects appreciated for their design and style; their *historical value* as "collectibles" (*koleksi*); their *biographical value* insofar as they are used in the construction of a sense of self in relation to others; and their *social value* in providing occasions for people to come together. So deeply can televisions become integrated into peoples' lives, that in spite of the considerable family investment their purchase requires, Iban may use them as grave goods, burying the television with a member of the family who particularly loved it (Postill n.d.).

Finally, there is the issue of the ways media may shape of everyday praxis. New media often initially adapt to preexisting divisions of time and space, of habit and aesthetic. Over time, however, they often begin to reshape our everyday lives, albeit not in predictable ways. For example, while television in Belize alters perceptions of time, in some ways the new periodicity liberates Belizeans from an older colonialist periodization that divided the world into the backward and the modern. The new TV time offers new ideas about culture and time that allow local goods to be "old fashioned" rather than backward, and local food to become "ethnic" cooking rather than "bush" food (Wilk 1996). In a very different context, Caldarola (1992b) argues that during the Gulf War, television's immediacy distorted the relationship between time and distance in such a way as to further the war agenda.[4]

Richardson and Meinhof (1999) argue that European broadcasting has seen three "eras" marked by distinct changes in the semiotics of time and space. Whereas television had previously accommodated itself to preexisting routines of everyday life, and then had itself become one of those routines, the new era is one of twenty-four hour broadcasting, unlimited reruns, and liveness as a hallmark of authenticity. And whereas television had originally been largely controlled by state agencies that made the "nation" the central fact of cultural space, contemporary television constructs audience identities in terms of markets and accepts no responsibilities to linguistic, cultural, or ethnic minorities.

Such theories assume that the ways media periodicize events or reconstruct spatial relations can introduce fundamental changes into the ways people perceive and act in the world around them. Conrad Kottak (1990) makes a case that people draw models from media-saturated domains of everyday life and apply them to other arenas. Kottak offers the example of the student reading while he lectured at the University of Michigan. The student turned out not to be enrolled in the class; having grown up with television, radio, and music players of various kinds, she could not read without background noise. Examining television in Brazil, Kottak argues that increasing levels of television saturation can be correlated with changes in the ways people talk about and act in the world.

Media's capacity to reshape public discourse, the values of objects, and the rhythms of daily life is a significant issue with far-reaching implications. Recognition that the media can reshape social life has led many scholars to speak of media as changing the ways people think. Writing about the ways media(ted) discourses of kinship intersect with preexisting discourses, Rodgers claims that they "restructure consciousness and social life in countries ... entering an age of nationally-controlled, urban-based modern communication systems" (1986). This is one of many essays postulating an emergent form of consciousness shaped by new forms of communications technology. This thesis postulates a media literacy or "mediacy" succeeding the earlier forms of orality and literacy, and shaping a new cultural-historical framework and new forms of cognition. This media literacy hypothesis arises by analogy with the thesis that the introduction of writing induces a shift from oral societies to literate societies, introducing profound changes not only in the ways people communicate but in the very ways they see the world. In this view, the rise of writing technologies in previously illiterate societies alters perceptions of time and space, replaces root metaphors in the worldview and modifies patterns of cognition. Originally introduced in a now-classic essay by Goody and Watt (1963), this thesis proposes that the technology of writing alphabetically[5] not only made it possible to "fix" speech and to create representations of the world but also changed the ways literate people see the world so represented.

This thesis states that whereas in oral societies, accounts of the past can be transformed to meet situational exigencies, writing produces records against which the past can be checked. The idea of history thus protrudes itself and with it a recognition that change is constant. New notions of objectivity, of abstract knowledge (removed from the contexts of everyday life), and of analytical thinking, in which records can be compared, emerge. These notions infiltrate cosmologies, with textual metaphors replacing older ways of seeing the world. The Word of God becomes not a spoken word but a written one. The world itself becomes understood as a text that can be read. These changes make possible new modes of knowledge. Oral modes of representation, it is claimed, are memory-based, empathetic and participatory, situational and collective. Literary modes of representation are record-based, objective and distanced, abstract and analytic (Ong 1982; Goody 1986, 1987).

A series of extended critiques of this deterministic view has led several of the leading theorists of this perspective to scale back their claims,[6] but the notion that technologies of representation shape the meanings of the messages remains a strong trend in media studies. In this view, the relationship between the written and the oral is being fundamentally transformed. New modes of cognition are emerging, although it may be too early to describe these clearly.

That new literacies emerge in response to the introduction of new media is an unavoidable conclusion. Among Aborigines "for whom all stories are true" (Michaels 1994), exposure to American westerns required the creation of a whole series of new interpretive codes and viewing practices.

> People were reading these movies as 'real' then; they wanted to know, for instance, what had happened to John Wayne's wife, who had appeared in one movie the previous week and now seemed to have disappeared. And where were his mother and father? His other kinsmen? (Hamilton 1997: 217)

These new codes involve not only learning how to decode the foreign text's narrative conventions—that kinship plays a minor role in the hero's identity, for example—but also the very idea of fiction, and the notion of "actors," real people who pretend to be one person in one film and another person in another.

Certainly it is not unreasonable to assume that with these new literacies will come new ways of seeing the world, new metaphors that can be extended beyond the act of viewing movies into other parts of the social world, such as the idea, perhaps, that people are sometimes like actors, or that not all stories are true. Rosalind Morris gives an extraordinary example of this in her account of changes in mediumship in Thailand. Mediums have embraced photography, radio, and television, not only using these forms as means of extending their client bases (or, in one important case, denouncing the whole institution as fraudulent), but also transforming traditional ways of speaking about mediumship by adopting the idiom of broadcasting. Instead of being "mounted" by spirits, the medium is now conceived of as the device through which spirits transmit messages to receivers on earth (Morris 2000).

It is important to recognize, however, that learning such new ways of seeing do not necessarily replace old ways of seeing, as the literacy hypothesis implies. David MacDougall (1987) points out that while Aborigines are capable of enjoying Western media when it is about non-Aboriginal subjects, when media is about them, they wish it to conform to indigenous aesthetics, as described in chapter 7. Production is performed with audiences in mind, and production and consumption thus shape one another. Among the Ernabella of Western Australia, certain locally produced materials can only be seen by particular initiates, while others are meant for wider distributions.

The empirical problems raised by the literacy thesis have led scholars to question whether literacy can be treated as a thing-in-itself. Increasingly, the move has been to see literate practices as emergent in cultural and historical processes, and embedded in specific cultural practices. Instead of "literacy" as a unique practice that produces particular modes of thought and action, scholars are writing of multiple, situated "literacies" (Heath 1983; Street 1984, 1991; Besnier 1991; Bloch 1998; Barton, Hamilton and Ivanic 2000). This approach recognizes that all written language is located in particular times and places, that literate activity is produced toward particular ends and shaped by broader social practices.

Summarizing a decade or more of work in the theory of situated literacies, David Barton and Mary Hamilton (2000) suggest six assumptions for understanding literacies as multiple and situated:

1. Literacy is best understood as a set of social practices; these can be inferred from events that are mediated by written texts.
2. There are different literacies associated with different domains of life.
3. Literacy practices are patterned by social institutions and power relationships, and some literacies are more dominant, visible, and influential than others.
4. Literacy practices are purposeful and embedded in broader social goals and cultural practices.
5. Literacy is historically situated.
6. Literacy practices change and new ones are frequently acquired through processes of informal learning and sense making.

Applying these principles to media allows us to begin situating ethnographic studies of media into communication ecologies and wider mediascapes (conceived here as networks of communications ecologies). In any social setting, types of media practices and kinds of events come to cluster around technologies. These sets of practices constitute a literacy. It is meaningful to speak, therefore, of television literacy, movie literacy, and so forth, for a given social milieu. These practices also differ with different social domains, such as religion, health, home, entertainment, public space, the workplace, the school, and so forth. Within each domain they serve different, and sometimes multiple, goals; these goals are related to wider social goals and cultural norms. These different uses of literacies require different cognitive and social skills.

Shanker and his friends are engaged in just such practices. For them, as for many of my Indian hosts, newspapers enable sociality. Far from being silent, cognitive acts, newspaper literacy in India often involves, and constructs, social relations. The ritual act of sharing newspapers daily reestablishes bonds between these four men. The content of the newspapers gives them something to talk about. The content changes from day to day, but this is not the central issue; what is significant is the connection that the talk creates between the men. Other aspects of press literacy in India come to the fore when one shifts domains to the home, or the office, or caste-specific public reading rooms.

But press literacy not only creates sociality; it also marks social distinctions. What newspapers one takes defines one in certain ways: English newspapers are of higher status than Hindi or Urdu newspapers, which are higher status than Punjabi. "Good" English newspapers like *Times of India* are of higher status than those written in "spicy" English like *Mid-Day*. Similar continua exist between chaste and spicy Hindi and Urdu. Nor is language the only such distinguishing feature: the price of one's paper, its political affiliation, and the kinds of advertisements it carries, all serve to place a person in a social field through the act of selecting and buying a newspaper.

These identities are obviously connected to wider cultural categories and social differences. They are distinctions that map social stratification in linguistic, political and economic dimensions. Using their media literacies, Shanker and his friends reestablish on a daily basis their position as middle-class shopkeepers, neither rich nor poor, educated but not highly educated, politically knowledgeable (and argumentative) but within the safe, nonradical parameters demarcated by their newspapers. Through their practices they experience themselves as friends, as citizens, as businessmen (the routine interruptions to see to customers ensures that), as Indians, and so forth.

Such literacies encompass the practices of both consumers and producers of media. Journalists imagine the audiences for which they write on the basis of these same sets of distinctions, and marketers toil over such problems as how to widen circulation without lowering one's language, or changing other markers of position. Many newspapers refuse certain kinds of lucrative advertising—lottery ads or even film ads—as vulgar and threatening to the face the paper presents in the social field. The work of editors, subeditors, and marketing professionals is always, at one level, maintaining the "place" of the newspaper in the social field, in accord with local press literacies.

The Intertextual Web

The notion of media literacies allows us to explicate the notion of a communications ecology as a network of media niches. Each niche is a "media world," consisting of the peoples and institutions that produce those events and objects which people define as media of a particular type: the media world of the telephone, the media world of television, the media world of radio, and so forth. Each such world is organized by

its own media literacies, modes of interpretation connected with specific practices, identities and varieties of experience.

For these worlds to form an ecology, however, they cannot be seen
as being each self-standing. They are interconnected by a number of different features: legal codes, regulations, shared technologies, linked
modes of production, similar sites of reception, and related forms of discourse. Jenny White (1999) offers an example of the interconnections
between niches in the communications ecology in her account of the
uses of television and telephone among working-class people in the
1991 Turkish national elections. Television was used to "package" various political positions and turn them into objects of scrutiny and
debate. It did not, however, seem to be effective in swaying voters.
Rather, it primarily offered voters crystallizations that helped confirm
and articulate what they already believed. The telephone, on the other
hand, was a powerful interpersonal medium that could be used to
extend personal networks based on trust and common community
interest. Parties with members in working-class communities could use
the telephone to rapidly exploit and extend existing networks and mobilize support for events and activities. What seems not to have been
effective was the use of the telephone as a broadcast medium; that is,
the use of the telephone by unknown persons at the party office calling
households to urge them to vote, boycott, or take other political action.

White's analysis does not merely compare two niches in the communicative ecology; it focuses on the flow of political information from
one to the other. She demonstrates that one of the most effective ways
of analyzing the connections and disconnections between local media
worlds is an examination of intertextual practice, the active social
process involving the extracting of a discourse or discursive element
from one setting (decontextualization) and inserting it into another
(recontextualization). In this section I want to go beyond intertextuality as a property of texts, which I discussed in chapter 3, to the notion
of intertextuality as an interpretive practice, a tool for linking the
processes of production with media texts, those texts with audience
consumption, media consumption with social intercourse and, finally,
social life with media production.

The essence of the approach I am advocating here is to treat intertextuality not as a property of texts but as a social strategy. In this view,
intertextuality is one among many strategies—reflexive and tactical as
well as unreflexive and habitual—by which people use the mass media
as part of their cultural capital, as part of the symbolic stuff they need
to accomplish the ordinary tasks of everyday life. To treat intertextuality as a strategy is to attempt to shift it from the realm of art or media
effects to the mundane practices of everyday life. An anthropology of

media that attempts to describe and explain the meanings of media in a society or community ought to be able to explain not only how cultural meanings are encoded in media texts but also the ordinary uses of media in everyday social interaction.

Such everyday social interactions include those that take place in the social fields of production. Many years ago at UCLA, I was told an anecdote about a graduate of the film program, now a famous director, who kept trying to get an actress to perform in a certain way by telling her, "You know, like in *Sunset Boulevard*" or "the way Shirley Temple smiled in *Heidi*." The actress kept saying, "I've never seen that movie" and "who is she?" The implication, of course, was that the director, as a film school graduate, had a vast knowledge of films that he drew on in constructing his own movies. The young actress's education derived from acting workshops and modeling; she had no systematic knowledge of film history and so could not understand the director. A secondary implication of this anecdote is that contemporary movie intertextuality is not only part of a playful aesthetic, or commercial pressures, but may be deeply institutionalized into the very processes by which film and television production personnel are professionalized. Even if the anecdote is exaggerated or untrue, the fact that film students tell it as true suggests that they recognize these implications.

Both White's ethnography and the film school anecdote emphasize the fact that intertextual play is not free but shaped by (and shaping of) media literacies. The strategic use of intertextuality involves the learning of *interpretive schemes* and *interpretive practices*. "Interpretive schemes," says Anthony Giddens (1979: 83), are "standardized elements of stocks of knowledge applied by actors in the production of interaction. Interpretive schemes form the core of mutual knowledge whereby the accountable universe of meaning is sustained through and in processes of interaction." Interpretive practices, on the other hand, are normative ways in which one's knowledge of those skills is put to use. While interpretive schemes may be appropriated directly from media texts, interpretive practices must be learned within a social milieu. Interpretive practices are one of the links between media consumption and everyday life. They involve social performances and, like all social performances, they accomplish multiple ends.

There are many ways in which intertextual webs bind together not only production and consumption within a media world but link media worlds into larger communicative ecologies. Consider, for example, the power of authorship in European cinema. The notion that texts have authors forms a powerful basis for intertextual play. In film, of course, it is typical among educated audiences in the west to speak of films as belonging to a director's *ouevre* just as we speak of novels as belonging to an author's *oeuvre*. Such interpretive practices are but a social convention; film production is such an enormously complex and multilayered activity that to speak of any single author is problematic. This being so, it is the conventions themselves that offer a site for ethnographic analysis. The ways in which people use author names to create intertextual references offers many insights into the ways meaning and authority are constructed. Bourdieu (1984) notes that in France recognition of directors goes up proportionally with the audience's educational level, and suggests that the cult of the *auteur* serves as one of the distinctions of taste that produce and reproduce the class system.

Legal, economic, social, aesthetic, and other codes organize communications ecologies by determining how (and with what modifications) texts can flow from one niche to another, and they are often linked to broader cultural principles. Indeed, this is often part of the strategic use of intertextuality: to make meaning by drawing connections between the unfamiliar and the familiar. Intertextuality is a standard tool for social actors to use when faced with ambiguity. Gumperz argues that participants in communications that violate expectations always search for explanations; in this search, they "rely on previous communicative experiences and their ability to establish intertextuality by remembering specific ways of talking and the situations and activities indexically associated with their use" (Gumperz 1996: 397). Intertextuality thus involves both personal and social constructions of meaning by active social agents who, in the process, shape and reshape mediascapes through their communicative behaviors.

Examining intertextuality as a means of describing the relations between niches in the communicative ecology raises a myriad of important questions, of which two have been particularly important in this discussion: (1) what does the recontextualized text bring with it from its earlier contexts and (2) what formal functional and semantic changes does it undergo as it is being recontextualized (Bauman and Briggs 1990: 72-75; Briggs and Bauman 1992: 141ff.). To this, I would now add a third: how is intertextual play organized into practices that seek to accomplish specific ends in particular social fields? The work of Walter Armbrust (1992, 1995, 1996a, 1996b, 1998a, 1998b, 1999, 2000a, 2000b) is rich in examples of uses of media intertextuality in everyday life that shed light on this problem.

Armbrust opens his book *Mass Culture and Modernization* (1996) with an incident in which a recent law graduate and her mother, unable to enter the overcrowded and disorganized swearing ceremony for the bar, quote lines from a popular song, "How Crowded is the World," by a "vulgar" Egyptian musician, Ahmad 'Adawiya. Contextualizing this quote takes him to the popular biography of the singer, the circulation of cassette music, both legitimate and pirated, the 1980 film *Shaban Below Zero*, in which the song appears, and the 1942 movie *If I Were Rich*, of which *Shaban* was a remake. Unpacking these indexical connections, and their connotations of class hierarchy, reveals a situation in which "middle class people feeling humiliated at the hands of an institution that is supposed to enable their upward mobility ... respond by reciting words from a song that the sort of people who control institutions such as the Bar Association, not to mention the establishment media, denounce" (1996a:2).

Armbrust tacks back in forth in this way from use of intertextuality in the situations of everyday life to the texts themselves, both the ways they represent society and the popular culture contexts in which they are consumed and interpreted. As he teases out the connotations that make media texts useful for making sense of life as lived, patterns emerge. One is an ordering of the communicative ecology into a "split vernacular" in which tensions between modernity, authenticity, and nation are played out.

Again we find the process identified by Peacock in 1968: the media provide a place in which and through which people meditate on, and come to terms with, modernity, "tradition," and the nation. In Armbrust's work, however, the role of the audience is not limited to participation *as* audience; audiences make active use of media representations, exploiting them as repertoires from which one can draw materials for the articulation of everyday dilemmas.

A key locus for the analysis of intertextuality, then, involves looking at the circulation of words, phrases, and discursive styles as they are appropriated from mass media and enter into social circulation. As Spitulnik (1998a) points out, such an approach has its origins in Bakhtin's (1981: 293) observation that certain forms of discourse have a "socially charged life" and Gumperz's recognition that "mass media and the prestige of their speakers tend to carry idioms far form their sources" (1971: 223). The circulation of such idioms in the United States is obvious; phrases like "Hasta la vista, baby," "Beam me up, Scotty," "Make my day," "I don't think we're in Kansas anymore, Toto," and so forth appear frequently in a variety of speech acts and become immediately recognizable even by people who have never seen the movies or television shows in question. Similar phrases abound among audiences in every media community.

This use of media discourse in everyday life has been explored ethnographically in a series of writings on radio in Zambia by Debra Spitulnik (1994, 1998a, 1998b, 1999, in press). Spitulnik looks at the decontextualization, recontextualization, and creative reworking of media discourses as they circulate *outside* the contexts of media reception. Arguing that mass media, "because of their extensive accessibility and scope, can serve as both reservoirs and reference points" (1998a: 161) for discursive elements to enter into the use of speech communities, Spitulnik offers a series of examples of the kinds of uses people make of these idioms in a variety of settings. The nature of the play can be extremely complex. In one example, Spitulnik describes the manner in which *chongololo* ("centipede" in ChiNyanja) has come to be used as a term for Zambians who try to speak (pretentiously) like Europeans. *Chongololo* is the title of a Zambian radio program about wildlife in which the host and discussants (including children) all speak with a slow and deliberate British Received Pronunciation accent (Spitulnik 1998a: 175). And while *chongololo* has entered into general use, such intertextual play has recursive effects for media consumption, as in the case of the 20-year-old student who Spitulnik quotes as saying, "Oh, today I'm going to listen to the news because it's not the chongololos reading it."

Spitulnik's ethnography is useful in its description of the formal conditions and functional effects of such decontextualizing and recontextualizing play. But her work goes beyond this to suggest that this intertextual play casts light both on the role mass media play in building national identity and on the transformation of language. Spitulnik argues that this circulation of recognizable idioms supports Benedict Anderson's general notion that mass media help create a sense of shared community, but at the same time she questions the verticality of his model of media consumption. The circulation of idioms she has mapped out suggests that national identities can result from the frequency of use and density of social communications *using* media without a high density of direct media saturation. The active intertextual play of audiences with radio discourses has also been a source for the emergence of a hybridized language of modernity she calls "town Bemba" a "set of Bemba-based multilingual practices which are iconic, indexical and symbolic of urbanity and modernity in Zambia" (Spitulnik 1999: 51). Such analysis offers a concrete and ethnographically accessible approach to the study of mass media in social change without the problematic assumptions that have characterized so many analyses of mass media and "modernization."

Intertextuality, then, can be seen as a form of social action through which people use media resources to achieve various ends. Far from being only an inherent property of texts, intertextuality can be seen as a strategically deployed practice through which producers and consumers construct meanings, frame activities and pursue outcomes. Such intertextual play is never free but takes place within a normative framework that both organizes and is organized by such interplay. In the patterns by which such interplay takes place, particularly legal, economic, and social codes guiding these interactions, the contour of the communications ecology are revealed.

Media Rituals and Social Dramas

Sometimes particular mediated events can seem to colonize large potions of a communications ecology for a period of time, such that they actively engage vast numbers of people. In the United States, for example, a president's speech may move rapidly from complete live coverage to an immediate television commentary in which quotations are discussed and given interpretations. Edited snippets will subsequently be aired in summary stories on the nightly news (but may first appear as advertisements for that news program). Following the news, late-night stand-up comedians may offer jokes based on the presidents words, and the jokes may further mutate over the course of the week as the writers of these jokes read commentaries. Stories will also be posted to Internet sites, many of them versions of materials that will appear the next day in newspapers. Many such sites invite public commentary. The following day, a transcription of the speech may appear in newspapers, as a sidebar to news stories that report what the president said in quotation and paraphrase, along with quoted comments by various selected supporters, opponents, and expert commentators. The speech will be further explored in newspaper editorials, and later may be taken up in news magazines. Parallel to all this is more intimate public talk, discussing the speech and the commentaries, traded interpersonally face-to-face and by telephone, letter, and e-mail. Each subsequent entextualization occurs within a unique situational context governed by the literacies peculiar to the media niche, yet each has intertextual connections to myriad others. A presidential talk is only a mild version of such a convergence of topics across the mediascape; a phenomenon like the 19910 Gulf War or the 2001 destruction of the World Trade Center multiplies this effect immeasurably.

Such a massive flow of intertextual elements across media niches is of interest not only because the transformations that occur allow us to map connections and disconnections between media worlds; such flows are also of interest because they are themselves a form of social action. They take on the status of a public ritual or social drama, through which social systems themselves may be reintegrated or transformed.

The social ritual approach to mass media derives from the work of Victor Turner. Turner understood the social to be constructed through the production of persons, particularly in ritual (1969). This is clearest in his extension of Van Gennep's (1960) classic work on *rites of passage*, rituals that are specifically about the production of persons, and the incorporation of individuals into the categories of social life. In the ritual process, individuals are transformed from one kind of person into another (from child to adult, for example) by first being removed from society to a *liminal* space. Betwixt and between social categories of person, neither one thing nor another, the normal rules of life that apply to either child or adult are suspended. During this period of transition, initiates receive instruction and training in their new status. The transformed members are then reincorporated into society as new kinds of persons.

The notion that media serves as part of a ritual process is not new. Many scholars have picked up on Turner's notions of ritual. What has made this research incomplete is that it usually assumes that such rituals are virtual experiences, of the sort described by Drummond (1996). Such theories get subsumed into the sender-message-receiver model, becoming one more theory of how media consumers are affected by media texts. This fails to adequately capture the anthropological sense of ritual as a social practice, a form of *action*, through which persons are made.

One exception is Hamid Naficy's (1993) work on exile television, which serves as an excellent example of the ways Turner saw this process as part of the larger social problem of the social production of persons. Asking how Iranian exiles living in Los Angeles become Iranian-Americans, Naficy sees a double-movement occurring amid both television producers and their audiences. Most of the producers of Persian television in Los Angeles were producers in Iran, where the economics involved state sponsorship and the media products involved particular visions of the society. As these producers became involved in American media production, they found themselves in a liminal state in which their former expertise was immaterial. To make it in the tough world of minority television, they had to learn about ratings, seeking advertisements from local businesses, advertising/content ratios, and the exactitude of timing. In so doing, they crossed over from being Iranian producers to being Iranian-American producers.

But this movement is only the backdrop to another ritual process. As the producers adapted to the minority television niche in their new communications ecology, the nature of their productions altered. The televisual worlds they constructed shifted between nostalgic, even fetishistic representations of the lost homeland, to advertisements for products available in Los Angeles. In between these stark contrasts were hybrid forms: English-language programs about Persian culture, Persian-language programs about the local Iranian exile community, talk shows, and Persian music videos. The result was the creation of a televisual liminal space through which viewers are gradually transformed from exiles into Iranian-Americans.[7] It is important to recognize that the virtual experiences of televiewing are not what produces these new persons out of old; it is media viewing in conjunction with social experience in the United States. The media offers resources for sorting out difference and for meditating on current experience through mediated symbols of the distant in time and space.

For Turner, one of the central elements of ritual, and of *communitas*, is its physicality. Most media theorists have tended to neglect the body for the mind. Turner's work on ritual offers a powerful alternative to textual and cognitive metaphors for understanding media in modern society, urging us to look instead at the interplay between imagination and bodily experience. Turner's approach differs from cognitive theories in which actors are psychologically interpellated through self-examination into the symbolic identities presented in texts, and also from many social constructionist versions that see texts as inscribing identities onto text-like minds and bodies. Turner suggests seeing ritual as a social process by which people co-construct their social and personal identities through physical and mental *activity*. Theorists following Turner have emphasized this element of seeing ritual always simultaneously as symbolic *and* performative, a social *and* a bodily practice (Bell 1992; Parkin 1992). This approach is consonant with recent arguments for seeing identities in terms of "bodily hexus" (Bourdieu 1977), "embodiment" (Csordas 1994), and "body-agency" (Connell 1995), views which see culture as experienced—and expressed—through the entire sensorium.

Media theorists have been slow to follow performance theorists down this route. The emphasis on the ethnography of situations of consumption in chapter 5 may be the start of a corrective. Ethnographers around the world have noticed the physical dimension to the media-consumption experience, and in a few cases have integrated this into their understandings of the meaning of media in particular sites. Liechty's account of proletarian Nepali filmgoers' body-agency offers a perfect example of Turner's *communitas*:

> For the often rural-born, poor, working class patrons of Hindi films the "satisfaction" and "enjoyment" of cinema going derives largely from the experience of shared emotions, of laughing, crying, and shouting in the company of hundreds of others who you know, in that instant, perfectly share your own strong feelings of pathos, fear, joy and anger. The real satisfaction of cinema lies in affirming one another's understandings and experiences of pleasure. (Liechty 1998: 102)

Like the audience at the Nepali cinema, physical activity and co-presence creates a sense of immediate shared bonds of community.

Turner's second project involves extending the ritual process from the production of social persons to the production of society itself. The concept of the *social drama* extends the ritual process into larger representational domains. Although they share the same structure, social dramas are different from rituals in that they are largely unplanned, and contingent aspects of social life.

Social dramas have four phases. The first phase begins when a *breach* of the social order takes place, usually in the form of breaking a law or some other violation of norms. This breach reveals the underlying conflicts of the social system. As a result of this breach, a *crisis* occurs. Overt conflict and antagonism arise as sides are taken and factions formed, resulting in a widening of the breach to include more and more members of the social group. *Redress* occurs as members of the group attempt to make use of formal and informal mechanisms (informal arbitration, ritual sacrifice, etc.) to limit the contagious spread of the breach. The social drama is completed when a *reintegration* of the opposed social groups occurs, or, if the redressive mechanisms are ineffectual, a *schism* occurs as the groups come to recognize that the gulf that separates them is unbridgeable.

Social dramas are significant because they are one of the central processes by which societies make themselves. They are political processes that produce systems of shared meanings. The breach initiates a society into antistructure, a situation of collective reflection and retrospection in which the values and norms of the society are suddenly on critical display. While they are occurring, of course, social dramas are contingent and messy. It is in the looking back at them in search of cohesion that they are made meaningful. The model of the social drama can be applied to a wide variety of events, from the murder of Thomas Beckett or the Mexican War of Independence of 1810 (V. Turner 1974a) to the American electoral crisis of 2000 (Beeman 2000).

The mass media are crucial actors in this process. Social processes can only become coherent by being turned into social accounts, representations such as news stories, documentaries, television docudramas, movies, jokes by stand-up comics, and so forth. This can only be done by drawing on symbols. Making the social coherent and meaningful requires a reliance on value systems and hence invokes—and creates or reproduces—structures of morality.[8]

It is the contingency of social dramas that makes them so fascinating. The social crises themselves are very real; the social, political, and economic cleavages they reveal are not imaginary. Social dramas are emergent, like social life itself, as people attempt to come to terms with what is occurring. And as people find meaning in what is occurring, they reshape their actions accordingly, producing further events that likewise require explication, and lead to further action. As a result, "it is hard to tell whether what one is observing at a given moment in the series is breach, crisis (when sides are being taken, coalitions formed and fissures spread and deepen through a number of coordinated and contiguous relationships between persons and groups), or the application of redressive machinery" (V. Turner 1974a: 79).

Contemporary news media begin accounts at the moment of breach and continue narrating them through redress, and usually into the final stage of completion. At every stage, efforts are marshaled to provide coherence to these unfolding events. Once events are completed, social dramas often produce retellings of events in a variety of media. As a result of these interventions, news media and other forms of social commentary cannot be seen merely as vehicles for the production of accounts of social drama; they must also be recognized as crucial actors in the ongoing, contingent process of making the society through such processes. This view requires us to see the social field of production in process, to watch stories evolve as producers, themselves always also consumers, react to their own productions and those of others.

The most complete application of the social drama approach to a media(ted) event is probably Robin Wagner-Pacifici's 1986 account of the 1978 kidnapping of Italian prime minister Aldo Moro by the Red Brigade. This took place at a time when Italy's political scene was in a shambles and Moro had patched together a shaky left-center government. For fifty-five days, this act and its aftermath dominated the mediascape, preempting most other discourses. The breach effectively revealed the country's underlying instability: "Italy was left without a government, without a credible and effective political class, without even a legitimate opposition to step into the breach" (1986: 63). The Red Brigade, a marginal, liminoid[9] group, suddenly occupied the center of political activity. A general strike was called. Wild accusations about foreign conspiracies abounded. Antistructure was thus ushered in as various factions sought to find something sensible and credible to say about the kidnapping and its meaning.

The drama moved into *crisis* stage as the various actors and agencies in the drama—contesting political parties, the mass media, the church, Moro (through communiqués released by the Red Brigade), his family, foreign political leaders, and the Red Brigade itself—began staking out their positions in the social field. The struggle became one of whose story was to count as *the* story. Most of these stories turned around the issue of recognizing the Red Brigade as a "real" political group with whom negotiations could be opened, rather than a band of inhuman criminals with whom no political relationship was possible.

Redress involved building a consensus around a series of national "root paradigms" or key metaphors: "the Resistance, the Reason of State, Democracy and Democratic Institutions, the Sanctity of Human life, the Working Class, and the Party" (Wagner-Pacific 1986: 169). Although different groups drew on different metaphors and employed them differently, they nonetheless managed to construct a common ground of discourse that rejected any possibility of negotiation with the terrorists. Moro became an expiatory sacrifice by the state. Ironically, almost the only voice raised against this interpretation of events was that of Moro himself, who in a series of forty-nine letters urged negotiations to restore him to liberty. Moro, and his letters, were systematically discredited, as was his family when they attempted to promote his expressed wishes.

The ritual sacrifice came to pass on May 9, when Moro's body was found on a street midway between two political party offices. This *completion* was neither fully redressive nor fully schismatic. Redress was symbolized by Moro's official state funeral. Yet schism was also symbolized, by Moro's private family funeral, which intentionally rejected national political figures because of their rejection of Moro's letters. This double funeral leads to one of Wagner-Pacifici's key points, which is that modern political spectacle and political theater are not really rituals in the sense of Turner's examples in preindustrial societies. Social dramas may be contingent but they are at the same time *handled*, and their effects are unclear. Mass audiences cannot be invoked in the same ways participatory audiences can. One can be invited to join in communitas, yet one need not. We seem to have come full circle back to the schism between producers and consumers.

And yet, something *does* happen. For a period of time, one event dominates the mediascape and extends into the everyday discourse of people's lives. Political actors, people on the street, journalists—all are joined together in a mutual production of discourses that construct, if not a shared meaning, a shared set of possible meanings, a universe of discourse that frames a set of acceptable ways for constructing accounts. This universe of discourse may itself alter and change with time. New retellings may push the boundaries of interpretation, not because they get closer to the "truth," but because they are responding to changed social conditions: changed presents produce changed accounts of the past.

Social dramas are crucial ways in which citizens of mass mediated societies come to know, make sense of, and decide how to act concerning political events. Social dramas are also about the process of struggle between orthodox and heterodox interpretations of events as they are represented by the media in particular niches in the communications ecology.

Conclusion

Communications ecologies, as I have tried to sketch them here, are complex and dynamic processes through and along which media texts are generated, circulated and consumed. Media texts have a dual existence. They are, on the one hand, configurations of symbolic elements, discourses whose meaning is constituted in the acts of interpretation by consumers. At the same time, media texts are always also materialized through physical objects—newspapers, televisions, radios—which also circulate in a variety of ways and which also carry significant social meanings.

The systems of codes by which texts and their vehicles are interpreted are embedded in media literacies, and can be seen as shared but unequally distributed systems of interpretative practice clustered around particular technologies. Literacies are not systems for applying passive codes to texts to constitute meaning, as many Western folk models of reading might suggest, but rather active processes through which interpretive practices are actively employed in many domains of everyday life to constitute meaning and pursue goals. Television literacies, then, in a particular time and place, would consist of all the interpretive practices that make television meaningful and constitute a basis for activities involving the television, of which viewing is only one.

These media literacies constitute the basis of connection and disconnection between producers and consumers of media. The meanings of media, the history of intertextuality, and understandings of media roles and effects in society serve as guidelines through which symbolic configurations are selectively appropriated and transformed by various culture industries. These culture industries, large and small, transform these symbolic configurations and return them to public circulation in new, textualized and commodified (or otherwise objectified) forms.

Production processes have their own dynamics, of course; they are shaped by the distribution of technology and the social organization of its uses, but also by struggles within the social relations of production over issues of status, wealth, pleasure, and meaning. Media producers often martial not only capital specific to their social field—expertise, aesthetics, competence, position—but draw on values more widely distributed across social domains—justice, gender, ethics—to pursue their ends within the social field of production. These struggles have consequences for the structures of the texts produced. This is as true of the production of home videos that are not really intended to be watched as it is of television news programs that are broadcast to millions.

Audiences often do not consume texts as discursive wholes. That is, attentive viewing or reading may make up only a small part of the interpretive practices by which people engage mass media. Rather, audiences selectively appropriate symbols from the sets of media texts available to them and employ these in their practices of social formation. Selection practices are shaped by media literacies, by forms of appropriateness. What features constitute genres, and what genres, times, and places are appropriate for persons of different ages, genders, classes, levels of education, and other social distinctions are crucial aspects of media literacy. Likewise, what elements of a media text consumers appropriate and what elements they ignore are partly determined by shifting but shared tastes and awareness of the social distinctions such tastes mark.

Media literacies also include norms for interpretive practice. Certain genres may demand different levels of attentiveness or verbal discussion. After-dinner family viewing of a video may be governed by very different norms than after-school viewing of a cartoon with friends, while simultaneously eating, joking, jumping on the sofa, and trying to do homework. Much of this behavior is habitual; some is strategized, as when one takes particular newspapers or purchases particular videos because they are believed to be "educational."

Media producers monitor and evaluate consumer choices through various means of surveillance (not the least of which are the observations and intuitions of producers who are also media consumers and members of other social fields than that of media production). This is equally true of the television companies who spend millions of dollars on audience profiling and the father who, having videotaped his first daughter's Girl Scout initiation, feels compelled to record those of subsequent daughters. Degrees of surveillance shift with the nature of the mode of production and the degree of distance between producers and consumers. Monopolistic culture industries put enormous effort into packaging media texts to "fit" with media literacies and to draw attention to them as products, to encourage, persuade, or compel audiences to attend to their messages of nationalism and consumption. Through this circuit, not only content but processes of selection and transformation may themselves be selectively transformed.

Media texts circulate not only between producers and consumers within the niches in the communications ecology but across them. This intertextuality is carried out both by media producers, who reproduce textual elements in multiple genres and media, but also by consumers, who use media as a repertoire of symbolic forms and employ them across different domains as part of the cultural processes of everyday life. Tracking these intertextual shifts reveals the contours of the communication ecology. Sometimes, a single text or set of texts comes to colonize entire sections of the communication ecology. These forms of intertext operate as public spectacles and rituals, challenging, transforming, and reconstituting the public spaces through which media circulate.

The notion that media texts circulate outside the communicative niches for which they were designed draws our attention to the capacity for media texts to move not only from media niche to media niche within the ecology of communicative forms but into entirely different ecologies organized by entirely different sets of literacies, networks of distribution, and interpretive practices. This form of intertextuality across national and other social and cultural boundaries is the subject of the final chapter of this book.

Notes

1. In 1992-19993, at the time of my fieldwork, the Registrar of Newspapers for India listed some 106 *daily* newspapers in New Delhi. These figures are skewed however, since *new* newspapers are required to register but no report is required when a newspaper folds. I can vouch for forty-four newspapers that I collected during my fieldwork, and some sixteen others were described to me.
2. *Paan* is a betel leaf stuffed with herbs and spices. People chew it for pleasure, and in the belief it produces health benefits.
3. Being an "educated" person does have certain status and symbolic values apart from education's purported but often unkept promise of a better life (Bach 1998). Television offers audiences a place to both feed on the fantasy of education as a ticket to a better life, and to reflect on the failures of that promise (see Armbrust 1996a; Abu-Lughod 1998a,).
4. The notion that time is a cultural, rather than natural artifact goes back at least to Evans-Pritchard (1940), and has been the focus of works by Fabian (1983), Gell (1992) and others. See Munn (1992) for an overview. This literature has been surprisingly silent on the role of the mass media.
5. A key aspect of this argument involves the phonetic alphabet as a unique intellectual technology, a system that is easy to learn because it emulates spoken discourse, as opposed to nonalphabetic writing systems like Chinese or hieroglyphic systems, which require intensive training and can be known only by a special class of literati.
6. See Collins 1995 for an overview of this debate.
7. Shryock (2000) points out that in the United States, state-supported media production, under the guise of "cultural activities," also leads to the production of "hyphenated" Americans. This provides additional evidence that the niches in a cultural ecology are never organized by the means or production (although they may be organized *around* a technology) but are framed by larger cultural and historical processes.

8. Recall Warner's comments on the newspaper as an instrument of moral discourse, quoted in chapter 2.
9. Turner makes a distinction between the liminal and the liminoid. Whereas the liminal is that aspect of ritual and social process in which creative play with the central myths of society is possible and through which communitas may be invoked, *liminoid* refers to elements in a society that embody antistructural elements and that dwell in the interstices, peripheries, and margins of society (V. Turner 1974b). The Red Brigade, a public yet secret group committed to the violent overthrow of the existing Italian state was certainly a liminoid group.

Chapter 10

MEDIATED WORLDS

Part of what it means to live in a modern society is to depend on representations of that society.

— John Durham Peters (1997)

O ur efforts to map the mediascape draws our attention to the wide variety of contexts from and through which media texts circulate, and the very diverse historical, economic, and social conditions that give those contexts shape and texture. Understanding the mediascape involves, in part, a shift of attention from texts to the processes of their circulation. We live in an age of instantaneous communication and rapid transportation that has condensed time and space in ways undreamed of by most of our predecessors. The term *globalization* refers to this "intensification of worldwide social relations which link distant localities in such a way that local happenings are shaped by events happening many miles away and vice versa" (Giddens 1990: 64). Globalization entails continuous ongoing practices of decontextualization and recontextualization not only of media texts, but of technologies, people, capital, and concepts. By compressing the human experience of time and space, globalization juxtaposes countless different cultural practices, beliefs, and symbolic forms. Through this process, globalization produces new cultural spaces in which these cultural forms become "fused," "hybrid," "syncretic," "translated," or "creolized." Globalization happens in the places anthropologists study—villages, boardrooms, laboratories, neighborhoods, schools, homes, temples, and so forth—but it transcends these localities in such a way that to study the local without reference to these larger worlds is to produce an incomplete understanding of the subject at hand.

Notes for this section begin on page 277.

Globalization is closely linked to the concept of *postmodernism*, a perceived breakdown of cultural orders in which the entire world is seen as diffuse, hybrid, unstable, and ephemeral. In a postmodern world, the isomorphism of people, place, and culture is no longer reliable (if it ever was), and symbols of identity and traditional cultural practices become disassociated from local references. Integrated into the capitalist world system, these cultural forms become commoditized. "The more social life becomes mediated by the global marketing of styles, images and places by global media, the more identities become detached—disembedded—from specific times, places, histories and traditions and appear free-floating" (Hall 1992: 303). Many of these changes have been wrought by communications media, including the so-called new media. Shifts in media technology, ways of using them, and ways of interpreting their products are often used as means of tracking the emergence of a postmodern world (much as media penetration was once used to track modernization).

Much of the literature on globalization presumes a chronology that runs from premodern to modern to postmodern. In the first stage, relatively homogenous communities circulated particular texts and images among themselves through ritual performances. This sharing of common symbols and practices helped maintain group cohesion and identity, and the rituals and myths also served as reflexive sources of creativity and innovation. In the modern stage, the circulation of images was rationalized, and separated from the social and cultural contexts of performance. Symbols and narratives were appropriated by a culture industry and returned transformed into commoditized texts that fused deeply held symbolic values with the discourses of the state and the market. In doing so, they reproduced the ideologies of the dominant classes that control the mechanisms of media (re)production, while still containing the seeds of resistance and transformation.

In postmodernism, the circulation of media images has slipped from the leash of the political economic structure and threatens to multiply, mutate, and transform itself at an inhuman speed. Not only do texts slip rapidly from context to context, but the contexts of consumption are themselves shifting in uncontrolled ways and at unparalleled rates. People and texts circulate simultaneously, old traditions are dismantled and new ones invented, and identities are constructed, deconstructed, and reconstructed in increasingly facile ways.

This model of social transformation is highly speculative, however, and is often based on unexamined assumptions rather than careful research.[1] Ethnographically speaking, these supposed premodernities, modernities and postmodernities seem to co-exist, not only in separate parts of the globe but even within the same societies. There are real limits to the extent to which identities become disembedded, and there are patterns by which such "global" phenomena become localized. Commodities, technologies, identities, styles, and people are distributed in unequal ways. The discussion of cottage culture industries in chapter 7 should lead us to confront theories of globalization and postmodernity with empirical questions about who the producers of media are, what kinds of media are being produced, which audiences are consuming what kinds of media, and what all of this has to do with culture, in ways that are far more complex than either the moribund modernist notions of the "impact" of Western technologies on "non-Western" peoples, or postmodern assumptions about free-floating symbols and identities. Instead of the easy stereotypes of Americanization, McDonaldization, Coca-Colonization, Disneyfication and so forth, we need to look at the complexity of the social processes through which media and their associated commodities spread globally, and to empirically examine the wide range of practices through which media is produced, distributed and consumed. At the same time, we must be careful not to get seduced by the postmodernist spectacle and its assumptions that cultural representation, systems of exchange, and social formations are easily disassociated.

How *do* processes of globalization actually work? Much contemporary ethnographic work involves exploring the cultural consequences of transnational flows of people, symbols, capital, and technology. Media play two key roles in this process. On the one hand, media are in circulation, not only as texts traveling along a bewilderingly complex system of satellite links and cable connections, but as objects: reels of film traveling through commercial distribution routes; videotapes, cassettes, CDs, legitimate and pirated, appearing as commodities in shops and kiosks around the world; tourist videos, home movies, video- and tape-recorded letters and other intimate portraits sent by mail and other means to link transnational families. On the other hand, media serve to mediate transnational flows of peoples, wealth, and technologies. Media provide links and grounds by which people can imagine themselves as maintaining continuity amid rapid transformation, while also providing new symbolic resources through which people can imagine themselves possessed of new identities with which to meet the changing world. In this chapter, I seek to develop a model for talking about these issues based on the notion that globalization is not so much about the superseding of the local but rather about connections between locales.

The Postmodern Spectacle

The difficulties of describing and understanding the contemporary world system have been explored by a series of social theorists of postmodernism. Postmodernism, as the name implies, is a term used to define a break with modernism. *Modernism* is an ideology defined by a positivistic, forward-looking approach to the world, a faith that the world is knowable through science, and that it is technologically perfectible through the rational application of that science. Capitalism and communism, development, progress, and social evolution are all modernist concepts. Modernism is based on the notion of a break with a past that was backward, unscientific, irrational, and unpleasant—"nasty, brutish and short," as Thomas Hobbes put it. *Postmodernism* in turn assumes a break with the postulates of modernity. It assumes a loss of faith in the certainty of progress and scientific rationality, and a recognition that all ideologies—including scientific knowledge—are culturally and historically specific, not natural and universal.

Postmodernism itself is as much an ideology as modernism, albeit it is sometimes an ideology that reflexively admits to being one, unlike ideologies that mask themselves as universal truths. Postmodernism assumes that modernism was a passing historical stage that is at an end. It seeks to go beyond the limitations of modernism by finding sciences of situated, local, and relativistic forms of knowledge, and of ironic and self-reflexive modes of representation that deny claims to realism, truth, abstract knowledge, and progress. Postmodern scholars reject traditional languages of scholarship that imply certain knowledge in favor of irony, and play with forms of writing.[2]

One need not subscribe to postmodernist epistemology, or write as a postmodernist, to study postmodernism as a cultural and ideological system. Many scholars understand *postmodernity* as the "culture of late capitalism," a period of global corporatism and mass consumption involving "a prodigious expansion of capital into hitherto uncommodified areas" (Jameson 1984: 78), leading to radically different cultural styles but operating according to the same underlying economic principles as earlier stages of capitalism.[3] As a culture, postmodernism is marked by simulation, fragmentation and loss of faith in explanation. It is thus possible to use standard social science and historical methods to understand the conditions that have given rise to such a culture, which is often localized as the culture of a particular transnational class of consumers. Globalization, transnationalism, commodification and mediation are seen as key processes in the rise of postmodernity.

For all the enthusiasm with which many Western scholars have embraced postmodernism, much of the world clearly does not see itself in postmodern terms. Many peoples and nations continue to be grappling with principles and conditions that could be classed as modernism (forging a stable nation-state, creating industry) or premodernism (kinship-based social organization). Whether or not one subscribes to the postmodern ideology, the idea of postmodernism has made it easier to look at the modern not as a universal human reality but as a specific historical and cultural construction. It thus becomes possible to describe *modernity* as a cultural system defined by a supposed historical break with "tradition." And if modernity is a break with a "traditional" past, Pieterse (1998) argues that it is necessary to speak of multiple modernities based on different *kinds* of pasts. The modernity of societies whose pasts are colonial will be different than the modernity of those European societies whose pasts are feudal, and these, in turn, will be different from the modernities of societies like Canada and the United States whose pasts more or less begin with the industrial revolution.[4] What's more, Pieterse argues, we should also expect to find differences between constructions of modernity based on the differences *within* such broad categories as feudal and colonial. The French experience of feudalism was different from that of the Dutch; the Algerian experience of colonialism was different from that of Egypt. Local modernities differ with these differences in the pasts from which they break.

If different territorial histories produce different experiences of modernity, this process is even more attenuated by the processes of deterritorialization and diaspora across cultural and national boundaries associated with globalization. A Houston oil executive transferring to Sumatra at the requirement of his multinational employer, or a Sudanese university student in Khartoum moving to Cairo because his village has been destroyed and he no longer has a home to which to return, or a Bombay woman traveling to Los Angeles to stay with her husband's brother's family so her soon-to-be born child will have U.S. citizenship; all these people move from place to place with ideas in their heads about the nature of the modern world, about their place in it, and about how their territorial mobility will (or at least might) lead to better lives. Arjun Appadurai calls the articulations of these relocated peoples making sense of their worlds *alternative modernities* (1996: 49). Appadurai emphasizes the roles played by mass media in helping them at once understand their new reterritorialized status while simultaneously constructing a nostalgic idea of their native land, one which becomes increasingly "invented" as they rely more and more on mediated ways of experiencing it. Brian Larkin extends the idea of multiple and alternate modernities by pointing out that multiple modernities may coexist within a single society and find expression in different kinds of media representations. He uses the term *parallel modernities* "to refer to the coexistence in space and time of multiple economic, religious and cultural flows that are often subsumed within the term 'modernity.'" He emphasizes the ways that media consumption allows local people to "participate in the imagined realities of other cultures as part of their daily lives" (Larkin 1997: 407). This brings us round again full circle to Pieterse, who emphasizes the ways various locations come to see other locations as models for their own modernity.

Media and mediation are clearly crucial to these theories of modernity and postmodernity. Modernist views assume the role of the media in connecting and integrating large groups of people ("masses") into nations, markets, and other formations. Postmodernist views assume the role of the media in offering symbolic resources for the construction and reconstruction of individual and group identities. Two key theoretical concepts in talking about media in these ways have been those of the *public sphere* and the *imagined community*.

Public Spheres and Imagined Communities

The social theorist Jurgen Habermas used the term *public sphere* to refer to that social domain in which "private people come together as a public" (1989: 27). Habermas describes the emergence of the public sphere as a particular historical moment in the development of modern liberal democratic society. In medieval society, the manorial lord's authority was expressed through public spectacles, such as parades, coronations, and executions, while actual political action took place through secret deliberations. The modern state, by contrast, makes its deliberations public, establishing its authority through appeals to reason and representation, and making rulers and ruled part of the same process. For Habermas, this change came about during the seventeenth and eighteenth centuries with the rise of coffee houses, literary societies, salons, and other public spaces, which became the centers of debate. Media play a significant role in this movement, as the first newspapers appear, and the production of political pamphlets and essays becomes a major publishing genre. These early mass media provide discursive connections between sites of public debate whose members might otherwise never meet. [5]

Contemporary writing on the public sphere involves extending this notion to contemporary sites of public opinion formation. Habermas believed that the public sphere, having emerged as a result of a rejection of feudalism, was at risk of being "refeudalized" by the state and the nation. For Habermas, criticism is a definitive aspect of public discourse, not only so that propositions about the world are tested by those who disagree with them, but because meanings are constructed by participants as a result of the deliberation process itself.[6] Both state ownership or control of media, and monopolistic control over the form and content of mass media, jeopardize this process, and thus reduce the power of the media to forge a public sphere. As a result, much of the writing on the public sphere is prescriptive, urging various modes of technological, economic or political reforms as means of "revitalizing" what is assumed to be a moribund or corrupted political sphere. Several authors (e.g. Rheingold 1993) have suggested that new modes of communication such as the Internet could fulfill the functions of the public sphere envisioned by Habermas. Other social scientists have sought to approach the public sphere from a descriptive perspective. Habermas's notion that sites of public discourse and the circulation of discourse in mediated form created "a living web of citizen-to-citizen communications" (Rheingold 1993: 13) lacks substantial theoretical and descriptive detail. What forms of sociality actually emerge in this system? Through what mechanisms is such sociality constituted? How do various forms of media control overdetermine the nature of social connectivity and, hence, the structure of the public sphere? In short, what does the public sphere look like as an empirical reality of human interconnectivity and how does it serve various constituencies? These are ethnographic questions.

Examined ethnographically, the public sphere proves to be a bewildering place full of disconnections as well as connections, in which various people struggle to make their voices heard. But mediated communication, even via the internet, is no simple thing. Jon Anderson (1995, 1999), for example, has described ways in which Muslims around the world have sought to use new media to stake out a place in the public sphere. While the *'ulama* (Islamic men of learning) have historically been defined through specific modes of authority to teach and interpret, the World Wide Web and other media have opened a series of new spaces in which Islam can be discussed, interpreted, and disseminated. Mass media have provided new vehicles for traditionally authorized teachers and institutions to communicate to ever wider publics. Such uses of media technologies have been slow to emerge in Islamic societies, however, partly because they raise questions about what happens when messages originally transmitted orally from teachers to students in defined religious contexts are disseminated to large publics with very different educational and devotional backgrounds.

On the other hand, new media like the World Wide Web offer opportunities for self-authorized persons to represent Islam to various publics (Muslim and non-Muslim), as well as to contest representations put forth by others. Thus we find engineers, schoolteachers, political protestors, bureaucrats, and other self-appointed spokespersons representing Islam on the Web. In reaching out to various publics, these communicators put into circulation ideas previously limited to much narrower circulations, and links discourses that were previously limited to specific times and places. Anderson calls this process *creolization*, a mixing of communicative codes and a linking (perhaps even a community-building) of the peoples that use them. Creolization, in this sense, refers to the formation of "special-purpose, intermediate communities of discourse that array in a continuum between otherwise (for example, socially) separate communities of communication" (J. Anderson 1999: 43-44).

Members of such communities of communication may share certain symbols and communicative practices but they do not share locations. The basis of their sense of community, if they have one, cannot involve face-to-face interaction; it is rather based on an imagining of others like themselves engaged in practices like those they are engaged in. Discussions of imagined forms of sociality created by media largely turn around Benedict Anderson's concept of the *imagined community*. Anderson coined the term to talk about the rise of the idea of the nation in the eighteenth century. Nations, he argues, are cultural artifacts. Nations are *imagined* in that most persons in even the smallest of them will never meet. They are *communities* in that members of a nation recognize a common bond with all other members. This bond of comradeship cuts horizontally across social hierarchies, and is so powerfully felt that men and women will kill and be killed for the sake of these people they have never met but with whom they feel a deep bond of national kinship. Such communities are imagined, but clearly not imaginary. They exist only as shared ideas but this does not make them any less real. As institutionalized products of a shared process of imagining, they have very real social and psychological effects.

Like Habermas, Benedict Anderson makes an historical argument, and he places the rise of the imagined community in the same era that Habermas places the rise of the public sphere. They are, in some ways, complementary concepts. But where Habermas depicts the newspaper, pamphlets, essays, novels, and other products of print capitalism as secondary to public gathering, Anderson foregrounds the role of these media, which argues created a heightened awareness of the "steady, anonymous, simultaneous experience" of readers (1991: 31).

Part of this simultaneity is produced by a shared set of meanings about the nation and those who belong to it. The media allow for a widespread circulation of common symbols, images, and language. Through media, it is possible for people to share—and to know they share—similar beliefs, values, sentiments, and practices. The media create a public sphere by linking the various sites where people gather to talk and think about the national community, and by providing them with common sets of symbols for doing so. As a result, media become sites of struggle where orthodox and heterodox representations vie for hegemony.

But the sharing of common ideas and values is not the only, or even the most important, role that media play in creating an imagined community. Media also create an experience of simultaneity through rituals of consumption, such as the reading of the daily newspaper or the viewing of the evening news. We are sharing not only the same images with millions of others but also the same experience.

These two strands are mutually reinforcing. As White says, "it is not reading or viewing or even listening that creates bonds between strangers, but their simultaneity—their shared bond of reading the same texts, seeing the same images and hearing the same words." But, she adds, "bonds created by simultaneity must derive legitimacy from the culturally specific meanings of reading, seeing and hearing" (White 1999: 175).

Although originated to explain the emergence of nations, the notion of imagined community has been used to describe or explicate many other groups or networks of people whose self-identities and discourses unite them with others they will never know on a personal basis. New media in particular have the capacity to increase this sense of simultaneity between "absent others" (Giddens 1990: 18). People in distant places can communicate about the same topic at the same time and in the same ways through Internet chat rooms and similar media forms. Much of the current interest in new media asks what kinds of forms of sociality they are forging in the contemporary world. What "imagined communities" exist, or are coming into existence *besides* nations?

A language for asking and answering these questions has been suggested by Arjun Appadurai, who extends and synthesizes the work of Habermas and Anderson. Appadurai suggests that an understanding of the cultural dimensions of globalization is based on the notion that people and mediated texts are in simultaneous circulation, and what links them is the work of imagination.

Caught up in this flow, people live not only in imagined communities but in *imagined worlds*, "multiple worlds that are constituted by the historically situated imaginations of persons and groups spread around the globe" (Appadurai 1996: 33). Appadurai sees these imagined worlds as comprised by a set of dimensions of cultural flows, or *scapes*. These scapes represent the kinds of things in motion in the contemporary global system: people (the *ethnoscape*), technologies (the *technoscape*), capital (the *financescape*), systems of media production and the representations they create (*mediascapes*), and the circulations of ideological discourses, both those of states and those of various social movements (*ideoscapes*).

Multiple Centers and Multiple Peripheries

Appadurai's language is an effort to move beyond the language of world systems theory, which organized earlier theoretical discussions of globalization. World systems theory, as articulated by Immanuel Wallerstein, is based on a Marxian emphasis on the primacy of economic relations. The modern capitalist world system, in Wallerstein's view, began in the fifteenth century with the rise of a worldwide mercantile and colonial system. Capitalism provided the basis for a world economy, which made "it possible to increase the flow of the surplus from the lower strata to the upper strata, from the periphery to the center, from the majority to the minority" (Wallerstein 1974: 15). Central to the entire theory is the notion that hegemonic ideologies and discourses flow from center to periphery while wealth flows from periphery to center.

World systems theory has provided a powerful basis for theories of globalization that assume imperialism, exploitation, rationalization, and homogenization. A wide range of metaphors have arisen to describe forms of combined symbolic and economic domination. *McDonaldization* refers to the application of the rational principles of the assembly line—uniformity, efficiency, predictability, preference for quantity over quality, and preference for nonhuman technologies over human labor—to such intimate aspects of everyday life as the cooking of meals (Ritzer 1993). *Westernization* refers to the replacement of local symbols, ideas, values, and practices with those that historically emerged in Western Europe and North America. A specific subtype of Westernization, *Americanization* sees America as *the* center of world modernity and an exporter of (highly profitable) forms of modernity to the rest of the world. *Disneyfication* refers to the marshaling of nostalgia and sentiment to construct sanitized and commodified cultural representations. *Coca-colazation* is an old term derisively referring to the movement of local economies into market systems following World War II, while the more recent *Coca-colonization* is often used to describe a recolonization of Third World countries by multinational corporations. All of these ways of imagining modernity assume an imperialistic dominance of economic and cultural peripheries by a corporate capitalist center whose cultural codes are predominantly Euro-American.

Without denying the very real inequities in the distribution of global wealth and power, or the role of the media in creating and sustaining such inequities, Appadurai wants to emphasize that the world economy is far more complex than world systems theory seems to treat it. Linear economic models can no longer accurately map the vast and rapid flows of credit, cash, capital, and labor across the financescape. Fears that Americans are buying up the world are matched by fears that

Japan is buying up America ("Nipponization") or fears in India in the mid 1990s that Arabs were buying up the city of Mumbai ("Arabization"). In each such case, the fear is not only that capital and property are changing hands but that the local is being transformed as a result. Appadurai offers a way of talking about globalization not as a coherent economic system but as an ever-changing technologically mediated flow of peoples, technologies, capital, ideas, and images across many different kinds of boundaries. Against the centralist model of center and periphery, Appadurai offers a model of multiple (and shifting) centers and peripheries.

Such a corrective is necessary because many scholars continue to take as an uninvestigated assumption the view that American culture, American institutions, and American media sit at the center of the world system and thus control relations with and between peripheral states. Treating the dominance of the periphery by the center as an established fact rather than an empirical question for investigation means, among other things, that we often "get the history of the impact of the center on the periphery, rather than the history of the periphery itself" (Hannerz 1992: 207). One of the most important empirical contributions of anthropologists to the study of the world system is the establishment of a body of descriptive work that makes it possible to avoid assuming the centrality of American cultural forms as the model for both modernity and postmodernity.

In film production, for example, Hollywood is not the center of the universe but only one of many centers. Bombay outproduces Hollywood in sheer quantity, and reaches as many markets (Pendakur and Subramanyan 1996); many other media production sites also distribute globally. Walk into a video store in Thailand, for example, and you will find the holdings divided between *nang Thai* (local films), *Chiin* (Chinese costume dramas from Singapore and gangster films from Hong Kong), and *farang* (foreign films). The latter consists primarily of Indian films, American action films and Japanese anime. Preference is for local vernacular films, and foreign films compete with one another more than they do with local productions. The foreign films are usually dubbed into local languages, and the dubbed version need not follow the story line of the original in all, or even many, particulars (Hamilton 1993).

The Thai video store draws our attention to two key sites for analysis, both of which we have discussed in previous chapters. The first is a shift of attention from production and consumption to distribution as a cultural practice. There is an enormous amount of work to be done tracking the complexes of connections, crossovers, and intersections by which media are circulated throughout the world—especially as these connections are often fortuitous, unplanned, and unexpected even by those engaged in the processes. When we take the trouble, however, simple theories of media imperialism and homogenization become harder to maintain.

In Egypt, for example, it is often claimed that the local film industry was destroyed in the 1950s by unfair competition—"media imperialism"—from American and European filmmakers. Examination of correspondence of that era between U.S. film executives and U.S. government representatives, however, demonstrates that neither Hollywood nor other foreign film industries ever dominated the market or destroyed local competition, much as they might have wished to. U.S. films occupied only a small part of the market, and competed primarily with other foreign films, mostly from Europe or the Soviet Union (Indian films also became popular but occupied a separate niche). Rather than being caused by Western media hegemony, the financial crisis the Egyptian film industry fell into was a result of its own poorly organized production and distribution system. The Egyptian film industry in fact could not meet the local demand for vernacular films; the Egyptian national production center, Studio Misr, could not even fill its own theater consistently (Vitalis 2000). The demand for local over foreign film continues unabated. If *Titanic* was the top grossing foreign film of all time in Egypt (as in many other parts of the world), it was immediately outgrossed domestically by two local products, *Saidi fi'l Gama'a al-Amrikiyya* and *Nasser 56* in the two years following.

What's more, texts that move from one site to another often undergo textual transformations in the process. Most theories of media hegemony and global homogenization assume textual coherence and the power of structures inherent in texts to dominate local consumers. I have already discussed at length the ways local interpretive frameworks may lead people to "read" media texts in very different ways in different settings. What still needs examination is the ways that new technologies increasingly enable local film industries to alter textual coherence and to give texts local inflections to better fit preexisting local media literacies. That is, not all mass mediations occur in the initial production of the media text; routes of distribution and sites of localization often involve additional mediating processes.

For example, when I watched the Disney television program *Ducktales* in the United States in 1990, I was amazed at how much the cartoons reflected the hegemony thesis put forward by Dorfman and Mattelart about Disney comic books. In *How to Read Donald Duck* ([1971] 1991), the authors argued that Disney comics, enormously popular worldwide, encoded messages of capitalist hegemony. The adventures of Donald Duck, Mickey Mouse, and especially Uncle Scrooge melded colonialist fantasies with Cold War ideologies. Stories often involved the Disney characters encountering savage tribes, stumbling into lost kingdoms, or being captured by desert nomads. The happy ending involved incorporating these others into the capitalist world system—for their own good and with their own eager participation, of course, but usually also to the profit of merchant prince Scrooge McDuck. Mattelart and Dorfman argue that the structure of the tales is such that children reading the texts almost necessarily side with either the very colonialist heroes, or with the happy converted savages.

But in 1993, when I watched the premiere of Disney's *Ducktales* in India, the cartoons were different. Doordarshan, the Indian state television, had dubbed the show with meticulous attention to detail. The cash-loving capitalist Scrooge McDuck, was given a Maharashtran accent, to make him sound like a Bombay businessman. The eccentric inventor Gyro Gearloose had an accent that places him as from Hyderabad, which is the center of India's information technology revolution. This approach is consistent with traditional Indian theatrical forms in which regional dialects are used to index character types. But it also localizes the ideology, casting India as a center exploiting peripheries. What happens to such colonialist texts when they are indigenized in such culturally intimate ways? How do Indian children understand such texts when the colonizers are turned into fellow Indians? The underlying structure of the episodes remains the same, but the range of meanings is refracted by localization.

These forms of technological intervention in processes of localization are far more widespread and thorough than is often recognized. Dubbing and other technologies for manipulating symbols offer far more thorough means of localizing texts than Doordarshan's careful dubbing. Back in Thailand, those *farangi* films that make it to the video store are not necessarily the same movies American viewers pick up at their local video stores:

> New Arnold Schwarzenegger or Sylvester Stallone movies could be found in video shops in the provinces even before their release in the Bangkok cinemas. Virtually all foreign films, however, were provided with a Thai sound track or, rather, with locally dubbed dialogue. The texts of these dialogues frequently did not follow the original language closely or, in some cases, did not follow it at all. "Dubbing" was a means by which a particular Thai slant could be given to unfamiliar situations and images. (Hamilton 1993: 524)[7]

New media technologies allow similar processes to take place with many kinds of images. In the past, *Superman* and *Batman* comic books in Asia and the Arab world were translated into indigenous languages by whiting out speech balloons and inserting new dialogue, leaving alone background text such as signs, sounds, and logos because these are drawn into the original artwork. These background images index Superman as American. Now image files are often transmitted electronically from the publishing corporation in the United States to the local entrepreneur in another country. These graphics can be manipulated by computers so that not only dialogue but images are translated; background text like exit signs, traffic symbols, and the logo of the Daily Planet newspaper can all be recast into local images, scripts and vernaculars.

Empirical accounts of the ways media are distributed and locally reconfigured are powerful tools for undermining commonsense notions of Westernization and modernity. These accounts serve to problematize the ways we view media by reminding us that the distribution and consumption of media involves the *production* of culture through human interaction. But this sort of problematization is only a first step. To successfully take the study of media beyond mere anecdotal accounts, scholars must develop new ways of handling mass media in a global, (post)modern world.

The Local in the Global

Globalization requires us to recognize that we live within a world system and that a great many of the things of our everyday lives are interconnected with the everyday lives of unknown others in distant places. There is nothing new in this discovery. Anthropologists have always been aware of, and interested in, the diffusion of cultural forms and material objects from area to area. They have been interested in trade, and warfare, in the development of pidgin and Creole language systems, and in *syncretism*, the merging of historically distinct cultural traditions into new, stable institutions. The crossing of cultural borders has always interested anthropologists because it is in the crossing of borders that cultural definitions about the nature of those borders become particularly amenable to study.

Globalization can be operationalized as what occurs when a local element is decontextualized and then rapidly distributed across myriad paths and multiplied recontextualized in a multitude of settings. Distribution and recontextualization do not happen simultaneously, but have histories, and these histories add to their meanings. In this process, each of these local recontextualizations leads to transformations of the element. Globalization is thus *about* localization. And localization is exactly the sort of thing ethnography is poised to study.

What is new in globalization is the *scope* of the phenomena. In the past, it was possible to see stability as normal, and the movement of a cultural form from one context to another as an isolable incident. Today, the rapid movement of peoples, technologies, capital, and symbols from context to context seems to be becoming the norm. What's more, these processes of decontextualization and recontextualization become defining elements of the contexts of consumption and interpretation. That is, contexts must increasingly be seen not as preexisting entities across and through which elements pass but rather as being constructed in the process of these shifts. The borders, in other words, are increasingly being defined by what crosses them and how they are being crossed.

This process poses two key dilemmas for ethnography. The first dilemma concerns how persons imagine themselves as parts of groups, systems, and networks outside their immediate face-to-face social worlds. This would seem to involve entire series of imagined communities of very different scope and scale. The second dilemma involves the ways that persons integrate the new images, events, persons, and objects that enter into their lives as a result of their participation in the world system into their everyday social worlds. To deal with these dilemmas, I will offer three principles concerning the ways the global and local mutually constitute one another. I call these the bifocal principle, the principle of localization, and the principle of indexicality.

The Bifocal Principle

The bifocal principle is based on the assumption that the peoples of the world, both as individuals and as social groups, are increasingly aware that they are embedded in larger social, political, and economic systems and that they have developed ways of making sense of these systems and their relative places in them. Like the person wearing bifocal glasses, we move from reading things close up to reading things far away and back again with a flick of our eyes. And like the person wearing bifocals, our capacity to do this is provided by technologies.

Bifocality, then, refers to this modern propensity to move back and forth between the local world of everyday experience and the larger world of virtual experience represented to us by various media. It further assumes that we relate these two dimensions of experience to one another. We understand the wider world presented to us in terms of our local worlds, and we understand our local worlds as shaped by forces in the wider world over which we have little or no control.

John Durham Peters argues that the bifocality of modern life requires us to expand our definitions of mass media to include not only "television, cinema, radio, newspapers and magazines" but also "all practices of social envisioning, reporting, and documentation, including statistics, accounting, insurance, census taking, polling, and the work of social services and of the social sciences" (1997: 79). I would extend this even further to the many forms of commodified goods and services that are linked to media images. In the modern world system, it is not only true that most media are commodified but also that most goods are mediated. The mass media are *all* those technological systems of representation through which the world is represented for us and to us.

Bifocality is not a universal, cognitive process, but a cultural, local one. It involves, first of all, local notions about how to be bifocal. As we saw in the previous chapter, communities have their own communicative ecologies, consisting not only of unequally distributed access to various modes of communication but normative ways of understanding how these modes of communication are appropriate or useful for what kinds of purposes or functions (even if these notions are always in flux). Second, communities have local notions of how to understand the information one gets from various media. Truth and falsehood, authentic and inauthentic, real and fake, authoritative and doubtful, sensible and ridiculous, and other modalities are applied to media in culturally specific ways.

The Egyptian villager who throws cellophane-wrapped processed foods to the pigs because they are not *real* food, cooked *for* someone *by* someone (Abu-Lughod 1997) is aware of a global system that she is at once in but not of, yet her experience of that system is very different than the Chiapas freedom fighters who slip reports of their rebellion out of Mexico to be uploaded to web sites by sympathizers around the world (Castells 1996, 1997; Cleaver 1998). Nor is it only consumers who are engaged in this bifocal awareness of the global system; producers of media and material goods have notions of world, regional and national markets that shape distribution and marketing. Advertising executives have defined ideas about what ads produced in one locale can be inserted into another, what ads need to be reshot with local actors, and which locales will require entirely new advertisements based on local cultural premises (O'Barr 1989).

Bifocality is always mediated. Peoples' notions of the world beyond their own are created through representations of that world supplied through a bewildering variety of sources. The Egyptian villager above is aware of the greater world through television programs and advertising, through the tales her children bring home from school, through her observations of the foreign tourists who come to visit the ancient ruins nearby. The Chiapas rebels understand the world beyond, and its relation to them, through intelligence reports, foreign and local news broadcasts, newspaper accounts, e-mail and web traffic. Advertising executives rely on reports by local representatives, market research, histories of prior successes and failures, as well as their own common sense understanding of how the world works.[8]

The Localization Principle

The localization principle concerns the ways we make use of the two worlds we see through our bifocal lenses. Giddens emphasizes that relations between the global and local are always dialectical: "Local transformation is as much a part of globalization as the lateral extension of social connections across time and space" (1990: 64). Indeed, globalization is essentially about the connections between localities and the ways these connections influence one another. The key point is that the ideas about the local—the nation, the neighborhood, the home—never cease to exist in globalization. On the contrary, they often take on a new importance. Globalization is thus not about the disappearance of the local but about the linking of locales. *Localization* refers to the processes of appropriation by which people decontextualize symbols, concepts, information, and images perceived through their mediated experience of the other locations and recontextualize them into the worlds of their everyday experience.

Examples of localization are all around us. James Watson and his colleagues describe the ways peoples in East Asia integrate McDonald's into their lifeways so that younger generations come to see McDonald's not as a global but a local entity, one which one visits on certain kinds of occasions for certain kinds of purposes (Watson 1997). Peter Donham (1998) describes the ways that upper-class South Africans who are engaged in same-sex relationships use the Internet to discover, and make their own, the idea of being "gay." Abu-Hashish and Peterson (1999) describe the ways Egyptians merge the idea and technology of "computer dating" with local urban marital matchmaking practices to create a new, hybrid institution.

These examples should help us come to see localization as not simply a linear process through which social processes from abroad are somehow imposed on local communities, but rather as social practices through which local agents actively engage in practices of appropriation and recontextualization. The upper-class South Africans involved in same-sex relations are not being "educated" by a more broad-minded Western culture; they are searching for an identity distinct from the traditional, "backward" identities offered for same-sex relations by traditional tribal culture. Entrepreneurs bring computer matchmaking to Egypt because they recognize the centrality of the local problem of finding a suitable match and the potential profit to be made from offering a solution. Entrepreneurs seek franchises because they recognize the attraction of the modernity and cosmopolitanism associated with McDonald's. Such practices are *motivated*, that is, they are employed toward particular ends. Practices may be carefully and specifically strategized, or they may be ad hoc, proceeding through analogies with preexisting practices. In either case, they involve people recognizing a cultural space for new practices, institutions, or identities, and appropriating symbols, technologies, or capital to inhabit that space. "Global" goods and services are always mediated by local actors—enthusiasts, entrepreneurs, visionaries, bureaucrats, and others—who act as cultural brokers.

Yet if people act with ends in view they are nonetheless not in control of actual outcomes. The consumption of goods and services may be rejected by consumers; alternatively, local restaurants may modify their own practices to resemble those of the new institutions. Loans accepted for immediate needs from donor agencies by bureaucrats may prove to cause national financial problems down the road. Adoption of alien identities as "modern" may be seen instead as pretentious and outlandish. What's more, each appropriation may have several *different* outcomes reflecting and affecting different local situations and interpretations.

The Indexical Principle

The indexicality principle attempts to understand the relations between the two dimensions of bifocality, and the values that elements express locally, by understanding these relations as indexical. In chapter 3, I briefly discussed the index as a sign in which signifier and signified are connected by relations of contiguity. Such relations include the intertextuality discussed in the previous chapter, as well as relations of cause and effect, as when smoke stands for fire; part-whole relations, as when Mickey Mouse comes to stand for the whole Disney empire; token-type relations, as when a particular film comes to be an exemplar of an entire genre; relations of adjacency, as when a journalist's question produces a source's answer, and many other forms of connectedness. *Indexicality* is about meaning something by being connected to it.

Contemporary global phenomena involve complex webs of indexicality. Consider again the example of McDonald's. A McDonald's restaurant is financed through franchising, a financial relationship that is also an indexical relationship involving flows of money and symbols. In many countries, McDonald's indexes the United States because the restaurant chain is known to have originated there. Yet McDonald's restaurants also index one another; great efforts are made to make every individual McDonald's like every other in significant ways. The value of the franchise to entrepreneurs is based on this indexical relationship—the new restaurant will open to a ready-made body of customers who know what to expect because they can rely on the restaurant being the same in all key particulars as every other McDonald's restaurant of which they have experience. Advertising is indexical because it is not only about the restaurant but ultimately derives from it. In addition, advertising can be created for the entire restaurant chain because this principle of indexicality allows ads to be nearly interchangeable. An advertisement for any McDonald's becomes in a sense an advertisement for all.

There are a number of reasons for paying attention to indexicality in processes of globalization and localization. For one thing, our ability to comprehend much of the world around us is based on interpretive frameworks rooted in indexicality. Labeling a film as "American," "Indian," or "foreign" is to index a place of origin as important to understanding what the film is, and how it should be interpreted (Armbrust 1998, 2000a). Such frameworks can be crucial not only to the ways in which people interpret texts but to forms of social and political action, such as boycotts or preferences for "foreign" goods. Peoples and goods that cross cultural boundaries usually retain a connection to their places of origin, and bear upon them the traces of the particular cultures, traditions, language, and histories by which they were shaped (Hall 1992: 310). This relation of contiguity serves as part of the interpretive framework by which they are interpreted, appropriated, and localized.

Second, indexicality is used to authorize media texts, to verify their status as authentic for those who seek to make sense of the world. When we attempt to understand news stories as reports on the real world on the basis of pictures, or of quotations by those who were "there," or to defend a movie's portrayal of another culture because "it's based on a true story," or to understand an advertisement's claims to be about the product we might buy, we are constituting knowledge on the basis of indexical relations. Indexicality is thus linked to the power representation has for us as we engage in our bifocal relationship with the world.

Third, media play a crucial role in what I will call here *metadeixis*. Metadeictic discourses are representations of indexical relationships, stories people tell about how things are connected. Metadeixis occurs when media accounts attempt to define or clarify the nature of indexical relations between a recontextualized cultural form and its original referents (real or imaginary). In 2000, when the United States was bombing Iraq, many Egyptian newspapers called on citizens to boycott McDonald's and imported American goods as a sign of protest. These newspapers constructed McDonald's as an American company and assumed that its indexicality through origin was also part of an economic flow. Other newspapers and magazines responded by pointing out that McDonald's in Egypt was locally owned, purchased its meat, vegetables, and bread from local sources and employed local people, so that boycotting McDonald's would hurt more Egyptians than it would Americans. These debates represented various interpretations of McDonald's indexical relations with the United States and sought to justify forms of social action. Explicating indexical relations is an increasingly important role played by media in the contemporary world.

Ethnographic Strategies

Using these principles to understand the contemporary world requires the development of new ways of gathering and interpreting data. Anthropologists have begun to explore a variety of strategies for handling this bifocal world. Ethnography has much to offer the study of media in a globalizing world. It focuses on the small-scale processes that make up most of human life as it is experienced, offering a powerful supplement and contrast to studies of macroprocesses. Ethnography challenges theory with empirical questions. At the same time, ethnography offers the opportunity to make connections between global and local, public and private, life experience and social structure.

One approach, suggested by George Marcus, involves *multisited ethnography*, a concept already introduced in chapter 6. Multisited ethnography involves a set of strategies in which an ethnographer follows a defined object of study—a people, a text, an individual, a story, a metaphor, an image—across a variety of sites. The goal is to follow the chain of decontextualizations and recontextualizations that occur as cultural forms flow across the scapes of the world system. To be done properly, multi-sited ethnography may well require a team of ethnographers, each working within contexts with which they are familiar.

One of the best examples of multisited ethnography is Emily Martin's *Flexible Bodies* (1994). In this book, Martin examines the flow of a single metaphor through a variety of unexpected sites, ranging from medical textbooks, to urban Americans' conversations about health, to economic discourses, to survivalist camps. In mapping this flow, Martin makes the interesting discovery that people often seize and integrate new metaphors into their thinking even before the media takes notice of them. However, Martin's work, like that of Manuel discussed in chapter 6, ultimately stays within national boundaries. The definitive multi-sited ethnography of a transnational or global media phenomenon is yet to be written.

A second strategy involves locating specific sites in which the global is particularly experienced. One name for such sites is *hyperspaces* (or *hyperplaces*), a term that refers to locations that are somehow experienced as the same regardless of where one is in the world, "environments such as airports, franchise restaurants, and production sites that, detached from any local reference, have monotonous universal qualities" (Kearney 1995: 553). A quintessential example is the bank teller machine, a "non-space" which seems to stand outside local space to give a similarity of experience regardless of location (Augé 1999). A related concept is that of *hyperreality*, a term coined to describe artificial environments that marshal symbols and technologies to create an experience of place that is "more real than reality." Hyperrealities include "places such as amusement parks and wax museums in which simulacra are seen as more real than the real thing" (Kearney 1995: 553). Disney's Epcot Center is one of the best exemplars. Epcot center creates simulated foreign locations that replicate all those elements—and just those elements—that most define a particular locale, while banishing all the troublesome contradictions and unpleasantries of real places. Disney's China simulacrum can be experienced as more real than China because it is condensed and distilled. But "real" travel can also share qualities of the hyperreal. Packaged tours to "exotic" places are designed to distill the experience of the place into a set of locations and events that deploy those elements tourists are most likely to imagine as what defines a place. Tourist experiences thus become managed simulacra very different from the lived experiences of those who dwell in a particular place.

A third strategy involves locating what David Hakken (personal communication) has called *metasites*, virtual places in which people in widely distributed locales socially interact with one another through various means of technological mediation. While conference calls and certain uses of television can be conceived as producing such metasites, the primary technology for the creation of the metasite is the computer. Chat rooms, MUDs (multiuser dungeons), usegroups, and other forms of computer mediated communication create possibilities for new forms of sociality through the development of new rules of interaction and modes of social formation, an "electronic vernacular" (Kirshenblatt-Gimblett 1996).

Chat rooms are a good example of a metasite. Like other media, chat rooms serve as sources that can be tapped to assist in the construction of identities and socialities in the everyday worlds to which those visiting belong. But Internet chat rooms are *more* than symbolic reservoirs—they are sites in which new forms of sociality are being forged. Internet chat rooms are virtual spaces defined by a particular topic or purpose. People in various parts of the world enter into chat rooms, create representations of themselves and interact with others. Chat rooms offer unique possibilities for social interaction. People can represent and re-represent themselves in radically different ways from visit to visit, changing their user names and claimed identities in ways usually impossible in face-to-face interactions. At the same time, real norms of interaction are emergent in every such chat room, created by the dynamic of different chat room members' collective interactions, and also by chat room censors—both human "hosts" and "bots," robot programs that watch for forbidden key words and evict users from the site. What such virtual socialities mean to their participants, and what the relation of chat room personas to other forms of identity may be is a matter of growing empirical interest (Hamman 1996; Hakken 1999; Bastani 2000).

The final strategy I will discuss here is that of seeking out specific groups of cultural brokers, persons who play crucial roles in the mediation of the global world. Ulf Hannerz has offered examples of two such types of people: cosmopolitans and foreign correspondents. He defines *cosmopolitans* as people whose own mobility has led them to develop particular modes of managing meaning and dealing with cultural difference, to accommodate their own continual decontextualization and recontextualization. Cosmopolitanism involves a "willingness to engage with the Other" and an "openness toward divergent cultural experiences," which leads to a set of competences for the "management of meaning" (Hannerz 1990: 238-239). Cosmopolitans use media to help them construct their transnational identities and to create a transnational culture that allows them to move more easily between territorial cultures.

Foreign correspondents are a subclass of cosmopolitans who produce the representations that form what most people know about the world. In Jerusalem, where Hannerz did fieldwork, these foreign correspondents form not so much a community as a *sodality*, a group bound together by common goals. These journalists dwell in "an elaborate information habitat, partly stable, partly quickly changing" (Hannerz 1998: 570) within which they seek to construct representations based on what they imagine an event "would look like to a member of an audience at home" (569). To Appadurai's observation that media and their audiences are both in simultaneous circulation, Hannerz's accounts of correspondents spurs the recognition that the producers are often also on the move.

Return to Pokémon

I began this book with Pokémon as an example of the new kind of phenomena with which theories of media must grapple, a world of commoditized media and mediated commodities. I suggested then that media theories needed better models of exchange than the sender-message-receiver model, and that the intense, intimate, long-term method of ethnography was well suited to analyze such phenomena. In this last section, I want to briefly return to Pokémon, and offer some examples of some of the ways this global mélange of movies, television, games, cards, clothing, school supplies, and other media operates in Cairo, Egypt, at the turn of the millennium.

As in most places in the world, schools are key sites for identity formation in Egypt, locations through which parents imagine their children's social futures. Schools in Cairo are hierarchically ranked according to the kinds of educations they can claim to provide. Egyptian schools, almost universally agreed to be in the midst of an "educational crisis" (*mushkilet at-ta'leem*) caused by "untrained teachers," "obsolete schooling practices," "crowded classrooms," and "private lessons,"[9] are at the bottom of this hierarchy. At the top are the "international schools," offering instruction in European languages and curricula based on American, British, French, or German models.[10]

The American School of Cairo (ASC)[11] is one of the most prestigious and expensive of these international schools. In 2000, the student body was comprised of 725 Americans, 284 other foreigners,[12] and 184 Egyptians.[13] Most of the American students come from middle-class families, the tuition being covered as a "dislocation expense" by a parent's employer. As the school's annual tuition was twelve thousand (U.S.) dollars, nearly ten times the mean average income in Egypt,[14] the Egyptian student body was made up of the sons and daughters of some of the wealthiest families in Cairo. These families send their children to ASC to learn cosmopolitan ways of managing meaning. Much of this involves learning American ways of speaking, ways of acting, and youth culture styles.

Although the Egyptian families at ASC are for the most part considerably wealthier than the U.S. citizens whose children make up the bulk of the student body, they are at a disadvantage in the school's institutional class structure, which is based on indexical links between commodities and place of origin. That is, goods of American origin are valued not only over local goods but over imported goods or locally manufactured goods of the same brand. The three tiers—"real" American, imported, and local—are clearly marked by the presence or absence of Arabic script. Egyptian local franchises of multinational brands like Coca-Cola carry the trademark in both English and Arabic script, while imports feature a white import sticker printed in Arabic. Script thus serves as a metadeictic sign explicating the relative value to be given goods on the basis of their relations to place or origin. This class system works because at least one-third of the Americans—all U.S. embassy families, military families, and some USAID-staff—have access to the military base commissary with its American goods at American prices.

Egyptians at ASC are generally limited in their access to such goods to what their families can bring back from infrequent trips to the United States and Europe. Managing status and identity at ASC involves nuanced awareness of what brands and items are most important so that students can maximize their use of such goods. Pokémon was such a good. Like other contemporary media phenomena, it consists of a multimedia, multiple-commodity system in which each component indexes the others. Pokémon is a perfect example of a *simulacrum*, a set of identical copies for which no original ever existed (Jameson 1984: 66). Whether as a Nintendo game in which players accumulate Pokémon, an animated series about a child accumulating Pokémon, or as cards, disks, plastic figures, and other objects that can be collected, Pokémon is about the acquisition of desirable commodities

Pokémon arrived at ASC in the form of commodities carried in by students as they arrived in Cairo in the fall of 1998, some newly arrived, some returning from the summer vacations that allow them to stay abreast of what's cool and what's not. Egyptians had an advantage with Pokémon over many other valued commodities—the commissary carried very few Pokémon paraphernalia. Possession of Pokémon artifacts was at first largely dependent on family members' trips abroad. Playing Pokémon on Nintendo Gameboys, collecting and trading cards, watching Pokémon videos and displaying notebooks, stickers, shirts, lunchboxes and backpacks became important ways of demonstrating one's cosmopolitan identity. Eventually, upscale toy stores became aware of Pokémon's popularity. Imported Pokémon stickers, Gameboys and the Pokémon cartridges, school supplies, posters and trading cards became available at upscale stores such as the new Cairo franchise of Toys"R"Us, and at some stationery stores in cosmopolitan suburbs like Ma'adi and Heliopolis.

The importance of Pokémon at ASC was already waning by December 2000, when Lays-Egypt, the local branch of the multinational food corporation Frito-Lay, began including small plastic disks, called *tazu* into their their Lay's and Ruffle's brand potato chips. The disks, used to play a game also called *tazu*, had pictures of Pokémon creatures on them, with the word "Pokémon" rendered in Arabic script. The English name of each monster was also rendered in Arabic script. There were twenty-four disks in all, and as with the American trading cards, some were easier to get than others. The promotion was immensely success-ful—far more successful than previous Lay's *tazu* campaigns featuring Teenage Mutant Ninja Turtles and Mighty Morphin Power Rangers—and the company extended the campaign for almost a year.

The extended success of the Lay's campaign was in part related to the arrival of Pokémon on Egyptian television. In response to the growth of satellite television, the local government channels had expanded children's programming. Where children's television had once been largely a Ramadan season phenomenon, Pokémon became among the first daily television programs for children "who can't get Cartoon Network" as one ministry official said. The appearance of an Arabic-language version of the cartoon show produced a small number of local spin-off products as well. While the selling of videos of the cartoons is apparently authorized, many of the others, such as Pokémon Crisps, a brand of locally manufactured corn chips, involve copyright pirating. Nor is all the pirating local. Kiosks near schools for several weeks carried packets of Pokémon treats imported from Turkey containing forged Pokémon cards, sticks of gum, lollipops, and stickers.

At the Modern Language School in south Cairo, collecting *tazu* and other Pokémon paraphernalia became, in the words of a school administrator, "an obsession." The MLS belongs to the second tier of Egyptian schools, the private "language schools" that use the national curriculum but offer their primary instruction in English, French, or German. Faculty and students at language schools are nearly entirely Egyptians of the upper middle classes. MLS's fees are one-third those of ASC, but still two and a half to three times the Egyptian mean national average income.

For students at MLS, Pokémon is in part about being current with the rest of the world, which they read about in regional children's magazines like *Bolbol, Majid,* and *Al Arabi Alsaghir*.[15] Through such media, students may enter into an imagined world of other children like themselves playing with Pokémon in America, Spain, and Japan. Students with the resources often branched out from Arabic *tazu* and videos into English booklets and trading cards. Some surfed the Web, learning more about Pokémon worldwide and about the commodities available.

The growing popularity of Pokémon among the Egyptian middle classes caught the attention of local newspapers and magazines, which began to offer comments on the nature of the indexical connections that Pokémon represented. At first, some were laudatory, emphasizing that Japan had broken into the Western hegemony of globalization. But soon the tenor became almost universally negative. It was charged that Pokémon was owned by Israelis (or American Jews backing Israel) and that the money made was spent on weapons used to kill Palestinians. It was also charged that the dyes used on the *tazu* were radioactive and poisonous. And again and again, journalists asked why the region could not produce its own culturally specific games and cartoons that would be as seductive to their children as those from abroad.

Criticism of Pokémon increased after the Grand Mufti of Saudi Arabia issued a *fatwa* against the game in March 2001, urging all Muslims to beware of the game and prevent their children from playing it so as to protect their religion and manners.[16] Although the primary reason given for the ban was that the game "resembled gambling," Sheikh Abdul Aziz Bin Abdullah Al Sheikh also mentioned that many of the commodities contained Zionist symbolism and that Pokémon promotes evolutionary theories, which are incompatible with Islam. Several Gulf states, including Saudi Arabia and the United Arab Emirates, banned all Pokémon commodities and seized and destroyed those already on the shelves. The Egyptian press covered all of this, and many editorials suggested Egyptian parents should do the same thing. Many did. Some schools invited parents to bring their children's Pokémon paraphernalia to the school to be burned.

Much of the criticism was enabled by a marketing choice that had important deictic consequences. The various culture brokers—entrepreneurs, bureaucrats, and so forth—who brought Pokémon to the Middle East chose to simply transliterate the English names of the characters into Arabic script, rather than translating the names into semantically significant local sounds. Whereas Nintendo and its subsidiaries and franchisers in North America and Europe had translated the Japanese names of most of the characters into foreign equivalents, in the Middle East market the American names were used. As a result, the names are strange and uncanny sounding to Arabic speakers, and could mean anything. Rumors began to circulate that the names were in fact blasphemies in some unspecified language. For example, the name of the fiery orange lizard Pokémon Charmander (derived from the English words /char/ and /salamander/) was said to mean "life without God."

Parents responded to this in various ways. One mother at MLS invited a group of her son's friends to a party, read them several stories from the newspapers, held a discussion, and took from them all a pledge to stop collecting and playing with Pokémon. Another mother examined the newspapers' claims, rejected them, and sought to defend her son's collection of Pokémon by emphasizing its educational value, particularly the fact that the websites he surfed and many of the texts he read were in English, a language of social mobility in Egypt. Both women were well-educated professionals, the former a medical doctor, the latter a corporate executive. The choice became one between linking a son's imagined social future to regionally specific identities or to a world consumer culture.

This brief (and incomplete) account of Pokémon in Egypt brings together many of the issues discussed in this chapter. Pokémon is in part about the making of the cosmopolitan class, the acquisition of skills in the management of meaning and cultural difference. Cosmopolitanism is a practical form of bifocality. But this is no simple matter of learning the status value of a few brands. It involves local interpretation of the ways locally available goods index places of origin or distribution and what that indexicality *means* for local identities. These interpretations are affected by the ways in which transnational products are localized—whether they are transliterated or translated, dubbed or re-edited. But interpretations are also affected by discourses from abroad—not only marketing discourses from Japan and America, but interpretations of Pokémon from other locales that are linked to Egypt by shared ethnic, religious, and regional identities. The public sphere is a place of contested discourses. Not all the foreign correspondents are Western, and metadeictic discourses abound as part of the entire region's larger problem of finding a place for Islam in the world system. In the end, playing with Pokémon involves not so much the free adoption of disembedded identities in a flexible world but a much more painful set of choices through which one must come to terms with conflicting regional, ethnic, religious, educational, linguistic, and class loyalties.

I return to the question I posed in chapter 1: what kind of a world is Pokémon? It is an indexical world, a complex web of meanings that link the local with other locales, in ways understood through a complex of sometimes contradictory cultural codes. It is a world in which the boundary between commodities and media is nonexistent, a world in which it makes no sense to even ask about such a boundary. It is a world in which the meanings of technologies are as important as what they do. It is a world in which people, the things they exchange, and the representations through which they construct meanings are all in simultaneous circulation.

It is one of the worlds we all now live in, and one that we are, perhaps, coming to understand. Because in the end, it remains a human world—social, meaningful, artifactual. If the social science models of fifty, or even twenty-five years ago, no longer serve, the fundamental building blocks of those models remain. The basic conceptual apparatus of anthropology—the interplay of representation, exchange, and social formation—is sound, and will see us through into the near future. Beyond that is anyone's guess.

Notes

1. Andrew Shryock points out that many contemporary scholars have an intellectual investment in the concepts of "globalization" and "postmodernity": "The sense of disruption and the lack of closure that mark the transnational narrative are *positively valued* by many of the analysts who invoke them" (2000: 37, emphasis in original).
2. Ironically, the most stylistically "postmodern" anthropological text on media, Carpenter's *Oh, What a Blow That Phantom Gave Me!* (1972), predates the term. Understanding anthropological representation as a mode of theft, and yet trying to write about the impacts of electronic media on communities in North America, Australia, New Guinea, and elsewhere in a way that would not also be theft, he presented his work as a series of interrelated, ironic vignettes, anecdotes, reports, and quotations, inviting the reader to interpret and locate meaning in their juxtaposition.
3. Jamison's definition of culture is not an anthropological one. For Jamison, culture is the superstructure that explains and rationalizes the social and economic systems. In postmodernism, culture is colonizing the social and economic, even as culture itself becomes increasingly commodified.
4. This is not to deny or ignore the realities of the aboriginal peoples displaced and transformed by these societies, but rather to draw attention to the culturally constructed nature of history as a record (and hence a representation) of a people's past.
5. In claiming that in the seventeenth century the press "was for the first time established as a genuinely critical organ of a public engaged in critical political debate: as the fourth estate," Habermas (1989: 60) is certainly romanticizing newspapers. Many early newspapers in America, Europe, and the colonies sought to avoid political controversy and the concomitant possibility of having one's types seized or presses destroyed (Schudson 1978; M. Peterson 1996).
6. Habermas quotes Manin: "A legitimate decision does not represent the will of all, but is one that results from the deliberation of all. It is the process by which everyone's will is formed that confers it legitimacy on the outcome, rather than the sum of already formed wills" (Habermas 1989: 446).
7. Of course, the very act of translation for dubbing raises issues of recontextualization. Word-for-word translation offers a poor approach, since verbal idioms and semantic reference are never completely homologous. Freddi (1999) offers an insider's view of the problems of dubbing English television programs into Italian, and the efforts made to capture the spirit of the original while ensuring that the language matches the movement of lips.
8. Local advertising agencies are often crucial in convincing transnational corporations of the need to inflect local products through advertising (Miller 1995).
9. This refers to the practice of teachers offering private tutoring for pay in addition to class work. Paid extremely low wages, many teachers make the bulk of their incomes through such lessons, and many parents fear that to refuse to pay for their child to receive tutoring means the teacher will downgrade their schoolwork.
10. There are also Korean and Japanese schools, but they do not seek Egyptian students, nor do Egyptians seem to desire to attend. Cosmopolitanism in Egypt is largely about knowing the West.
11. I have changed the names of both schools.
12. The largest foreign group after the United States is Canadian (seventy-three students), followed by Korean (forty-nine), then Swedish, Indian, Israeli, and British, all with twenty to twenty-five students.

13. These figures are imprecise as they refer to one specific moment in time in an extremely fluid and changing population. The figures are also somewhat mislead- ing, since dual passport holders often declare their foreign citizenship rather than their local citizenship. The school is complicit in this activity. It is not uncommon for members of wealthy Egyptian families, for example, to travel to the United States to give birth, since children born in the United States are automatically rec- ognized by the United States as citizens. Egypt, on the other hand, recognizes citi- zenship as passed down through fathers. Many of the students, although raised in Egypt, declare themselves as Americans.

14. A Sept. 1991 report of the World Bank pegged the average Egyptian income at between $1140 and $1490 per year.

15. *Bolbol* is published in Egypt, *Majid* in the Emirates, and *Al Arabi Alsaghir* in Kuwait, but all are available at newsstands throughout the region. The bright, enter- taining magazines cost between one and one and a half pounds (thirty-five to forty cents in 2001), and offer news, games, stories, and lots of cartoons. In addition to featuring Islamic religious and historical narratives, they keep Arab children up-to- date on computers, commodities, and worldwide popular culture for children (the first Harry Potter book was summarized in the January 2001 issue of *Al Arabi Alsaghir*, for example).

16. The *fatwa* is not necessarily binding on Egyptians, whose authoritative interpreta- tions of Islamic law come from Al-Azhar University. Nonetheless, the Mufti is a highly respected and influential figure throughout the Gulf region and his pro- nouncements are covered by the press and followed by many people in Egypt and throughout the world.

REFERENCES

Abrahamson, Mark. 1978. *Functionalism*. Englewood Cliffs, NJ: Prentice Hall.

Abu-Hashish, and Mark Allen Peterson. 1999. "Computer *Khatbas*: Databases and Marital Entrepreneurship in Modern Cairo." *Anthropology Today* 15(6): 7-11.

Abu-Lughod, Lila. 1989 "Bedouins, cassettes and technologies of public culture." *Middle East Report* 159: 7-11, 47.

_____. 1993a. "Finding a Place for Islam: Egyptian Television Serials and the National Interest." *Public Culture* 5(3): 493-513.

_____. 1993b. "Editorial Comment: On Screening Politics in a World of Nations." *Public Culture* 5(3): 465-467.

_____. 1993c. "Islam and Public Culture: The Politics of Egyptian Television Serials." *Middle East Report* (January/February): 25-30.

_____. 1995a. "The Objects of Soap Opera: Egyptian Television and the Cultural Politics of Modernity." In *Worlds Apart: Modernity through the Prism of the Local*, ed. Daniel Miller. New York: Routledge.

_____. 1995b. "Movie Stars and Islamic Moralism in Egypt." *Social Text* 42: 53-67.

_____. 1997. "The Interpretation of Culture(s) after Television." *Representations* 59: 109-134.

_____. 1998a. "Television and the Virtues of Education: Upper Egyptian Encounters with State Culture." In *Directions of Change in Rural Egypt*, ed. Nicholas Hopkins and Kirsten Westergaard. Cairo: American University in Cairo Press.

_____. 1998b. "The Marriage of Feminism and Islamism in Egypt: Selective Repudiation of Postcolonial Cultural Politics." In *Remaking Women: Feminism and Modernity in the Middle East*, ed. Lila Abu-Lughod. Pp. 243-269. Cairo: American University in Cairo Press.

Adams, Richard Newbold. 1970. *Crucifixion by Power: Essays on Guatemalan National Social Structure, 1944-1966*. Austin: University of Texas Press.

Adorno, Theodor. 1973. *Negative Dialectics*. New York: Seabury Press.

Adorno, Theodor and Max Horkheimer. 1976. "The culture industry: Enlightenment as mass deception." In *The Dialectic of Enlightenment*. Pp. 120-167. Trans. John Cummings. New York: Continuum.

Agar, Michael, and Jerry Hobbs. 1985. "How to Grow Schemas out of Interviews." In *Directions in Cognitive Anthropology*, ed. Janet W.D. Dougherty. Urbana: University of Illinois Press.

Ahmed, Akbar S. 1986. "Death in Islam: The Hawkes Bay Case." *Man* 21(1): 120-134.

_____. 1991. "Bombay Films: The Cinema as a Metaphor for Indian Society and Politics." *Modern Asian Studies* 25(2).

Alasuutari, Pertti. 1992. "'I'm Ashamed to Admit It, but I Have Watched Dallas': The Moral Hierarchy of Television Programmes." *Media, Culture and Society* 14: 561-582.

Al-Korey, Amina. 2001. "Pokémon Conquers the World." *Egypt's Insight Magazine* (May): 49-51.

Allison, Anne. 2001. "Cyborg Violence: Bursting Borders and Bodies with Queer Machines." *Cultural Anthropology* 16(3): 237-265.

Althusser, Louis. 1972. "Ideology and the Ideological State Apparatuses." In *Lenin and Philosophy, and Other Essays*. Trans. Ben Brewster. New York: Monthly Review Press.

Alvarez-Cáccamo, Celso. 2001. "Codes." In *Key Terms in Language and Culture*, ed. Alessandro Duranti. Oxford: Blackwell.

Alverson, Hoyt. 1978. *Mind in the Heart of Darkness: Value and Self-identity among the Tswana of Southern Africa*. New Haven: Yale University Press.

Amit-Talai, Vered and Helena Wulff, eds. 1995. *Youth Cultures: A Cross-Cultural Perspective*. London and New York: Routledge.

Andersen, Robin. 1995. *Consumer Culture and TV Programming*. Boulder: Westview.

Anderson, Benedict. 1991. *Imagined Communities: Reflections on the Origin and Spread of Nationalism*. Revised and updated edition. London and New York: Verso.

Anderson, Jon. 1995. "Cybarites, Knowledge Workers and New Creoles on the Information Super Highway." *Anthropology Today* 11(4): 13-15.

_____. 1999. "The Internet and Islam's New Interpreters." In *New Media in the Muslim World: The Emerging Public Sphere*, ed. Dale Eickelman and Jon Anderson. Bloomington: Indiana University Press.

Ang, Ien. 1985. *Watching Dallas: Soap Opera and the Melodramatic Imagination*. London and New York: Methuen.

Appadurai, Arjun, ed. 1988. *The Social Life of Things: Commodities in Cultural Perspective*. Cambridge: Cambridge University Press.

_____. 1996. *Modernity at Large: Cultural Dimensions of Globalization*. Minneapolis: University of Minnesota Press.

Armbrust, Walter. 1992. "The Nationalist Vernacular: Folklore and Egyptian Popular Culture." *Michigan Quarterly Review* 31: 525-542.

_____. 1995. "New Cinema, Commercial Cinema and the Modernist Tradition." *Alif Journal of Contemporary Poetics* 15: 18-129.

_____. 1996a. *Mass Culture and Modernization in Egypt*. Cambridge: Cambridge University Press.

_____. 1996b. "Popular Culture and the Decline of the Egyptian Middle Class." *Journal of the International Institute* (University of Michigan) 3 (3) (Spring/Summer): 8-9.

_____. 1998a. "Terrorism and Kebab: A Capraesque View of Modern Egypt." In *Images of Enchantment: Visual and Performing Arts of the Middle East*, ed. Sherifa Zuhur. Pp. 283-299. Cairo: American University in Cairo Press.

_____. 1998b. "When the Lights Go Down in Cairo: Cinema as Secular Ritual." *Visual Anthropology* 10: 413-442.

_____. 1999. "Bourgeois Leisure and Egyptian Media Fantasies." In *New Media and the Muslim World: The Emerging Public Sphere*, ed. Dale Eickelman and Jon Anderson. Pp. 106-132. Bloomington: Indiana University Press.

_____. 2000a. "The Golden Age before the Golden Age: Commercial Egyptian Cinema before the 1960s." In *Mass Mediations: New Approaches to Popular Culture in the Middle East and Beyond*, ed. Walter Armbrust. Berkeley: University of California Press.

_____. 2000b. "Introduction: Anxieties of Scale." In *Mass Mediations: New Approaches to Popular Culture in the Middle East and Beyond*, ed. Walter Armbrust. Berkeley: University of California Press.

Ascroft, Joseph, and Sipho Masilela. 1994. "Participatory Decision Making in Third World Development." In *Participatory Communication: Working for Change and Development*, ed. Shirley A. White, K. Sadanandan Nair and Joseph Ascroft. Pp. 259-294. New Delhi: Sage.

Askew, Kelly. 2002. "Introduction." In *The Anthropology of Media*, ed. Kelly Askew and Richard Wilk. Oxford: Blackwell.

Associated Press. 1999. "Canadian Student Stabbed over Pokémon." Wednesday, October 27, 9:30 PM ET.

Aufderheide, Patricia. 1993. "Latin American Grassroots Video: Beyond Television." *Public Culture* 5(3): 579-592.

_____. 1995. "The Video in the Villages Project: Videomaking with and by Brazilian Indians." *Visual Anthropology Review* 11(2): 82-93.

Augé, Marc. 1986. "Telecultural Heroes; or a Night at the Embassy." *Current Anthropology* 27(2): 184-188.

_____. 1999. *An Anthropology for Contemporaneous Worlds*. Stanford: Stanford University Press.

Babb, Lawrence, and Susan Wadley. 1995. *Media and the Transformation of Religion in South Asia*. Philadelphia: University of Pennsylvania Press.

Bach, Kirsten Haugaard. 1998. "The Vision of a Better Life: New Patterns of Consumption and Changed Social Relations." In *Directions of Change in Rural Egypt*, ed. Nicholas Hopkins and Kirsten Westergaard. Cairo: American University in Cairo Press.

Bacon-Smith, Camille. 1992. *Enterprising Women: Television Fandom and the Creation of Popular Myth*. Philadelphia: University of Pennsylvania Press.

_____. 2000. *Science Fiction Culture*. Philadelphia: University of Pennsylvania Press.

Bakhtin, Mikhail. 1981. *The Dialogic Imagination: Four Essays*, ed. Michael Holquist, trans. Caryl Emerson and Michael Holquist. Austin: University of Texas Press.

_____. 1984. *Problems of Dostoevsky's Poetics*, trans. Caryl Emerson. Minneapolis: University of Minnesota Press.

_____. 1986. *Speech Genres and Other Essays*, ed. Caryl Emerson and Michael Holquist, trans. Vern McGee. Austin: University of Texas Press.

Ballew, Tad. 2001. "Xiaxiang for the '90s: The Shanghai TV Rural Channel and Post-Mao Urbanity amid Global Swirl." In *China Urban: Ethnographies of Contemporary Culture*, ed. Nancy Chen et al. Pp. 242-273. Durham: Duke University Press.

Baron, Naomi. 1999. "History Lessons: Telegraph, Telephone and E-Mail as Social Discourse." In *Dialogue Analysis and the Mass Media: Proceedings of the International Conference, Erlangen, April 2-3, 1998*, ed. Bernd Naumann. Pp. 1-34. Tübingen: Niemeyer.

Barthes, Roland. 1973. *Mythologies*. Trans. Annette Lavers. New York: Noonday Press.

_____. 1986. "The Reality Effect." In *The Rustle of Language*. Pp. 141-148. New York: Hill and Wang.

Barton, David, and Mary Hamilton. 2000. "Literacy Practices." In *Situated Literacies: Reading and Writing in Context*, ed. David Barton, Mary Hamilton, and Roz Ivanic. Pp. 7-15. New York: Routledge.

Barton, David, Mary Hamilton, and Roz Ivanic, eds. 2000. *Situated Literacies: Reading and Writing in Context*. New York: Routledge.

Bastani, S. 2000. "Muslim Women Online." *Arab World Geographer* 3 (Spring).

Bateson, Gregory. 1943. "Cultural and Thematic Analysis of Fictional Films." *Transactions of the New York Academy of Sciences*, series 2, vol. 5: 72-78. Reprinted in Douglas G. Haring, ed. *Personal Character and Cultural Milieu*. Syracuse: Syracuse University Press.

_____. 1972a [1942]. "Morale and National Character." In *Steps to an Ecology of Mind*. Reprint, New York: Ballantine.

_____. 1972b [1942]. "A Theory of Play and Fantasy." In *Steps to an Ecology of Mind*. Reprint, New York: Ballantine.

_____. 1980. "An Analysis of the Nazi Film 'Hitlerjunge Quex.'" *Studies in Visual Communication* 6(3): 20-55.

_____. 2000 [1953]. "An Analysis of the Nazi Film 'Hitlerjunge Quex.'" In *The Study of Culture at a Distance*, ed. Margaret Mead and Rhoda Métraux. Pp. 302-316. New York: Berghahn.

Bauman, Richard. 1977. *Verbal Art as Performance*. Rowley, MA: Newbury House.

_____. 1986. *Story, Performance, and Event: Contextual Studies of Oral Narrative*. New York: Cambridge University Press.

Bauman, Richard, and Charles Briggs. 1990. "Poetics and Performance as Critical Perspectives on Language and Social Life." *Annual Review of Anthropology* 19: 59-88.

Bean, Susan. 1981a. "Towards a Semiotics of 'Purity' and 'Pollution' in India." *American Ethnologist* 8: 575-595.

_____. 1981b. "Soap Operas: Sagas of American Kinship." In *The American Dimension*, ed. William Arens and Susan Montague. Van Nuys, CA: Alfred Publishing.

Becker, Howard S. 1976. "Art Worlds and Social Types." *American Behavioral Scientist* 19(6): 703-719.

_____. 1982. *Art Worlds*. Berkeley: University of California Press.

_____. 1990. "*Art Worlds* Revisited." *Sociological Forum* 5(3): 497-502.

_____. 1996. "A New Art Form: Hypertext Fiction." In *Cultural and Economia*, ed. M. Lourdes Lima dos Santos. Pp. 67-81. Lisbon: Edicoes de Instituto de Ciencias Socials.

Beeman, William O. 1982. *Culture, Performance and Communication in Iran*. Tokyo: Institute for the Study of Languages and Cultures of Africa and Asia.

_____. 1983. "Images of the Great Satan: Representations of the United States in the Iranian Revolution." In *Religion and Politics in Iran*, ed. Nikki Keddie. New Haven: Yale University Press.

_____. 1984. "The Cultural Role of the Media in Iran." In *The News Media in National and International Conflict*, ed. Andrew Arno and Wimal Dissanayake. Boulder: Westview.

_____. 1986. "Freedom to Choose: Symbolic Values in American Advertising." In *The Symbolization of America*, ed. Herve Varenne. Omaha: University of Nebraska Press.

_____. 2000. "Social Drama of Election Deadlock Points to a True American Culture." *Prince Georges County Journal*, December 21.

Beeman, William O., and Mark Allen Peterson. 2001. "Situations and Interpretations: Explorations in Interpretive Practice." Special issue of *Anthropological Quarterly* 74(4).

Bell, Allan. 1991. *The Language of News Media*. Oxford, UK and Cambridge, MA: Blackwell.

_____. 1994. "Telling stories." In *Media Texts, Authors and Readers: A Reader*, ed. David Graddol and Oliver Boyd-Barrett. Pp. 100-118. Clevedon, UK: Multilingual Matters Ltd.

_____. 1998. "The discourse structure of news stories." In *Approaches to Media Discourse*, ed. Allan Bell and Peter Garrett. Pp. 64-104. Oxford, UK and Malden, MA: Blackwell.

Bell, Allan and Peter Garrett, eds. 1998. *Approaches to Media Discourse*. Oxford, UK and Malden, MA: Blackwell.

Bell, Catherine. 1992. *Ritual Theory, Ritual Practice*. Oxford: Oxford University Press.

Bellah, Robert N., ed. 1965. *Religion and Progress in Modern Asia*. New York: Free Press.

Belo, Jane. 2000. "The Father Figure in Panique." In *The Study of Culture at a Distance*, ed. Margaret Mead and Rhoda Métraux. New York: Berghahn.

Benedict, Ruth. 1934. *Patterns of Culture*. Boston: Houghton Mifflin.

_____. 1946. *The Chrysanthemum and the Sword*. Boston: Houghton Mifflin.

Bennett, John. 1967. "Microcosm-Macrocosm Relationships in North American Agrarian Society." *American Anthropologist* 69(5): 441-454.

Benthall, Jonathan. 1993. *Disasters, Relief and the Media*. London: I.B. Tauris.

Benveniste, Emile. 1971. *Problems in General Linguistics*. Coral Gables, FL: University of Miami Press.

Berger, Peter, and Thomas Luckman. 1966. *The Social Construction of Reality: A Treatise in the Sociology of Knowledge*. Garden City, NY: Doubleday.

Bergman, Brian. 1996. "TV that Protects the North from the South." *Maclean's* 109(21): 46.

Berlo, David K. 1960. *The Process of Communication: An Introduction to Theory and Practice*. San Francisco: Rinehart.

Bernstein, Matthew, and Gaylyn Studlar, eds. 1997. *Visions of the East: Orientalism in Film*. London: I.B. Tauris.

Bertalanffy, Ludwig von. 1968. *General Systems Theory*. New York: George Braziller.

Besnier, Niko. 1991. "Literacy and the Notion of Person on Nukulaelae Atoll." *American Anthropologist* 93(3): 570-587.

Bhabha, Homi, ed. 1990. *Nation and Narration*. New York: Routledge.

_____. 1994. *The Location of Culture*. New York: Routledge.

Bharati, Swami Agehananda. 1977a. "Anthropology of Indian Films, part one." *Folklore* 18(8): 258-266.

_____. 1977b. "Anthropology of Indian films, part two." *Folklore* 18(9): 288-300.

Bhatia, Nandi. 1998. "'Shakespeare' and the Codes of Empire in India." *Alif* 18: 96-126.

Bickerton, Derek. 1975. *Dynamics of a Creole System*. London: Cambridge University Press.

Bloch, Maurice. 1998. *How We Think They Think: Anthropological Approaches to Cognition, Memory, and Literacy*. Boulder: Westview.

Boas, Franz. 1911. *Handbook of American Indian Languages*. Washington, DC: Smithsonian Institution.

Bourdieu, Pierre. 1977. *Outline of a Theory of Practice*. Cambridge: Cambridge University Press.

_____. 1979. "The Kabyle House, or the World Reversed." In *Algeria 1960*. Cambridge: Cambridge University Press.

_____. 1984. *Distinction: A Social Critique of the Judgment of Taste*, trans. Richard Nice. Cambridge: Harvard University Press.

_____. 1998. *On Television*. New York: New Press.

Bourdieu, Pierre and Loïc J.D. Wacquant. 1992. *An Invitation to Reflexive Sociology*. Chicago: University of Chicago Press.

Boyer, Dominic C. 2001. "On the Sedimentation and Accreditation of Social Knowledges of Difference: Mass Media, Journalism and the Reproduction of East/West Alterities in Unified Germany." *Cultural Anthropology* 15(4): 459-491.

Briggs, Charles. 1986. *Learning How to Ask: A Sociolinguistic Appraisal of the Role of the Interview in Social Science Research*. Cambridge: Cambridge University Press.

Briggs, Charles, and Richard Bauman. 1992. "Genre, Intertextuality and Social Power." *Journal of Linguistic Anthropology* 2: 131-172.

Brisebois, Debbie. 1983. "The Inuit Broadcasting Corporation." *Anthropologia* 25(1): 103-118.

Brunsdon, Charlotte and David Morley. 1978. *Everyday Television: Nationwide*. London: British Film Institute.

Buck-Morss, Susan. 1977. *The Origin of Negative Dialectics: Theodor W. Adorno, Walter Benjamin, and the Frankfurt Institute*. New York: MacMillan.

Buckingham, David. 1987. *Public Secrets: Eastenders and its Audience*. London: British Film Institute.

Caldarola, V.J. 1992a. "Reading the Television Text in Outer Indonesia." *Howard Journal of Communication* 40(1-2): 28-49.

_____. 1992b. "Time and the Television War." *Public Culture* 4(2): 127-136.

Carael, M., and John B. Stanbury. 1983. "Birth Spacing on Idjwe Island, Zaire." *Studies in Family Planning* 14: 134-142.

_____. 1984. "A Film Program in Health and Family Planning in Rural Zaire." *Human Organization* 43(4): 341-348.

Carpenter, Edmund. 1972. *Oh, What a Blow That Phantom Gave Me!* New York: Holt, Rinehart and Winston.

Castells, Manuel. 1996. *The Rise of the Network Society*. Cambridge, MA: Blackwell.

_____. 1997. *The Power of Identity*. Malden, MA: Blackwell.

Caton, Steven C. 1999. *Lawrence of Arabia: a Film's Anthropology*. Berkeley: University of California Press.

Caughey, John L. 1984. *Imaginary Social Worlds: A Cultural Approach*. Lincoln: University of Nebraska Press.

_____. 1985. "Social Relations with Media Figures." In *Inter/Media: Interpersonal Communication in a Media World*, ed. Gary Gumpert and Robert S. Cathcart. Pp. 219-252. Oxford: Oxford University Press.

_____. 1994. "Gina As Steven: The Social and Cultural Dimensions of A Media Relationship." *Visual Anthropology Review* 10 (1): 126-135.

_____. 1995. "Imaginary Social Relationships." *Media Journal: Reading and Writing About Popular Culture*, ed. Joseph Harris and Jay Rosen. Pp.121-146. Boston: Allyn and Bacon.

Chapin, Francis Stuart. 1979 [1920] *Field Work and Social Research*. New York: Arno.

Charlot, John. 1998. "Pele and Hi'iaka: The Hawaiian-Language Newspaper Series." *Anthropos* 93: 55-75.

Chopyak, James D. 1987. "The Role of Music in Mass Media, Public Education and the Formation of a Malaysian National Culture." *Ethnomusicology* 31(3): 431-454.

Clark, Katerina, and Michael Holquist. 1984. *Mikhail Bakhtin*. Cambridge: Harvard University Press.

Claus, Peter J. 1982 [1976]. "A Structuralist Appreciation of Star Trek." In *Anthropology for the Eighties*, ed. Johnetta B. Cole. New York: Free Press.

Clayman, Steven E. 1990. "From Talk to Text: Newspaper Accounts of Reporter-Source Interactions." *Media, Culture and Society* 12(1): 79-103.

Cleaver, Harry M. 1998. "The Zapatista Effect: The Internet and the Rise of an Alternative Political Fabric." *Journal of International Affairs* 51(2): 621-640.

Clerc, Susan J. 1996. "DDEB, GATB, MPPB, and Ratboy: *The X Files* Media Fandom, Online and Off." In *Deny All Knowledge: Reading The X Files*, edited by David Lavery, Angela Hague, and Marla Cartwright. Pp. 36-51. Syracuse, NY: Syracuse University Press

Clifford, James, and George Marcus, eds. 1986. *Writing Culture: The Poetics and Politics of Ethnography*. Berkeley: University of California Press.

_____. 1988. *The Predicament of Culture*. Cambridge: Harvard University Press.

Clover, Carol. 1992. *Men, Women, and Chain Saws: Gender in the Modern Horror Film*. Princeton: Princeton University Press.

Cohen, Percy. 1968. *Modern Social Theory*. New York: Basic.

Coldevin, Gary O., and Thomas C. Wilson. 1985. "Effects of a Decade of Satellite Television in the Canadian Arctic: Euro-Canadian and Inuit Adolescents Compared." *Journal of Cross-Cultural Psychology* 16(3): 329-354.

Coleman, Patrick. 1986. "Music Carries a Message to Youths." *Development Communication Report* 53.

Colle, Raymond. 1992. "A Radio for the Mapuches of Chile: From Popular Education to Political Awareness." In *Ethnic Minority Media: An International Perspective*, ed. Stephen Harold Riggins. Newbury Park, CA: Sage.

Collins, James. 1995. "Literacy and Literacies." *Annual Review of Anthropology* 24: 75-93.

Connell, R.W. 1995 *Masculinities*. Cambridge, UK: Polity.

Coombe, Rosemary. Coombe, Rosemary J. 1996. Embodied Trademarks: Mimesis and Alterity on American Commercial Frontiers. *Cultural Anthropology* 11(2): 202-224.

_____. 1997. The Demonic Place of the 'Not There': Trademark Rumors in the Postindustrial Imaginary. In Gupta, Akhil and James Ferguson, eds. *Culture, Power, Place: Explorations in Critical Anthropology*. Pp. 249-274. Duke University Press.

_____. 1998. *The Cultural Life of Intellectual Properties: Authorship, Appropriation, and the Law*. Durham: Duke University Press.

Cotter, Colleen. 1999. "From Folklore to 'News at 6': Managing Language and Reframing Identity through the Media." In *Reinventing Identities: From Category to Practice in Language and Gender Research*, ed. Mary

Bucholtz, A.C. Liang, and Laurel Sutton. Pp. 369-387. Oxford University Press.

Cotter, Colleen. 2000. "Story Meetings": The Negotiation of News Values in the Journalistic Discourse Community." Paper presented at Georgetown University Round Table on Language and Linguistics, Washington, DC, May 2000.

Coutin, Susan Bibler and Phyllis Pease Chock. 1995. "'Your Friend, the Illegal': Definition and Paradox in Newspaper Accounts of U.S. Immigration Reform." *Identities* 2(1-2): 123-148.

Crawford, Peter I. 1995. "Nature and Advocacy in Ethnographic Film: The Case of Kayapo Imagery." In *Advocacy and Indigenous Filmmaking*, ed. H.H. Philipsen and B. Markussen. Denmark: Intervention Press.

Csordas, Thomas, ed. 1994. *Embodiment and Experience: The Existential Ground of Culture*. Cambridge: Cambridge University Press.

Culler, Jonathan. 1975. *Structuralist Poetics; Structuralism, Linguistics and the Study of Literature*. London: Routledge and Kegan Paul.

Danielson, Virginia. 1997. *The Voice of Egypt: Umm Kulthum, Arabic Song, and Egyptian Society in the Twentieth Century*. Chicago: University of Chicago Press.

Das, Veena. 1973. "The Structure of Marriage Preferences: An Account from Pakistani Fiction." *Man* 8(1): 30-45.

_____. 1995. "On Soap Opera: What Kind of Anthropological Object is It?" In *Worlds Apart: Modernity through the Prism of the Local*, ed. Daniel Miller. New York: Routledge.

Davila, Arlene. 1998. "El Kiosko Budweiser: The Making of a 'National' Television Show in Puerto Rico." *American Ethnologist* 25(3): 452-470.

de Certeau, Michel. 1984. *The Practice of Everyday Life*. Berkeley: University of California Press.

DeFleur, Melvin L., and Susan Ball-Rokeach. 1975. *Theories of Mass Communication*. New York: David McKay.

Deregowski, Jan. 1980. *Illusions, Patterns and Pictures: A Cross-Cultural Perspective*. New York: Academic.

Derrida, Jacques. 1978. *Writing and difference*. Chicago: University of Chicago Press.

_____. 1998. *Of Grammatology*. Baltimore: Johns Hopkins University Press.

Deutsch, Karl. 1961. "Social Mobilization and Political Development." *American Political Science Review* 55: 463-515.

Diawara, Manthia. 1994. "On Tracking World Cinema: African Cinema at Film Festivals." *Public Culture* 6: 385-396.

Dickey, Sara. 1993. *Cinema and the Urban Poor in South India*. Cambridge: Cambridge University Press.

_____. 1997 "Anthropology and its Contributions to Studies of Mass Media." *International Social Science Journal* 154: 413-427.

_____. 2001 Opposing faces: film star, fan clubs and the construction of class identities in South India. In Rachel Dwyer and Christopher Pinney, eds.

Pleasure and the Nation: The History, Politics and Consumption of Popular Culture in India. New Delhi: Oxford University Press.

Dolgin, Janet, David S. Kemnitzer, and David M. Schneider. 1977. "Commentary on 'Cézanne's Doubt.'" In *Symbolic Anthropology: A Reader in the Study of Symbols and Meanings*. P. 91. New York: Columbia University Press.

Donham, Donald L. 1998. "Freeing South Africa: The 'modernization' of male-male Sexuality in Soweto." *Cultural Anthropology* 13(1): 3-21.

Dorfman, Ariel and Armand Mattelart. 1991[1971]. *How to Read Donald Duck: Imperialist Ideology in the Disney Comic*, trans. David Kunzle. New York: International General.

Dornfeld, Barry Evan. 1998. *Producing Public Television, Producing Public Culture*. Princeton: Princeton University Press.

Douglas, Mary, and Baron Isherwood. 1981. *The World of Goods*. New York: Basic.

Douglass, H. Paul. 1924. *1000 City Churches: Phases of Adaptation to Changing Environment*. New York: George H. Doran.

_____. 1928. *How to Study the City Church*. Garden City: Doran and Company.

Drummond, Lee. 1980. "The Cultural Continuum: A Theory of Intersystems." *Man* 15: 352-374.

_____. 1984. "Movies and Myths: Theoretical Skirmishes." *American Journal of Semiotics* 3(2): 1-32.

_____. 1986. "The Story of Bond." In *Symbolizing America*, ed. Herve Varenne. Pp. 162-186. Lincoln: University of Nebraska Press.

_____. 1992. "Media and Myth: Theoretical Skirmishes." *Semiotica* 3(2): 1-32.

_____. 1996. *American Dreamtime: A Cultural Analysis of Popular Movies and Their Implications for Humanity*. Lanham, MD: Littlefield, Adams.

DuBois, Cora. 1944. *The People of Alor*. Minneapolis: University of Minnesota Press.

Duclos, Denis. 1998. *The Werewolf Complex: America's Fascination with Violence*. New York: Berg.

du Gay, Paul. 1996. *Consumption and Identity at Work*. London and Beverly Hills: Sage.

du Gay, Paul, Stuart Hall, Linda Janes, Hugh Mackay and Keith Negus. 1997. *Doing Cultural Studies: The Story of the Sony Walkman*. London and Beverly Hills: Sage.

Durkheim, Emile. 1915. *Elementary Forms of the Religious Life*. New York: Macmillan.

Dyer, Gillian. 1989. *Advertising as Communication*. London: Routledge.

Eco, Umberto. 1979. *The Role of the Reader*. Bloomington: Indiana University Press.

_____. 1989. *The Open Work*, trans. Anna Cancogni. Cambridge: Harvard University Press.

_____. 1990. *The Limits of Interpretation*. Bloomington: Indiana University Press.

Eickelman, Dale, and Jon Anderson, eds. 1999. *New Media in the Muslim World: The Emerging Public Sphere*. Bloomington: Indiana University Press.

Enzenberger, H.M. 1970. "Constituents of a Theory of the Media." *New Left Review* 64: 13-36.

Erikson, Erik. 1950. "The Legend of Maxim Gorky's Youth: A Study of the Soviet Film *The Childhood of Maxim Gorky*." In *Childhood and Society*. New York: W.W. Norton.

Evans-Pritchard, E. A. 1940. *The Nuer: A Description of the Modes of Livelihood and Political Institutions of a Nilotic People*. Oxford: Clarendon.

Fabian, Johannes. 1983. *Time and the Other: How Anthropology Makes Its Object*. New York: Columbia University Press.

Faris, James C. 1992. "Anthropological Transparency: Film, Representation and Politics." In *Film as Ethnography*, ed. Crawford, Peter and David Turton. Pp. 171-182. Manchester: Manchester University Press.

Fernandez, James. 1986. *Persuasions and Performances: The Play of Tropes in Culture*. Bloomington: Indiana University Press.

Fienup-Riordan, Ann. 1988. "Robert Redford, Apanuugpak, and the Invention of Tradition." *American Ethnologist* 15(3): 442-455.

Fischer, Claude S. 1992. *America Calling: A Social History of the Telephone to 1940*. Berkeley: University of California Press.

Fisherkiller, JoEllen. 1997 Everyday Learning About Identities Among Young Adolescents in TV Culture. *Anthropology and Education Quarterly* 28(4): 467-492.

Fishman, Mark. 1980. *Manufacturing the News*. Austin: University of Texas Press.

Fiske, John. 1987. *Television Culture*. London and New York: Methuen.

Foucault, Michel. 1978. *The History of Sexuality*. New York: Pantheon.

_____. 1984a. "What Is an Author?" In *The Foucault Reader*, ed. Paul Rabinow. Pp. 101-120. New York: Pantheon.

_____. 1984b. "Truth and Power." In *The Foucault Reader*, ed. Paul Rabinow. Pp. 51-75. New York: Pantheon.

Frank, Andre G. 1969. *Latin America: Underdevelopment or Revolution*. New York: Monthly Review Press.

Freddi, Maria. 1999. "Dialogue Analysis and Multimedia Translation." In *Dialogue Analysis and the Mass Media: Proceedings of the International Conference, Erlangen, April 2-3, 1998*, ed. Bernd Naumann. Pp. 149-158. Tübingen: Niemeyer.

Fry, Charles Luther. 1924. *Diagnosing the Rural Church*. New York: George H. Doran.

_____. 1925. *A Census Analysis of American Villages*. New York: Institute of Social and Religious Research.

Fuglesang, Minou. 1994. *Veils and Videos*. Stockholm: Stockholm Studies in Social Anthropology.

Fukui, Nanako. 1999. "Background Research for the Chrysanthemum and the Sword." *Dialectical Anthropology* 24(2): 173-180.

Gallois, Dominique T., and Vincent Carelli. 1993. "Video in the Villages: The Waiapi Experience." *CVA Newsletter* 1993(2)/1994(1): 7-11.

Gans, Herbert. 1980. *Deciding What's News*. New York: Vintage.

Geertz, Clifford. 1973. "Thick Description." In *The Interpretation of Cultures*. New York: Basic.

Gell, Alfred. 1992. *The Anthropology of Time: Cultural Constructions of Temporal Maps and Images*. Oxford: Berg.

Ghei, Kirin. 1988. "Accessible Choreographies: Hindi Cinema on Videotape in Los Angeles." *UCLA Journal of Dance Ethnology* 12: 18-31.

Giddens, Anthony. 1979. *Central Problems in Social Theory*. Berkeley: University of California Press.

_____. 1990. *The Consequences of Modernity*. Cambridge, UK: Polity.

Gillespie, Marie. 1995. *Television, Ethnicity and Cultural Change*. London: Routledge.

Gilligan, Carol, and Lyn Mikel Brown. 1992. *Meeting at the Crossroads*. Cambridge: Harvard University Press,

Ginsburg, Faye. 1991. "Indigenous Media: Faustian Contract or Global Village?" *Cultural Anthropology* 6(1): 92-112.

_____. 1993a. "Aboriginal Media and the Australian Imaginary." *Public Culture* 5(3): 557-578.

_____. 1993b. "Station Identification: The Aboriginal Programs Unit of the Australian Broadcasting Corporation." In *Visual Anthropology Review* 9(2): 92-96.

_____. 1994a. "Culture/Media: A (Mild) Polemic." *Anthropology Today* 10(2): 5-15.

_____. 1994b. "Production Values: Indigenous Media and the Rhetoric of Self-Determination." In *The Rhetoric of Self-Making*, ed. Deborah Battaglia. Berkeley: University of California Press.

_____. 1994c. "Embedded Aesthetics: Creating a Discursive Space for Indigenous Media." *Cultural Anthropology* 9(3): 365-382.

_____. 2002a. "Screen Memories: Resignifying the Traditional in Indigenous Media." In *Media Worlds: Anthropology on New Terrain*, ed. Faye Ginsburg, Lila Abu-Lughod and Brian Larkin. Berkeley: University of California Press.

_____. 2002b [1995]. "Mediating Culture: Indigenous Media, Ethnographic Film and the Production of Identity." In *The Anthropology of Media*, ed. Kelly Askew and Richard Wilk, Pp. 210-235. Oxford: Blackwell.

Gitlin, Todd. 1983. *Inside Prime Time*. New York: Pantheon.

Gledhill, John. 1994. *Power and its Disguises: Anthropological Perspectives on Politics*. London and Boulder: Pluto.

Goffman, Erving. 1986. *Frame Analysis: An Essay on the Organization of Experience*. Reprint edition. Boston: Northeastern University Press.

Goldman, Robert and Stephen Papson. 1998. *Nike Culture: The Sign of the Swoosh*. London: Sage.

Goody, James. 1986. *The Logic of Writing and the Organization of Society.* Cambridge: Cambridge University Press.

_____. 1987. *The Interface between the Oral and the Written.* Cambridge: Cambridge University Press.

Goody, James, and Ian Watt. 1963. "The Consequences of Literacy." *Comparative Studies in Society and History* 5: 304-326, 332-345.

Gore, Charles. 1998. "Ritual, Performance and Media in Urban Contemporary Shrine Configurations in Benin City, Nigeria." In *Ritual, Performance, Media,* ed. Felicia Hughes-Freeland. Pp. 66-84. New York: Routledge.

Gorer, Geoffrey. 1946. "Japanese Character." *Science News* 1: 26-51.

_____. 2000 [1953]. "National character: Theory and Practice." In *The Study of Culture at a Distance,* ed. Margaret Mead and Rhoda Métraux. Pp. 61-89. New York: Berghahn.

Granzberg, Gary. 1982. Television as storyteller: The Algonkian Indians of central Canada. *Journal of Communication* 32(1): 43-52.

Granzberg, Gary, and Jack Steinbring, eds. 1980. *Television and the Canadian Indian: Impact and Meaning among Algonkians of Central Canada.* Winnipeg: University of Winnipeg Press.

Granzberg, Gary, Jack Steinbring, and John Hamer. 1977. "New Magic for Old: TV in Cree Culture." *Journal of Communications* 27(4): 155-177.

Gross, Joan, David McMurray, and Ted Swedenburg. 1992. "Rai, Rap and Ramadan Nights: Franco-Maghribi Cultural Identities." *Middle East Report* 178: 11-24.

Grossberg, Lawrence. 1987. "The In-Difference of Television." *Screen* 28(2): 28-45.

Gumperz, John J. 1971. "The Speech Community." In *Language and Social Context,* ed. Pier P. Giglioli. Pp. 219-231. New York: Viking.

_____. 1996. "The Linguistic and Cultural Relativity of Conversational Inference." In *Rethinking Linguistic Relativity,* ed. John J. Gumperz and Stephen C. Levinson. Pp. 374-406. Cambridge: Cambridge University Press.

Gupta, Akhil and James Ferguson, eds. 1997. *Culture, Power, Place: Explorations in Critical Anthropology.* Durham: Duke University Press.

Habermas, Jurgen. 1985 [1981]. *Theory of Communicative Action, Vol. 1: Reason and the Rationalization of Society.* Boston: Beacon.

_____. 1989. *The Transformation of the Public Sphere.* Cambridge: MIT Press.

Hakken, David. 1999. *Cyborgs@Cyberspace? An Anthropologist Looks to the Future.* New York and London: Routledge.

Halbfinger, David M. 1999. "Suit Claims Pokémon Is Lottery, Not Just a Fad." *New York Times,* September 24.

Hall, Stuart. 1977. "Culture, the Media and the 'Ideological Effect.'" In *Mass Communication and Society,* ed. James Curran, Michael Gurevitch, and Janet Woolacott. London: Edward Arnold.

_____. 1982. "The rediscovery of 'ideology': The Return of the Repressed in Media Studies." In *Culture, Society and the Media,* ed. Michael Gurevitch, T. Bennett, James Curran, and Janet Woolacott. London: Methuen.

_____. 1992. "The Question of Cultural Identity." In Modernity and Its Futures, ed. Stuart Hall, David Held and Tony McGrew, eds. Cambridge: Polity Press.

Hall, Stuart, and Paddy Whannel. 1965. *The Popular Arts*. New York: Pantheon.

Halleck, Dee Dee, and Nathalie Magnan. 1993. "Access for Others: Alter(Native) Media Practice." *Visual Anthropology Review* 9(1): 154-163.

Hallowell, A.I. 1960. "Ojibwa Ontology: Behavior and Worldview." In *Culture and History*, ed. Stanley Diamond. New York: Columbia University Press.

Hamilton, Annette. 1993. "Video Crackdown, or the Sacrificial Pirate." *Public Culture* 5: 515-532.

_____. 1997. "Comments." *Current Anthropology* 38(2): 216-217.

Hamman, Robin B. 1996. "Cyborgasms: Cybersex among Multiple Selves and Cyborgs in the Narrow-Bandwidth Space of America Online Chat Rooms." MA Dissertation, Department of Sociology, University of Essex, [http://www.socio.demon.co.uk/Cyborgasms.html]. [Accessed Feb. 9, 2002].

Hannerz, Ulf. 1971. "The Study of Afro-American Cultural Dynamics." *Southwestern Journal of Anthropology* 27: 181-200.

_____. 1990. "Cosmopolitans and Locals in World Culture." In *Global Culture: Nationalism, Globalization, Modernity*, ed. Michael Featherstone. Pp. 237-253. London: Sage.

_____. 1992. *Cultural Complexity: Studies in the Social Organization of Meaning*. New York: Columbia University Press.

_____. 1998. "Reporting from Jerusalem." *Cultural Anthropology* 13(4): 548-574.

Hardt, Hanno, and Bonnie Brennan, eds. 1995. *New Workers: Toward a History of the Rank and File*. Minneapolis: University of Minnesota Press.

Hartmann, Paul, B.R. Patil, and Anita Dighe. 1989. *The Mass Media and Village Life: An Indian Study*. New Delhi: Sage.

Hawkes, Terence. 1977. *Structuralism and Semiotics*. Berkeley: University of California Press.

Heath, Shirley Brice. 1983. *Ways with Words: Language, Life and Work in Classrooms and Communities*. Cambridge: Cambridge University Press.

Hebdige, Dick. 1979. *Subculture: The Meaning of Style*. London: Methuen.

Hedebro, Goran. 1982. *Communication and Social Change in Developing Nations: A Critical View*. Ames: Iowa State University Press.

Henry, Jules. 1963. *Culture against Man*. New York: Random House.

Herzfeld, Michael. 1997. *Cultural Intimacy: Poetics and Politics of the Nation State*. New York: Routledge.

_____. 2001. *Anthropology: Theoretical Practice in Culture and Society*. Oxford: Blackwell.

Heyer, Virginia. 2000 [1953]. "Relations between men and women in Chinese stories." In *The Study of Culture at a Distance*, ed. Margaret Mead and Rhoda Métraux. Pp. 241-255. New York: Berghahn.

Hirsch, Eric. 1989. "Bound and Unbound Entitites: Reflections on the Ethnographic Perspectives of Anthropology vis-à-vis Media and Cultural Studies." In *Ritual, Performance, Media*, ed. Felicia Hughes-Freeland. Pp. 208-228. London: Routledge.

Hoberman, J., and Jonathan Rosenbaum. 1981. *Midnight Movies*. New York: Harper and Row.

Hobson, Dorothy. 1982. *Crossroads: The Drama of a Soap Opera*. London: Methuen.

Hockett, Charles. 1977. "Logical Considerations in the Study of Animal Communication." In *The View from Language: Selected Essays 1948-1974*. Pp. 124-162. Athens: University of Georgia Press.

Hodge, Robert, and Gunther Kress. 1988. *Social Semiotics*. Ithaca, NY: Cornell University Press.

Hodgkinson, Neville. 1994. "Conspiracy of Silence." *The Sunday Times* (London), April 3.

Hoffman, Barbara G. 2000. *Griots at War: Conflict, Conciliation and Caste in Mande*. Bloomington: Indiana University Press.

Holquist, Michael. 1986. "Answering as Authoring: Mikhail Bakhtin's Translinguistics." In *Bakhtin: Essays and Dialogues on His Work*, ed. Gary Saul Morson. Chicago: University of Chicago Press.

Honigman, J., and M. van Doerslaer. 1955. "Some Themes from Indian Film Reviews." In *Studies in Pakistan National Culture 2*. Institute for Research in Social Science, University of North Carolina.

Horkheimer, Max, and Theodor Adorno. 1994. "The Culture Industry: Enlightenment as Mass Deception." In *Dialectic of Enlightenment*. New York: Herder and Herder.

Huizinga, Johann. 1955. *Homo Ludens: A Study of the Play Element in Culture*. London: Beacon.

Hymes, Dell. 1977. *Foundations of Sociolinguistics*. Philadelphia: University of Pennsylvania Press.

_____. 1984. *"In Vain I Tried to Tell You": Essays in Native American Ethnopoetics*. Philadelphia: University of Pennsylvania Press.

Jakobson, Roman. 1960. "Concluding Statement: Linguistics and Poetics." In *Style in Language*, ed. T. Sebeok. Pp. 350-377. New York: Wiley.

_____. 1990. *On Language*, ed. Linda R. Waugh and Monique Monville-Burston. Cambridge: Harvard University Press.

Jameson, Fredric. 1984. "Postmodernism, or the Culture of Late Capitalism." *New Left Review* 146: 53-92.

Jay, Martin. 1973. *The Dialectical Imagination: A History of the Frankfurt School and the Institute for Social Research, 1925-1950*. Boston: Little, Brown.

Jenkins, Henry. 1992. *Textual Poachers: Television Fans and Participatory Culture*. New York: Routledge.

Jhappan, C. Radha. 1990. "Indian Symbolic Politics: The Double-Edged Sword of Publicity." *Canadian Ethnic Studies* 22(3): 19-39.

Johnson, Richard. 1987. "What is Cultural Studies Anyway?" *Social Text* 16(1): 38-80.

Joyce, Cynthia. 1999. "Give Pokémon a Chance." www.salon.com. July 6. [Accessed July 9, 1999].

Juhasz, Alexandra. 1995. *AIDS TV: Identity, Community and Alternative Video*. Durham: Duke University Press.

Karp, Ivan. 1981. "Good Marx for the Anthropologist: Structure and Antistructure in 'Duck Soup.'" In *The American Dimension*, ed. William Arens and Susan Montague. Pp. 37-50. Sherman Oaks, CA: Greenwood.

Katz, Elihu, Jay Blumler and Michael Gurevitch. 1974. *The Uses of Mass Communications: Current Perspectives on Gratifications Research*. Beverly Hills: Sage.

Kearney, Michael. 1995. "The Local and the Global: The Anthropology of Globalization and Transnationalism." *Annual Review of Anthropology* 24: 547-565.

Keesing, Felix. 1956. "Recreative Behavior and Culture Change." In *Selected Papers of the Fifth International Congress of Anthropological and Ethnological Sciences*. Pp. 130-133. Philadelphia: University of Pennsylvania Press.

Kemnitzer, David S. 1977. "Sexuality as a Social Form" In *Symbolic Anthropology: A Reader in the Study of Symbols and Meaning*, ed. Janet Dolgin, David S. Kemnitzer, and David Schneider. New York: Columbia University Press,

Kent, Pauline. 1999. "Japanese Perceptions of *The Chrysanthemum and the Sword*." *Dialectical Anthropology* 24(2): 181 - 192

Kent, Susan. 1985. "The Effects of Television Viewing: A Cross-Cultural Perspective." *Current Anthropology* 26(1): 121-126.

Kertzer, David. 1980. *Comrades and Christians: Religion and Political Struggle in Communist Italy*. Cambridge: Cambridge University Press.

Kirshenblatt-Gimblett, Barbara. 1996. "The Electronic Vernacular." In *Connected: Engagements with Media*, ed. George Marcus. Chicago: University of Chicago Press.

Kondo, Dorinne. 1996. "Shades of Twilight: Anna Deavere Smith and *Twilight: Los Angeles 1992*." In *Connected: Engagements with Media*, ed. George E. Marcus. Chicago: University of Chicago Press.

Kottak, Conrad. 1982a. "Structural and Psychological Analysis of Popular American Fantasy Films." In *Researching American Culture: A Guide for Student Anthropologists*, ed. Conrad Phillip Kottak. Pp. 87-97. Ann Arbor: University of Michigan Press.

_____. 1982b. "The Father Strikes Back." In *Researching American Culture: A Guide for Student Anthropologists*, ed. Conrad Phillip Kottak. Pp. 87-97. Ann Arbor: University of Michigan Press.

_____. 1990. *Prime Time Society*. Belmont, CA: Wadsworth.

Krech, Shepard. 1999. *The Ecological Indian*. New York: W.W. Norton.

Kroeber, Alfred L. 1948. *Anthropology*. Rev. ed. New York: Harcourt Brace.

Lacan, Jacques. 1968. *The Language of the Self: The Function of Language in Psychoanalysis*. Baltimore: Johns Hopkins Press.

Landsman, Gail. 1987. "Indian Activism and the Press: Coverage of the Conflict at Ganienkah." *Anthropological Quarterly* 60(3): 101-113.

_____. 1988. *Sovereignty and Symbol: Indian-White Conflict at Ganienkah*. Albuquerque: University of New Mexico Press.

Larkin, Brian. 1998. "Theaters of the Profane: Cinema and Colonial Urbanism." *Visual Anthropology Review* 14(2): 46-62.

Lasswell, H.D. 1960. *The Classical Law of India*, trans. D.M. Derrett. Berkeley: University of California Press.

Latour, Bruno. 1993. *We Have Never Been Modern*. Cambridge: Harvard University Press.

Leach, Edmund. 1961. *Rethinking Anthropology*. New York: Humanities.

Lembo, Ron. 2000. *Thinking through Television*. Cambridge: Cambridge University Press.

Leuthold, Steven. 1998. *Indigenous Aesthetics: Native Art, Media, and Identity*. Austin: University of Texas Press.

Levi-Strauss, Claude. 1963. *Structural Anthropology*. New York: Basic.

_____. 1973. *Totemism*. Boston: Beacon.

Liebes, Tamar and Elihu Katz. 1994. *The Export of Meaning: Cross-cultural Readings of Dallas*. Oxford: Polity.

Liechty, Mark. 1995 "Media, Markets and Modernization: Youth Identities and the Experience of Modernity in Kathmandu, Nepal." In *Youth Cultures : A Cross Cultural Perspective*, ed. Vered Amit-Talai and Helena Wulff. London ; New York : Routledge.

_____. 1998. "The Social Practice of Cinema and Video-viewing in Kathmandu." *Studies in Nepali History and Society* 3(1): 87-126.

Lipsitz, George. 1986. "The Meaning of Memory: Family, Class and Ethnicity in Early Network Television Programs." *Cultural Anthropology* 1(4): 355-387.

Locke, Liz. 1999. "Don't Dream It, Be It: 'The Rocky Horror Picture Show' as Cultural Performance." *New Directions in Folklore 3*. http://www.temple.edu/isllc/newfolk/rhps1.html. [Accessed July 1, 2001].

Lodge, David. 1988. *Nice Work*. London: Secker and Warburg.

Lord, Albert B. 1960. *The Singer of Tales*. Cambridge: Harvard University Press.

Lukács, Georg. 1968 [1922]. *History and Class Consciousness*. Cambridge: MIT Press.

Lull, James. 1988. *World Families Watch Television*. Newbury Park, CA: Sage.

_____. 1990. *Inside Family Viewing: Ethnographic Research on Television's Audiences*. London: Routledge.

Lutz, Catherine and Jane Collins. 1993. *Reading National Geographic*. Chicago: University of Chicago Press.

Lynd, Robert. 1937. *Middletown Revisited*. New York: Harcourt Brace.

Lynd, Robert, and Helen Merrell Lynd. 1929. *Middletown*. New York: Harcourt Brace.

Lyons, Andrew. 1990. "The Television and the Shrine: Towards a Theoretical Model for the Study of Mass Communication in Nigeria." *Visual Anthropology* 3(4): 429-456.

Lyons, Harriet D. 1990. "Television in Contemporary Urban Life: Benin City, Nigeria." *Visual Anthropology* 3(4): 411-428.

Mabee, Carleton. 1987. "Margaret Mead and Behavioral Scientists in World War II: Problems of Responsibility, Truth, and Effectiveness." *Journal of History of the Behavioral Sciences* 23: 3-13.

MacDougall, David. 1987. "Media Friend or Media Foe?" *Visual Anthropology* 1(1): 54-58.

Madan, T.N. 1987a. "Asceticism and Eroticism." In *Non-Renunciation: Themes and Interpretations of Hindu Culture*. Pp. 72-100. Delhi: Oxford University Press.

_____. 1987b. "The Desired and the Good." In *Non-Renunciation: Themes and Interpretations of Hindu Culture*. Pp. 101-118. Delhi: Oxford University Press.

Maddox, Richard. 1997. "Bombs, Bikinis and the Popes of Rock 'n' Roll." In *Culture, Power, Place: Explorations in Critical Anthropology*, ed. Akhil Gupta and James Ferguson. Durham: Duke University Press.

Malinowski, Bronislaw. 1922. *Argonauts of the Western Pacific: An Account of Native Enterprise and Adventure in the Archipelagoes of Melanesian New Guinea*. London: Routledge.

_____. 1944. *The Scientific Theory of Culture and Other Essays*. New York: Oxford University Press.

_____. 1953. "Introduction." *Argonauts of the Western Pacific*. New York: E. P. Dutton.

_____. 1966. *The Father in Primitive Psychology*. New York: Norton.

Mankekar, Purnima. 1993. Television Tales and a Woman's Rage: A Nationalist Recasting of Draupadi's Disrobing." *Public Culture* 5(3): 469-492.

_____. 1999. *Screening Culture, Viewing Politics: An Ethnography of Television, Womanhood, and Nation in Postcolonial India*. Durham and London: Duke University Press.

Manuel, Peter. 1993. *Cassette Culture: Popular Music and Technology in North India*. Chicago: University of Chicago Press.

Marcus, George. 1998. *Ethnography through Thick and Thin*. Princeton: Princeton University Press.

Marcus, George, ed. 1996. *Connected: Engagements with Media at the Century's End*. Chicago: University of Chicago Press.

Marcus, George, and Michael M.J. Fischer. 1986. *Anthropology as Cultural Critique: An Experimental Moment in the Human Sciences*. Chicago: University of Chicago Press.

Martin, Emily. 1992. *The Woman in the Body: A Cultural Analysis of Reproduction*. New York: Beacon.

_____. 1994. Flexible Bodies: *Tracking Immunity in American Culture From the Days of Polio to the Age of AIDS*. Boston: Beacon.

Marx, Karl and Friedrich Engels. 1963 [1869]. *The 18th Brumaire of Napoleon Bonaparte*. New York: International.

_____. 1967 [1867]. *Capital: A Critique of Political Economy*. New York: International.

_____. 1968 [1895]. "Preface to a Contribution to the Critique of Political Economy." In *Selected Works*. London: Lawrence and Wishart.

McCreery, John L. 2001. "Getting to Persuasion." *Anthropological Quarterly* 74(4): 163-169.

McLagen, Meg. 1996. "Computing for Tibet: Virtual Politics in the Post-Cold War Era." In *Connected: Engagements with Media at the Century's End*. Pp. 159-194. Chicago: University of Chicago Press.

McLelland, David C. 1967. *The Achieving Society*. New York: Free Press.

McLuhan, Marshall. 1989. *The Global Village: Transformations in World Life and Media in the 21st century*. New York: Oxford University Press.

McQuail, Denis. 1992. *Media Performance: Mass Communication and the Public Interest*. London: Sage.

_____. 1994. *Mass Communication Theory: an Introduction*. London: Sage.

Mead, Margaret. 1951. "What Makes Soviet Character?" *Natural History* 60(7): 296-303, 336.

_____. 1961. "The Institute for Intercultural Studies and Japanese Studies." *American Anthropologist* 63(1): 136-137.

_____. 2000a [1942]. *And Keep Your Powder Dry: An Anthropologist Looks at America*. New York: Berghahn.

_____. 2000b. "The Study of Culture at a Distance." In *The Study of Culture at a Distance*, ed. Margaret Mead and Rhoda Métraux. Pp. 3-58. New York: Berghahn.

Mead, Margaret and Rhoda Métraux, ed. 2000 [1953]. *The Study of Culture at a Distance*. New York: Berghahn.

Mead, Margaret, Geoffrey Gorer and John Rickman. 2001 [1949]. *Russian Culture*. New York: Berghahn Press.

Mead, Margaret, et al. 2001. *Methods of Research on Contemporary Cultures*. New York: Berghahn.

Meadow, Arnold. 1944. *An Analysis of Japanese Character Structure Based on Japanese Film Plots and Thematic Apperception Tests*. New York: Institute for Intercultural Studies.

Medvedev, Pavel N., and M.M. Bakhtin. 1992. *The Formal Method in Literary Scholarship: A Critical Introduction to Sociological Poetics*. Baltimore: Johns Hopkins University Press.

Melkote, Srinivas R. 1991. *Communication for Development in the Third World: Theory and Practice*. Delhi: Sage.

Merleau-Ponty, Maurice. 1977. "Cézanne's Doubt." In *Symbolic Anthropology: A Reader in the Study of Symbols and Meanings*, ed. Janet Dolgin, David S. Kemnitzer, and David M. Schneider. Pp. 91-105. New York: Columbia University Press.

Métraux, Rhoda. 2000 [1953]. "Informants in Group Research." In *The Study of Culture at a Distance*, ed. Margaret Mead and Rhoda Métraux. Pp. 155-236. New York: Berghahn.

Meyer, Birgit. 1999. "Popular Ghanaian Cinema and the African Heritage." *WOTRO Working Papers*, No. 4. The Hague.

Michaels, Eric. 1994. *Bad Aboriginal Art: Tradition, Media and Technological Horizons*. Minneapolis: University of Minnesota Press.

Michaels, Eric, and Francis Jupurrula Kelly. 1984. "The Social Organization of an Australian Video Workplace." *Australian Aboriginal Studies* 1: 26-34.

Mikulak, Bill. 1998. "Fans versus Time Warner: Who Owns Looney Toons?" in *Reading the Rabbit: Explorations in Warner Bros. Animation*, ed. Kevin S. Sandler. Pp. 193-208. New Brunswick, N.J.; Rutgers University Press.

Miller, Cristanne. 1987. *Emily Dickinson: A Poet's Grammar*. Cambridge: Harvard University Press.

Miller, Daniel. 1994. *Modernity — An Ethnographic Approach: Dualism and Mass Consumption in Trinidad*. London and New York: Berg.

_____. 1995. "Introduction: Anthropology, Modernity and Consumption." In *Worlds Apart: Modernity through the Prism of the Local*, ed. Daniel Miller. Pp. 1-22. New York: Routledge.

_____. 1997. *Capitalism: An Ethnographic Approach*. London and New York: Berg.

Mitchell, J. Clyde. 1966. "Theoretical Orientations in African Urban Studies." In *The Social Anthropology of Complex Societies*, ed. Michael Banton. London: Tavistock.

Modell, Judith. 1999. "The Wall of Shame: Ruth Benedict's Accomplishment in the *Chrysanthemum and the Sword*" *Dialectical Anthropology* 24(2): 193-215.

Modleski, Tania. 1988. *The Women Who Knew Too Much: Hitchcock and Feminist Analysis*. New York: Routledge.

Mody, Bella. 1991. *Designing Messages for Development Communication*. New Delhi: Sage.

Moerman, Michael. 1988. "Society in a Grain of Rice." In *Talking Culture: Ethnography and Conversation Analysis*. Philadelphia: University of Pennsylvania Press.

Moffatt, Michael. 1990. "Do We Really Need Postmodernism to Understand Ferris Buehler? A Comment on Traube." *Cultural Anthropology* 5(4): 367-373.

Moores, Shaun. 1993. *Interpreting Audiences: The Ethnography of Media Consumption*. London: Sage.

Morley, David. 1980. *The Nationwide Audience*. London: British Film Institute.

_____. 1986. *Family Television: Cultural Power and Domestic Leisure*. London and New York: Comedia.

Morris, Rosalind C. 2000. "Modernity's Media and the End of Mediumship? On the Aesthetic Economy of Transparency in Thailand." *Public Culture* 12(2): 457-475.

Morson, Gary Saul. 1986. "Introduction to Extracts from 'the Problem of Speech Genres.'" In *Bakhtin: Essays and Dialogues on His Work*, ed. Gary Saul Morson. Chicago: University of Chicago Press.

Mulvey, Laura. 1981. "On *Duel in the Sun*: Afterthoughts on 'Visual Pleasure and Narrative Cinema.'" *Framework* 15-17: 12-15.

_____. 1989 [1975]. "Visual Pleasure and Narrative Cinema." In *Visual and Other Pleasures*. Bloomington and Indianapolis: Indiana University Press.

Munn, N.D. 1992. "The Cultural Anthropology of Time: A Critical Essay." *Annual Review of Anthropology* 21: 93-123.

Naficy, Hamid. 1993. *The Making of Exile Cultures: Iranian Television in Los Angeles*. Minneapolis: University of Minnesota Press.

Nash, June. 1979. *We Eat the Mines and the Mines Eat Us: Dependency and Exploitation in Bolivian Tine Mines*. New York: Columbia University Press.

Neiburg, Federico, and Marcio Goldman. 1998. "Anthropology and Politics in the Study of National Character." *Cultural Anthropology* 13(1): 56-81.

Nightingale, Virginia. 1993 [1989]. "What's 'Ethnographic' about Ethnographic Audience Research?" In *Nation, Culture, Text: Australian Cultural and Media Studies*, ed. Graeme Turner. Pp. 164-177. London: Routledge.

Nobuhiro, Nagashima. 1998. "The Cult of Oguricap: Or, How Women Changed the Social Value of Japanese Horse-Racing." In *The Worlds of Japanese Popular Culture: Gender, Shifting Boundaries and Global Cultures*, ed. D.P. Martinez. Cambridge: Cambridge University Press.

O'Barr, William. 1989. "The Airbrushing of Culture: An Insider Look at Global Advertising." *Public Culture* 2(1): 1-19.

_____. 1994. *Culture and the Ad: Exploring Otherness in the World of Advertising*. Boulder: Westview.

Oliveira, O.S. 1991. "Mass Media, Culture and Communication in Brazil: The Heritage of Dependency." In *Transnational Communication: Wiring the Third World*, ed. J. Lent and G. Sussman. Pp. 200-214. Newbury Park, CA: Sage.

Öncü, Ayse. 1995. "Packaging Islam: Cultural Politics on the Landscape of Turkish Commercial Television." *Public Culture* 8: 51-71.

Ong, Walter. 1982. *Orality and Literacy: The Technologization of the Word*. London: Methuen.

Ortner, Sherry. 1995. "Resistance and the Problem of Ethnographic Refusal." *Comparative Studies in Society and History* 2: 173-193.

Pace, R. 1993. First-Time Televiewing in Amazonia: Television Acculturation in Gurupa, Brazil. *Ethnology*. 32(2): 187-205.

Pack, Sam. 2000. "Indigenous Media Then and Now: Situating the Navajo Film Project." *Quarterly Review of Film and Video* 17(3): 273-287.

Packard, Vance. 1959. *The Status Seekers*. New York: D. McKay Co.

Painter, Andrew. 1994. " On the Anthropology of Television: A Perspective from Japan." *Visual Anthropology Review* 10(1): 70-84.

_____. 1996. "The Telerepresentation of Gender in Japan." In *Re-Imaging Japanese Women*, ed. Anne E. Imamura. Pp. 46-72. Berkeley: University of California Press.

Palmgreen, Philip, and J.D. Rayburn. 1985. "An Expectancy Value Approach to Media Gratifications." In *Media Gratifications Research*, ed. K.E. Rosengren et al. Pp. 61-72. Beverly Hills: Sage.

Parenti, Michael. 1993. *Inventing Reality*. New York: St. Martin's Press.

Parezco, Nancy J. 1983. *Navajo Sandpainting: From Religious Act to Commercial Art*. Tucson: University of Arizona Press.

Parkin, David. 1992. "Ritual as Spatial Direction and Bodily Division." In *Understanding Rituals*, ed. Daniel de Coppett. New York and London: Routledge.

Peacock, James. 1968. *Rites of Modernization: Symbolic and Social Aspects of Indonesian Proletarian Drama*. Chicago: University of Chicago Press.

_____. 1969. "Religion, Communication and Modernization: A Weberian Critique of Some Recent Views." *Human Organization* 28(1): 35-41.

_____. 1979. *Consciousness and Change: Symbolic Anthropology in an Evolutionary Perspective*. Oxford: Halstead.

Peacock, James and A. Thomas Kirsch. 1970. *The Human Direction: An Evolutionary Approach to Social and Cultural Anthropology*. New York: Meredith.

Pedelty, Mark. 1993. "Making Use of the (Alternative) Media." *Practicing Anthropologist* 15(3): 29-30.

_____. 1995. *War Stories: The Culture of Foreign Correspondents*. New York: Routledge.

_____. 1998. "Coors World Culture War: Multicultural Conservativism in Advertising." *The Socialist Review* 26 (3-4).

_____. 1999. "Bolero: the Birth, Life and Decline of Mexican Modernity." *Latin American Music Review* 20 (1): 30-58.

Peirce, Charles Sanders. 1960. *Collected Papers, Vol. 2*, ed. Charles Hartshorne and Paul Weiss. Cambridge: Belknap.

Pendakur, Manjunath, and Radha Subramanyan. 1996. "Indian Cinema beyond National Borders." In *New Patterns in Global Television: Peripheral Vision*. New Delhi: Oxford University Press.

Pendergrast, Mark. 1993. *For God, Country, and Coca-Cola*. New York: Scribners.

Perin, Constance. 1977. *Everything in its Place: Social Order and Land Use in America*. Princeton: Princeton University Press.

Peters, John Durham. 1997. "Seeing Bifocally: Media, Place, Culture." In *Culture, Power, Place: Explorations in Critical Anthropology*, ed. Akhil Gupta and James Ferguson. Pp. 75-92. Durham: Duke University Press.

Peterson, Leighton C. 1997. "Tuning in to Navajo: The Role of Radio in Native American Language Maintenance." *Teaching Indigenous Languages*, ed. Jon Reyhner. Pp. 214-221. Flagstaff: Northern Arizona University.

Peterson, Mark. 1996. "Writing the News in India: Press, Politics and Symbolic Power." Ph.D. dissertation, Brown University.

_____. 1998. "The Rhetoric of Epidemic in India: News Coverage of AIDS." *Alif: The Journal of Comparative Poetics* 18: 237-268.

_____. 2001. "Getting to the Story: Off-the-Record Discourse and Interpretive Practice in American Journalism." *Anthropological Quarterly* 74(4): 163-173.

Pfaffenberger, Brian. 1992. "Social Anthropology of Technology." *Annual Review of Anthropology* 21: 491-516.

Piccini, Angela. 1996. "Filming Through the Mists of Time: Celtic Constructions and the Documentary." *Current Anthropology* 37 (Supplement): S87-S111.

_____. 1997. "Comments." *Current Anthropology* 38(2): 219-222.

Pieterse, Jan Nederveen. 1998. "Hybrid Modernities: Mélange Modernities in Asia." *Sociological Analysis* 1(3): 75-86.

Pool, Ithiel de Sola, ed. 1977. *The Social Impact of the Telephone*. Cambridge: MIT Press.

_____. 1983. *Forecasting the Telephone: A Retrospective Technology Assessment*. Norwood, NJ: Ablex.

Portes, Alejandro. 1976. "On the Sociology of National Development: Theories and Issues." *American Journal of Sociology* 82(1): 55-85.

Postill, John. n.d. "The Life and Afterlife Crises of Saribas Iban Television Sets. MEDIA@LSE Working Papers. http://www.lse.ac.uk/collections/media@lse/mediaWorkingPapers/ewpNumber5.htm (accessed Aug. 2003).

Powdermaker, Hortense. 1947. "An Anthropologist Looks at the Movies." *Annals of the American Academy of Political and Social Science* 254: 80-87.

_____. 1950. *Hollywood: The Dream Factory*. New York: Grosset and Dunlap.

_____. 1962. *Coppertown: Changing Africa*. New York: Harper and Row.

_____. 1966. *Stranger and Friend: The Way of an Anthropologist*. New York: W.W. Norton.

Prakash, Gyan. 1990. "Writing Post-Orientalist Histories in the Third World: Perspectives from Indian Historiography." *Comparative Studies in Society and History* 32(2): 383-408.

Price, David. 1998. "Gregory Bateson and the OSS: World War II and Bateson's Assessment of Applied Anthropology." *Human Organization* 57(4): 379-384.

Price, Monroe E. 1999. "Satellite Broadcasting as Trade Routes in the Sky" Public Culture 11(2): 387-390.

Pritchett, Frances. 1995. "The World of Amar Chitra Katha." In *Media and the Transformation of Religion in South Asia*, ed. Lawrence Babb and Susan Wadley. Philadelphia: University of Pennsylvania Press.

Propp, Vladimir. 1928 [1969]. *The Morphology of the Folktale*, trans. Lawrence Scott. Austin: University of Texas Press.

Rabinow, Paul. 1997. *Making PCR: A Story of Biotechnology*. Chicago: University of Chicago Press.

Radway, Janice. 1983. "Women Read the Romance: The Interaction of Text and Context." *Feminist Studies* 9(1).

_____. 1984a. "Interpretive Communities and Variable Literacies: The Functions of Romance Reading." *Daedalus* (Summer).

_____. 1984b. *Reading the Romance: Women, Patriarchy and Popular Literature*. Chapel Hill: University of North Carolina Press.

_____. 1988. "Reception Study: Ethnography and the Problems of Dispersed Audiences and Nomadic Subjects." *Cultural Studies* 2(3): 359-376.

_____. 1991. "Introduction: Writing *Reading the Romance*." In *Reading the Romance: Women, Patriarchy and Popular Literature*. Rev. Ed. Chapel Hill: University of North Carolina Press.

Redfield, Robert. 1941. *The Folk Culture of Yucatan*. Chicago: University of Chicago Press.

_____. 1964 [1947]. "The Folk Society." In *Readings in Anthropology*, ed. Morton H. Fried. New York: T.Y. Crowell.

Redfield, Robert, and Milton Singer. 1954. "The Cultural Role of Cities." *Economic Development and Cultural Change* 3: 53-73.

Reuters. 1999. "Pokémon License Boosting Topps Co. Sales." Monday, October 25 11:28 A.M. ET.

Rheingold, Harold. 1993. *The Virtual Community: Homesteading on the Electronic Frontier*. Reading, MA: Addison-Wesley.

Richardson, Kay, and Ulrike H. Meinhof. 1999. *Worlds in Common? Television Discourse in a Changing Europe*. London and New York: Routledge.

Ricouer, Paul. 1981. *Hermeneutics and the Social Sciences*. Cambridge: Cambridge University Press.

Ritzer, George. 1993. *The McDonaldization of Society*. Thousand Oaks, CA: Pine Forge.

Rodgers, Susan. 1986. "Batak Tape Cassette Kinship: Constructing Kinship through the Indonesian National Mass Media." *American Ethnologist* 13(1): 23-42.

Rosaldo, Renato. 1986. "From the Door of His Tent: The Fieldworker and the Inquisitor." In *Writing Culture: The Poetics and Politics of Ethnography*, ed. James Clifford and George Marcus. Berkeley: University of California Press.

Rose, Arnold M. 1970. "Sociological Factors Affecting Economic Development in India." In *The Human Factor in Political Development*, ed. Monte Palmer. Waltham, MA: Ginn.

Rosen, Lawrence. 1984. *Bargaining for Reality: The Construction of Social Relations in a Muslim Community*. Chicago: University of Chicago Press.

Rosenblum, Mort. 1979. *Coups and Earthquakes: Reporting the World to America*. New York: Harper and Row.

Rosengren, Karl Erik, Philip Palmgreen, and Lawrence A. Wenner, eds. 1985. *Media Gratification Research: Current Perspectives*. Beverly Hills and London: Sage.

Rostow, Walter W. 1960. *The Stages of Economic Growth: A Non-Communist Manifesto*. Cambridge: Cambridge University Press.

Roth, Lorna, and Gail Valaskakis. 1989. "Aboriginal Broadcasting in Canada: A Case Study in Democratization." In *Communication for and Against Democracy*, ed. Marc Raboy and Peter Bruck. Pp. 221-234. Montreal: Black Rose.

Rotha, Raul, and Basil Wright. 1980. "Nanook and the North." *Studies in Visual Communication* 6(2): 33-60.

Rubey, Dan. 1997. "Not So Long Ago, Not So Far Away." *Jump Cut* 41: 2-130.

Ruby, Jay, ed. 1982. *A Crack in the Mirror: Reflective Perspectives in Anthropology*. Philadelphia: University of Pennsylvania Press.

Ruby, Jay. 1991. "Speaking For, Speaking About, Speaking With, or Speaking Alongside- An Anthropological and Documentary Dilemma." *Visual Anthropology Review* 7(2): 50-67.

_____. 1995. "The Viewer Viewed: Watching Ethnographic Film." In *The Construction of the Viewer: Media Ethnography and the Anthropology of Audiences*, ed. Peter Crawford and Sigurjon Hafsteinsson. Pp. 192-206. Hojbjerg: Intervention Press.

Ryles, Gilbert. 1984. *The Concept of Mind*. Chicago: University of Chicago Press.

Sahlins, Marshall. 1976. *Culture and Practical Reason*. Chicago: University of Chicago Press.

Said, Edward. 1978. *Orientalism*. New York: Vintage.

_____. 1980. *The Question of Palestine*. New York: Vintage.

_____. 1981. *Covering Islam: How the Media and the Experts Determine How We See the Rest of the World*. New York: Pantheon.

_____. 1985. "Orientalism Reconsidered." *Race and Class* 27(2): 1-15.

Sapir, Edward. 1985a [1932]. "Cultural Anthropology and Psychology." In *Selected Writings in Language, Culture and Personality*, ed. David Mandelbaum. First paperback edition. Pp. 509-521. Berkeley: University of California Press.

_____. 1985b [1938]. "Why Cultural Anthropology Needs the Psychiatrist." In *Selected Writings in Language, Culture and Personality*, ed. David Mandelbaum. First paperback edition. Pp. 569-577. Berkeley: University of California Press.

Sartre, Jean Paul. 1963. *Search for a Method*. New York: Alfred A. Knopf.

_____. 1970. *Existentialism and Humanism*. London: Methuen.

Saussure, Ferdinand de. 1983. *Course in General Linguistics*. London: Duckworth.

Scherer, Joanna Cohan. 1988. "The Public Faces of Sarah Winnemucca." *Cultural Anthropology* 3(2): 178-204.

Schieffelin, Edward. 1976. *The Sorrow of the Lonely and the Burning of the Dancers*. St Martin's Press, New York

Schramm, Wilbur. 1964. *Mass Media and National Development*. Stanford: Stanford University Press.

_____. 1971. "The Nature of Communication between Humans." In *The Process and Effects of Mass Communication*, ed. Wilbur Schramm and Donald F. Roberts. Pp. 3-53. Urbana: University of Illinois Press.

_____. 1976. "The End of an Old Paradigm." In *Communication and Change*, ed. Wilbur Schramm and Daniel Lerner. Pp. 45-48. Honolulu: University Press of Hawaii.

Schudson, Michael. 1978. *Discovering the News: A Social History of American Newspapers*. New York: Basic.

_____. 1987. "Deadlines, Datelines and History." In *Reading the News*, ed. Robert K. Manoff and Michael Schudson. New York: Pantheon.

Schwartz, Vera. 2000 [1953]. "An Analysis of the Soviet film *The Young Guard*: Comparison of the Novel and the Film." In *The Study of Culture at a Distance*, ed. Margaret Mead and Rhoda Métraux. Pp. 326-331. New York: Berghahn.

Scott, James. 1985. *Weapons of the Weak: Everyday Forms of Peasant Resistance*. New Haven: Yale University Press.

Sebeok, Thomas, and Marcel Danesi. 2000. *The Forms of Meaning: Modeling Theory and Semiotic Analysis*. Berlin and New York: Mouton de Gruyter.

Shannon, Claude E., and Warren Weaver. 1949. *The Mathematical Theory of Communication*. Urbana: University of Illinois Press.

Shaviro, Steven. 1993. *The Cinematic Body*. Minneapolis: University of Minnesota Press.

Shostak, Marjorie. 1981. *Nisa, the Life and Words of a !Kung Woman*. Cambridge: Harvard University Press.

Shryock, Andrew. 2000. "Public Culture in Arab Detroit: Creating Arab/American Identities in a Transnational Domain." In *Mass Mediations*, ed. Walter Armbrust. Berkeley: University of California Press.

Silverstein, Michael, and Greg Urban. 1996. "The Natural History of Discourse." In *Natural Histories of Discourse*, ed. Michael Silverstein and Greg Urban. Pp. 1-17. Chicago: University of Chicago Press.

Simensky, Melvin, Lanning G. Bryer, and Neil J. Wilkof, ed. 1999. *Intellectual Property in the Global Marketplace*. New York: Wiley.

Singer, Benjamin D. 1981. *Social Functions of the Telephone*. Palo Alto, CA: R and E Research Associates.

Singer, Milton. 1960. "The Great Tradition of Hinduism in the City of Madras." In *Anthropology of Folk Religions*, ed. Charles Lesley. New York: Random House.

_____. 1966. "Modernizing Religious Beliefs." In *Modernization: The Dynamics of Growth*, ed. Myron Weiner. New York: Bass Books.

_____. 1972. *When a Great Tradition Modernizes: An Anthropological Approach to Indian Civilization*. New York: Praeger.

Singhal, Arvind, and Everett Rogers. 1989. *India's Information Revolution*. New Delhi: Sage.

Smith, Bruce L., and Jerry C. Brigham. 1992. "Native Radio Broadcasting in North America: An Overview of Systems in the United States and Canada." *Journal of Broadcasting and Electronic Media* 36(2): 183-195.

Soysal, Levent. 1999. "Projects of Culture: An Ethnographic Episode in the Life of Migrant Youth in Berlin." Ph.D. Dissertation, Department of Anthropology, Harvard University.

Spitulnik, Debra. 1993. "Anthropology and Mass Media." *Annual Review of Anthropology* 22: 293-315.

_____. 1994. "Radio Cycles and Recyclings in Zambia: Public Words, Popular Critiques and National Communities." *Passages* 8: 10, 12, 14-16.

_____. 1998a. "The Social Circulation of Media Discourse and the Mediation of Communities." *Journal of Linguistic Anthropology* 6(2): 161-187.

_____. 1998b. "Mediated Modernities: Encounters with Electronic Technologies in Zambia." *Visual Anthropology Review* 14(2): 63-84.

_____. 1999. "The Language of the City: Town Bemba as Urban Hybridity." *Journal of Linguistic Anthropology* 8(1): 30-59.

_____. 2000. "Documenting Radio Culture as Lived Experience: Reception Studies and the Mobile Machine in Zambia." In *African Broadcast Cultures: Radio and Public Life*, ed. Richard Fardon and Graham Furniss. London: James Currey.

Spivak, Gyan Chakravorty. 1988. "Can the Subaltern Speak?" In *Marxism and the Interpretation of Culture*, ed. Cary Nelson and Lawrence Grossberg. Urbana: University of Illinois Press.

Sreberny-Mohammadi, Annabelle and Ali Mohammadi. 1994. *Small Media, Big Revolution: Communication, Change and the Iranian Revolution.* Minneapolis: University of Minnesota Press.

Srinivas, S.N. 1973. "Comments on Milton Singer's 'Industrial Leadership, the Hindu Ethic and the Spirit of Socialism." In *Entreneurship and Modernization of Occupational Cultures in South Asia*. Program in Comparative Studies on South Asia, ed. Milton Singer, monograph no. 12. Pp. 279-286. Durham: Duke University Press.

Stam, Robert. 1989. *Subversive Pleasures: Bakhtin, Cultural Criticism and Film*. Baltimore: John Hopkins University Press.

Steward, Julian H., et al. 1956. *The People of Puerto Rico: A Study in Social Anthropology*. Urbana: University of Illinois Press.

Street, Brian. 1984. *Literacy in Theory and Practice*. New York: Cambridge University Press.

_____, ed. 1991. *Cross-Cultural Perspectives on Literacy*. New York: Cambridge University Press.

Strom, Susan. 1999. "Japanese Family Values: I Choose You, Pikachu!" *New York Times*, November 7.

Tannen, Deborah. 1984. *Conversational Style: Analyzing Talk among Friends*. Westport, CT: Ablex.

Thomas, Rosie. 1985. "Indian Cinema: Pleasures and Popularity." *Screen* 26(3-4): 116-131.

Toumey, Christopher. 1994. *God's Own Scientists: Creationists in a Secular World*. New Brunswick, NJ: Rutgers University Press.

Traube, Elizabeth. 1989. "Secrets of Success in Postmodern Society." *Cultural Anthropology* 4(3): 273-300.

_____. 1990. "Reply to Moffatt." *Cultural Anthropology* 5(4): 374-379.

_____. 1991. "Transforming Heroes: Hollywood and the Demonization of Women." *Public Culture* 3(2): 1-28.

_____. 1992. *Dreaming Identities: Class, Gender and Generation in 1980s Hollywood Movies*. Boulder: Westview.

_____. 1993. "Family Matters: Post-feminist Constructions of a Contested Site." *Visual Anthropology* 9(1): 57-73.

Tuchman, Gaye. 1972. "Objectivity as Strategic Ritual: An Examination of Newsmen's Notion of Objectivity." *American Journal of Sociology* 77: 660-670.

_____. 1978a. *Making News*. New York: The Free Press.

_____. 1978b. "Professionalism as an Agent of Legitimation." *Journal of Communication* 28: 106-113.

Tulloch, John, and Albert Moran. 1986. *A Country Practice: Quality Soap*. Sydney: Currency Press.

Turner, Terrence. 1991. "Representing, Resisting, Rethinking: Historical Transformation of Kayapo Culture and Anthropological Consciousness." In *The History of Anthropology: Colonial Situations*, ed. George W. Stocking, Jr. Pp. 285-313. Madison: University of Wisconsin Press.

_____. 1992a. "Defiant Images: The Kayapo Appropriation of Video." *Anthropology Today* 8(6): 5-16.

_____. 1992b. "The Kayapo on Television: An Anthropological Viewing." *Visual Anthropology Review* 8(1): 107-112.

Turner, Victor. 1967. *The Forest of Symbols: Aspects of Ndembu Ritual*. Ithaca, NY: Cornell University Press.

_____. 1969. *The Ritual Process: Structure and Anti-structure*. Ithaca, NY: Cornell University Press.

_____. 1974a. *Dramas, Fields and Metaphors: Symbolic Action in Human Society*. Ithaca, NY: Cornell University Press.

_____. 1974b. "Liminal to Liminoid in Play, Flow and Ritual." *Rice University Studies* 60: 53-92.

_____. 1980. "Social Dramas and Stories about Them." *Critical Inquiry* (Autumn): 141-168.

_____. 1982. *From Ritual to Theater*. New York: Performing Arts Journal Publications.

Tyler, Stephen. 1987. *The Unspeakable: Discourse, Dialogue, and Rhetoric in the Postmodern World*. Madison: University of Wisconsin Press.

Urciuoli, Bonnie. 1998. "Acceptable Difference: The Cultural Evolution of the Model Ethnic Citizen." In *Democracy and Ethnography: Constructing Identities in Multicultural Liberal States*, ed. Carol Greenhouse. Albany: State University of New York Press.

Valaskakis, Gail and Thomas Wilson. 1985. *The Inuit Broadcasting Corporation: A Survey of Viewing Behavior and Audience Preferences Among the Inuit of Seven Communities in the Baffin and Keewatin Regions of the Northwest Territories*. Montreal: Concordia University.

Van Dijk, Teun A. 1985. *Discourse and Communication: New Approaches to the Analysis of Mass Media Discourse and Communication*. Berlin and New York: Walter de Gruyter.

_____. 1988. *News Analysis: Case Studies of International and National News in the Press*. Hillsdale, NJ: Erlbaum.

_____. 1991. *Racism and the Press*. London: Routledge.

Van Gennep, Arnold. 1960. *Rites of Passage*. Chicago: University of Chicago Press.

Vitalis, Robert. 2000. "American Ambassador in Technicolor and Cinemascope: Hollywood and Revolution on the Nile." In *Mass Mediations: New Approaches to Popular Culture in the Middle East and Beyond*, ed. Walter Armbrust. Berkeley: University of California Press.

Wagner-Pacifici, Robin Erica. 1986. *The Moro Morality Play*. Chicago: University of Chicago Press.

Wallace, Anthony F.C. 1954. "Review of the Study of Culture at a Distance." *American Anthropologist* 56: 1142-1145.

_____. 1961. *Culture and Personality*. Philadelphia: University of Pennsylvania Press.

Wallerstein, Immanuel. 1974. *The Modern World System*. New York: Academic Press.

Wang, Georgetter and Wimal Dissanayake. 1984. "Indigenous Communication Systems and Development: A Reappraisal." In *Continuity and Change in Communication Systems*, ed. Georgetter Wang and Wimal Dissanayake. Pp. 21-33. Norwood, NJ: Ablex.

Wapshott, Tim. 1999. "Pokémon: Back to the Playground." *The Times* (London), September 29.

Warner, William Lloyd. 1953. *American Life: Dream and Reality*. Chicago: University of Chicago Press.

_____. 1959. *The Living and the Dead: A Study of the Symbolic Life of Americans*. New Haven: Yale University Press.

_____. 1962. *American Life: Dream and Reality*. Revised edition. Chicago: University of Chicago Press.

Warner, William Lloyd and Paul S. Lunt. 1941. *The Social Life of a Modern Community*. New Haven: Yale University Press.

Warner, William Lloyd and W.E. Henry. 1948. "The Radio Daytime Serial: A Symbolic Analysis." *Genetic Psychology Monographs* (37).

Watson, James, ed. 1997. *Golden Arches East: McDonald's in East Asia*. Stanford: Stanford University Press.

Weakland, John. 1956. "Lusin's *Ah Q*: A Rejected Image of Chinese Character." *Pacific Spectator* 10: 137-146.

_____. 1966. "Themes in Chinese Communist Films." *American Anthropologist* 66(3): 477-484.

_____. 2000 [1953]. "An analysis of seven Cantonese films." In *The Study of Culture at a Distance*, ed. Margaret Mead and Rhoda Métraux. Pp. 321-325. New York: Berghahn.

Weber, Max. 1964. *The Sociology of Religion*. Boston: Beacon.

Weiner, James F. 1997. "Televisualist Anthropology: Representation, Aesthetics, Politics." Current Anthropology 38(2): 197-235.

Wendl, Tobias. 1999. "*The Return of the Snakeman*: Horror Films Made in Ghana." *Revue Noir* 31(2).

White, Jenny. 1999. "Amplifying Trust: Community and Communication in Turkey." In *New Media in the Muslim World: The Emerging Public Sphere*, ed. Dale Eickelman and Jon Anderson. Pp. 162-179. Bloomington: Indiana University Press.

Wilk, Richard. 1995. "'It's Destroying a Whole Generation': Television and Moral Discourse in Belize." *Visual Anthropology* 5: 229-244.

_____. 1996. "Colonial Time and TV Time: Television and Temporality in Belize." *Visual Anthropology Review* 10(1): 94-102.

Williams, Linda. 1989. *Hard Core: Power, Pleasure and the Frenzy of the Visible*. Berkeley: University of California Press.

Williams, Raymond. 1958. *Culture and Society*. New York: Doubleday.

_____. 1974. *Television and Technological Form*. London: Fontana.

Wittgenstein, Ludwig. 1975. *Tractatus Logico-Philosophicus*. New York: Routledge.

Wolfenstein, Martha. 2000 [1953]. "Movie Analysis in the Study of Culture." In *The Study of Culture at a Distance*, ed. Margaret Mead and Rhoda Métraux. Pp. 293-308. New York: Berghahn.

Wolfenstein, Martha, and Nathan Leites. 1950. *Movies*. Glencoe, IL: Free Press.

Wood, Daniel B. 1999. "Pokémon: New Scourge of the Schoolyard." *Christian Science Monitor*, Oct. 4.

Worth, Sol. 1966. "Film as Non-art: An Approach to the Study of Film." *The American Scholar* 35: 322-334.

_____. 1972a. "Toward an Anthropological Politics of Symbolic Forms." In *Reinventing Anthropology*, ed. Dell Hymes. New York: Random House.

_____. 1972b. "Review of You Are on Indian Land." *American Anthropologist* 74 (4): 1029-1031.

Worth, Sol, and John Adair. 1970. "Navajo Filmmakers." *American Anthropologist* 72: 9-34.

_____. 1972. *Through Navajo Eyes: An Exploration in Film Communication and Anthropology*. Bloomington: Indiana University Press.

_____. 1997. *Through Navajo Eyes: An Exploration in Film Communication and Anthropology*. Rev. Ed. Albuquerque: University of New Mexico Press.

Yang, Mayfair Mei-hui. 1993. "Of Gender, State Censorship, and Overseas Capital: An Interview with Director Zhang Yimou." *Public Culture* 5: 297-313.

_____. 1994. "State Discourse of a Plebeian Public Sphere? Film Discussion Groups in China." *Visual Anthropology Review* 10(1): 47-60.

_____. 1997. "Mass Media and Transnational Subjectivity in Shanghai: Notes on (Re)Cosmopolitanism in a Chinese Metropolis." In *Ungrounded Empires: The Cultural Politics of Modern Chinese Transnationalism*, ed. Aihwa Ong and Donald M. Nonini. Pp. 287-321. New York: Routledge.

Yano, Christine. 1997. "Charisma's Realm: Fandom in Japan." *Ethnology* 36(4): 335-349.

INDEX

Berghahn Books

GIRL MAKING

A Cross-Cultural Ethnography on the Processes of Growing up Female

Gerry Bloustien

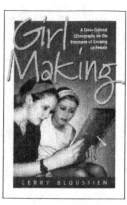

Through the innovative methodology of asking them to record their experiences on videotape, this book offers an evocative and fascinating cross-cultural exploration into the everyday lives of a number of teenage girls from their own broad social, cultural and ethnic perspectives. The use of the video camera by the girls themselves reveals their exploration and experimentation with possible identities, highlighting their awareness that the self is not ready made but rather constituted in the process of continuous performance. The result is an active self-conscious exploration of the continuous "art" of self-making. Through their play, the teenagers are shown to strategically test out various possibilities, while keeping such explorations within the bounds of what is acceptable and permissible in their own micro-cultural worlds. The resulting material challenges previous findings in those feminist and youth anthropological studies based on too narrow a concept of class, ethnicity or populist approaches to culture.

From the Contents: Ceci n'est pas une jeune fille — Camera Power — My Body, Myself — *Whose* Private Space? — (Public Space Invaders — Learning to Play It "Cool" — "Music is in My Soul" — Global Girl Making: 10 + 6

Gerry Bloustien is a senior lecturer in Communications at the University of South Australia.

Berghahn Books
604 West 115th Street
New York, NY 10025, USA

3 Newtec Place, Magdalen
Rd. Oxford OX4 1RE, UK

2003. 312 pages, 21 ills., bibliog., index
ISBN 1-57187-425-6 hardback
ISBN 1-57181-426-4 paperback

orders@berghahnbooks.com ～ www.berghahnbooks.com